A RELATIONAL APPROACH PSYCHOTHERAPY

CW01084246

A Relational Psychoanalytic Approach to Couples Psychotherapy presents an original model of couples treatment, integrating ideas from a host of authors in relational psychoanalysis. It also includes other psychoanalytic traditions as well as ideas from other social sciences. This book addresses a vacuum in contemporary psychoanalysis devoid of a comprehensively relational way to think about the practice of psychoanalytically oriented couples treatment.

In this book, Philip Ringstrom sets out a theory of practice that is based on three broad themes:

- the actualization of self-experience in an intimate relationship
- the partners' capacity for mutual recognition versus mutual negation
- the relationship having a mind of its own.

Based on these three themes, Ringstrom's model of treatment is articulated in six nonlinear, non-hierarchical steps that wed theory with practice—each powerfully illustrated with case material. These steps initially address the therapist's attunement to the partners' disparate subjectivities, including the critical importance of each one's perspective on the "reality" they co-habit. Their perspectives are fleshed out through the exploration of their developmental histories with focus on factors of gender and culture and more. Out of this arises the examination of how conflictual pasts manifest in dissociated self-states, the illumination of which lends to the enrichment of self-actualization, the facilitation of mutual recognition, and the capacity to more genuinely renegotiate their relationship. The book concludes with a chapter that illustrates one couple treated through all six steps and a chapter on frequently asked questions ("FAQs") derived from over 30 years of practice, teaching, supervision, and presentations during the course of this book's development.

A Relational Psychoanalytic Approach to Couples Psychotherapy balances a great range of ways to work with couples, while also providing the means to authentically negotiate their differences in a way which is insightful and invaluable. This book is for practitioners of couples therapy and psychoanalytic practitioners. It is also aimed at undergraduate, graduate, and postgraduate students in the fields of psychiatry, psychology, marriage and family therapy, and social work.

Philip A. Ringstrom, PhD, PsyD, is a Senior Training and Supervising Analyst and faculty member at the Institute for Contemporary Psychoanalysis in Los Angeles. He is a member of the editorial boards of both the *International Journal of Psychoanalytic Self Psychology* and *Psychoanalytic Dialogues*. He is also a member of the International Council of Self Psychologists, and on the Board of Directors of the International Association of Relational Psychoanalysis and Psychotherapy.

Relational Perspectives Book Series
Lewis Aron & Adrienne Harris
Series Co-Editors

Steven Kuchuck & Eyal Rozmarin
Associate Editors

The Relational Perspectives Book Series (RPBS) publishes books that grow out of or contribute to the relational tradition in contemporary psychoanalysis. The term *relational psychoanalysis* was first used by Greenberg and Mitchell (1983) to bridge the traditions of interpersonal relations, as developed within interpersonal psychoanalysis and object relations, as developed within contemporary British theory. But, under the seminal work of the late Stephen Mitchell, the term *relational psychoanalysis* grew and began to accrue to itself many other influences and developments. Various tributaries—interpersonal psychoanalysis, object relations theory, self psychology, empirical infancy research, and elements of contemporary Freudian and Kleinian thought—flow into this tradition, which understands relational configurations between self and others, both real and fantasied, as the primary subject of psychoanalytic investigation.

We refer to the relational tradition, rather than to a relational school, to highlight that we are identifying a trend, a tendency within contemporary psychoanalysis, not a more formally organized or coherent school or system of beliefs. Our use of the term *relational* signifies a dimension of theory and practice that has become salient across the wide spectrum of contemporary psychoanalysis. Now under the editorial supervision of Lewis Aron and Adrienne Harris, with the assistance of Associate Editors Steven Kuchuck and Eyal Rozmarin, the Relational Perspectives Book Series originated in 1990 under the editorial eye of the late Stephen A. Mitchell. Mitchell was the most prolific and influential of the originators of the relational tradition. He was committed to dialogue among psychoanalysts and he abhorred the authoritarianism that dictated adherence to a rigid set of beliefs or technical restrictions. He championed open discussion, comparative and integrative approaches, and he promoted new voices across the generations.

Included in the Relational Perspectives Book Series are authors and works that come from within the relational tradition, extend and develop the tradition, as well as works that critique relational approaches or compare and contrast it with alternative points of view. The series includes our most distinguished senior psychoanalysts along with younger contributors who bring fresh vision.

Vol. 1
CONVERSING WITH UNCERTAINTY
Practicing psychotherapy in a
hospital setting
Rita Wiley McCleary

Vol. 2
AFFECT IN PSYCHOANALYSIS
A clinical synthesis
Charles Spezzano

Vol. 3
THE ANALYST IN THE INNER CITY
Race, class, and culture through
a psychoanalytic lens
Neil Altman

Vol. 4
A MEETING OF MINDS
Mutuality in psychoanalysis
Lewis Aron

Vol. 5
HOLDING AND PSYCHOANALYSIS
A relational perspective
Joyce A. Slochower

Vol. 6
THE THERAPIST AS A PERSON
Life crises, life choices,
life experiences, and their
effects on treatment
Barbara Gerson (ed.)

Vol. 7
SOUL ON THE COUCH
Spirituality, religion, and morality in
contemporary psychoanalysis
*Charles Spezzano &
Gerald J. Gargiulo (eds.)*

Vol. 8
UNFORMULATED EXPERIENCE
From dissociation to imagination in
psychoanalysis
Donnel B. Stern

Vol. 9
INFLUENCE AND AUTONOMY
IN PSYCHOANALYSIS
Stephen A. Mitchell

Vol. 10
FAIRBAIRN, THEN AND NOW
Neil J. Skolnick & David E. Scharff (eds.)

Vol. 11
BUILDING BRIDGES
Negotiation of paradox in psychoanalysis
Stuart A. Pizer

Vol. 12
RELATIONAL PERSPECTIVES
ON THE BODY
*Lewis Aron & Frances Sommer Anderson
(eds.)*

Vol. 13
SEDUCTION, SURRENDER,
AND TRANSFORMATION
Emotional engagement in the
analytic process *Karen Maroda*

Vol. 14
RELATIONAL PSYCHOANALYSIS
The emergence of a tradition
Stephen A. Mitchell & Lewis Aron (eds.)

Vol. 15
THE COLLAPSE OF THE SELF
AND ITS THERAPEUTIC
RESTORATION
Rochelle G. K. Kainer

Vol. 16
PSYCHOANALYTIC PARTICIPATION
Action, interaction, and integration
Kenneth A. Frank

Vol. 17
THE REPRODUCTION OF EVIL
A clinical and cultural perspective
Sue Grand

Vol. 18
OBJECTS OF HOPE
Exploring possibility and limit
in psychoanalysis
Steven H. Cooper

Vol. 19
WHO IS THE DREAMER, WHO
DREAMS THE DREAM?
A study of psychic presences
James S. Grotstein

Vol. 20
RELATIONALITY
From attachment to intersubjectivity
Stephen A. Mitchell

Vol. 21
LOOKING FOR GROUND
Countertransference and the problem of
value in psychoanalysis
Peter G. M. Carnochan

Vol. 22
SEXUALITY, INTIMACY, POWER
Muriel Dimen

Vol. 23
SEPTEMBER 11
Trauma and human bonds
*Susan W. Coates, Jane L. Rosenthal,
& Daniel S. Schechter (eds.)*

Vol. 24
MINDING SPIRITUALITY
Randall Lehman Sorenson

Vol. 25
GENDER AS SOFT ASSEMBLY
Adrienne Harris

Vol. 26
IMPOSSIBLE TRAINING
A relational view of psychoanalytic
education
Emanuel Berman

Vol. 27
THE DESIGNED SELF
Psychoanalysis and contemporary
identities
Carlo Strenger

Vol. 28
RELATIONAL
PSYCHOANALYSIS, II
Innovation and expansion
Lewis Aron & Adrienne Harris (eds.)

Vol. 29
CHILD THERAPY IN THE
GREAT OUTDOORS
A relational view
Sebastiano Santostefano

Vol. 30
THE HEALER'S BENT
Solitude and dialogue in the clinical
encounter
James T. McLaughlin

Vol. 31
UNCONSCIOUS FANTASIES AND
THE RELATIONAL WORLD
Danielle Knafo & Kenneth Feiner

Vol. 32
GETTING FROM HERE
TO THERE
Analytic love, analytic process
Sheldon Bach

Vol. 33
CREATING BODIES
Eating disorders as self-destructive survival
Katie Gentile

Vol. 34
RELATIONAL
PSYCHOANALYSIS, III
New voices
*Melanie Suchet, Adrienne Harris,
& Lewis Aron (eds.)*

Vol. 35
COMPARATIVE-INTEGRATIVE
PSYCHOANALYSIS
A relational perspective for the
discipline's second century
Brent Willock

Vol. 36
BODIES IN TREATMENT
The unspoken dimension
Frances Sommer Anderson (ed.)

Vol. 37
ADOLESCENT IDENTITIES
A collection of readings
Deborah Browning (ed.)

Vol. 38
REPAIR OF THE SOUL
Metaphors of transformation in Jewish
mysticism and psychoanalysis
Karen E. Starr

Vol. 39
DARE TO BE HUMAN
A contemporary psychoanalytic journey
Michael Shoshani Rosenbaum

Vol. 40
THE ANALYST IN THE INNER CITY,
SECOND EDITION
Race, class, and culture through a
psychoanalytic lens
Neil Altman

Vol. 41
THE HERO IN THE MIRROR
From fear to fortitude
Sue Grand

Vol. 42
SABERT BASESCU
Selected papers on human nature and
psychoanalysis
George Goldstein & Helen Golden (eds.)

Vol. 43
INVASIVE OBJECTS
Minds under siege
Paul Williams

Vol. 44
GOOD ENOUGH ENDINGS
Breaks, interruptions, and terminations
from contemporary relational perspectives
Jill Salberg (ed.)

Vol. 45
FIRST DO NO HARM
The paradoxical encounters of
psychoanalysis, warmaking, and resistance
*Adrienne Harris & Steven
Botticelli (eds.)*

Vol. 46
A DISTURBANCE IN THE FIELD
Essays in transference-countertransference
engagement
Steven H. Cooper

Vol. 47
UPROOTED MINDS
Surviving the politics of terror in
the Americas
Nancy Caro Hollander

Vol. 48
TOWARD MUTUAL RECOGNITION
Relational psychoanalysis and
the Christian narrative
Marie T. Hoffman

Vol. 49
UNDERSTANDING AND TREATING
DISSOCIATIVE IDENTITY DISORDER
A relational approach
Elizabeth F. Howell

Vol. 50
WITH CULTURE IN MIND
Psychoanalytic stories
Muriel Dimen (ed.)

Vol. 51
RELATIONAL
PSYCHOANALYSIS, IV
Expansion of theory
Lewis Aron & Adrienne Harris (eds.)

Vol. 52
RELATIONAL
PSYCHOANALYSIS, V
Evolution of process
Lewis Aron & Adrienne Harris (eds.)

Vol. 53
INDIVIDUALIZING GENDER AND
SEXUALITY
Theory and practice
Nancy Chodorow

Vol. 54
THE SILENT PAST AND THE
INVISIBLE PRESENT
Memory, trauma, and representation
in psychotherapy
Paul Renn

Vol. 55
A PSYCHOTHERAPY FOR THE
PEOPLE
Toward a progressive psychoanalysis
Lewis Aron & Karen Starr

Vol. 56
HOLDING AND PSYCHOANALYSIS
A relational perspective
Joyce Slochower

Vol. 57
THE PLAY WITHIN THE PLAY
The enacted dimension of
psychoanalytic process
Gil Katz

Vol. 58
TRAUMATIC NARCISSISM
Relational systems of subjugation
Daniel Shaw

Vol. 59
CLINICAL IMPLICATIONS OF
THE PSYCHOANALYST'S
LIFE EXPERIENCE
When the personal becomes professional
Steven Kuchuck (ed.)

Vol. 60
THE ORIGINS OF ATTACHMENT
Infant research and adult treatment
Beatrice Beebe & Frank M. Lachmann

Vol. 61
THE EMBODIED ANALYST
From Freud and Reich to relationality
Jon Sletvold

Vol. 62
A RELATIONAL PSYCHOANALYTIC
APPROACH TO COUPLES
PSYCHOTHERAPY
Philip A. Ringstrom

A RELATIONAL PSYCHOANALYTIC APPROACH TO COUPLES PSYCHOTHERAPY

Philip A. Ringstrom

Routledge
Taylor & Francis Group

NEW YORK AND LONDON

First published 2014
by Routledge
711 Third Avenue, New York, NY 10017

and by Routledge
27 Church Road, Hove, East Sussex BN3 2FA

Routledge is an imprint of the Taylor & Francis Group, an informa business

© 2014 Philip A. Ringstrom

British Library Cataloguing in Publication Data
A catalogue record for this book is available from the British Library

Library of Congress Cataloging-in-Publication Data
Ringstrom, Philip A.
A relational psychoanalytic approach to couples psychotherapy/
Philip A. Ringstrom.
pages cm
Includes bibliographical references.
1. Couples therapy. 2. Marital psychotherapy. 3. Couples–Psychology.
I. Title.
RC488.5.R55 2014
616.89'1562–dc23
2013038158

ISBN: 978-0-415-88924-7 (hbk)
ISBN: 978-0-415-88925-4 (pbk)
ISBN: 978-0-203-83097-0 (ebk)

Typeset in Times New Roman
by Cenveo Publisher Services

MIX
Paper from
responsible sources
FSC
www.fsc.org   FSC® C013604

Printed and bound by CPI Group (UK) Ltd, Croydon, CR0 4YY

To Marcia, who taught me how to hate*…
To Lena, who taught me about development …
To Crouton, who taught me that if you need unconditional love,
get a dog.

---

*(The original acknowledgment added, "so that I would truly know how to love…" Marcia said, "Too wordy".)

CONTENTS

Preface   xii
Acknowledgments   xiv

Introduction   1

1 Theoretical overview   7

2 Step One   37

3 Step Two   65

4 Step Three   89

5 Step Four   118

6 Step Five   146

7 Step Six   177

8 Michael and Carmen: an illustration of the Six Steps   214

9 Frequently asked questions   239

Appendix A: A brief summary of four models of family
systems theory and their implications   258
Appendix B: Practice questions   265
References   269
Index   281

PREFACE

> It is too late to turn back. Having read the opening words of this book, you have already begun to enter into the unsettling experience of finding yourself becoming a subject who you have not met, but nonetheless recognize. The reader of this book must create a voice with which to speak (think) the words (thoughts) comprising it ... Reading involves a far more intimate form of encounter. You must allow me to occupy you, your thoughts, your mind, since I have no voice with which to speak other than yours. If you are to read this book, you must allow yourself to think my thoughts and in that moment neither of us will be able to lay claim to the thought as our own exclusive creation.
>
> (Ogden, 1994, p. 1)

Thomas Ogden's quote is perhaps my favorite opening of any book in psychoanalysis. It informs the beginning passages of this book, a book about marital therapy or, more precisely, the treatment of any long-term committed relationship. Pursuant to Ogden's quote, this is a book about "a meeting of minds" (Aron, 1996). In this moment, the meeting begins with a potential relationship between you, the reader, and me, the author, representing a potential "marriage of our minds."

Beginning to read a book involves a kind of courtship, if you will. As the reader, you of course have the prerogative at any time to close the book's cover, and the relationship will be over. If you continue, however, some kind of ineffable collaboration of our minds will have to be taken more seriously. For a while, each time you pick up this book, we will be on a kind of "date," gradually interpenetrating one another's minds. Over time, we will become more deeply "engaged"— engaged, that is, in a kind of private and intimate discourse. By the time you finish the book, some aspects of both of us will forever be married, "for richer or poorer, in sickness and in health, until death do us part."

Reading should be an emotional activity, at times even conceivably a passionate one. You may hate some things that I write and possibly love others. Were I to have direct access to your mind, I might both love and hate the ways in which you construe me to make sense of what I write. The ultimate irony is that neither of us will ever know our assessments of the other. Still, our encounter will reveal a plethora of truths about each of us, something heretofore unknown.

As is true of long-term committed relationships, our thoughts will come to both comfort and disturb us; we will never grow if there is not enough common ground for our safety or enough intermittent disturbance to stimulate our growth. As Ogden noted, for you to read my text, you must allow it to give direction to your thoughts and your feelings and, in so doing, we are both likely to be changed. As you are the interpreter of my text, I must surrender to what meanings it will have for you, just as you will have to surrender some of your own most strongly held convictions to take in some of mine. If we can allow this to happen, neither of us will be the same. This is the paradigm of marriage, of long-term intimate commitment that will be discussed throughout the remainder of this book.

In the Introduction, I will tell you about me—but who prospectively are you? You must be someone at least somewhat interested in models of couples therapy, or else you would not have picked up this book. But hopefully you are interested in even more. Your professional backgrounds may vary, as well as your specific training and how that shapes your orientation to this book's topic. If you are of a family systems theory background, you may be hungering for a model that is congenial to your systems sensibility, but that also embraces the intricate conundrum of our experiential subjective sense of self, especially in all the ways that it exhibits itself unwittingly both before and after we enter into any long-term intimate commitment. This model of treatment will hopefully pique your curiosity about human beings as subjects, anchored in the gravity of deeply personal narratives that are forever challenged by and challenging to the relational systems of which any human subject is a part.

Some of you, on the other hand, may be informed by any of the multiple psychoanalytic perspectives and therefore are deeply ensconced in the unconscious realms of the experiential self. For you, this book will hopefully introduce you not only to the intrasubjective nature of human being, but also to numerous versions of intersubjective and interpersonal relating especially found in the intersubjective and relational perspectives, which will deepen your grasp of contemporary psychoanalysis. Also included in this text are other ideas simmering in the stew of contemporary psychoanalysis, presented to you in a way to apply them to couples as well.

Whether you are a couples therapist or not, hopefully you will discover ideas that enrich how you think about your individual cases, since, after all, individual psychotherapy is itself a marriage of the minds of both therapist and patient. Furthermore, as this model of treatment is embedded in the relational psychoanalytic canon, many of the ideas will apply to individual psychotherapy as well. This book will also facilitate your thinking about the extra-transferential relationships in your patients' lives outside of therapy in terms of how they richly inform the intimate dance of the patient's transference and the analyst's countertransference. Ultimately, as human beings, we are inextricably related from birth until death. The goal of this book, therefore, is to shed some light on how our all too brief existence can be enhanced through all of its relational forms.

ACKNOWLEDGMENTS

This book owes its creation to all the authors whose thinking has deeply influenced my own. There are far too many to mention individually but their names will no doubt become recognizable throughout the text. On top of my debt to all of them there are also many others who over many years volunteered their time to read early drafts of its chapters. Some were in classes I taught, some in study groups, quite a few simply having expressed an interest in reading chapters and giving me feedback. Their comments have spanned enumerable drafts that have been written and rewritten over the span of close to a decade. So to the following I say many thanks: Roberto Angelo, George Bermudez, David Blackstone, Edie Boxer, Kati Breckenridge, Sally Cassidy, William Coburn, Terry Cooper, Sona Delurgio, Stan Dudley, Stuart Ende, Glen Gabbard, Christina Griffin, Holly Hardgrove, Tyler Howard, Lynne Jacobs, Judy Van Dixhorn Kent, Chris Loeb, June Maize, Claudia Miller, Medford Moreland, Jean Wolfe Powers, Cindy Rubin-Brown, Chris Ann Vallier, and Todd Walker.

I want to also thank my wife Marcia Steinberg, my dear friend Estelle Shane, and of course Lewis Aron, co-editor of the Relational Psychoanalytic Book Series of Taylor & Francis. All three of them gave my final draft of this manuscript a very careful reading. Their feedback was indispensible to my editing the volume as it currently exists. Thanks also go to Kristopher Spring for his very helpful final editing touches, as well as to Kate Hawes, Editor at Routledge for all of her assistance in seeing this volume to its completion.

I also want to thank so many dear friends whose unflagging interest spirited me along throughout all the years I have been involved in this project. I can't remember a time when I was with them that they did not, in one fashion or another, ask: "So how's the book coming along? When is it going to be published?" And, perhaps most importantly, "When are we going to have a book signing party?!" So many thanks to John and Starr Wayne, Glen Gabbard, Fred Schlussel, Susie and Jay Jurkowitz, Gita Zarnegar, Kaj and Diane Stromer, Warren Garner, Vicki Marx, Judy Ferrari, Bobbie Berger, and Stephen Naifeh.

Everything written in this book has been professionally "field-tested" with hundreds of couples that I have either treated or supervised the treatment of for over 30 years. But even more so it has been inspired greatly by my marriage to Marcia

Steinberg for 30 years. I don't think that there is very much in this book that hasn't been witnessed and or experienced in our relationship. Her support and inspiration have taught me more than I could have ever learned without her. Lastly I want to thank our daughter Lena, who couldn't have been a cooler kid growing up and from whom I have also learned so much.

INTRODUCTION

Several years ago, I was listening to an economist on National Public Radio anguishing over the extraordinary complexity of his field. With gathering frustration, he confessed, "We know what works in practice! The question is, will it work in theory?!" I suddenly found myself in the same shoes as the commentator as I reflected upon over 30 years of theorizing about my clinical practice in couples and family therapy, as well as psychoanalysis with individual patients. As I pondered writing this book, I recognized that I seemed to be onto something in my work with couples, though I hadn't been able to make it "work" in theory. My odyssey in seeking a meaningful explanation for what I did clinically began in the early 1970s, when I was in social work graduate school at the University of Kansas. My second-year internship was at the Menninger Foundation in Topeka, one of four or five meccas of psychoanalytic training in the world. At Menninger, psychoanalysis reigned supreme. Unfortunately, the isolated, one-person psychology of that era was at least a decade away from the revolution in contemporary psychoanalysis from the intersubjective and relational perspectives, not to mention advances in infancy research, attachment theory, neuropsychology, and more.

Being at Menninger in the early 1970s, however, was quite confusing. My college life away from it was bombarded by the political climate of turmoil regarding civil rights, feminism, gay rights, the Vietnam War, and ecological imbalances. Virtually all of these problems were being understood systemically and contextually. Thus, they presented mighty challenges to the Americanized one-person, ego-psychological version of psychoanalysis in which I was being trained. To say that I was a fish out of water in the traditional psychoanalytic context underappreciates the hunger I had for ideas that linked systems and subsystems and all versions of contextualist thought about the complexity of human existence and relationality.

In my early twenties at the time, I shared the "angry young man" sensibility of many of my generation, and along with it a deep suspicion of authority.[1] No doubt this prejudiced me against many worthwhile aspects of traditional psychoanalytic thinking. Still, like a youthful revolutionary, I turned to the burgeoning family systems theories of the day. For a half-dozen years thereafter, I kept returning to these theories no matter what I was studying or practicing. This included two and a half years working in the Kansas Correctional Ombudsman's Office as an Ombudsman Associate, investigating complaints from prisoners and staff members and making recommendations for change throughout the adult penal system. When I graduated from my PhD program in Social Work from the University of Southern California in 1981, I returned to work in a hospital setting, treating adolescents and their families. As much as my appreciation of family systems theory informed me, I began to develop a new appreciation for psychoanalysis, since it was immediately apparent that although you can take the teenager out of the family you cannot take the family out of the teenage patient. By this, I mean that the adolescent patient's personality will typically reenact the dynamics of his family of origin. In these initial years of hospital work, I also began a private practice while teaching part-time at the University of Southern California Graduate School of Social Work, the University of California at Los Angeles Graduate School of Social Welfare, the Loyola Marymount University Graduate School of Clinical Art Therapy Program, and the California Institute for Clinical Social Work (subsequently renamed The Sanville Institute).

Among the broad range of courses I taught for over a decade was a course on four models of family/couples therapy. These "schools"[2] involved: a) Bowenian Family Therapy at the Georgetown Family Study Institute in Washington, DC; b) structural family therapy by Minuchin (1974) and his colleagues from the Philadelphia Child Guidance Clinic; c) the Interactional approach, which is an amalgamation of the works of Bateson, Haley, Watzlawick, Satir (1967), and many others, coalescing in the writings of the Mental Research Institute in Palo Alto; and d) another amalgamation of writings by authors such as Dicks, Boszormenyi-Nagy, Framo, and Slipp, who were shaping family and couples therapy in terms of psychoanalytically informed object relations theory. Since each theory plays at least some beginning role in the ideas that organize the work I am presenting in this book, I have briefly outlined their basic ideas in Appendix A as I both understood and taught them.

In the course of teaching all four models, my attempts at creating an integrative model from this system of generalizations was never very satisfactory to me. While the models spoke brilliantly of the systematic issues complexly entwining human beings, they never quite captured the passions of being human. As family therapists Fred and Bunny Duhl once averred, "You can't kiss a system." As much as these theories informed parts of my practice, none alone or in combination really covered it. Paraphrasing the economist's protest, I sensed what worked in my practice, though not how it worked in theory.

By the early 1980s, as my attitude toward psychoanalytic theory shifted, I became primed for the explosion in contemporary psychoanalytic theory and practice. By the end of the 1980s, I discovered *Psychoanalytic Treatment: An Intersubjective Approach* by Stolorow, Brandchaft, and Atwood (1987). Although a book about psychoanalytic treatment of individuals, it supplied conceptually important elements missing in my ideas about conjoint therapy.

I began translating many salient principles into concepts that fit with my mode of treatment. It was from their seminal offerings that the beginnings of my model of conjoint psychotherapy began.

In the early 1990s, I also became familiar with the works of the Relational psychoanalysts referenced throughout this text. Those initially shaping my thinking were Stephen Mitchell, Lewis Aron, Jody Davies, Jessica Benjamin, Irwin Hoffman, Donnel Stern, and Philip Bromberg, as well as many, many more. On top of all of these authors, I also have drawn from the rich treasure trove of ideas from infant research, attachment theory, complexity theory, mentalization theory, gender and cultural studies, and the empirical observations of John Gottman's group at the University of Washington.

The culmination of my theoretical research is organized around three themes that are operationalized in Six Steps, outlining a method for thinking about and practicing conjoint psychotherapy, in Chapters 2 through 7. The three themes include what I refer to as:

1. the actualization of self-experience in the context of a long-term, committed intimate relationship;
2. mutual recognition of both partners' subjective experiences;
3. the relationship having a mind of its own.

The Six Steps are outlined as follows:

Step One: How the therapist's attunement to each spouse's subjectivity instills hope, perspective, and the possibility for renewed growth.

Step Two: The therapist's assertion that none of the three participants in the therapy has a more correct (i.e., more "objective") view of reality than any of the others, while supporting each one's needs to be seen as the arbiter of what is true (i.e., "fits") within her/his experience in the moment.

Step Three: The exploration of how each partner's complaint arises from a multi-variant developmental history that contextualizes what each partner brings to their relationship.

Step Four: Awakening of the "slumbering giant": when the "dread to repeat" repetitive transference states shifts into the "dread not to." This step examines how partners reenact their conflictual pasts in the service of "trying to remain the same while changing" (Bromberg, 1998). It further explores phenomena regarding dissociated self-states, finally emerging only after other self-states become actualized by the progress of the treatment. For these dissociated states to emerge, they must be enacted.

Step Five: The enrichment of each partner's capacity for self-actualization through enhanced introspection in the presence of the other. This step also accentuates each partner's sense of ownership of the multiplicity of their personality, along with learning to negotiate seemingly irreconcilable aspects of each one's sense of selfhood.

Step Six: The facilitation of each partner's capacity to attune to and support the other's introspection and personal growth. It follows the progress of the intrasubjective work of Step Five regarding recognition of and negotiation between multiple self-states, including sometimes having to surrender to that which is non-negotiable. As such, Step Five prepares the couple to engage in comparable processes intersubjectively. Thereafter, Step Six enhances the couple's capacity to negotiate their *relational* conflicts where possible and to come to terms with those that are non-negotiable. All of this builds to the internalization of this conjoint treatment model, allowing for the facilitation of each partner's capacity to attune to and support each other's introspection and personal growth. This then leads to their self-actualization, increased capacity for mutual recognition, and the relationship developing a creative mind of its own. This last idea serves the couple in both maturing and growing old together, while facing the vicissitudes of losses that come with aging and eventually facing their mortality.

Since I first published the earliest version of this model over two decades ago, the use of the term *steps* has never felt completely comfortable, though I have never been able to come up with a suitable alternative. Others have suggested terms such as *dimensions*, *layers*, *phases*, *movements*, *acts*, *tasks*, and so on. Still, all of these also suffer similar problems. The problem with *steps*, as well as with these other terms, is that they connote and denote different things.

Steps, for example, is powerfully suggestive of a linear and hierarchical progression. That, however, is at odds with a model that in practice is dynamically nonlinear and that fits more in the contemporary tradition of thinking of theory and practice in terms of complexity theory. On the other hand, at least conceptually, *steps* does capture a progression of ideas that follow one another. For example, the model begins with fostering reciprocal attunement as a means of repairing ruptures (Step One). This process is furthered by the active engagement and encouragement of "perspectival realism," meaning the fostering of each partner's subjective perspective (Step Two). Fostering this epistemological stance is assisted through the persistent illumination of the backgrounds of the partners (Step Three). Understanding the partners' backgrounds helps in appreciating the emergence of enactments, especially ones that are resistant to attunement and therefore must be enacted (Step Four). Enactments are necessary in exposing multiple dissociated self-states that need to be worked with so that they are no longer split off and projected from one partner onto the other (Step Five). All of this lends to the partners' enhanced ability to collaborate and negotiate a third way of relating that differs from their historical penchant to degenerate into "doer and done-to" (right/wrong, dominant/submissive) binaries (Step Six). The model coalesces in this premise: *That which needs to be negotiated between the partners has to first be negotiated within each of them.* Clearly, this view of the steps does suggest a kind of progression, an arch, if you will.

Still, from a complexity theory standpoint, it is possible for all Six Steps to emerge in a session and, furthermore, that the ideas articulated in each of the steps chapters could, through "soft assembly" (Harris, 2009), belong in other steps as well. A very important understanding of the model includes that the steps recycle over and over throughout the treatment.

In short, a stepwise model like this one is a bit messy. While it implies conceptually a kind of linear progression, in practice it is inherently more of a nonlinear, dynamic process. As a result, a compelling metaphor for the Six Steps is to think of them much like the famous staircases in the M. C. Escher print titled *Ascending and Descending* (Locher, 1971). In this etching, the uppermost staircase landing paradoxically ends its "ascent" right back at the beginning staircase landing. Around and around the staircases ascend, endlessly taking the viewer back to the beginning. In a comparable fashion, a marriage or other long-term commitment suffers the recurrence of ruptures born of emerging personal differences that result from the partners' continual growth and development. This requires going back through cycles of rupture and repair, which culminate in new meanings about each partner and their relationship. All of this is inevitable relative to the partners' pursuit of self-actualization. In their pursuit of these, they will inevitably stub one another's toes, much like learning (negotiating) a new dance routine. Even the best attempts at being empathically attuned and supportive of one another will inevitably be fraught with disruptions. No matter how much partners may hope for it to be otherwise, they simply cannot always accommodate one another without violating their own needs and wishes.

While *self-actualization, mutual recognition,* and *the relationship having a mind of its own* provide the three fundamental organizational themes of the book, there is an additional question that will infuse the Six Steps, and that is the question posed by Stephen Mitchell (2002) in his posthumously published volume *Can Love Last? The Fate of Romance over Time.* In it, Mitchell challenged that our conventional explanation for why passion in many long-term relationships eventually fades—that romance is childish and immature and that attachment love is what is mature—is problematic at best and, quite possibly, mostly erroneous. As will be taken up in greater detail in the next chapter, Mitchell posits that attachment love and its presumptive role as the "real" relationship is as illusory as is romantic love. For love to last, Mitchell says, we must come to terms with both illusory systems and that, in so doing, we must learn to hold them in dialectical tension. They represent less of a problem to be solved than a paradox to be managed. Many additional relational authors will also weigh in on this paradox throughout the book.

The first chapter presents a theoretical overview, while the six chapters following it each embody one of the Six Steps. Practice questions for each of the steps are articulated in Appendix B as probe questions and ideas germane to each step. They create a kind of summary way of thinking about the issues taken up in each of the steps. Chapter 8 presents a case illustration of a couple, Michael and Carmen, that progresses through all Six Steps of treatment. The final chapter involves my responses to "frequently asked questions," which I have been asked for over 30 years of teaching, supervising, and presenting at conferences.

Notes

1 Mitchell (1993) noted in *Hope and Dread in Psychoanalysis* that, in the context of countercultural changes in the 1960s and 1970s (including more critical views of authority), contemporary analysts have learned that it is as important to question the patient's over-compliance to authority as it once was to question the patient's resistance to it.
2 Many other theoreticians were surveyed, such as Ackerman (1958, 1966), Wynne (1970), and Whitaker (1977). I settled on a deeper investigation of the four schools, however, because the conceptual core of each was sufficiently unique to be replicated by the works of others working in their own comparable systems.

1

THEORETICAL OVERVIEW

Beginning with the last half of the nineteenth century, and concurrent with the massive socio-cultural-economic changes coming out of the Industrial Revolution, a monumental change in the institution of marriage occurred, when it shifted from an arrangement agreed upon by the two families of the prospective bride and groom to a decision made on their own (Mitchell, 2002; Perel, 2007). Historically, the conscious needs of the family social system, often following the traditions of the community of which it was a part, determined the criteria for selection. By contrast, for the first time in human history, a new system introduced the potential for unconscious choice to be a primary factor in mate selection. Of course, for many years, this newer way of selecting a spouse was still likely occupied with conscious agendas, such as those reflecting the needs and interests of the intended's social networks. But the very allowance of the personally intimate factors of love, passion, and desire as determining criteria opened the door for the unconscious mind to play a powerful role in the ultimate selection of a mate. I believe the ripple effect of this dramatic social change potentially insinuates itself into virtually every marital couple—or otherwise long-term committed relationship—entering conjoint therapy. As such, every system of couples therapy ultimately grapples with the ramifications of this choice.

Over many years of treating couples, providing consultations to other clinicians, and teaching seminars, I have stated that the goal of my approach is to enable two "'real selves' to intimately connect under that same roof." I have added, however, that in so doing the partners will inevitably "stub one another's toes," and that central to my thesis is their developing the capacity to repair inevitable ruptures.

The conceptual basis for all of this begins with three themes, representative of qualities that are optimal for the functioning of long-term committed relationships. The three themes pertain to *self-actualization in a committed intimate relationship, mutual recognition,* and *the relationship having a mind of its own.*

The actualization of the self in the context of an intimate relationship

> The distinguished neurologist Kurt Goldstein (1995) said, "There's only one drive by which human activity is initiated: the drive for self-actualization" (p. 67). To actualize oneself means to express what is uniquely one's own: actualization of the expression of agency.
>
> (Modell, 2008, p. 351)

To capture something of what Modell is asserting, I begin with a story about our daughter, Lena, at the age of 5. One afternoon, my wife Marcia and I decided that we wanted to have some time alone, and decided to see if her grandparents would take Lena for a sleepover. We called them early in the afternoon and left our request on their answering machine. As evening approached, however, having not heard from them, we had all but given up hope, when they called and said they would be glad to accommodate our wish.

Elated, we went to Lena and announced with joy that she was going to get to have a sleepover with grandma and grandpa. Our elation stemmed from selfish motives for sure, but it also drew from the anticipation that Lena too would be thrilled, since she loved time with her grandparents. To our dismay, however, Lena burst into tears. Knowing implicitly that we would have normally discussed this matter earlier in the day, and that she might have had some input about it, she retorted to our gleeful solicitations with "You didn't give me time to know my own *mind*!"

It was the first time she had uttered this expression, and it certainly was not one (at the tender age of 5) we could have imagined she would have. It was possible that she had overheard our conversations about what it means to have "a mind of one's own," as well as to "know one's 'mind,'" but it seemed unfathomable that she could grasp this meaning, though at least on some implicit level she surely did. Embedded in her assertion are several critical assumptions. First, in this particular space/time coordinate, she grasped that from the standpoint of her *sense of self* she was unprepared to react to what had confronted her. Furthermore, she implicitly knew that if her parents had given her the time to consider something related to her, as she would normally expect, she could better know what it is that *she* wanted to do, that she would be able to know "her own mind." Hence, her statement implied some recognition that she had the capacity to make her choice vis-à-vis her desires, and that if she did not know what she wanted to do in a particular moment, she could, if allowed, know it soon enough. (Five minutes later, Lena decided that she did want a sleepover at her grandparents, and we, relieved of our guilt, scampered off to our film.)

The fulfillment of self-actualization in a long-term committed relationship to which each partner is drawn arises out of a longing to accomplish something incomplete in their upbringing—that is, to fulfill what has felt deficient, or to repair what has felt fundamentally broken. This involves the hope to become who they have not yet become, though it also entails, albeit unconsciously, the emancipation of a highly self-centered if not a seemingly selfish perspective.[1] This latter point argues that their hopes for self-fulfillment are uniquely counterbalanced by their dreads that what they desire may very well be withheld or, even worse, that there will be a repetition of the profound disappointments about which their developmental narrative of hurt, pain, and vulnerability are "writ large." This makes the hunger for actualization fraught with risk. Consequently, to control against being disappointed by the whims of the other, sometimes partners paradoxically act in manners so fraught with the anticipation of their *not* getting the thing they seek, they engage in an unconscious self-fulfilling prophecy, wherein they reject what might be offered even before it is. Given this vulnerability to self-fulfilling defeat, we might wonder why partners take any risks at all. And yet, it is the press of self-actualization that truly enlivens a marriage by "pushing" each partner to seek for something more. Actualization can therefore be a hotbed for passionate discord, though a powerful motivating force for being together at all.

In employing the term *actualization*, I am, of course, relating it to Maslow's (1943) hierarchy of needs, wherein only after a basic foundation of physical needs has been cemented can one's attention finally turn to the fullest realization of a sense of selfhood. While I believe that some of the work of self-actualization occurs in instances of solitude (Storr, 1988), I am focusing this book on how, in life and in therapy, each partner's actualization is experienced as being both thwarted and fulfilled in the context of connections with intimate others.

The actualization of self is a theoretically complex notion. Chief among many of these ideas is our possessing a sense of *agency*, which is definitive in terms of capturing how each of us is unique. So what *is* agency? Fonagy (2003) notes:

> Sometime during their second year, infants develop an understanding of agency that is already mentalistic: They start to understand that they are intentional agents whose actions are caused by prior states of mind, such as desires. At this point, they also understand that their actions can bring about change in minds as well as bodies: For example, they clearly understand that if they point at something, they can make another person change their focus of attention ... this point marks when the two-year-old child comes to be able to distinguish his own desires from those of the other person.
>
> (p. 421)

What Fonagy is positing is what Damasio (1994, 1999) and Bucci (2002) refer to as "core-consciousness." That is, the state of consciousness that lends to experiences of having a core self and out of which "extended consciousness" develops, lending to one's sense of an "autobiographical self." All of this consolidates into our having a sense of identity, personhood, and personal narrative. And all of these elements operate on multiple levels of complexity, involving comparisons of the past with fantasies about the future, which become instrumental to our understanding of each marital partner's wishes, longings, expectations, and of course disappointments.

Thus, agency suggests that, despite our biological determinism, we remain agents of "free will." We can choose, and in so doing, at least in some manner define what it means to be ourselves. Still, fluidity of development over our lifetime dictates that many of those choices will likely change over time. Understanding this requires our capacity for self-reflection, which is a topic taken up in greater detail later, referring to the ability to "meta-cognize" and not simply react to our experience.

Meanwhile, though the description of these processes may seem terribly conscious, in fact much of what undergirds our sense of agency is unconscious. Thus, our intentions, our sense of purpose, derive from our unconscious self (i.e., extended and autobiographical memory). This complex memory system involves first declarative memory, which is typically accessed through verbal symbolization. A second memory system involves our implicit (nonverbal) and procedural memory (the "autopilot" of our personality organization). This system involves our more automatic ways of doing things, such as driving and riding a bike, as well as the routine, almost automatic ways in which we react to different relational contexts. Agency, however, also pertains to our capacity to reflect upon our experience, and in particular the meaning that such reflection conveys to us, as well as the choices such reflection avails to us. Still, we thrive upon and are enlivened by being spontaneous, while we also make agentic choices as outgrowths of being reflective. These principles relate to one another in an endless Möbius loop, wherein being spontaneous in very vitalizing ways folds seamlessly into processes of reflection that then add material for more spontaneous existence.

The Möbius loop model helps us understand one of the most profound evolutions in conceptualizing agency, arising from the neurosciences, which provocatively argues that agency is an illusion, albeit a necessary one. Modell (2008) writes:

> We can accept the idea that the feeling of agency is a construction of our brain and in this sense is illusory, if we consider that all our mental constructions are in a certain sense illusory. If illusion is defined as a false appearance, a belief that does not have its correspondence in the physical world, the current view in neuroscience is that everything the brain constructs is an illusion. Selves do not exist in the physical world; our perception of the self is a construction of our brain. We essentially imagine ourselves. But we should not depreciate or disparage belief in illusions as false conceptions; if the self is an illusion and the feeling of agency is an illusion, these are illusions without which we cannot live.
>
> (p. 362)

Despite agency being an illusion, it is one upon which we rely in determining our intentions and the intentions of others, for that matter. In this vein, neuroscientists also inform us that unconscious intentionality *de facto* precedes conscious intentionality.[2]

Now, if what I am positing so far seems too dry and too theoretical, consider that every disagreement, every argument, every discordant moment in the life of a couple is taking up dueling versions of reality. This can lead to mini-wars, the stakes of which are no less than the preservation of each party's sense of sanity— that is, their sense of what constitutes their version of mind, and how that version makes sense of what they interpret constitutes reality. It is this that makes the principles of "perspectival realism" (discussed in Step Two) the lynchpin of this model of treatment, for it is perspectival realism that argues that everyone has their own unique, subjective perspective on reality, or what I refer to as "great-big-altogether-everything-else-both-beyond-and-including-me." This is what we commonly refer to as "reality."

The thing about our "illusions," however, is that we can get stuck in them—that is, constrained in our capacity to choose and act, or to be relatively free of them (Weisel-Barth, 2009). Thus, our personal sense of agency functions in a most gratifying way when we feel less constrained in how we determine and pursue personal goals in work, love, and play. By contrast, it founders to the extent that our sense of agency functions more for defensive purposes, and in fact serves to "pervert" (Gentile, 2001) our pursuit of work, love, and play. This perversion of agency pertains to the degrees of freedom in our capacity to imagine and to make living choices.[3]

From all of this, we begin to see that agency, however individualistic it may seem philosophically, is psychologically a very relationally oriented phenomenon. Greenberg (1991) and elsewhere Aron (1996) argue that often our sense of agency is measured by our sense of being able to *effect* things in life (*effectance*). However, that feeling hinges upon the degree to which we feel *safe* doing so. Both authors argue that the crucible of agency is found in our conflicting needs as human beings to be effective—that is, to be impactful while also feeling safe and secure in our attempts to be agentic.[4]

In all these ways, agency is clearly not an isolated mind phenomenon, but one that can only be understood in terms of the reciprocal impact that one experiences in the relational field of others, of which one is a part (Stern, 2004). As Benjamin (1995) notes, agency requires, "the other's confirming response, which tells us that we have created meaning, had an impact, have revealed an intention" (p. 33). Thus, while agency appears to arise intrasubjectively (from within), Benjamin (1999) asserts that it requires another's confirming response regarding our meaning, the impact it has, and what it reveals about what we intended. This then places agency within the intersubjective field of mutual need, mutual responsibility, and mutual recognition.

The intersubjective field in which each partner's sense of agency arises is therefore an additional factor in establishing the horizons of each partner's self-actualization (Stern, 1997). It means that how one lives out one's sense of agency in terms of self-actualization must be perpetually renegotiated in intimate relationships (Pizer, 1998). These points will be elaborated more in the second theme of this book, regarding mutual recognition of both partners' subjectivity.

The mutual recognition of each partner's subjectivity

This theme hinges to a large extent on Jessica Benjamin's ideas about mutual recognition, which is a foundational concept to her theory of intersubjectivity. Benjamin presents a scholastically creative treatise involving, among important others, Hegel's philosophy (1807), Winnicott's developmental theory, and Beebe and Lachmann's infancy research. Concurring with Daniel Stern (1985), Benjamin sees intersubjectivity as a developmental achievement,[5] the first evidence of which arises around 8–9 months of life.

Intersubjectivity is a condition of our human nature. It is an innate, primary motivational system (Stern, 2004). The desire for intersubjectivity is one of the major motivations that drives psychotherapy forward. Patients want to be known and to share what it feels like to be them. Evolutionarily, this intersubjective tendency also strongly favors species survival. As Slavin and Kriegman (1992, 1998a, 1998b, 1998c) note: "Intersubjectivity makes three main contributions to assuring survival: 1) it promotes group formation, 2) it enhances group functioning, and 3) it assures group cohesion by giving rise to morality. The same impulse that contributes to species survival can also make psychic intimacy among friends possible" (p. 98).

Broadly speaking, the intersubjective motivational system concerns regulating psychological belonging versus psychological aloneness. The poles of the spectrum are, at one end, cosmic loneliness, and at the other, mental transparency, fusion, and the disappearance of the self. The intersubjective motivational system regulates our comfort, thriving somewhere between these two poles. The exact point of comfort depends on one's role in any group with whom one has a personal history. The point on the continuum must be negotiated continually. Too much is at stake for it not to be.

Returning to Benjamin (1999), what is critical is that her ideas represent a bold departure from mainstream psychoanalytic theories such as ego psychology, object relations, self psychology, and Kleinian theory, insofar as Benjamin argues that an emerging sense of selfhood (i.e., subject) occurs not simply in relation to the regulatory supplies and provisions of the other (i.e., object), but also in *discovering the subject in the other*—that is, in discovering how the other is different from oneself. In fact, to my way of thinking, Benjamin's (1992) argument represents a true evolutionary step in psychoanalytic theorizing. She boldly reshapes Freud's dictum of "where id is, ego shall be," as well as the object relationists' dictum of "where ego is, objects must be," to her own dictum, "where objects were, subjects must be." Clearly, this last dictum is imperative to childhood development, but, to truly thrive, marital dyads need to develop the critical capacity for *subject-to-subject* relating amidst the inevitability and sometimes advantage of *subject-to-object* relating.

Benjamin points out that mutual recognition is often mired in a *paradox of recognition*, which embodies conflicts between each party's *assertion of self* versus *recognition of the other*. Slavin and Kriegman (1992, 1998a, 1998b) and Slavin (2007), in fact, argue that the tension of this paradox is actually in the makeup of our genetically structured evolutionary plan. By that, they are suggesting that there is always some potential tension between conflicts of self-interest colliding with our biological imperative to relate. Slavin (2007) argues that this conflict is fundamental to our understanding of the adaptational strategies embedded in our propensity for "self-deception," on the one hand, and our "adaptive skepticism" about others' authenticity, on the other.

Slavin notes that the roots of this psychosocial conflict began approximately 150,000 years ago. It was about this time when our predecessors started to develop language along with a capacity to communicate via symbols. This evolutionary feat set in motion an extraordinary schism between human beings' raw experience of nature and our intimate relationship to it, and our capacity to reflect upon and communicate about both our sense of nature as well as our experience of it. As these cognitive processes evolved, there developed a greater capacity of individuals to reflect on their experience, hence the emergence of a more complex sense of self than had heretofore existed in the animal kingdom. Of course, what accompanied this evolutionary change also set in motion the beginnings of human beings' psychological conflict. By this, I mean that our self-needs and desires (our self-actualization) often clashes with the needs and interests of the group, family, tribe, community, society, culture, or whatever variant of affiliation one is studying. Attempts at mastering this conflict often entail the denial of selfhood strivings in the form of "self-deception." Such deception is managed through key ego defense mechanisms such as repression and dissociation. And yet, there still remains some implicit sense of conflict between the human being's felt sense of selfhood and its meaning (whether real or imagined) to the group of which she is a part, and with whom she shares a language and symbol system.

What is fascinating about human beings is our capacity to imagine how our state of mind may very well apply to others. In this manner, human beings are burdened with an implicit sense of others' proneness to self-deception. This realization, then, lends to a sense of "adaptive skepticism" regarding the authenticity of others. On this note, Slavin writes that exploring the authenticity of the other often requires a

> probing of the [other's] otherness ... [in a manner that] entails a bit more active taking apart or breaking down of aspects of the [other's] subjectivity—a process that entails more of some type of adaptive aggression than anything that is encompassed by the ways we usually conceptualize the signaling and provision of selfobject needs.
>
> (p. 26)

What Slavin is suggesting is that there is a fair degree of aggression involved in self-assertion as well as in dealing with the aggression of others. Thus, when the romantic idealization or "honeymoon phase" is over, the real work of the relationship begins. And that work entails a potential battleground over the competition of each partner's actual needs and desires, which are far more threatening to take up, since what has presumably settled down is loath to be stirred up once again. This conflict arises over both concrete provisions as well as psychological ones. It is adjudicated through conflicts over the respective systems of meaning which each partner brings to the relationship, which becomes fundamental to how needs and desires—both practically and psychologically—will be negotiated or not.

Returning to Benjamin, the road to mutual recognition involves a developmental process of finding the subjectivity in the other, a process whereby (from the standpoint of actual child development) the child's omnipotent fantasy organization regarding herself and the other transforms into the recognition of the other as subjectively different, a center of his own initiative, a relative agent of "free will." This is a huge achievement, one that entails the child's fantasy-based worldview undergoing an interpersonal encounter that compels its accommodation of a new way of seeing and experiencing himself *and* the other.

In her conceptualization of the achievement of an attained capacity for mutual recognition, Benjamin finds considerable explanatory power in Winnicott's theory of the importance of ruthless, sometimes "destructive" play that the child enacts in her fantasy "destruction of the other."[6] The term *ruthless* frequently confuses readers, because it is often linked in conventional language with concepts like treachery. In this case, however, ruthlessness means simply that one is not exhibiting "ruth"—that is, a response that is occupied by care and concern for the other, the literal translation of *ruth*. Transient moments of ruthlessness in intimately committed relationships are quite commonplace, unless it is the kind of relationship that is phobic about aggression.

Meanwhile, "killing" the other off through ruthless treatment—first in infant/child development, and later on in adult treatment—enables individuals to realize that the actual (real) external other (whether parent or analyst) survives the ruthless attack. Indeed, she may even flourish independently of the one's omnipotent fantasy control. This process is especially cemented when the recipient of ruthlessness responds in a minimally defensive manner that neither lashes out nor abandons the person being ruthless.

Following Hegel's logic, Benjamin argues that the paradox of this entirely self-centered assertion is that one cannot fully appreciate being recognized by another, if that other is only experienced as an object—that is, only as a narcissistic extension of one's own fantasy world of needs and desires. If I only see myself in your eyes in the manner that I have coerced *you to see me*, then I will never have a true reflection of how I am seen by an independent other, for it is only through the independent other's recognition—outside of one's solipsistic fantasy—that one feels truly recognized.

By contrast, feeling that one has ultimate control over the object, in fantasy or in reality, lends to a person becoming readily bored. It underscores why narcissistically organized adults end up leapfrogging from one relationship to another.

Meanwhile, by not recognizing the degree to which narcissists coercively control others (frequently in the service of unconsciously attempting to make themselves feel safe and cohesive), they drain (in due time) any semblance of "otherness" and difference from the other. As will be illustrated in case material throughout this book, this process also manifests over and over in marriages, especially in moments of mutual negation—the necessary precursor state to mutual recognition.

The antidote to this solipsistic position is to be able to embrace the difference and "otherness" (alterity) of the other. Of course, the problem in couples therapy is that recognizing one's partner's uniquely different subjectivity often entails some threat to one's own sense of selfhood, especially when one is constrained by *transference convictions* that provide cohesion to one's worldview through rigidly attributing what one's partner thinks and feels, irrespective of how untrue those attributions are to one's partner's own experience. Overcoming the constraints of an omnipotent solipsistic worldview can be especially daunting for those whose fundamental organization has been traumatized by the caregiving others in their lives.[7]

The therapeutic question remains, then: How does each partner overcome the tenacious grip of their own repetitive transference organization from constraining both getting and giving the quality of recognition that each of them needs and desires? Elaborating upon Winnicott's ideas, Benjamin (1992) writes: "in the mental act of negating or obliterating the object, which may be expressed in a real attack on the other, we find out whether the real other survives" (p. 51). Survival here optimally means that the other responds relatively non-defensively (it's impossible to expect one not to defend oneself at least to some degree when feeling attacked) yet holds to his own boundaries and needs. It means, for example, that I develop the ability to stand firm, while not retaliating or abandoning or pulling rank on you, despite the fact that the version of me that you are asserting is born out of your fantasy of who I am, instead of actually recognizing who I experience myself to be. In successful patterns of rupture and repair, marital partners do exactly this. It is through the assertion of our own self-centered ways of relating, without necessarily insisting on their fulfillment, that we come to discover something—not only about ourselves, but about each other. In the course of doing so, each comes to relinquish his or her internal fantasy relationship of the other, while coming to recognize something about the other (at least for that moment) that was heretofore unrecognizable.

To develop both personally and relationally, we have to expose ourselves and the other to how our omnipotent fantasies—those tiny incessant daydreamed dress rehearsals about how things are supposed to be—are over-determining our relationship. It is against this backdrop that novel emerging patterns of self-actualization result in bursts of self-assertion, which often necessitate moments of ruthlessness. To invoke Winnicott's notion, these are emergent patterns of new "true-self" experiencing that frequently can only come forth from temporarily not recognizing the other. Furthermore, because development is not static, this process occurs over and over. Recognition in general, and therefore mutual recognition in particular, is perpetually ruptured, requiring repair. Mutual recognition, Benjamin avers, is at best accomplished and lost, re-accomplished and lost, and so forth. This model of conjoint therapy also recognizes that subject-to-object relating can represent modes of enlivening a relationship in a manner that the pure constancy of subject-to-subject relating might ultimately dull,[8] a point taken up momentarily on the topic of "can love last?"

The problem that Benjamin (2004) keenly notes is that when there is not the ability to repair and restore mutual recognition, relationships devolve into structures of "split complementarity" (i.e., dominance and submission). Taken to the extreme, such relationships exemplify qualities of sadomasochism (Aron, 2003), wherein the "submissive" loses his or her ability to even mentalize long enough to know his or her position of self-assertion. He or she becomes subsumed under the subjective order of the dominant partner, though this latter position is seldom very gratifying. It is during rigidly fixed stretches of split complementarity that the relationship begins evincing structured patterns of relating that suggest it has developed "a dysfunctional mind of its own." Split complementarity rapidly devolves into "reversible complementarity," in which the positions of dominance and submission rapidly trade places, like scenes from Edward Albee's *Who's Afraid of Virginia Woolf?* (1962). Such a dysfunctional relational mindset requires a different version of the "relationship having a mind of its own" to break out of this rigid patterning. In contemporary psychoanalytic literature, this epiphenomenon has been discussed richly, complexly, and often confusedly in terms of the "psychoanalytic third."[9]

The relationship having a mind of its own

What is critical about the relationship having a mind of its own is that, up to this point, the concepts of self-actualization and mutual recognition pertain principally to the individual partners of the relationship, as well as what bearing their recognition of one another's individual subjective experience has upon their becoming ever more actualized. These ideas, while critical to this model of conjoint therapy, do not quite capture the unique quality that each relationship has on its own—that is, what distinguishes it from all other relationships.

For a relational mind to emerge in a relationship requires what Benjamin refers to as surrendering to the "thirdness" of the relationship. Here, Benjamin's (2004) ideas involve an elaboration of Emmanuel Ghent's (1990) seminal concept of "surrender." Ghent's treatise on surrender articulates its difference from submission, and even more to the point, its distinction from the masochistic position. Instead, Ghent sees surrender as allowing for the co-constructive, co-authorial aspect of each partner to the other—each being open to allowing themselves to transiently identify with one another's projections without this devolving into a rigid pattern of projective identification. When the latter occurs, the couple degenerates into a rigidified pattern of dominance and submission. This helpful

16

delineation also clears up some of the confusion that may arise in Ogden (1994) ascribing both positive and negative functions of the "subjugating third."

Benjamin's differentiation of surrender from submission helps distinguish how relationships can maintain a climate of playfulness from patterns of split complementarity. In thirdness, partners surrender positions of dominance while not engaging in submission. Both parties' surrender is ultimately additive to their relationship. It represents something synthesizing, indeed organic, in their creation of a living relationship that is truly greater than the sum of the two of them. This also helps distinguish the conditions under which mutual recognition can occur and those under which it cannot. Indeed, Benjamin (2002) notes a circularly reinforcing process, whereby:

> [W]e might say that the third is that to which we surrender, and thirdness is the mental space that facilitates or results from surrender. In my thinking, the term surrender also implies the aspect of mutual recognition, of accepting the other's separateness and difference rather than interacting with the intent to control or coerce … The other's recognition is what helps create the space of thirdness that makes surrender possible. Then again, we might think of surrender as making recognition possible— allowing the outside, different other to come into view as we let go of the preconceived internal other. We are then able to negotiate differences in the space of the thirdness.
>
> (pp. 2, 4)

Perhaps the simplest way to think of the psychoanalytic third in relation to the relationship having a mind of its own is to think of the "positive third" versus the "negative third." The former represents an intersubjectively co-constructed relational mindset that allows for more "degrees of freedom" in the field (Stern, 2012) (e.g., openness to possibility and variance)—that is, more variance versus the latter, in which there is great invariance and rigidity of patterns of interacting. When a couple is open to positive thirdness, they become a veritable playhouse of improvisational theater, versus a more constrained relationship preoccupied by fixed roles, scripts, even props, this latter manner of behaving simulating the staging of classical theater, wherein each participant's character constricts their mode of relating. Indeed, more pathological family systems embody "rules" that constrain participants' capacity to even define their relationships, sometimes including making them impossible to define (Palazzoli et al., 1978). The treasure trove of family therapy concepts briefly outlined in Appendix A of this book captures a variety of rules that govern processes of differentiation, obfuscation, triangulation, projection, and identification, not to mention collusions and blurred boundaries.

The collapse of thirdness in a relationship periodically occurs in even the best of marital relationships. Thus, in couples therapy, *the therapist must become the embodiment of thirdness*, by being the one party in the room that can recognize the subjective realities of both partners, especially when one's developmental strivings become frightening to the another. As a transitional representative of mutual recognition, the therapist becomes the exemplar of the steps illustrated in the next six chapters, which over the course of treatment ideally becomes internalized by the marital partners.

Can love last?

In his final book, *Can Love Last: The Fate of Romance over Time*, published posthumously[10] in 2002, Stephen Mitchell raised the question that has dogged psychoanalysis from its inception. He notes that Freud (1957a/1912) intoned, "Where they love, they have no desire, where they desire they cannot love." In his inimical fashion, Mitchell does not directly answer the question his title poses so much as reveal his thoughts about it, and therein challenge others to contemplate the fate of love in modern times. Likewise, in a tradition that is more noted for the questions with which it confronts psychoanalysis than the solutions it arrives upon, a number of authors within the relational canon (Blechner, Crastnopol, Frommer, Goldner, Slavin, Stein, Stern, Wrye; all 2006) embraced Mitchell's challenge, positing a fascinating array of responses of their own. Some of their thoughts, along with Mitchell's, will be initially introduced here, but thereafter latticed throughout this volume, giving momentum to the arch of ideas covered in the Six Steps of this model of conjoint therapy. What is apparent from each author's contribution is that there is no "one-size-fits-all" answer that speaks to the question "Can love last?" Instead, there are a plethora of ideas that compel our attention and that provide responses that inform us of a wide variety of circumstances in which modern couples find themselves.

Ever the dialectical thinker, Mitchell posed romance and attachment as being in contention with one another. If romance is the launch vehicle for starting a relationship, it is attachment that tethers the couple together as they voyage into the deep dark space of the unknowable vicissitudes of every couple's relationship. But here is the rub: Attachment seems in many cases to kill romance and, with it, desire, hence Freud's cynicism. Romance, Mitchell avers, invokes synonymous ideas such as love, desire, novelty, excitement, arousal, mystery, spontaneity, transcendence, adventure, childlikeness, passion, danger, risk, and always the unknown. By contrast, attachment weds with words such as stability, safety, predictability, commitment, control, continuity, certainty, and at least the conviction that the future is knowable. It is hard to find two systems of ideas more divisive and conflicted.

Mitchell points out that conventional thinking, especially governed on the cultural convention of Western heterosexual marriage, appears to latch onto the attachment pole. Conventional wisdom's bias is that romance, though desirable in the beginning, is ultimately rather illusory, ephemeral, and fleeting. In place of its childlike disposition, partners scramble in an effort to make their relationships committed, safe, stable, predictable, and known—known in the sense that, after the courtship and honeymoon, the couple settles down and each really gets to know each other. Romance is a young person's game (whatever the actual partners' ages), not for the steadily married, who have higher procreative and other life-consolidating ambitions in mind. Yet it is the myth of the "reality" of the predictable, known attachment that Mitchell provocatively calls into question.

Attachment, and all that it presumes, especially the idea that partners are knowable and known to one another, is as big a myth as romance itself. In short, in dialectical tension are actually two illusory systems. Furthermore, Mitchell avers the latter illusion, attachment, is in many ways as potentially problematic as the so-called illusion of romance, because both are actually frequently defensive strategies against the fearful vicissitudes of love. The attachment conceit becomes a mechanism for obscuring how partners are afraid to know themselves as well as be known by each other. Any way we slice it, everything we think about romance/love versus attachment are equal parts illusion. At the very least, they are constructions of our own subjective sensibilities and not by any means a god's eye, objective view of reality. On this latter point, Mitchell is quick to encourage that we disabuse ourselves of any thoughts of objectivity about ourselves, our partner, our relationship, and lastly, what we blithely cast about as being love.

Mostly, our convictions involve deeply personal, private ideas, often "unformulated experiences" (Stern, 1997) and "unthought knowns" (Bollas, 1989). All of this is scary in that we know so little about them. In short, the attachment illusion is in place to ward off the very elements of danger and risk that romance invites—that once my partner really gets to know me, I will be found lacking, potentially humiliated, if not even abandoned. Love is dangerous stuff, certainly not for sissies. Mitchell warns, "It is not that romance fades over time, but it does become riskier."

Perhaps the author who conducted the most elaborate investigation of the theme that drove Mitchell's *Can Love Last?* is Esther Perel (2007), whose monumental book *Mating in Captivity: Unlocking Erotic Intelligence* is not only an extremely thorough examination of the conundrum that Mitchell raises, but also an equally thoroughly entertaining exploration of the subject matter. In this way, much like Mitchell's book, it is as appropriate for an educated lay audience as it is for a professional one.

Like Mitchell, Perel argues that there is much to be taken up regarding romantic, passionate love versus attachment love, especially because of their penchant to cancel out each other. But Perel takes the theme into another important dimension that is critical to the relational canon, not only regarding sex but larger issues as well—that is, that somewhere along the line, partners will have to face what can manifest as their spontaneous, ruthless, selfish aspects of unbridled desire (sexual and otherwise) versus their accommodative potential to operate and revere more selflessly (i.e., with more "ruth," if you will) all of what they see as fundamental to the illusory domain of attachment. (Much of this echoes Benjamin's ideas introduced earlier in this chapter.) Perel's book is an entire treatise on the complexities of these contradictory elements. Like many other authors in the relational canon, Perel sees this "as a paradox to be managed, not a problem to solve" (p. 82).

How these ideas are key to this book on couples treatment is in how they relate to the oscillating worlds of the experience of mutual recognition versus the experience of mutual negation. As is discussed throughout this volume, mutual recognition is a means of subject-to-subject relating, wherein both partners experience their subjective point of view recognized by the other. By contrast, mutual negation involves more of a quality of subject-to-object relating, wherein partners treat one another as objectified extensions of themselves, often in a manner that is quite at odds with how the other subjectively experiences him- or herself.

Mutual recognition is crucial to the repair of ruptures in relationships; however, it should not necessarily be thought of as the idealized state of the relationship to be pursued all of the time. Indeed, subject-to-object relating has a very normal place in human relationships, and this can especially be the case in sex. Indeed, as will soon become apparent, it is a vehicle for discovering unknown aspects of ourselves as they are projected in sexual fantasy regarding the object (i.e., the other).

Regarding subject-to-object relating, Perel is quite outspoken. Desire and egalitarianism are seldom very compatible. Indeed, too much democracy and equality makes sex boring. Meanwhile, our human need to feel safe can make us do practically anything not to lose our primary contacts (beginning first with our parents and all ones thereafter), including suppressing our aggression, renouncing our needs, and becoming more self-reliant and consequently more and more estranged. All of this, however, flies in the face of yet another powerful human need: our self-actualization through the articulation and expression of our sense of agency. This innate motivational sphere constantly threatens attachment.

These contradictions are palpable, for as Perel notes, there can be no genuine love where there is no possibility for hatred.[11] Sexual love always teeters precariously on shifting themes of dominance and submission. Ultimately, although Mitchell went to considerable lengths to challenge psychoanalysis' historical foundation in its dual instinct theory of sex and aggression driving all of human behavior (Greenberg & Mitchell, 1983), he (2002) never stopped seeing how sex *and* aggression remained strange bedfellows, writing: "The degradation of romance, the waning of desire, is due not to the contamination of love by aggression, but to the inability to sustain the necessary tension between them" (p. 144). Perel (2007) notes, "We must integrate our aggression, not eradicate it" (p. 63). The question is: How? Perel notes that answers cannot come easily, if at all in any steady, consistent way, though she has some useful ideas.

She notes that our entire culture is uncomfortable with vulnerability and dependency, and yet good intimate sex requires both. It is not surprising that she argues that our sense of desire lies deeply buried in the details of our childhood upbringing. Whether we were rejected, humiliated, abandoned, held, rocked, or soothed will loom large in the unformulated experiences and the unthought knowns that haunt our bedchambers. What turns us on or off, draws us in or leaves us cold, has its roots in childhood, along with how much closeness we can or cannot feel.

Part of "unlocking our erotic intelligence" very much relies upon our use of our human imagination, which Perel avers is the "central agent of eroticism." Erotic imagination fuels our fantasy life, and it is here that what we typically are prohibited to see about ourselves is writ large, when we are finally able to bravely face it. For it is here that we come to terms with versions of our self we are less wont to see: the more ruthless, selfish, at times sadistic and cruel versions that can powerfully fuel our sense of desire, but are frightening to reveal and are frequently, according to Perel, often better off not disclosed, unless and until there is an atmosphere in which we can tell our truths safely. This atmosphere is a prerequisite for the kinds of intimate disclosures that the erotic imagination might reveal.

Still, sexual fantasy (whether disclosed or not) can, according to Perel, be a wellspring for renewal and healing. She notes from Michael Bader (2002) that fantasy is the sanctuary of the erotic mind, wherein inhibitions and fears imposed by the culture of one's upbringing can get a second chance at being challenged. Fantasies are like scripts, repetitively dictating what the subject is to think and feel. But, likewise, the individual, in relationship to his fantasy, is also author, director, producer, and leading star in his repetitive mini-dramatic series. It is, however, potentially also a drama that can be played with, once it is understood and no longer so over-determining. Indeed, Perel sees considerable promise in partners learning to play with their fantasies or, as I would argue, play with them improvisationally—that is, to learn how to play-off-of-and-with them with one another. This is the world of the improvisatory, wherein what happens next is never known, hence it is *de facto* mysterious, so long as the couple can stand taking the risk—the risk that Mitchell notes we most fear.

Slavin (2006) situates the dilemma that Mitchell and Perel articulate as being an artifact of our evolutionary heritage. Whereas *Eros* has been typically seen in a transgressive light, he argues that it serves a crucially important existential and relational role in aiding us to face many of the broad adaptive strategies that human beings are heir to. As noted earlier in the chapter, Slavin argues that our early ancestors—proto-human beings—began shifting from an exclusive focus on raw and prereflective experience of being to starting to form symbols. Thereafter, they became more capable of reflection, from which emerged the declarative processes of shared symbolization by which more and more sophisticated language systems developed upon which socialized communities could take form.[12]

These evolutionary advances culminated in new social arrangements along with burgeoning new technologies, all of which led to the symbolic introduction of rules and roles that would inform prospective attachment systems. But, along with this, individual human beings began to develop something approximating the rudimentary processes that underscore our human capacity for having minds of our own, and with this began the earliest origins of psychosocial conflict—that is, between the emerging sense of individuals having their own self-interests, needs, agendas, and of course desires that would prospectively put them at odds with their surrounding attachment systems. It made apparent the potential risk of disclosing their individual inclinations, especially whenever these might be construed as a threat to the tribe and reciprocally therefore a threat to themselves. In the face of such conflict, it is likely that early humans—and frankly humans ever since—developed the capacity to sequester these potentially "threatened-me" experiences, fearing that their disclosure might be cataclysmic. Wherever a whiff of a sense of selfhood arose, so too would a powerful sense of its prospective meaning to the other(s)—enter the earliest origins of transference.

In the face of this powerful countervailing force to accommodate the surround, Slavin argues, humans are universally vulnerable to "over-accommodation" and to "over-socialization."[13] Still, notwithstanding our penchant for accommodation, we human beings simply could not, cannot, and will not eradicate our sense of selfhood. It is our inescapable relationship to this force of human nature that Slavin argues makes *Eros* our private antidote to our human penchant for over-accommodation. *Eros*, and the erotic imagination it entails, remains one of the most private and priceless aspects of our sense of individuality. *Eros* potentially provides us with a sense of transcendence over our daily battles with all of the sexual prohibitions and injunctions with which we grew up. For Slavin, *Eros* is a key means for maintaining our sense of aliveness and hope in relationship to our dreaded fear of our existential annihilation of our "true self" experiences.

The price of *Eros* and its transcendent and enlivening aspect, however, is that our psyches must manage the tension of the dialectic between romance and attachment. Slavin (2006) notes: "The fact that we sometimes become stuck in that tension and even stagnate there, should not blind us to the unimaginable costs that would be incurred by an over-accommodating human sexuality" (p. 822). Without the maintenance of this tension, our very personhood is at risk of being swallowed up in the banalities of the everyday otherness of what Heidegger (1927) refers to as "*das man*," which translates into "the they." The *they* determines what we should be thinking, feeling, and doing, in terms of the dictates of what *they* are all thinking, feeling, and doing in contrast to our "ownmost" sense of our unique sense of being.

How we sequester aspects of experience such as *Eros* is a subject of real importance to the relational canon, most commonly addressed in terms of multiple self-states. In terms of the canon, each of us has a multiplicity of self-states, mostly linked together unconsciously through the process of dissociation. Bromberg (1998) notes, "We feel like one while being many." Although dissociation is most often linked with trauma, Donnel Stern and Philip Bromberg (among a sea of other relational voices) see dissociation as a fundamentally normal human process, likely, as Slavin suggests, a part of our evolutionary inheritance for managing conflicts between self and other(s).

Through dissociation, we can sequester those aspects of ourselves, including in particular our thoughts and feelings about sex, from other aspects of ourselves more in line with accommodation. Dissociation is so common that Stern (2006) writes: "Normal dissociation is relative and often situational … It makes life more comfortable, that's all" (p. 751). A great deal more will be mentioned about dissociation, but for now the important idea is that through dissociation we create "firewalls" between our unconscious sexual desires and the prohibitions and injunctions about them that we took in growing up. Indeed, we will see later that these clashes play out in all forms of enactments in long-term committed relationships.

Still, some sequestered states are wellsprings of data about ourselves with regard to our struggle with the tensions between romance and attachment. Indeed, several of the relational authors see *Eros*, eroticism, lust, and the erotic imagination as in many ways seeking to help us grasp something about ourselves that we feel is lacking or deficient. In effect, in sex and in sexual fantasy, we—at least some of us some of the time, if not most of us most of the time—need to use the other as a vehicle for discerning what we have always felt as fundamentally missing.

One way in particular that we do this, according to Martin Frommer (2006), is through our sense of lust towards another. Lust is usually a very private matter, more typically eschewed by the conventional contract of enduring love and attachment. Frommer sees our encounters with lust as fortuitous breakthroughs of our normative dissociative, sequestering processes—that is, the dissociative processes that prevent us from feeling the shame and humiliation of having discovered, whether by self or other or both, the prurient manner in which we might lust for another, a manner that defies social convention and societal prohibition. Lust, after all, is often quite opposite from love.

Whereas love values more of a mutual recognition, subject-to-subject mode of relating, lust is typically more self-absorbed, more self-preoccupied—simply, more selfish. It is therefore frequently at odds with the societal conventions of love. Furthermore, lust enables us to objectify ourselves and others and fantasize about any dominance and submission distribution that in other conscious self-image states might mortify us. These ideas recall Robert Stoller's (1985, 1991) recommendation that analysts closely follow their patient's masturbatory fantasies for object relational clues about their dominance and submission wishes.

Lust experiences are mini-breakthroughs that enable us to envision something about ourselves that has felt missing. Frommer (2006) writes: "If desire is found on lack, or what is absent, then the painful yearning that is part of the erotic is itself a quest to both imagine and experience what goes missing from the self" (p. 641). In lust, we "tap into images and fantasies that are less well-known or unknown to one's more familiar sense of self, yet still companionable with it" (p. 641). If lust defines what it is that we crave from the other, it becomes likewise a portal for looking at what is "other" about ourselves. In this regard, Frommer echoes Mitchell's theme that only through the other can one discover the otherness of oneself.

This otherness, whether ascribed to another or adhering to something within ourselves, is typically enigmatic, mysterious, and fraught with the unknown. It is therefore fertile territory for what drives romance, passion, and the like. Frommer notes that in lust we typically privilege the otherness of the other—that is, *their* mysteriousness over our own, because phenomenologically it is their "mystique" that initially provokes our sense of lust. Still, Frommer suggests,"part of the other's allure ... is our experience of them as holding the key that can unlock our own lustful selves" (p. 645). In so doing, Frommer argues, we gradually note that the mystique of the other gives way to an enlivened ability to revisit or perhaps rediscover some otherness within and about our self—some mystique about our self that we would normatively not be aware, that normally would lie sequestered behind some dissociative firewall. But what is it we are seeking?

Frommer argues that lustful states of mind frequently give us access to:

> both feared and actual narcissistic injuries and psychic traumas ... Lust seeks, with a variety of motives, to re-engage problematic aspects of self-experience. It seeks to repair a damaged sense of self, reclaim disavowed aspects of self, resolves or subverts the psychic conflicts that emanate from early wounds to one's sense of self, and/or retaliate for the wrongs that have been done.
>
> (p. 643)

In a sense, lust seems to involve an unwitting reparative venture to the ruptures caused within one by one's very own developmental attachment system. Of course, that is most commonly our family of origin, upon which we typically experience the greatest dependency experience of our lives. Indeed, this becomes the experience that will be repeated by analogy in other relationships the rest of our life. It is not so hard, then, to see how confusing it is to attempt to sustain lust in the attachment system of a long-term committed relationship, bearing in mind lust's function is to raise the ghosts of one's development and to engage them in a manner about which we are primarily unconscious and often threatened to realize. All of this lurking just beneath is perhaps the reason that Perel argues there can be no real love without there also being real hatred.

Jeanne Wolff Bernstein (2006) takes up another way in which our conscious approach to love is often actually a cover story, diverting our attention from our unconscious use and objectification of the other. Desire, Bernstein asserts, is a "hide-and-seek game of narcissistic illusions" (p. 711). To hammer home her point, she invokes Lacan's famous admonition (which Mitchell also did in *Can Love Last?*): "Love is giving something you do not have, to someone you do not know." Lacan's thesis is that, while we are born in a state of fragmentation (the calamity of the baby's lack of coordination of his central nervous system), we develop an extremely early and illusory sense of "wholeness" from what is mirrored back to us, both visually and by others, especially mother. Literally, the baby sees a whole image of himself in the mirror, different from his experience of his immature lack of coordination in a world occupied by seemingly coordinated beings. On the psychological plane, the baby experiences a sense of wholeness in the eyes of his mother, in particular through her "gaze," a gaze that completes him

24

and makes him feel whole. Compounding this, it is what the mother imagines the baby desires that she attempts to fulfill and, as a result, she communicates to him what it is he desires, irrespective of how off the mark she might be in terms of his actual experience. Nevertheless, what becomes the mother's interpretation of the infant's desire telecasts what the baby (and thereafter developing self) imagines that the (m)other desires from him. Of course, all of this is illusion and therefore illusory, what Lacanians would call the register of the imaginary; nevertheless, it forecasts with whom we fall in love and what follows as the inherent complications of our choices.

To the degree to which this is the trajectory upon which love may be taking us, we are forever seeking a sense of completeness through our involvement with others. That is, we are filling in what we lack (similar to Frommer's idea) by desiring something of another that we assume will lend us that completeness. As mentioned, prominent among the experiences that we assume will be fulfilling is what Lacan called the gaze, which in the realm of the imaginary both informs us of who we are as well as our value, or perhaps our lack thereof.

The illusion of the power of the gaze—the "smoke-and-mirror" effect, if you will—is that it is fraught with risk. That is because it just about guarantees—to some extent frequently and maybe to a very great extent in most cases—that we are ascribing an illusory, objectified version of our desire that our partner is presumably supposed to meet. And yet, just as frequently, our partners are people who may have little or no notion, or perhaps even any inclination, to play the desiring object roles in which they are being cast. Furthermore, from this perspective, it is clear that we never desire the whole person, only a fragment of him or her—in essence, a fragment to complete a fragment of our self, like the popular jewelry that is half of a heart (severed along an uneven broken line) that lovers can each wear with the understanding that when they put these two halves together, they are suddenly whole. Wolff Bernstein (2006) quotes Mitchell: "love by its very nature is not secure, we just keep wanting to make it so (p. 49)".

Though one might assume the trend of this thesis broaches a kind of cynicism, Wolff Bernstein ends her article on a vastly more upbeat note: there is great purpose to our recognizing our misspent efforts in love, such as pursuing the fallacy of projecting upon the other who we expect/need them to be to fulfill our lack of completeness. Wolff Bernstein advises that much can be gained by our coming to recognize that we don't know our partners, though now, with this recognition, possibly we can start to. This creates a whole new worldview of love. In essence, the partners stop attempting to seek out the other as a mirror and now seek out the other who is, as Wolff Bernstein poetically puts it, "a mirror that *sees*" (p. 723, italics in original). She notes the transition to this awareness can be terribly frightening; after all, a mirror that sees does not simply echo how we narcissistically wish to be seen, it also discerns our every flaw. Nevertheless, this is a path to a kind of mutual recognition, the kind that other relational authors have proposed in relationship to Mitchell's challenge.

Of course, we can't and shouldn't try to go very far in this entire discussion without recognizing the cultural bias in which it is embedded. Blechner (2006) provocatively questions:

> I wondered whether the healthfulness of sustaining love, sex, and romance within a single relationship through the lifespan might be just one of those presumptions that will not survive the next century. What percentage of the population will achieve it? If most do not, or if a significant proportion do not, should we still postulate it as a sign of mental health? And, should we, in our clinical practices, try to help patients achieve that goal?
>
> (p. 784)

I can't think of any relational authors who wouldn't find merit in Blechner's questions. And the statistics that support his argument are even more sobering, with over 50 percent of marriages in the US ending in divorce and close to 75 percent of second marriages dissolving comparably. For all our reverence of the intact nuclear family, less than 25 percent of families abide this pristine 1950s illusion of the intact heterosexual couple and their 2.5 offspring. Culture marches on irrespective of our societal proclivities. This may very well be why more Orthodox cultures and even the religious right in the US are extremely frightened of the onslaught of Western secular ideology. Still, several other relational authors have some fascinating thoughts about how any couple might at least attempt to talk about and engage in how their love might last.

Goldner (2006), for example, appreciates Mitchell's argument that attempting to sustain romance in long-term committed intimate relationships gets riskier, at least in terms of increased vulnerability to what might make any of us fearful of being hurt, betrayed, or abandoned. But Goldner takes more of a "black diamond" approach to skiing this proverbial love slope. In effect, Goldner is saying that it is the mysteriousness of the other that challenges and prospectively inspires us to risk attempting to deepen what we believe we know about the other, as well as making ourselves comparably available to be known. It's a warts-and-all proposition for sure.

Arguing against Mitchell's premise that it is primarily the foreign and unfamiliar that excite us, Goldner takes up a somewhat different relational trajectory, writing: "It is not necessarily the (re)discovery of the lover's ultimate alterity that turns the heat on, but the (re)finding of the *deeply known* person we love and need, and the thrill and relief of discovering that they are also reaching out for us, that turns on the tap" (p. 627, italics in original).

This takes on many forms, notably Davies (2006) pointing out that love can only be vivified to the extent that we can bear the emotional vicissitudes of oscillating between the periodic narcissistic fulfillment of the idealization of our lover in relationship to the waning moments of our comparative de-idealization. This sounds a lot like another iteration of Bernstein's mirror that sees, but regarding the extent to which we can do this Goldner (paraphrasing Benjamin) speaks of the thirdness of mutual recognition. This encompasses for both partners a thirdness that I think may be comparable to my third theme in this book, the relationship having a mind of its own. As Benjamin asserts, couples fail when they fail to build this thirdness, because it is formative to their capacity to mutually embrace their excitement and their let-downs, along with facing their inevitable ruptures.

Clearly, part of how this thirdness occurs is how our bodies work together (or not). Perel (2007) states: "The body is the purest, most primal tool we have for communicating. As Roland Barthes wrote, 'What language conceals is said through my body. My body is a stubborn child; my language is a very civilized adult'" (pp. 111–112). So, whether our bodies are in sync or not has huge implications. Crastnopol (2006) argues on behalf of what might arguably be taken as a fruitful United Nations conference on multiple self-states. Multiple self-states embody lust, romantic love, attachment, and dependence—all self-states arguably in this context of discourse as potentially opposing one another, but ones that, according to her, can more or less overlap in ways that are passionate, intimate, adaptive, and defensive. Depending on how they play out, they can be constructive, though also destructive.

Crastnopol joins others in aligning with the ineluctable erotic intelligence of the human body. She reminds us of something ironically forgotten in the developmental emphasis of contemporary psychoanalysis: It is through sexual intercourse that we engage in the most literally pronounced act of interpenetration. We engage in an act that simultaneously—through its act of thrusting in and out, in and out—brings us face to face or, more to the point, genital body part to genital body part, while experiencing both our oneness and our separation.

Crastnopol sums this up in the very evocative image of "the rub." By this, she means both literally and symbolically the essential friction that is part and parcel to our human existence of rubbing up against each other—a daily rubbing, if you will, that asserts our differences and our similarities (though we are not likely aware of it on this level). In her poetic evocation of friction captured in rubbing, Crastnopol finds the essence of relationality. In rubbing up against each other, we both attempt to find out who we are and who the other is. It is the friction in the rub that reveals conflict, pressure, influence, sometimes directed force, all of which is sometimes synchronous and sometimes not. By all of these means, however, we have the opportunity of discovering what is unique about the partners of a long-term committed relationship.

From an evolutionary perspective, perhaps this is part of what Mitchell was referring to as "designed interdependence." Pushing up against each other is a way through which we take up what is essential to our human inheritance, both in terms of our sexuality and our aggression, without necessarily reducing them to Freud's primary drives, instead elevating them in manners that inform us of both our subject and object relating.

In the end, the question of *Can Love Last?*, at least as taken up in this book, will depend on how the question takes form in relationship to each partner and each coupling—all of which makes it centrally important to take up the question of sex in a couple's relationship as candidly and as tactfully as is possible relative to being sensitive to the couple's capacity to discuss their sex life. Where there is timidity or other aversive reactions, the therapist must make a mental note of this while looking for potential entry points that may arise metaphorically in the ways in which the couple displays other forms of constricted communication.

Most importantly, however, is that, notwithstanding the couple's sex life can be demonstrative of a host of deeper issues (seemingly deeper that is than sexual behavior itself) such as conflicts around intimacy, attachment and object relations, it is an error for the couples therapist to simply defer to these issues and bypass more directly addressing the actuality (or lack thereof) of the couple's sexuality. As Perel (2007) notes, many therapists pass over discussing the couple's sex life because of their own countertransference awkwardness with the topic. The idea that sex is merely a symptom of deeper psychological issues can make it too easy for the topic to be neglected, thereby sparing all parties' discomfort. The degree to which this occurs, however, involves a potentially pernicious enactment in which the couples therapist is as culpable as the two partners for avoiding what can be a most fertile topic. In fact, it is not lost upon the couple, even if, more implicitly (unconsciously) than explicitly, the degree to which their therapist is at ease with discussing sex versus colluding in warding off the topic.

Meanwhile, the relational canon as described above clearly provides a powerful array of ideas that help stimulate how the analytically oriented couples therapist can engage the couple in encouraging their curiosity. (Tactful and even playful ways to address a couple's sex life will be taken up in Chapter 9, "FAQs"). At the very least, these ideas can have the power to elevate the couple out of their more concrete assumptions about what their difficulties entail, into beginning to see that there is much, much less than meets the eye (that can be informed entirely by the conscious mind) and much, much more about each of us that we may be unconsciously seeking. Getting to this, however, also means facing the problematic ways in which partners induce one another into unwitting roles to fulfill something of each other—roles that are also frequently unwanted ones. To the extent to which this happens, our desire's attempts at inspiring our mate's desire potentially misfire horribly.

Meta-theoretical framework: complexity theory and improvisation

Thus far, this chapter has been grounded in three themes (self-actualization, mutual recognition, and the relationship having a mind of its own), along with a host of theoretical conceptualizations that organize a framework for thinking about couples treatment. There remains, however, a broader meta-theoretical framework regarding an important improvisatory mode of therapeutic action that is informed to a large extent by complexity theory. Complexity, and its related nonlinear dynamic systems and chaos theories, pose formidable challenges to some of the constrained ways—predominantly linear, one-person psychological modes of conceptualization—in which psychoanalytic theory has been historically embedded.

This section takes up a fundamental paradox that arises from our efforts to articulate the actualization of selfhood along with all its individualistic, deeply personal strivings. The paradox is that our sense of selfhood is so deeply embedded in the sense of selfhood of the other (and vice versa) that it can, at times, be hard to know where we all "begin" and "end" in human relationships. Coburn (2002) notes, "We can no longer say (with certainty) this is yours and this is mine" (p. 662). As will be seen in all of the Steps, this paradox underscores the critical importance of collaboration and negotiation between intrasubjectively organized multiple self-states ("within" each partner), on the one hand, and collaboration and negotiation of intersubjectivity between the partners, on the other. It is this latter condition that ultimately lends to the thirdness of the relationship having a mind of its own.

In what follows, I am wedding the ideas of complexity theory to those of an improvisatory perspective. This is especially important, since little has been written about how to put complexity theory into practice. It is therefore to an improvisatory perspective that I turn, to put flesh and blood on the sterile bones of these theories. In agreement with my project, Daniel Stern (2007) wrote in a discussion of my article on improvisation (Ringstrom, 2007a, 2007b) in psychoanalytic treatment:

> An improvisational view is a logical next step in the field. In the last decades we have seen the application of chaos and complexity theory, along with dynamic systems theory, open up our clinical eyes to various features of the therapeutic situation, such as: the emphasis on process; the approximate equality of the contribution of patient and therapist, i.e., the notion of co-creativity; the unpredictability of what happens in a session from moment to moment, including the expectance of emergent properties; a focus on the present moment of interaction; and the need for spontaneity and authenticity in such a process.
>
> (p. 101)

As Coburn (2002) notes, complexity theory "helps us understand the highly contextualized nature of emotional experience and the meanings that we attribute to it" (p. 659). Further, "it revolutionizes concepts of human development, so-called psychopathology and the process of change" (p. 659). There are enumerable key elements to complexity theory, descriptive of how systems operate. For the purposes of a psychoanalytic model of couples therapy, the primary systems of examination include the two partners, the therapist, and the couple's relationship, as well as their relationships to the therapist.

Key elemental features, regarding the therapeutic triangle that couples therapy constitutes, include how systems are self-organizing in manners that are nonlinear and are therefore complex (chaotic) and largely unpredictable. This means that, while many of the theories of development upon which psychoanalysis is based[14] provide a rich cornucopia of metaphors that are powerfully descriptive of human beings' experience, they nevertheless impart linear design models that complexity, chaos, and nonlinear dynamic theories eschew. Neither individuals nor couples and families as systems are quite as design- or rule-driven as these traditional psychoanalytic theories suggest. Instead, systems, on whatever level one parses them—whether that be individual, couple, or a triad—are far more complex. Their complexity, however, also reflects their relative degrees of invariance (i.e., rigid stochastic [repetitive] processes) in contrast to variant, "transformative," non-predictable "emergent" states. As will be elaborated shortly, of chief concern is that a system, on whatever level of abstraction we observe, is neither too rigidly organized so as to prohibit growth, development or change, nor too loosely organized to support any of these conditions (Schore, 1994; Siegel, 1999).

Elaborating key ideas from complexity theory, Coburn (2002) states:

> [It] can be talked about in different ways. Indeed, each author who has written about it seems to highlight one or a few specific aspects of the idea in the course of applying it to psychotherapy and psychoanalysis, and there are many facets from which to choose. Some highlight the importance of 1) initial conditions, some the 2) property of self-organization, some focus on the concept of 3) self-criticality (or a particular system's propensity toward hovering around the "tipping point," some underscore the 4) dynamism, fluidity, and unpredictability of a system, others the 5) role of perturbation in altering the trajectory of a system, and still others the 6) characteristic of emergence and the idea that nonlinear systems are not rule-driven or design-driven. There are many other descriptive aspects of the theory that theorists draw from as useful metaphors for understanding human experiencing and therapeutic action.
>
> (p. 675)

All of these ideas capture how the unconscious works, not simply in fixed and stochastic ways, but also in fluidly open and highly unpredictable ways. This can be the case especially when contexts allow for the unconscious mind to be open to possibility and less constrained by defensive strategy. I believe an improvisatory stance optimizes the former possibility. Either way, partners are vulnerable to contextual permutations that can set them on all sorts of unpredictable trajectories. Some may entail good consequences and some bad, often determined by the cultural and psychological lens from which they hail.

What is unavoidable is that as the couple advances through further stages of adult development, the stasis of any given phase is perturbed by the onset of a new one. Indeed, such perturbations are simply a matter of a developing procreative family system, since, with the addition of each offspring, the complexity of relationships in the family is no longer simply additive, it is geometric: Whereas the arrival of the first offspring creates a three-relationship family system, the arrival of the second creates a six-relationship family system! Finally, couples are especially vulnerable to the inherently stasis-disruptive processes that emerge from couples psychotherapy. Thus, although systems (individuals, dyads, and triads) "self"-organize in all sorts of seemingly predetermined ways (often referred to as "stable attractor states"— i.e., stable patterns of relating to which people seem drawn to engage), they also can rapidly reorganize in relation to seemingly indiscernible conditions to which they are sensitive.

In sum, couples are compelled to change by virtue of the host of conditions that alter their lives as they move through a myriad of life cycle phases. For the procreative couple, this takes place from the origins of their coupling, to the family they create, to how all of this affects their families of origin and vice versa. As a system, the long-term intimately committed dyad is always on the brink of some perturbation from within and from without.

Though couples may imagine how all of this will unfold, typically it does so with the "dynamism and fluidity and unpredictability" that challenges all elements of partners' self-actualization, mutual recognition, and their relationship having a mind of its own. Finally, along this trajectory, there are "tipping points" (self or system "criticality") where unarticulated, indeed likely unformulated issues have been building over time. They then unpredictably emerge in a manner that "puts the couple over the edge." Here the adage "the straw that broke the camel's back" speaks to humankind's intuitive sense of complexity long before any iteration of systems theory had ever been conceived.

Having briefly introduced a few of the key elements of complexity theory, the question is: What does all of this have to do with an improvisatory approach to treatment? The kinship of improvisation to complexity theory is that in improvisational modes of engagement, each party *plays-off-of-and-with* each other's unconscious minds. For this to happen, however, the key issue—both in the life of the couple and in the course of their treatment—is the partners' (and the therapist's) degree of openness to playing with one another. By play, I am not suggesting anything frivolous or silly, or necessarily "fun"—though at times it may be some of both. I am actually taking up the idea that our capacity to play is critical to the quality of our lives and our ability to be creative in all ways. That includes untying the relational knots within which we find ourselves entangled. Play introduces the idea that, instead of repeating the same strategy of reacting over and over, we begin to imagine (play within our minds) new possible ways of relating that then literally can get played with interpersonally. This enables us to develop new strategies of relating within ourselves and with one another.

Understandably, couples coming to treatment often exhibit constraints, sometimes severe, in their ability to play. Nevertheless, Winnicott's (1971) admonition regarding psychotherapy remains as true for couples treatment as it does for individual treatment. He argued that if the therapist cannot play, then he is not suitable to work. If the patient cannot play, then something needs to be done to enable him to become able to play, after which psychotherapy may begin. Accordingly, if the

31

couple cannot play, something needs to be done to enable them to play, and this requires the therapist's capacity to play.

This meta-theoretical overview lends perfectly to the implementation of an improvisatory stance to treatment. Contrary to what people might think, improvisation is not random. Instead, it plays with the inherently chaotic flux of unpredictable events that are always impinging upon the structure of the couple's relationship. By structure, I mean the history of expectations the couple has grown accustomed to as to how things will be. Improvisation involves playing off of the "always already" (Stern, 2013) unconscious minds of the partners and the therapist. Via the unconscious, each participant is steeped in associations to vast resources of psychic material. When this material can be creatively played with, things open up, and new possibilities ensue. Conversely, such material often defensively constrains, inhibits, and closes things down. It is in this latter closed-down state that most couples come to treatment, a state manifesting their key issues of conflict. It is, however, equally important for the therapist not to become too attached to the couple's often profoundly depressing perception about their conflicts, so that she remains attentive to areas of their life together that are not so arrested. These latter areas are potentially fertile for play, and it is from them that the couple can be drawn out of their overly constrained world of interaction.

So, how does improvisational play in psychoanalytic treatment work? To begin with, the cardinal rule of improvisation (when used artistically in theater or music or any number of endeavors, including the high-speed exchanges between athletes) is not about acting, but about *listening*—that is, to always respond in a manner that recognizes what has been asserted by the other, off of which then one plays, developing further possibility. It should be apparent that getting to this state will require a lot of work in couples treatment, since listening to one another is a skill that is rapidly lost at the commencement of most long-term committed relationships, if it ever existed to begin with! What this proposition means is that each participant engages in a kind of *yes/and* mode of relating—that is, taking something of what the other says and building upon it. This mode contrasts with what in improvisational workshops is referred to as *yes/but blocking*. In this manner, improvisationally playing-off-of-and-with each other is not only an *in vivo* antidote to how each partner becomes mired in their own narcissism, it also creates a quality of psychoanalytic thirdness (Benjamin, 2004; Ogden, 1994), thus lending to the cultivation of the relationship having an open/creative mind of its own.[15]

It involves the participants allowing themselves to play with whatever emerges spontaneously from their unconscious (recognizing that there is no time for preparation or "scripting" in improvisation; there are "no time outs," as Hoffman, 1994, notes). It further involves the guideline to agree to play-off-of-and-with whatever each offers. Doing so involves following the implicit "suggestions" born of their respective subjective unconscious states of mind, while adding something original to each other's in a manner that does not negate either one's "suggested reality" of who they are to one another, as well as what the hell they are doing with one another. All of this is what allows for an emergent property of thirdness. It reflects something that they have creatively co-authored, something that neither can take exclusive ownership for, especially since each has been building upon the other's suggested subjective reality—that is, each one's temporal version of you-me-us-ness.

In contrast to this optimal improvisatory condition, couples enter treatment negating one another. This implies another process, one that would adhere to another type of complexity if you will, though one likely mired in static states of adaptive defensiveness, resistance, and repetitious scripted-ness. It is suggestive of a kind of seemingly "non-complex" complexity. By this, I mean a host of ways of being that involve a powerful "gravitational" pull, attempting to thwart uncertainty and control the inherent complexity of any human relationship—especially the long-term committed one. Much of this latter mode is in fact an attempt to control the system from being perturbed, though in its proclivity towards invariance and rigidity it is more reflective of psychopathology, both on the individual and couple's level.

Where such constraint (i.e., psychopathology) exhibits itself, we see a powerful "attractor state" that organizes both the self-systems and relational system of the couple. The term *attractor* speaks to the inherent movement or flux that any biological—and therefore information-based—system is always in; that is, some potential state of flux relative to the context(s) of which it is a part. Galatzer-Levy (2009) talks about two attractor states that organize any psychopathological system under examination, and avers that on one end of the continuum are chaotic attractor states, which are simply too disorganized to provide a repetitive structure for individuals to live in any state of expectancy, predictability, and order. Chaos rules, anxiety disorders flourish. Conversely, an opposing attractor state of the dyadic system adopts patterns of repetition and rigidity that severely constrain the evolutionary range of the system. Galatzer-Levy writes: "Psychological health involves involvement with attractors that are neither too rigid nor too disorganized. These attractors are sufficiently complex that rich, even creative possibilities exist in them" (p. 986). Obviously, it is this latter state to which Galatzer-Levy is relating, one that is most open to an improvisatory mode of engagement.

When the dyad (or treatment triad) is unable to be improvisational, it usually means one of the self-states within one party "takes over" the system. Not only does it dominate the other multiple self-states within one party, but it also begins to dominate the intersubjective field. Such domination arises from processes of dissociation, which then manifests into processes of "mutual inductive identification" (elaborated in detail in Step Four). In so doing, it compromises the field of non-conscious play necessary for improvising.

Without access to one's other self-states, the predominant self-state behaves as the "spokesperson" for all the rest (e.g., a domineering "chair" of the "committee of the mind"). Such experience is suggestive of a state of mind in which self-states are incommunicado (i.e., beyond the reach of play both within and between the participants). These states represent sub-symbolic experiences that cannot be mentalized (Fonagy, 2003; Fonagy & Target, 1997)—that is, connected to making symbolic meaning of one's emotional experience. Absent the capacity for such self-state formulation, and therefore absent the capacity for symbolic articulation, a prevailing sense or version of "reality" comes to dominate all other self-states. Eventually, this one *must* be enacted (Bromberg, 2006). And, it must be done in a manner that involves both parties' participation or, in the case of couples treatment, all three participants. Indeed, when mentalization is impaired, the very capacity to generate new and vitalizing narratives is equivalently impaired. Thus, impaired mentalization connotes a "hostage-taking" of the mind—often embodying the shackles of old identifications with caregivers (Brandchaft, 1994, 2007; Grotstein, 1997) in which only old scripts rule.

Notes

1　A curious thing about the accusation of one being "selfish" is that it often arises from someone who is disavowing their own selfishness, since the accusation typically accompanies the accuser's argument that the accused is not doing something the way the accuser wishes it to be done!

2　Consciousness, as Jaynes (1990) argues, is a thin boundary between the enormity of organizing input from unconscious memory and the enormity of chaotic input of stimuli from the external world. Consciousness is the reflective space that unconscious organization attempts—through complex comparisons of what is in unconscious memory—to make sense of the infinite swirl of potential data arising from our immediate experience of the so-called external world. How each of us comes to understand the relationship between our unconscious organization and our conscious apprehension of our inner and outer world experiences becomes formative in developing a sense of self-actualization in life in general and in intimate relationships in particular.

3　A notable point addressed throughout the rest of this book is that the sequelae of traumatic experience is a radical diminution in our ability to create new meaning and therefore encumbers our sense of agency. As Modell (2008) notes, "We lack a sense of agency when we are unable to transform the meaning of trauma, when we are involuntarily drawn to interpret experiences the same way over and over again. Our imagination is constricted and directed by the past" (pp. 358–359).

4　Bowen's family systems theory (see Appendix A) is an especially cogent model for capturing the intensity of anxiety that emerges when one attempts to differentiate from one's family of origin, anxiety that is not only felt by the individual differentiating, but by many if not all the other members of the family.

5　While Benjamin's and Stolorow et al. (2002)'s theories share much in common with all relational theories, they can be critically distinguished by their relative attention to this topic. Stolorow et al.'s version of intersubjectivity primarily involves a systems theory of mutual regulation and influence between subjectivities (Aron, 1996). The subjectivities of both parties are contextually intertwined, mutually shaping each other's subjective sense of self-experiencing. Mutual recognition is not critical to their definition of intersubjectivity. Indeed, they argue that when intersubjectivity is operationally defined by the developmental achievement of mutual recognition, it risks enforcing the analyst's subjectivity being recognized, as importantly as that of the patient (Coburn, personal communication). Elsewhere, I have argued that this interpretation of relational psychoanalysis is incorrect (Ringstrom, 2010a, 2010b, 2010c).

6　For example, most parents are familiar with periodic episodes in their child's development that involve the child's ruthless *assertion of self* in relation to her parent. Such episodes can culminate in the requirement of the parent to simply assume the role of dutifully subjugated need-fulfilling other—in short, the required "object" or psychological functionary. At such times, parents—especially psychologically savvy ones, who pride themselves on being child-centered in their family decision-making—can become taxed trying to figure out how to best negotiate their own needs in relation to their child's. And, at such times, the child is loath to give up this heady experience of omnipotent control, though under optimal developmental circumstances she will soon enough discover why she must.

7 A rather sobering point in this vein comes from the Bowenian Family Therapy Group, which has concluded from years of research (Bowen, 1978) that each member of the partnership picks the other based upon similar levels of self differentiation (or lack thereof).

8 Subject-to-subject relating pertains to both parties' recognition of one another's subjectivity (i.e., subjective experience of reality), whereas subject-to-object relating pertains more to how one subject "uses" the other, in essence treats the other as an extension of oneself. This often leads to the experience of negation of the other's sense of subjectivity. However, there is also a multiplicity of gratifying experiences of performing as another's object. Examples include the gratification of the maternal experience of breastfeeding, or even one's performative role in lovemaking. Subject-to-object relating devolves into experiences of one-up and one-down split complementarity when the person in the object position experiences him- or herself as dominated, and that submission is required to preserve one's relationship.

9 The *psychoanalytic third* is a relatively new and popular term in psychoanalysis that is unfortunately riddled with all the vagaries and multiplicities of meanings as are other high level abstractions, such as the concept of transference and projective identification. Some authors, those of a more Lacanian persuasion, seem to treat it like a system of rules that preexist the union of the dyad and as the unconscious medium, usually through the deep structure of language, that enables them to relate and that therefore also "structurally grounds them" (Wolff Bernstein, 1999; Muller, 1999); for others, it is an unconsciously co-created state of intersubjectivity that is unpredictable and therefore seems less tied to an emphasis on *a priori* structure than upon the *a posteriori* engagement of the dyad (Ogden, 1994); while for others it seems to be a theory of mind and/or professional association to which the analyst is "married" and therefore imposes some form of symbolic Oedipal partnership with the analyst, that *de facto* must be addressed by the analyst and/or analysand alike (Aron, 1999; Crastnopol, 1999; Hoffman, 1994, 1998).

10 Stephen Mitchell died at age 54 of a sudden heart attack on December 20, 2000. He was a long-distance supervisor of mine from 1994 to 1996 on my third psychoanalytic training control case. After 1996, Stephen progressively involved me, along with many others, in the burgeoning new association he and others were creating, the International Association of Relational Psychoanalysis and Psychotherapy (IARPP), of which I am a founding board member.

11 Her work follows historically in terms of what Gabbard (2000) notes: From the origins of psychoanalysis, Freud saw an inextricable bond between love and hatred.

12 Slavin notes that current evolutionary psychology sees the rapid growth in size and cognitive complexity of the human brain as less about the introduction of working with tools (the more traditional "opposing thumb" hypothesis of early man's evolving brain; Bronowski, 1974) and more arising from working cooperatively (e.g., socially) through an advancement in symbolic communication. This latter development was perfectly suited for the purposes of cooperative hunting as well as the mutual protection and nurture of the developing human species.

13 If one needs evidence of this, we need only to look at the fact that the preponderance of nations around the world are still not free societies, many of them running in terms

of the followership of people to political ideologies, such as fascism and communism, or of orthodox religions, all of whose ideological or biblical tenets govern all aspects of social as well as spiritual life. This notwithstanding, we must also acknowledge the perpetual history of revolt against this crushing of individualism.

14 For example, Freud's psychosexual stage theory (oral, anal, phallic, genital); or Mahler's theory of separation-individuation stage theory; or Erikson's epigenetic life cycle theory; or conventions such as pre-Oedipal and Oedipal stages.

15 Working improvisationally may also be a means for facilitating "moral thirdness," a further elaboration of Benjamin's seminal work on psychoanalytic thirdness. Benjamin (2006) notes that moral thirdness entails a mutual shouldering of responsibility for the co-creative activity of psychoanalytic enactments—what I am calling "scene work"—insofar as neither one must end up the doer or done-to, the abuser or victim, but recognize their joint participation. Benjamin notes that when the analyst is constrained by the conventional wisdom of being the "container" of the patient's "bad object" projections, her act of containment often becomes mystifying to the patient, since the latter often accurately detects the former's distress masked behind a stance of analytic opacity. In effect, by working improvisationally, neither actor remains the exclusive creator or holder of the "hot potato" but can toss it back and forth in a manner that can ultimately "cool it down." In this manner, *improvisational moments* capture the most heightened moments of relational authenticity (Donnel Stern, personal communication).

2

STEP ONE

The therapist's attunement to each partner's subjectivity instills hope, perspective, and new possibility

> All happy families are alike, each unhappy family is unhappy in its own way.
>
> Tolstoy

> Falling in love is easy, staying in love is the hard part.
>
> Anonymous

Couples enter therapists' consulting rooms for the first time exhibiting a wide variety of problems. When they are deeply in conflict, they typically arrive highly agitated, frightened, and profoundly threatened. Not uncommonly, they are convinced that their partner is "nuts" (though sometimes privately they often wonder if they are, too). As a result, they are often full of hopelessness and despair. It is in this manner that they present the therapist with a priceless moment of intervention that, if lost, can spell defeat for the couple and therefore the couple's therapy.

The conjoint therapist has precious little time to get the couple out of this sinkhole and back to being capable of seeing each other's point of view. Doing so requires a rapid attunement to the subjective experiences of each of the partners. This means capturing the same aspect of hopes and dreads that brought them together in the first place, which have now taken form in whatever conflict they are initially presenting to the therapist. The "surface structure" of their complaints can be rather commonplace, entailing such issues as disputes over spending money, rearing children, initiating and participating in sex, taking vacations, regulating degrees of involvement with extended family members, renovating, remodeling, or relocating. Of greater salience, however, is what these manifest issues mean to each of them. Just as importantly, how do these issues influence each one's sense of *self-actualization*, their capacity to mutually recognize one another, and the quality of their relationship—that is, will it be one that is opening and vitalizing, or closing down through perpetual vying for dominance against the terror of submission?

My initial session with a couple is very open-ended. I ask them how I can help them, or what brings them to me, or what seems to each to be the problem. I make it immediately clear that I am interested in each of their perspectives, which I regard as just that—their own subjective points of view about their presenting issue. I do not assume, therefore, that their statements will correspond with their partner's point of view, unless of course their partner agrees that it does. In this manner, I underscore that we each have our own unique subjective experience and perspective on our shared reality.

An interesting finding in my 30 years of practice is that today's cultural leitmotif seems to more readily accept a "perspectivalist" premise—that is, that each one has his or her own independent feelings, perspectives, and attitudes. This seeming acceptance, however, is mostly intellectual, since once the partners become emotionally reactive to each other they typically revert to some claim of the "objectivity" of their position. As quickly as possible, I begin pointing out that much of what they refer to as objective fact, especially about each other, involves both interpretations and judgments, veritable "prejudices" about one another's version of reality. I also assert that such prejudices (however normal) begin to have a shaping effect on how they listen and interact with one another, resulting in unwitting self-fulfilling prophecies.

An example of such a self-fulfilling prophecy came when a wife introduced that she had been reading a lot about "narcissistic personality disorders," and that she was amazed how much what she read fit her husband "to a tee." I cautioned that she was on a path of making a case against her husband and that this likely would doom their marriage. I said that the only way that this might be helpful to her would be if she was determined to in fact leave him and not seriously entertain our couples therapy. Otherwise, I said, she would simply be isolating the problem to her husband, making herself an ineffectual victim, and would become devoid of any sense of agency.

Shortly thereafter, we began taking up the purpose of her reading. It became immediately clear that she was looking for some tonic to her shame and anger with herself for passively allowing things to have gone so badly in their marriage, without calling attention to her concerns. In this latter self-reflective manner, she was restoring a place of self-actualization rather than simply blaming and shaming her husband. Shaking off his initial "narcissistic wound," her husband agreed that he too had let things slide, and that he was eager to change things if she too was willing to. Their pattern is emblematic of many couples. For this reason, I frequently discourage, if not downright insist, that they cease and desist judging one another, as this almost guarantees their spiraling into a mutually destructive pattern of engagement. With couples who actively inflict wounds through contempt and criticism and "character assassination," I tell them that we will have a daunting enough task treating the history of wounds they have already inflicted, and that I beseech them to do their best to not add further wounds to those we are trying to heal. I also tell them that I don't expect they will likely be able to comply with my request, but I want them to be reflecting more and more about their participation in perpetuating their vicious circle. To understand their part in their struggles, each partner has to develop a deeper understanding of his or her personality organization, which takes us to the topic of organizing principles.

Organizing principles

Attunement to each partner's subjectivity begins with an understanding of how each one's personality is organized, and this is where Step One begins. The subjectivity of each party, while always a part of an intersubjective relationship, is constituted by "organizing principles"—that is, thematic patterns of experiencing (Stolorow, Brandchaft, & Atwood, 1987). Organizing principles are recursive patterns of personality organization that are theoretically very much like those proposed by Slap-Shelton's "schemas" (1994), Stern's (1985) RIGs ("representational interactions generalized"), Piaget's (1973) "cognitive schemas," Breger's (1974) "affect schemas," and Kernberg's (1991a, 1991b, 1993) self-affect-object relational units, that represent thematic organizational assumptions about oneself in relation to another.

Organizing principles serve as essential information processing systems for filtering the morass of sensory information data bombarding us every moment of experience. Organizing principles make micro determinations of what is and isn't meaningful (whether practically, philosophically, spiritually, or whatever mode of meaning-making in which one finds oneself). What is critical in both development throughout life and in psychotherapy is that these schemas are amenable to change when necessary.

Understanding when organizing principles are or are not amenable to change involves adoption of Piaget's theory of learning (Atwood & Stolorow, 1984), as it pertained to cognitive schemas. Piaget suggested that schemas (organizing principles) will *assimilate* data (i.e., the constant input of information) in as orderly and coherent a fashion as possible. As such, they assimilate new experience in terms of the inherent set of assumptions the schemas embody, and continue to do so until these schemas begin to fail to make sense of new experience. Piaget noted that, when the latter occurs, the subject is often thrown into a state of *disequilibration*, a state of chaos, if you will (and therefore often anxiety). This will be the case until one can *accommodate* new organizing principles to make sense of the data; it is in this latter sense that all systems of learning thrive.

Piaget's ideas are particularly helpful in underscoring how *prereflectively invariant organizing principles* may end up being treated as unquestioned "knowns" (i.e., as matters of certainty). This is a fallacy that is repeatedly encountered in couples therapy. When it rears its ugly head, it is evidence that the individual has forgotten (or never recognized) his inherent role as a constructor as well as discoverer of his subjective version of reality. And, when this happens, he falls prey to the illusion that he is simply seeing reality as it is, what Fonagy (2003) refers to as the state of "psychic equivalence."

Admittedly, few of us stop to consider that it is our construction of reality with which we are engaging and not the great imponderable "model-independent reality" (Hawking, 1988) itself. When one commits the all too common error of assuming one's perspective *is* reality, one engages in a *concretization* (Atwood & Stolorow, 1984)—that is, the "absolutizing" of a point of view, rather than seeing it as just another point of view, albeit one with which there may well also be real merit with disagreeing (Cavell, 1998; Gabbard, 2000).

My own study of organizing principles has led me to propose that there should be two broad classes of organizing principles. The first class I call "variant organizing principles," most frequently associated with organizing principles pertaining to development and repair. The second class pertains to "invariant organizing principles." Variant, developmental, reparative organizing principles constitute the structure upon which fluid experiencing is organized because they supply organization to the onslaught of information that would otherwise overwhelm any human being.[1] Variant organizing principles remain open to adaptation and change, and herein lay their critical distinction from invariant organizing principles. Variant organizing principles are open to the process of accommodation, which may come in slow accretions of trial and error over time or sometimes even in an instant of restructuring needed to accommodate for rapid shifts in context. In this latter sense, such accommodation allows for responsiveness to unpredictable "elements" of spontaneity. It is in this vein that an improvisatory mode of engagement can be most useful.

By contrast, invariant organizing principles are the more rigidified, highly constrained information processing structures that automatically constrain us moment to moment, disallowing us from a more fluid engagement with our surround. The order they impose on experience also radically constrains our ability to be more spontaneous, free, and creative, to become more improvisational in our lives. In their most pernicious form, invariant organizing principles fundamentally resist any form of change—that is, any form of accommodation. Or in a particularly, uniquely human manner, they adapt strategies that rigidly and repetitively involve processes of "pathological accommodation" (Brandchaft, 1994, 2007): By persistently accommodating to the other, one undermines one's own self-actualization. Either way, invariant organizing principles not only radically constrain how we see and experience ourselves, but also how we see and experience one another. Such organizing principles can dominate us with a kind of oppressive order—an order, however, which we may also be loath to be rid of because it serves to "bind" our plethora of anxieties.

There are multiple ways by which invariant organizing principles provide us with the illusion of security, but they are most vexing in their omnipotent-like attempt to halt time, to institute fictional states of permanence, to forbid the acknowledgment of loss, and to institutionalize ritualized substitutions to the experience of emptiness through forms of addictive/compulsive behavior. But as constraining as they can be, they are also all that we may have to fall back upon when we anticipate a lapse in intersubjective recognition from an important other, such as our analyst or spouse, a friend or a lover, whether this occurs in reality or in our imagination.

In sum, while variant organizing principles operate in the realm of probability and possibility, invariant organizing principles operate in the realm of absolutes and certainty. Since human nature is nothing if not constituted by a great deal of uncertainty, the invariant organizing principles create illusions of security that can end up massively limiting who we are, who we can be to ourselves, and who we come to be with one another. In this manner, each partner's invariant organizing principles set in motion what becomes a process of complementarity (wherein each becomes the opposite of the other, e.g., passive versus active, etc.) and the instantiation of binaries in their relationship: Who is "good" and who is "bad"? Who is "right" and who is wrong"? Who is the "victim" and who is the "victimizer"? Who is the "doer" and who is the "done-to"? And so forth.

A fundamental question that presses upon the marital dyad is: What are the "degrees of freedom" within the relationship that allow each partner to more fully express and experience him- or herself (i.e., fulfilling self-actualization versus constraining it)? Perhaps the greatest asset a couple can have is for its partners to be able to play (improvise) with their respective subjectivities, to take them both seriously and lightly, enabling the invocation of humor *and* aggression that stimulates their vitality, repair, and renewal.

Hopefully, what will become clear in subsequent chapters is that my style of intervention with a couple is to explore how they communicate meaning via subjectively important symbols and signifiers that arise within each partner as well as between partners. Their manner of communication conveys information through a huge array of forms, including verbal, nonverbal, paraverbal (tonal), and proxemic (spatial) styles of communication. It is a veritable impossibility for us to attend to all of these tiny permutations of communication. Therefore, what more typically gets explored and understood in this model of conjoint therapy is what I am proposing as the broader relational assumptions of each partner's *bidimensional forms of transference* (the developmental, selfobject dimension versus the repetitive, conflictual dimension).

Bidimensional transference

Returning to the initial assessment, I listen closely to how each partner expresses the following unconscious conviction: "With this partner, I hope that I will be able to actualize what heretofore I have not been able to (including my future strivings). However, with this partner, I also anticipate the dread of revisiting some unpleasant if not traumatizing experience from my past." This conviction of course embodies the *hope* to reconstitute one's growth or to repair what was traumatically broken, as counterbalanced by the *dread* that these hopes will be crushed, leading to retraumatization. The organization of such hopes and dreads take on their characteristic organizational forms of bidimensional models of transference (Stolorow, Brandchaft, & Atwood, 1987), wherein the first dimension embodies qualities of longed for reparation, reconstituted development, and a host of longings for selfobject attunement and the provisions of certain responses.

Comparable to Stolorow et al.'s bidimensional transference model is Tolpin's (2002) concept of the "forward versus trailing edge" of transference. Both sets of authors capture how, in contemporary psychoanalytic theories of transference (especially those influenced by Kohut's self psychology revolution), the longing for developmental experiences that were missing or insufficient during formative years is challenged by dreaded repetitions of experience of thwarted development.

By selfobject experiences, of course, the authors are referring to different versions of attuned responsiveness to key affect (emotional) states throughout all phases of one's life. Conversely, repetitive transference experiences pertain to fears and dreads of a repetition of selfobject failures. Tolpin captures how the selfobject dimension, or what she refers to as the forward edge, often represents the most barely noticeable tendrils of stunted growth. Her poetic depiction aptly describes the fragility and vulnerability of the partners exposing their longings, and it is here that the toes of the marital partners are routinely stubbed, if not periodically crushed. Since pointing this out in my first publication on conjoint therapy (Ringstrom, 1994), these points have been further elaborated in both couples and family therapy by authors influenced by the self-psychological and intersubjective systems theory traditions (Leone, 2001; Livingston, 2007; Shaddock, 1998, 2000) to which I have responded (Ringstrom, 2012c).

These longings echo the inextricable role caregivers play in the development of the personality, not only in the earliest stages of life, but in fact throughout adult life as well (Kohut, 1984). Many of the very same longings and needs that are instrumental to a child's development become some of the central functions of a couple's relationship, albeit hopefully operating on a more mature level. Nevertheless, it is in the failings of selfobject attunement and provisions that virtually every marital complaint can at least initially be understood. This understanding can be relayed fairly easily to the couple in a manner that both experience as attuned to their subjective sensibility. Other experiences, more resistant to attunement and therefore more prone to needing to be enacted, will emerge later in the model.

From an attuned perspective, however, it is easiest for me to begin by thinking of complaints in terms of the experiential failure of selfobject functions that would otherwise enable self-experiences of cohesion, continuity, and worth. While Kohut (1959, 1977) based his self-psychological theory on three selfobject functions, Stolorow et al. (1987) have aptly noted that the list of potential selfobject functions is limitless, corresponding to the unique organizational needs of any given individual. Nevertheless, there are a number of selfobject functions that merit brief enunciation, given the sheer frequency with which they organize the substance of so many marital complaints.

Kohut's original tripartite of functions included *mirroring, idealization,* and *twinship.* Mirroring is a critical function in development, reflecting the parents' recognition and affirmation of the child's subjective experience, especially those

42

pertaining to experiences of expansiveness and ambition in the world, along with related affect states of pleasurable excitement and pride in these activities. The critical function of idealization that Kohut proposed was to provide the child with a sense of others upon whom he could trust for their provision of strength, security, leadership, values, and guidance. Finally, in twinship, otherwise known as the "alterego" selfobject function, Kohut identified the importance of feeling known via the other's conveyance of a comparable experience of the world.

More contemporary theoreticians, influenced by Kohut's self psychology, took up where Kohut stopped. Stolorow et al. (1987) forwarded several more selfobject functions critical to affect integration, including "affect differentiation and self-articulation," "synthesizing affectively discrepant experiences," "affect tolerance and the use of affects as self-signals," and finally "desomatization and cognitive articulation of affect." Similarly, others promoted noteworthy functions, such as Bacal's (1994) "fantasy self object function," wherein through the power of imagination one "creates" the image of a selfobject provider and what he or she or "it" might entail in terms of the conveyance of a selfobject function in the absence of its occurrence from a real caregiver. Wolf (1988) even alerted us to the potential longing for an "adversarial selfobject function," wherein the other could be needed as a worthy source of opposition who can withstand our outpourings and with whom we can safely "fight" about our respective takes on reality.[2]

Meanwhile, a fundamental premise in self psychology is that the more such attuned responsiveness occurs in development (or in analysis, or in marriage), the more an individual's archaic selfobject needs potentially transform into more mature ones. Where these mature ones come to constitute a lifelong pattern of psychological reorganization, an individual may be found to be less prone to fragmentation on those occasions of inevitable disappointments that occur in a marriage, as well as through the vicissitudes of adult development.

Still, listening for the selfobject longings and their failure is only one half of the puzzle regarding each partner's self-actualization. The other half pertains to the *repetitive, dreaded, resistive dimension of each partner's unconscious models of transference*. This dimension of organization embodies all of the themes that prereflectively shape how self and other are seen in relation to one another, particularly in relationship to disappointment, if not retraumatization. All of these modes of organization predate the relationship, and will serve to contextualize each other's experience—that is, how each partner's schematic ways of being in the world contextualize the others.

Eventually, over time, each one's schematic organization becomes more and more reenacted by their partner. In this sense, the partners are not simply discovering something about their partner, they are each co-constructing the other's reaction. In essence, they are unconsciously scripting one another as to who they are in any given scenario. Ironically, there really is no alternative to this happening. In fact, to work with the hopes and dreads each has brought to the relationship, each partner will inadvertently and unwittingly lend themselves to enacting familiar, old "self" and "other" configurations (Shane, Shane, & Gales, 1997), pertaining to the hopes and dreads that each partner brings to their relationship that soon become reciprocally reenacted. Indeed, it is in the manner of "present moment remembering" (Stern, 2004) that parts of the past can become animated, out of which, with the help of couples therapy, prospectively welcome new modes of relating can develop.

Having stipulated that the repetitive dimension of transference often entails the *dread of repeating* past selfobject failures (Ornstein, 1974), the repetitive dimension can also entail the *dread not to repeat* past patterns of engagement, no matter how ostensibly unwanted these repetitive dreads are claimed to be. It is at these junctures that the greatest potential for change and reorganization is possible. The quest of such dreaded familiar patterns may surface especially when either of the partners are threatened by change—even change they profess to want to occur. As Bromberg (1998) notes, many patients come to our practices unwittingly asking us to help them to change while wishing to remain the same. Anxious over being truly able to trust change within themselves and their partners, they can easily revert to primitive fears of unknowns, of disloyalties, and to a host of common anxieties that arise when facing greater senses of vulnerability and intimacy. In the face of the latter terror, partners are compelled to repeat the failings of their development, despite conscious wishes to the contrary.

This can result in the unfortunate tendency for partners to respond to each other defensively, often precisely in the manner for which they anticipate being attacked. Instead of presenting each other with a new experience of difference, and therefore a new potential reality, they fortify each other's rigid, repetitive transference fantasy system about the badness inherent in intimate relationships.

With some couples I have learned to playfully label this kind of repetitive engagement as involving "The Jack Story," which is a shorthand way of noting when one or both are engaging in modes of prereflectively invariantly organized repetitive transferences. "The Jack Story" comes from a familiar joke about the city slicker whose car has a flat tire on a country road in the middle of the night. Bereft by his realization he left his car jack at home, the man sets out towards the singular lit-up farmhouse he can see. In the course of walking closer and closer to the farmer's door, the helpless driver's fantasies move from hopefully imagining the farmer will graciously assist him, to fearing the farmer will shamefully rebuke him for his ill-preparedness (similar to what he would have anticipated from his early caregivers). The joke is told with considerable tension building over each of the driver's ever-worsening fantasies. The punchline finally explodes with the driver ascending the farmer's front porch and screaming at the shocked and horrified farmer, "You can keep your *fucking* jack!" When couples learn to say about themselves that "this feels like a 'Jack Story,'" they are alerting each other that their respective fantasies about one another are becoming dominated in a negative fantasy about each other, which may involve something that the other is not at all experiencing—at least not yet.

Vicious circles

Ultimately, armed with the complementary constructs of the selfobject and repetitive dimensions of transference, I listen closely for the failing of the former and how and what triggers in the latter. Furthermore—and this is a critical component of couples therapy—I also listen for how each one's selfobject longings is a likely source for triggering each other's repetitive dimension transference, and that whenever this happens the couple rapidly devolves into a *vicious circle* escalating their madness and pain. Momentarily, I will address the affect regulating activities the therapist must also engage during such crushing episodes, but an illustration of the assessment of each partner's bidimensional transference, as well as how they trigger one another, might be most helpful at this point.[3]

Tom and Jane

Tom and Jane came to me as a couple in their late fifties. They had two grown daughters, both of whom were university graduates exhibiting considerable promise of doing well as adults. Tom had maintained a successful CPA practice for close to 30 years, while Jane had been both a homemaker and part-time interior decorator. Until their recent crisis, their marriage had been a reasonably harmonious one, which, though lacking in sparks, was sufficient to making them both feel secure and reasonably fulfilled in life.

The crisis in their marriage arose when Tom announced to Jane that he was seriously contemplating selling his practice and pursuing his real life's passion, which was to become an inventor. Jane was sure that Tom had either been "abducted by aliens" or "gone stark raving mad," since this was not the sort of behavior of the "straight-arrow" Tom that she had married.

Beneath his straight-arrow manner, however, Tom had always sequestered his passion for examining what made things work and his love for tinkering with them to see if he could make improvements. His avocation in this regard was always dismissed by his wife and daughters as "Dad's little hobby." Nevertheless, in his youth, he had won several science fairs, and had created a few inventions that aroused some potential commercial interest. Absent any mirroring of his passion from his immigrant parents, he was insecure about pursuing it. Instead, he followed his father's admonition that America will always need accountants, and as a child who never disrespected his parents he went to night school to obtain his degrees while working as a bookkeeper by day. When he met Jane, he never gave her any reason to think he would be anything but a stable and devoted provider to his family—a requirement for her to marry any man.

Jane's own upbringing was anything but stable. Her charismatic father had a drinking and gambling problem that perpetually undermined the stability of his family life. Clean and sober for a few years at a time, his relapses would cast the family into economic chaos, usually requiring their relocating to stay just ahead of the creditors. When he wasn't in trouble, Jane's father was very loving and much loved by his family, but the chaos this created powerfully influenced Jane's choice for a future mate. One asset from all the moving was that Jane had developed a keen eye for decorating, as well as how it could be done on a shoestring budget. This, in combination with her extroverted qualities, provoked Tom's youthful ardor, not to mention a part-time career of her own.

Of course, in an initial session, a couple does not immediately supply such information. In fact, the personality organizations that underscore their calamity can take some time to discern. Furthermore, their "affect storms" can create chaos in data gathering. In the midst of Jane's accusations that Tom had lost his mind, and his that Jane suddenly had become selfish and greedy, it became especially important to listen for their underlying longings, their derailments, and the history of disruptions these replicated. As I listened closely, I began to pick up threads of each one's histories, which became part of the weave in my formulation of the vicious circle of their respective transferences.

Of course, modern models of affect regulation underscore that individuals are impaired in their ability to learn when they are in the extremes of either hyper- or hypo-arousal (Beebe & Lachmann, 1994; Lillas & Turnbull, 2009; Schore, 1994; Stern, 1985), so it behooves the therapist to actively intervene and bring down the tension level by pointing out that accusatory behavior only promulgates unremitting defensiveness and counter-accusatory behavior. Without this intervention, I find that it is very hard for either partner to make meaning of their own experience, much less each other's. Tom and Jane certainly were not in much position to make much use of my interpretations.

As with many couples, I had to help Jane and Tom with regulating their affect. I did this by interrupting them and asking them to take a few deep breaths. While I had them pause for a moment or two, I described their physiological appearance in their state of mutual emotional dysregulation.[4] I pointed out that, while each is able to see the other's face, they are unable to see their own. To ease some of their agitation and to try to inspire them to realize that they likely knew less about what they are communicating affectively than they think, I joked with them that God's greatest omission was to not give us rearview mirrors with which to see our own expressions. This kind of intervention typifies a manner in which I attempt to improvise off of what they are saying, and to infuse a property of playfulness to open up possibility in the face of rigidity, scriptedness, and repetition. In like manner, I mentioned to Tom and Jane that research on nonverbal communication indicates that our faces are a primary mode of emotional communication. As a consequence, our faces are often betrayers of our unformulated thoughts and feelings.

Once Tom and Jane calmed down, I was able to offer the following interpretation, which typifies the kind that I try to make in an initial session. I began with Tom, saying, "So here's what I think that I am hearing. It seems, Tom, that all of your life you have been sitting on your desire to be an inventor. You are more aware of your mortality than ever before, especially having told me that both of your parents died in the past five years. You see that your time to pursue your passion is running out, but to do it, you really need Jane's support, affirmation, and encouragement [e.g., the mirroring selfobject transference]. Absent that, you are not only disappointed, you feel threatened, because this revisits the absence of support from your parents that undermined your passion from its inception [e.g., the repetitive transference]. It's not easy for you to convey this to Jane, I'm sure, because to want something so badly, and to imagine its rejection, can make one feel vulnerable. *And*, it's also not easy for her to hear what you want, because of what it triggers in her.

"For you, Jane, Tom has disrupted the very thing you have always relied upon in him, and that is his stability, his predictability, and the security those qualities lent to you [e.g., the idealizing selfobject transference] that have been so reparative of the chaos of your childhood [e.g., the repetitive transference]. Indeed, it makes perfect sense to me that you feel thrown, maybe even betrayed, since you have come to count on this from Tom.

"The calamity I think that the two of you have brought to me is that what you each long for is provoking something threatening in the other. In your case, Tom, wishing for Jane's support of this new life project comes too close in her mind to revisiting the chaos that came from her father's drinking and gambling. I know that you are set financially, from what you describe, but I am wondering if Jane has fears that the cost of your inventions could jeopardize this, so that at least is a part of her fear. Meanwhile, Jane, your wish, even need for continuity in Tom's behavior triggers for him a threatening aspect of his past—that he will never have support to grow and to become the man he has always wanted to be. What makes so much sense to me is that each one of your perfectly understandable strivings is tragically serving as a major threat to the other because of what they are arousing historically within each of you. How does this all sound to the both of you? Does this fit? Does it make sense?"

Now if the conjoint therapist's interpretation is close enough to the mark for both partners, many things rapidly begin to happen—for example, affective coloration in their faces changes. There also can be an increased state of calm as they start to listen less defensively to what each other is saying. Indeed, they begin talking to one another, at least momentarily, rather than at one another. This is exactly what happened with Tom and Jane. With this affect containing framework came the restoration of their capacity to reflect rather than simply react. This enabled them to communicate the following. Tom queried Jane, "Did you really fear that I would use *our* money on my inventions? I wouldn't use anything more than drafting some plans, but full model work-ups would require venture capital, which, by the way, you know I have connections to pursue through my accounting practice." Jane replied, "I never thought of that; all I could see in my mind was, 'Here I go again, losing everything.'"

Most importantly, when the couple grasps what the therapist has formulated, several important elements have already been set in motion. First, the therapist becomes someone who can actually understand both of them, no matter how mad or crazy they each seemed to the other before they walked through the consulting room door. Second, the therapist represents someone who can deeply, empathically, and compassionately capture what is at stake in each one's self-actualization, as well as what threatens it. Third, the therapist's interpretations begin to model the quality of mutual recognition involved in intersubjective relating. That is, that two different mindsets can be recognized, appreciated, and even seen to be inextricably intertwined in their dynamics. Finally, all of this potentially cultivates an amazing quality of hope that had begun to feel all but lost to the couple.

Assuming all goes as I have stated, another curious thing happens: Each partner begins to form their own idealizing transference to the therapist, notwithstanding that much of the repetitive dimension of the transference remains focused on each other, though somewhat mitigated by a renewed sense of hope. The idealization of the conjoint therapist has all sorts of ramifications down the line, but for now it serves as a potentially powerful bonding agent for the couple.

The therapist instantly becomes a critical point of view, offering an alternative to their right/wrong, black/white, doer/done-to binary modes of relating (Benjamin, 2004). What will become of greater importance in subsequent chapters is examining the fact that now there are at least six levels of transference operating at any given moment in the room. That is because there is each partner's bidimensional transference with each other, as well as each one's bidimensional transference to the therapist, and the therapist's bidimensional countertransferences to each of them. Whew![5]

The visual image of all of this can seem a bit like the confluence of interstate highways at a Los Angeles Freeway overpass. In truth, though, aspects of all parties' transferences and countertransferences move in and out of the experiential foreground and background, deriving their impetus more by how different issues the couple faces activate themes relevant to each parties' personality organization. If, for example, farther down the line in treatment it is discovered that Jane is freer with sex but tighter with money, and Tom is just the opposite, each one's constricted versus freer qualities will surface along the lines of what I call *context dependent issues*, meaning that differing contexts of engagement give rise to certain issues which have the potential of provoking different self-state reactions in the respective parties. This concept becomes crucial in discerning legitimately different self-states within each partner and aiding in their illumination. This becomes especially important in underscoring the effect of different self-states in what appears to be inconsistency or, even worse, hypocrisy, when in fact what is getting represented are multiple states of authenticity, albeit ones disconnected through dissociation.

As will be examined in Step Four, the concept of context dependent issues also helps explain why enactments can have a temporal sequence—that is, that an issue can initially perturb one partner more than another, at least until the latter is drawn into the enactment. It is because of this reciprocating process that I have coined the term *mutual inductive identification*. The point to all of this is, while enactments may seem to begin asymmetrically, they move very quickly to operating symmetrically (i.e., with each partner now at the other's throat).

Handling disappointments: attunement to the secondary selfobject function

Sometimes partners are unresponsive to each other's selfobject longings simply because they do not fit with their normal self-centered agentic need not to provide them, as in each preserving their sense of autonomy and authenticity. In couples with whom a degree of personal and relational maturity has been accomplished, it is not necessarily the disappointment of the longed-for primary selfobject function (Stolorow, Brandchaft, & Atwood, 1987) that is the greatest difficulty to manage. The real source of disruption usually entails a failure in the secondary selfobject function, which is measured by a lack of attunement by each partner to the other's emotional reaction over the disappointment of the primary selfobject function. A typical example of a failed response on the secondary level is when the disappointed partner is now shamed for having her negative reaction to the primary disappointment. This arose in the case of Helena and Theo.

Helena and Theo

Helena and Theo entered their session mutually enraged. Theo, an amateur artist, discovered an impressionistic oil painting class at a local art institute that was being held in the evening after his workday. He was eager to take it, though loath to tell Helena about it, since he knew that she could readily become anxious after nightfall if she was all alone. This had been the case since she was 8 years old, when her parents had left her with a babysitter and went out for the evening. Well after nightfall, the babysitter received an urgent call that her father had had a medical emergency. Distraught in her own fears and not thinking clearly, she told Helena to sit tight, keep the door locked, and that she, the babysitter, would go home for a few minutes to make sure everything was all right and then come right back. Once she got home and saw the paramedics surrounding her father, she realized that she couldn't leave her father's side. She quickly called another neighbor who she presumed to be home, and left a message on her answering machine asking her to go attend to Helena. Unfortunately, the neighbor was also out for the evening and didn't receive the message until many hours later. Meanwhile, the minutes that Helena was to be left alone soon turned into hours, though it was unclear how long she was actually alone. Nevertheless, when her parents returned home, they found their 8-year-old completely traumatized. In this historical context, Helena's night fears made considerable sense. However, they had also made it difficult for Theo to ever leave home at night.

Given the magnitude of Theo's desire to take the painting class and his anticipation of this desire being shot down, Theo approached Helena in a preemptively defensive manner. He announced his wish to Helena in the form of an angry demand. Expectantly, Helena's nonverbal lack of enthusiasm uncorked him. In truth, Helena had come a long way in terms of being alone at night, but the residue of trauma still could reveal itself in her implicit forms of expression. Instantly taking offense at this, Theo blasted, "Oh great, I guess your night fears will kill this for me too! I guess I am on permanent babysitter duty!" Helena felt instantly ashamed.

What we finally teased out was not that Helena needed Theo to stay with her (e.g., fulfilling a kind of primary idealizing protective selfobject function). After all, she had come to recognize and even admire the degree of self-actualization Theo accrued from his art classes. What she needed instead was some understanding that she could have her initial hesitation, her initial disappointed expression, even if nonverbal, without needing or wishing to kill Theo's dream. Instead of Theo's shaming response, she needed a secondary selfobject response recognizing her difficulty but also trusting in her increasing capacity to tolerate her fears, rather than a response that shamed her for whatever residue of them she still harbored. When Theo understood this, he quickly apologized for shaming Helena, and did then confirm that he had seen her getting better and better with managing her fears. He also appreciated her affirming the self-actualization he got from his art and he thanked her for all of her support.

There are a number of couples with whom I have worked over the years in which learning to respond in an attuned manner as a secondary selfobject response to the primary selfobject rupture becomes a kind of tool that they utilize effectively for holding to their own desire while not denigrating their partners. This occurs through their finding a means of recognizing the disappointing impact their primary selfobject failure could have for their partner. This helps build a bridge for mutual recognition between them, and therein also develop a kind of structure of thirdness, that makes their relationship more readily open to repair.

Agency

While transference captures the organization of one's personality, *agency* captures a nascent sense of personal authorship, wherein we are the writers, directors, producers, and actors in the psychodramas of our existence. It is through our sense of agency that our lives are writ large or small. On the most basic level, we bring to the world not only our perceptions of it, but our imaginings as well.

As Loewald (1980, 1988) noted, fantasy and perception inextricably inform one another. Grotstein (1997) referred to this most basic form of authorship as "autochthony," wherein the basic intrapsychic reality of any individual begins in the omnipotent fantasy of having created the universe. As the child matures, she learns that such fantasy is gradually at odds with the humbling realization that, instead of the omnipotent source of creation, an individual is merely one participant among many fellow co-creators of a vision of the universe.[6]

Still, for some people, relinquishing one's sense of omnipotence can be very difficult, especially when their real life experiences were so traumatizing as to make it impossible for them to step very far out of the constraints of their fantasy life. Worse yet, their fantasy system often must preemptively imagine the worst, to be prepared for its occurrence. Relinquishing omnipotent fantasy is all the more difficult when it is intensely entwined with a kind of vitalizing affectivity.

Despite all of this, it appears that our personal sense of agency functions in a most gratifying way when we feel least constrained in how we determine and pursue personal goals in work, love, and play. By contrast, agency founders to the extent it functions more for defensive purposes, which, as Gentile (2001) notes, arises in what she refers to as the "perversion of agency" that appears to agentically undermine or to "pervert" our pursuit of work and love and play.

While agency appears to arise intrasubjectively, it actually requires another's confirming response, indicating that they grasp our meaning and, even more importantly, that they experience the impact our sense of agency has in revealing what we intended (Benjamin, 1995). This makes agency only discernible within an intersubjective field of mutual need and mutual responsibility. Partners feel efficacious and recognized, to the extent that their sense of agency registers an impact upon one another. The intersubjective field in which each partner's sense of agency arises is therefore a crucial factor in establishing the horizons of each partner's self-actualization (Stern, 1997). It means that how one lives out one's sense of agency in terms of self-actualization must be perpetually renegotiated in intimate relationships (Pizer, 1998).

All of this means that, beginning with Step One and continuing throughout the treatment, it is important to listen for the manner in which each partner's desires and goals for self-actualization manifest. In a similar vein, this involves assessing how much each partner looks to the other for recognition and affirmation of his or her personal goals, as well as how threatened each is by the other's sense of agency. All of these ideas are germane to an assessment of how much each partner is able to take responsibility for their sense of agency, versus requiring the other to assume that responsibility.

Meanwhile, both dimensions of the transference are profoundly influenced by acts of agency, insofar as an individual's selfobject dimension of the transference is organized around seeking responsiveness to his sense of agency, while the repetitive dimension of his transference is often scanning for how it will be thwarted. (The examination of the "perversion of agency" in Step Four covers how agency is sometimes perversely employed by inducing the other to actually thwart it—in short, to replay a version of "The Jack Story.") This manifests in ways in which partners sometimes not only actively constrain one another, but, less visibly, they actively collude with helping each other in undermining work, love, and play in their relationship. A key pathway to both personal liberation and empowerment in one's relationship comes from each partner embracing his and her sense of agency, and not holding the other responsible for it.

Each time the therapist successfully takes the couple through a systemic understanding of what got ruptured, she simultaneously provides them with a model for "rupture and repair," one of the key "curative" ingredients in all psychotherapies, according to Beebe and Lachmann (1994). A reparative interpretation captures several salient properties: a) recognition of each partner's stake in their problem;

b) how their rupture makes perfect sense to the therapist in terms of its content (e.g., the vicious circle entanglement of their bidimensional transferences); and c) their distressing affect states including shame, blame, and guilt. The therapist also captures their fear of being caught in the impossible dilemma that they must either lose one another or lose their minds (Davies, 2003). This cycle of rupture and repair lends to a rapid mitigation of the partners seeing each other only in terms of their projections (and therefore negation of one another). In this manner, it is instrumental to developing a working model of mutual recognition. The repetition of rupture and repair gradually creates a new relational structure that is refined throughout the couple's therapy.

Mutual recognition

As Bromberg (1998) notes, non-recognition "is equivalent to relational abandonment. It is that which evokes the familiar though often bewildering accusation 'you don't know me'" (p. 258). In this context, assessing the couple's capacity for mutual recognition is critical. (In Step Three, other crucial ideas germane to this assessment regarding attachment patterns and mentalization will be elaborated in far greater detail.) Couples lacking capacity for mutual recognition inevitably lapse into experiences of fixed states of asymmetrical dominance and submission, or oscillating ones of reversible complementarity with its symmetrically ceaseless patterns of mutually destructive competition. As will become clearer in Step Two, it is important that the therapist not jump to judging who the dominant is and who the submissive is, since both will likely lay claim to feeling dominated.

Tim and Valerie

Tim and Valerie exemplified a couple perpetually caught up in such dominance and submission struggles. They came to me as a separated couple, a mere pen stroke away from signing divorce papers. As parents of three children all under the age of 5, they both wished for reconciliation, but could barely tolerate staying in the same room with one another. Each professed that the only time they remotely got along with one another was when they lapsed into a submissive position—that is, each proclaimed, "It only works when I give up all hope of getting anything that I want, and just give in to him/her." The irony that both were making exactly the same claim seemed completely lost on them. Nevertheless, each one's experience was that his or her sense of agency not only went unrecognized, but that it was a major source of traumatic threat to the other. This threat corresponded with each one's upbringing.

In Valerie's case, this entailed physical and sexual abuse from several uncles. This went unrecognized for years, and later, when disclosed, resulted in her being blamed for being a seductress. On top of this, she was constantly told that, unlike her brother, who was the apple of the parents' eye, she would not amount to anything. The absence of recognition in general, coupled with the shaming attribution of her "participation" in the sexual interludes, flooded Valerie with hateful spite—a typical *modus operandi* in the service of self-righting. She literally strove with a vengeance to succeed throughout her adulthood. In so doing, however, she found little sense of pleasure in her personal agency, mastery, and competency. Ultimately her achievements were less about doing something for herself than they were about her being hell-bent on showing her family her highly enviable qualities. The only thing meaningful to her about her substantial success was that, relative to their rather low station in life, she could flaunt that which none of them would ever be able to achieve, while also depriving them of sharing her success by holding them at arm's length through her vitriolic estrangement.

Comparably, Tim's only experience of mutual recognition—with his mother—abruptly terminated when she died shortly following his 10th birthday. His estranged relationship with his father only worsened as his father quickly introduced a "wicked" stepmother to their household. Tim's learning disabilities made him a constant source of ridicule in his otherwise academic family, so, much like Valerie, he left home at an early age to make his way in the world, which he did with huge financial success as an entrepreneur.

Though each had been wildly successful in their own vocations, Tim and Valerie were terribly challenged as to how to succeed in cultivating an intimate relationship. It was immediately apparent that each one's sense of agency was a source of threat to the others. From the vantage point of the organization of their bidimensional transferences, each longed for recognition (in both cases an admixture of mirroring and idealization) and some accommodation from the other, while also expecting their longings to be thwarted in manners similar to that which occurred in their upbringings (repetitive transference dimension). As is common with so many couples, the repetitive dimensions of each one's transference shaped their expectation of being dominated by the other, and their manner of protecting themselves resulted in a co-constructed "self-fulfilling prophecy" of this nightmare scenario. Couples beset with such impasses develop a quality of "negative thirdness"—that is, their relationship devolves into a mutually negating mind of its own. This is in distinct contrast to the kind of positive thirdness or opening of potential space for personal and interpersonal growth.

The relationship having a mind of its own

Tim and Valerie's dilemma spelled out a mutually despairing sense of futility. Locked in their experience of simultaneous dominance and submission, they foundered in a mutual negation of each other's sense of agency. As with many such couples, their affective states readily flipped into hyper-arousal mode, making it almost impossible for them to find any room to mentalize—that is, reflect on what it is about themselves that contributes to the mess they are in, as well as to be able to reflect upon their partner's feelings as independent of their own. The more agitated they became, the less they could do anything but accuse and abuse one another.

Tim and Valerie were the kind of couple that require extraordinary early intervention that includes containing the extremes of their hyper-aroused affectivity, and interpreting the condition of their relationship (i.e., of its having a negating mind of its own). This often must happen *before* attempting to point out their bidimensional transference conflicts, since otherwise they are vulnerable to hearing such interpretations as sources of individual blame.

Helping Tim and Valerie required a style of confrontation that pretty much throws the psychoanalytic treatment ideals of abstinence, anonymity, and neutrality right out the window (not that they have typically ever had a place in couples treatment of the psychoanalytic variety). It required my insisting on *my* being the authority in the room, not in terms in the veridicality of my interpretations, but in terms of my insistence on our rules of engagement. I had to insist that I would be the only one allowed to interrupt, and that I would do so when it appeared to my best judgment that they were deviating back on a path of destruction and mutual annihilation. Frequently, when one would go off into rants of mutual accusations, I would tell them to "knock it off," and when they would obliterate my attempts at containing their rant, I would lean far forward in my chair and repeat, over and over, "[Tim/Valerie], find my eyes, find my eyes, find my eyes!" (This is a technique I had learned in working with children and adults suffering from Attention Deficit Disorder.) In this manner, I was calling them out of their dissociated states of vitriolic ranting, into which each would frequently lapse in moments of narcissistic rage.

Once Tim and Valerie would calm down, I would quickly talk about how the climate of their relationship was one that had become mutually traumatizing. It can be very important to make this assertion, so as to lessen the focus on either one or the other being the culprit in their derailment, or in that moment the dominating/obliterating party. Confronting the specifics of their individual styles of being bullying and domineering may come later, but if it is taken up too soon in the treatment, it can be experienced as too provocative, too blaming, and too shaming. By contrast, when the onus is placed on the mutually negating thirdness of the relationship, it is less about each one, and more about the pernicious "grip of the field," to quote Donnel Stern (1997, pp. 191–193). "Breaking the grip" entails questioning what is going on between the two participants. Couples in severe distress often have difficulty doing this. Their attitudes towards one another are, for the moment, what Stern describes as "autocentric," where each one experiences the other as an object to be used, or often an object whose needs threaten their own. By contrast, cultivating an allocentric attitude requires cultivating curiosity that is part of the restoration of the analytic thirdness of intersubjective mutual recognition.

It is not uncommon for this to seem impossible with some couples, and in effect, as with Tim and Valerie, it had to be demonstrated by me. In this case, a recurrent dimension of their argument was about Valerie's return to Los Angeles from what was Tim's country dream home, a place in which she no longer felt safe or welcome. Having lived there for a number of years, she wanted to return to a metropolitan area to raise their children, whereas Tim's vision remained to rear their children in the safety of country far from the turmoil of urban life, away from its corrupting culture, not to mention its unhealthy air.

What is apparent on the surface is the clash of each one's sense of agency. Tim's life plan had been temporarily fulfilled by Valerie's willingness six years before to move to his country estate. While Valerie tried to make the best of it, the subjugation of her own personal strivings, along with the perpetual acrimony in their relationship, left her feeling that Tim was being "in total control," and that she was "totally dominated." Compounding this, she perceived others in their social circle as turning against her, much like her family had in her youth at the disclosure of her incest. All of this led to her taking their children and abruptly moving to Los Angeles. Tim now felt that he was the dominated party, forced to forsake his dream and to move back to Los Angeles.

Modeling the shift from negating thirdness to intersubjective thirdness meant grasping what was at stake in their respective senses of agency. Before they could hear that, however, I had to paradoxically enjoin them by asking them to accept my invitation to do something impossible (Watzlawick et al., 1974): to see what it might feel like momentarily to set aside their own version of reality without discarding it; that is, to "walk in one another's moccasins," if only for a moment, and to try to entertain the other's subjective experience. In effect, I was inviting them into a kind of improvisational exercise, wherein they'd set aside their predetermined scripts and attempt to play off-of-and-with one another's "suggested" version of reality, much like what is described in the previous chapter. In the course of doing this, they each began to hear within themselves some possibility that had heretofore been foreclosed in their minds.

Having bracketed my comments and temporarily enlisted their willingness to go along with my suggestion, I then returned to the clash in their respective sense of agency. I pointed out to Tim that as much as I understood his vision for his family, I also understood that it was his dream and his alone. Unfortunately, I ventured, that, while Valerie initially went along with his dream, she had lost her sense of self in it, as it was his dream and not hers. In fact, his agency had cut against the grain of hers.[7] From this standpoint, I said that it made perfect sense to me that Valerie could feel dominated, having lost her sense of control. I suggested that this might be especially trying for her because she may well experience anger at herself for having ceded control over to him.

Having previously already gone over how much each could simultaneously feel dominated by the other, Tim could see what I meant, even if only momentarily. Meanwhile, Valerie felt especially recognized by my interpretations. I then commented to her that, while she had gone along with Tim's dream against her own, her reversal now made it perfectly understandable to me that Tim would feel dominated by her sense of agency at the expense of his own. Now it was he who had to return to Los Angeles—a place that he loathed—to be a part of rearing his children. She was, for the moment, able to grasp this. Of course, it is hard from such initial interpretations to have too much lasting impact. That which challenges them is the background (invariant organizing principles) each partner brings that then potentially constrains one another's sense of agency.

Multiple self-states

A critically important topic that will be expanded upon throughout the remainder of the book is that patients present with multiple versions of self, or more precisely, multiple self-states. These include multiple relational models regarding multiple versions of self and other. Frequently, these versions are dissociatively detached from one another and therefore are not readily recognizable. One of the paradoxes of this model is that "who oneself experiences him- or herself to be" can entail multiple versions of self, as well as, over time, mutative experiences of oneself, especially as a result of the therapy. Still, a sense of what feels real or true or authentic permeates the multiplicity of experiences that leads eventually to coming to terms with inner conflicts, as well as reckoning with internal aspects of oneself not so easily negotiated.

The problem of unwitting or unformulated multiple self-states outlines two key disruptions in the marital dyad. The first disruption pertains to ruptures of selfobject states (i.e., the dread of repeating historical ruptures) that has been explored earlier in this chapter. The second relates to the dread of change, wherein a patient's initial desire to change devolves into what Bromberg (1998) calls "the wish to stay the same while changing" (p. 170). It is critical that, over the course of treatment, each partner's manner of dissociation be addressed. This becomes especially important to constituting safety in the therapeutic matrix, lest one version of self affirm a partner, while another takes this affirmation away. Such oscillations breed a treacherous sense of "gaslighting," which breeds the upsurge of tragic mistrust right in the midst of the couple's attempts at creating tendrils of trusting connection.

Listening stances

Up to this point, Step One has emphasized the therapist's highly empathically attuned listening stance vis-à-vis the partners as individuals, as well as to their relationship as a couple. All of this pertains to recognition of the individual partners' sense of self, self-actualization, agency, and so forth, as well as how these states are optimized for both partners under the circumstances of mutual recognition and the relationship having (an open) mind of its own. From what we understand about multiple self-state theory, however, the experience of selfhood can manifest in a host of different states configured by a sense of self, a sense of other, and the affect that links the two. For most of Step One, the focus has been on how the therapist and the partners learn about each other's subjective experiences through listening from what Fosshage (1997) refers to as the "subject-centered listening perspective" (self psychology's and intersubjective systems theory's privileged listening stance). To expand this view even more, however, I find it enormously useful to engage in what Fosshage introduces as the "other-centered

56

listening perspective" (frequently the emphasis of object relations, interpersonal, and relational stances of psychoanalysis).

For purposes of reiteration, when one (whether partner or therapist) listens to another from the subject-centered listening perspective, one is engaged in a form of empathic inquiry, involving affective resonance, vicarious introspection (the search for like experiences in one's own life), and reflectivity—all focused on the patient's subjective experience. When accurate, this creates a powerful sense of being subjectively recognized.[8]

Still, Fosshage argues that along with the subject-centered listening perspective, we are naturally predisposed to engaging in an other-centered listening perspective. This entails listening to one *not* from a position *within* their experience of themselves, but as listening to their experience from *without* (i.e., listening for how the listened-to individual impacts others)—in short, what it is like to be an "other" in the patient's life. This can result in their creepy experience of being suspected for "reasons" about which they are clueless.[9]

Couples therapy creates an extraordinary therapeutic circumstance that, in certain ways (though not all), is vastly more complex (and therefore clinically economical) than individual treatment. This is because the same therapist can be both empathizing with one's spouse's subjective experience while also experiencing what it is like to be another (object) to him or her.

Fosshage (1997) emphasizes:

> Relationships in general entail a natural oscillation between these two perspectives as one listens to another person. In the analytic situation [as well as in couples therapy], I am proposing that the subject-centered and other-centered modes are two principle [sic] methods of listening to our analysand's experiences and that important data are gathered through each listening stance.
>
> (p. 35)

None of this, of course, obviates that the therapist is listening from her own subjective personality organization. Historically, her experience of the patient was referred to as her countertransference. This term typically emphasized the role of the patient's transference on the analyst, her reaction to it, and therefore her countertransference. More contemporary psychoanalytic theory, however, has come to emphasize the analyst's own transference organization as a key element of influence in the intersubjective field.

The latter point creates an important complexity in the dynamics of any couples therapy, one that is not easily resolved but is important to grapple with. The question is: When is what the therapist is experiencing—from either of the partners—emblematic of how they each experience one another (and how others in their lives experience them)? Or, when is what the therapist is experiencing idiosyncratic of her own personality organization and therefore having less to do with the other listening perspective?

Typically, though not always, patients prefer the therapist, and their partner for that matter, to listen from the subject-centered position, to attempt to recognize what it is like to "walk around in their moccasins," so to speak. This assiduous attunement stance usually, though again not always, reduces the risk of introducing information that might be experienced as shaming or blaming a partner for the impact he or she has upon the spouse. For this reason, both self psychology and intersubjective systems theory have strongly eschewed the role of the other-centered listening stance, deferring instead to the empathic attunement position. By contrast, relational psychoanalysis' strong affiliation with both object relations theory and interpersonal psychoanalysis results in an assumption that, somewhere in the analysis, material has to come up not simply about the patient's experience of others, but also how the patient might be experienced by others, especially in ways that are largely unconscious and also prone to shame him when realized. What concerns relational psychoanalysts is that the evasion of such material risks reinforcing a patient's solipsism and undermining an increased capacity for relationality through mutual recognition.

The complexity of relational psychoanalysis is that, while it is never advocating an objectivist view of reality, it is also *not* throwing out the analyst's subjectivist experience of the patient as being sometimes critically informative of the manner in which the patient relates to others. The relational perspective ultimately sees an other listening perspective as indispensible, a thoroughgoing investigation of the patient's total world of experience, including his multiple self-states and all the ways that these states imply something about one's self, the other, and the relational affective theme being evoked in any particular issue dependent context that gives rise to it. I will now turn to the case of Claire and Simon, examining how both listening perspectives were involved in an episode of treatment.

Claire and Simon

Claire and Simon are a couple in their early forties whose relatively intact and loving relationship was beset with a particularly menacing problem: the omnipresence of what had been Claire's lifelong anxiety disorder. Though typically not present during our sessions, their reports of her anxiety conveyed how extraordinarily burdensome it was for both of them. Medication and individual therapy had to some extent been helpful, but when Claire's symptoms "reared their ugly head" they rapidly became a relationship issue. This had very much to do with how Simon would respond to Claire and what she would take of his response that was helpful, or—more often not—even exacerbating of her anxiety.

Claire's anxiety disorder could be activated by any number of causes. She was an admitted germaphobe, and with small children constantly being exposed to bacteria and viruses—coupled with the virtual impossibility of keeping their hands clean for more than a few minutes—Claire was constantly vulnerable to feeling under assault.

Simon, on the other hand, was not anxious in the same concrete sense as his wife; everyday triggers like hygiene or fear of flying (another of Claire's phobias) did not make him anxious. However, it had become apparent in recent years, by way of high blood pressure and other physical reactions to stress, that Simon was harboring his own pervasive anxiety, though not experiencing it so much in a conscious sense as in a psychosomatic one. In short, as a couple, Claire and Simon could rapidly become a mutually reverberating anxiety amplifying system, wherein the isolation of symptoms to either of their minds—likely a diagnosis from psychoanalysis of the past—was irrelevant.

In one sense, Claire and Simon could fit neatly into the profile of a Step One couple. Clearly, to some extent, it could be interpreted that Claire longed for an idealizing selfobject function from her husband, one in which she felt taken care of. However, one of their painful dynamics was that—try as he might—Simon perpetually failed in his efforts to soothe his wife. His failing typically arose over Claire disbelieving Simon having any "authoritative basis of knowledge" about whatever was making her anxious. Likewise, when his efforts at protecting and attempting to soothe his wife failed miserably, Simon was left demoralized, dejected, and filled with self-loathing. This latter state unfortunately came out in contempt towards Claire, making her hate him. This of course resulted from his wife's negative mirroring of him (i.e., the failure of a mirroring selfobject function) that would restore Simon's sense of goodness as a man.

As readily imaginable, each one's failing of the other's selfobject longings produced deepening senses of repetitive dimension transference reactions towards one another. Claire experienced Simon treating her contemptuously for her symptoms of anxiety in a manner both dismissive and debasing of them, which echoed what she experienced from all her family members growing up. Meanwhile, Simon felt "castrated" by Claire in his efforts at being a powerful, strong, "erect" presence to help her. All he really hungered for was attempting to be her hero.

My Step One interpretations about their failed selfobject longings, their triggered repetitive transference reactions, and the vicious cycle that arose from this helped Claire and Simon better understand their reactions to their hurt feelings and to even begin to see the anxiety defining aspects of both of their personalities as well as their relationship. They were, in short, a self-perpetuating system of anxiety. I found, however, that in listening to them I oscillated between the subject-centered and other-centered listening perspectives, and sharing this was especially useful.

A model scene characterizing the unabated anxiety symptom came up in a session that began with Simon describing the extraordinarily depressing state in which he found their relationship. The precursor episode involved flying home from the East Coast and barely speaking to one another for the entire six-and-a-half-hour flight. Simon and Claire both had highly responsible professional jobs, and with a household full of youngsters and pets they rarely had any time to speak intimately with one another. In the context of this deprivation, Simon found it especially heartbreaking that they could not take advantage of being on a flight in which they had no responsibilities and could therefore have had ample time to engage one another.

Claire agreed, but then offered that she was, first, engrossed in her fear of flying, and second, that she was still reeling from an insulting exchange between them that then jettisoned her into a plane ride of "silent treatment" lest she publically explode. It was clear that, feeling fed up with feelings of impotence in helping his wife, Simon had said something that Claire found very degrading regarding her state of anxiety.

As we unpacked the moment, the following story unfolded. During an early part of the flight, the pilot came on the loudspeaker and announced that sometime within the next 15 to 30 minutes their flight could be encountering turbulence, and therefore he requested that passengers remain seated with their seatbelts fastened. Knowing that turbulence disturbs Claire more than anything (strangely, take-off and landing do not especially bother her), Simon reached over to take her hand, which Claire anxiously pulled away so as to not be distracted from her panicky ruminations. She obviously was beginning to dissociate, as she didn't even remember this part of what occurred. In conjunction with this, Simon also tried to soothingly speak to her, but again she was unable to metabolize this. Instead, she anxiously kept pressing the flight attendant button and, upon the attendant's arrival, Claire pressed her for more information involving the details of what the captain had communicated. Of course, there was nothing definitive the attendant could convey, but Claire pressing her led to her speaking with the captain, who finally came out and attempted to reassure Claire.

Meanwhile, Simon was seething from his sense of both public and private humiliation over his impotence in attempting to soothe this wife. To her credit, Claire readily understood what Simon was going through, though during the flight she had no access to this thought. What was apparent was that, notwithstanding his desire to soothe Claire, she was unable to be soothed, at least in the manner that Simon attempted.

I decided to improvisationally engage Claire by beginning to play-off-of-and-with ways of engaging her exploring exactly what she might find soothing. When I asked her what might help, she said that she needed to hear something authoritative (e.g., omnipotent) from some credible authority who would reassure her that everything with the flight would be all right, to which I attempted to "play" the role of the authority she longed for. Very quickly, however, this became an example of how improvisation doesn't always work. Indeed, at times, attempts at improvisation can spur an enactment. Acting as the sought after "authority," I lamely responded in the fashion that, retrospectively, can often backfire in treating those with fear of flying: attempting to reassure them of the exceedingly high safety record of air transportation and the infinitesimal chances of an in-flight accident. I said, as is commonly and also lamely noted, that there is much higher incidence of accidents occurring on the way to and from airports.

Claire's eyes widened like two large marbles and she urgently said, "Stop, I need you to stop. This is really, really making me anxious." Taken aback by her urgent protest, I was also thrust into the other-centered listening position that corresponded with Simon's recurrent sense of being ineffectual precisely at the time that he most wanted to be helpful. I also got a sense, for the first time, how petrified Claire could become, as well as becoming petrifying to the other.

I then asked her what she wanted to hear, and she said, "I want to hear someone say that there is no way that the plane is going fall out of the air" (which ironically I had heard from a few other patients over the years and that is the irrational assumption that the plane might simply, and suddenly, fall out of the sky, much like if one held a baseball high over one's head and released it to its inevitable vertical plunge to the ground). Improvising—that is, taking her "suggestion" of who I was to be in this scene for her to play with—I said firmly (omnipotently) and authoritatively, "Claire, I promise you, the plane will *not* fall out of the sky!" She immediately relaxed and, within seconds, we began analyzing the meaning of our engagement. She said that, as irrational as it is, it took an authority (clearly of the transferential-fantasy variety) to speak to her, and it didn't matter whether his comments made any rational or scientific sense. What mattered was the degree to which the authority spoke confidently and unequivocally, a privileged position that Simon had lost years before. Offering ideas about the infinitesimally tiny percentages of airline accidents simply lacked the certitude of omnipotence she sought.

Most importantly, however, it was from my other listening perspective that I could quickly resonate with Simon's exasperation and humiliation, especially in my own failed attempts to soothe Claire. Hence our enactment served an important function in helping one develop greater empathic resonance to Simon's experience. This model scene (Lichtenberg, Lachmann, & Fosshage, 1992, 1996) illustrated the accretions of such experiences that over many years had led to Simon's contemptuous responses, comments that bore a quality of what Gottman (1999) has referred to as "the sulfuric acid of love." Consequently, I could also readily resonate with Claire's building hatred of her husband.

Clearly, my shifting in and out of the two listening perspectives facilitated Claire, and Simon beginning to engage in their own other-centered listening perspective vis-à-vis each other. Suddenly, this enabled them to hear something about themselves—that is, as they were experienced by their partner—that was part of what was perpetuating their problems. Claire acknowledged how castrating Simon must have experienced her rejection of his efforts to soothe her. And Simon relinquished his heretofore defensive position, now embracing how alienating and hurtful his contemptuous outpouring could be for Claire.

We then took up how there might be some circumstances that are beyond their control (e.g., when they are on an airplane). Recognizing these as extraordinary times allowed them to consider bracketing them in a kind of humility about inevitable mutual failings. We also were able to recognize many other times that, with some fine-tuning, Simon's efforts at soothing Claire might be more effective. All of this moved us away from the zero-sum binary of "nothing ever working" to a host of conditions that, given different approaches, could yield satisfying results for both.

Summary

Given the degree of despair and hopelessness with which some couples enter treatment, the therapist has little time to reconstitute their sense of hope. Instilling this means articulating early in the first session how each brought unconscious hopes and dreads to this relationship that are manifesting in their bidimensional versions of transference, ones in which the selfobject dimension of each readily triggers the repetitive dimension in each. Being able to demonstrate this to them, as well as the vicious circle in which they are caught, conveys that the therapist actually understands both of them and will not side with one against the other. Furthermore, by modeling mutual recognition through her capacity to empathize with each, no matter how much each seems "crazy," she rekindles hope and curiosity. In this manner, she also models a methodology for repairing ruptures, which she further clarifies are the inevitable result of each partner's self-actualization needs.

The therapist in Step One is also listening for themes pertaining to each partner's sense of agency. If transference is the organization of self-actualization, agency is its impetus. It represents each partner's sense of authorship in each one's life, and becomes a means for accessing how well each one can take responsibility for his or her thoughts, feelings, and behaviors versus attributing responsibility to their partner.

Additionally, in Step One, the capacity for mutual recognition also needs to be assessed early on and may represent a prognostic indicator for the course of treatment. Relationships evincing little capacity for mutual recognition tend to reflect the quality of negative thirdness that in the relational field is highly constricted, making self-actualization a serious threat. Breaking out of the grip of the field will require early modeling by the therapist of what subject-to-subject relating looks like, as opposed to the couple's exclusive mode of subject-to-object relating.

Finally, while Step One begins by examining how selfobject failures trigger repetitive dimensions of transference, it also recognizes that the versions of self that are evidenced in such moments represent only a part of self-experiencing, and that in the context of different issues those same selfobject failures may not be present or may not be as fragmenting. This then introduces the idea that each partner can have multiple self-experiences, and thereby multiple relational schemas. The elucidation of this helps mitigate accusations of inconsistency and hypocrisy, while elevating a treatment leitmotif that emphasizes empathic engagement and curiosity.

Introduced in the preceding chapter is the question of how a couple manages the dialectical tension between the pole of romantic, passionate, sexual love and the often sex-diminishing pole of attachment love and its penchant for undermining the mystery of romance and replacing it with predictability and presumed knowness of one's partner. Of course, this dialectic actually exposes that these opposite poles are both illusory, and the assumption that one truly knows one's partner can be as much an illusion as romantic love is frequently cast as being.

What is germane about this question in Step One is that lurking beneath the conscious attempts to identify failed selfobject functions, along with the repetitive transferences that each partner's selfobject longings can generate, is a whole world of the unconscious mind, struggling with deeper questions about bodies, sex, and sexuality, and, as profoundly as anything, the question "Who am I?" much less "Who is my partner?" As noted in Chapter 1, many relational authors see that it is in sexual fantasy, and various sexual enactments, that partners seek to discover something about themselves that has been split off and remains unknown. It is through *Eros* and sometimes lust that we seek out something in our partner that is actually a disavowed, unknown, or unrecognized aspect of our self—something about our otherness that remains inaccessible to us, and that is thereby sought out in the otherness of the other. But all of this usually has to be ferreted out through enactments, or what I refer to as mutual inductive identification.

The attunement model proposed in this chapter is often not equipped to uncover this unconscious material, as it stays closer to *experience-near* evidence, which is typically more of the conscious mind's grasp of immediate experience. No doubt such attunement is a critical beginning place, for, as Grotstein avers, psychotherapy typically needs to begin *symmetrically* (i.e., in the therapist's powerful identification with the patient's conscious experience), but to progress it ultimately must culminate in *asymmetry*—that is, processes in which differences between therapist and patient, as well as within the patient, come to be recognized and managed. On this latter note, differences in each partners' multiple self-states come more and more into evidence throughout the treatment, sometimes through attunement, though frequently through enactments. And the differences that exist within one self become more and more clarified, along with taking up the conflict that may ensue from this recognition.

Notes

1 They involve the necessary process of assimilation, a kind of healthy repetitiveness that flows from a sense of what works in one's life born of trial and error. In fact, as Magid (2001, 2008) has noted in his study of Zen Buddhism, this kind of repetitiveness enables one to be freer from the obsessional self-consciousness of "second-guessing" one's life. One can act and simply enjoy one's actions without the hyperconsciousness of over-deliberation and self-doubt.
2 In many respects, these and other selfobject functions dovetail with the works of British object relational authors, such as Winnicott's (1971) "holding function," wherein the caregiver non-intrusively lends herself to the child's ruthlessness, while neither retaliating with abuse or abandonment. Her actions ultimately reassure the child that his illusion of destructive omnipotence wasn't real as the object remained intact. Additionally, Bion's (1967) "containing function" can be seen as a version of assisting with negative affective regulation, as well as facilitating affective differentiation, articulation, and reintegration.
3 For those skeptical about couples' capacity for taking up the topic of transference, 30 years of experience has led me to conclude that many patients are able to quickly adapt to a psychoanalytic mode of treatment in couples therapy that is otherwise impossible

for them to achieve in an analytically oriented individual psychotherapy. This is because many patients remain clueless about the construct of transference, especially in relation to their analytically oriented psychotherapist. This makes it exceedingly difficult for them to develop a "transference neurosis" in relation to their analyst, from which they can come to grasp central organizing themes regarding their personality. Efforts to encourage such a working alliance can founder in a process that feels very alienating to the patient, if not downright crazy. This is because the analyst inquires about a host of plausible feelings and reactions that the patient might be having towards her that the patient simply is not conscious of. Meanwhile, such patients—who might require years to become analytically engaged in developmental and repetitive transference dimensions with their therapist—quickly come face to face with both these dimensions as they instantaneously arise in relation to their spouse. This makes it much easier for the analytically oriented therapist to point out in very convincing and compelling ways. Tom and Jane are illustrative of such a couple.

4 Of course, I do not interrupt at every emotional outburst—far from it—and oftentimes I let them run their course for a while to find out what natural repair strategies they may have that I can capitalize upon. Following Gottman's (1999) admonition, however, I do point out to them early on that contemptuous interactions are the "sulfuric acid of love" and the number one predictor of divorce. Correspondingly, I ask their permission for me to point out when they are engaging one another contemptuously—a point they are often unaware of—so that I can help them begin right away to mitigate further damage to one another.

5 For example, every moment of treatment is potentially structured by six levels of transference that are constituted by each of the partners' and the therapist's bidimensional transference organizations. When we add the concept of multiple self-state theory, the potential levels become mathematically imponderable. The objective of this model of therapy is to augment the therapist's repertoire of flexible and fluid ideas for facilitating self-actualization, recognition, and the quality of thirdness.

6 Grotstein notes that humans have a nascent curiosity about creation and our place in it emerging from a primary "epistephilic instinct" (Klein, 1946, 1952) that is part of an important step towards recognizing that others also possess their own sense of subjectivity and initiative. As such, in every human encounter, we are all observers/participants as well as co-constructors/interpreters, unconsciously attempting to unravel one another's intentions (Stern, 2004, 2007).

7 I do not typically use words like *agency* with patients because they are too fraught with jargon. Instead, I spoke more in terms of their dreams, wishes, desires, and so on.

8 Racker (1968) referred to this as the first of two forms of identification between the analyst and the patient. By this he meant that the analyst identified with something profound going on with the patient. Racker referred to this state as one of "concordant identification," a state synonymous with the two persons linked through the process of empathy.

9 Racker (1968) referred to this second mode of listening as a *complementary* mode of countertransference, in which the therapist is not identifying with the patient's subjective state of being so much as she is identifying with how the patient is "casting" the therapist in a role of the other (object) in some transference scenario.

3

STEP TWO

The therapist's assertion that none of the three participants in the therapy has a more correct (i.e., "objective") view of reality than any of the others, and that each is the arbiter of what is true within her/his experience in the moment.

> Even the perception of the senses is governed by mechanisms which make our knowledge of the outside world highly inferential. We do not receive impressions that are elemental. Our sense impressions are themselves constructed by the nervous system in such a way that they automatically carry with them an interpretation of what they see and feel.
>
> Jacob Bronowski

> It must be remembered that the object of the world of ideas as a whole (e.g., a map or a model PAR) is not the portrayal of reality—this would be an utterly impossible task—but rather to provide us with an instrument for finding our way about more easily in the world.
>
> Hans Vaihinger

> A map is not the territory it represents, but, if correct, it has a similar structure to the territory, which accounts for its usefulness.
>
> Alfred Korzybski

In the peak of their distress, couples often present a dilemma about which Davies (2003) writes, "To feel sane I must forgo love and to feel loved, I must forgo my sanity." Such high stakes in any intimate dyad can make arguing over whose version of reality is the correct one an extremely precarious venture, into which the conjoint therapist is inevitably ensnared. A conjoint therapy model based upon relational intersubjectivity therefore has as its lynchpin the reconciliation of this problem.

Perhaps the greatest evolution in contemporary psychoanalytic thinking has been to move away from its heritage of authoritative, "objectively" rendered interpretations of the clinical "facts" regarding a patient. Today, the real crucible of our work rests in interpreting to our patients their unique subjective perspectives on reality. It also entails helping them grasp how their beliefs constrain both self-actualization and mutual recognition.

The shift from objectivist claims to more perspectival ones has not been without considerable controversy. It also has involved numerous misunderstandings about perspectivalist claims. The most frequent misunderstanding is that it makes all interpretations of reality "equal" in a relativistic sense—that is, a person's sense of reality is merely relative to how they experience it, and from this view all perspectives are essentially equal. Instead of a relativist perspective, this chapter adheres to what is called "perspectival realism" (Stolorow, Orange, & Atwood, 2002) and elsewhere "perspectival constructivism" (Aron, 1996; Hoffman, 1991; Stern, 1992). This latter argument states that not all perspectives, in any given momentary context, are of equal merit; sometimes, one perspective is better than another. And, ultimately, when a couple is working well together, they frequently find that "two heads can be better than one." This is because once what is at stake emotionally is understood, the merits of each one's arguments can be appreciated, which lends to greater collaboration and negotiation.

The basic premise of perspectival realism is that reality exists independent of how we interpret "it," or as Hawking (1988) refers to "it," a "model independent reality." Hawking is asserting that our models of reality are just that, only models, and they necessarily never completely capture the totality of reality.[1] Bronowski (1974) shows us how perception is not elemental, but is an inference constituted by the nervous system. Vaihinger (1924) states that "ideas as a whole never portray reality"—an "utterly impossible task"—but that ideas "provide us with an instrument for finding our way about more easily in the world." Korzybski (1933) reminds us that our "maps" (language systems) are never exact representations of the world or of our experience of it, but are useful to the extent that they are similar to the territory of the world we inhabit. Finally, Einstein[2] notes that we all inhabit "a kind of optical delusion of his consciousness" and that "our task must be to free ourselves from this prison" (e.g., this delusion), though "Nobody is able to achieve this completely, but the striving for such achievement is in itself a part of the liberation and foundation for inner security."

Nevertheless, for many people, it is terrifying to realize that no human being can grasp the totality of reality—at best, we infer it. This may account in modern times for the powerful gravitation pull many fundamentalist religions exert, wherein absolute convictions about reality and about how men and women should accord themselves arise from doctrines that provide a comforting sense of certitude. Donnel Stern (1997) argues poignantly, however, that ideas about reality are inexhaustible. As evidenced in great works of art and scientific theories, our models or beliefs about reality both enable us to recognize many things as well as constrain our points of view. Hence, both the arts and sciences are always "works in progress" that never achieve any measure of certainty. From the point of view of this book, that can be a useful way for individuals to examine their own beliefs about reality, which can be quite bountiful, so long as we understand that they are simply our perspectives.

As such, truth claims, from the standpoint of perspectival realism, are just that: propositional claims of what appears to be the best version of truth or the best model of a given aspect of reality in a given period. Cavell (1998) writes:

> What we take to be truth can always be called into question at another time, or under other circumstances; that our claims to truth must always be provisional; that a truth claim is always that, a claim, requiring support; that between the best evidence and what is the case there will always be a gap; that a justified belief and a true belief are, unfortunately, not necessarily the same; that talk about "the truth," especially "sincere" and self-righteous talks, is often a way a dignifying one's own blind spot; that the conversational move which says "you're wrong" or "that is not true" is often a conversation-stopper.
>
> (p. 450)

Clearly, truth is always provisional. As such, each partner's assertion involves a propositional truth (e.g., argument) about how any given circumstance is to be made sense of and ultimately what must be done in terms of it. Even the silliest of arguments, such as the rules of toilet seat etiquette—leave the seat up after using it versus always putting it down—are saturated with what Stolorow, Orange, and Atwood (2002) refer to as "emotional convictions," which become the royal road for investigating each partner's organizing principles and the foundation of their bidimensional models of transference. The seemingly innocuous toilet seat example actually underscores that these emotional convictions bear not only the stamp of a history of personal experiences, but are also deeply endowed with cultural (or in this case gender) biases, a point of further elaboration in Step Three.

Cavell proposes that in any argument truth claims arise in what she refers to as a "triangulation of perspectives." Thus, in any couple's argument about what is true, arriving at the best perspective necessitates the participants recognizing that each is only offering his or her perspective on a third point; that is, on the issue at hand, which commonly involves such things as how to raise their children, invest their money, make love, and negotiate time together as well as time apart. Perhaps the biggest problem a couple runs into is when the partners are unable to see that their beliefs are just beliefs. This requires a theory of mind that recognizes each individual has a mind of his or her own, organized in part by his or her own prejudices about the nature of things. In short, it requires mutual recognition of each partner's mind (Orange, 2005; Stern, 1997).

Cultivating such a dialogical quality of communication in couples therapy assumes certain epistemological attitudes on the parts of all of its participants. As stated at the beginning of this chapter, it entails the therapist's assertion that none of the three participants in the therapy has a more correct (i.e., "objective") view of reality than any of the others, and that each is the arbiter of what is true within

67

her/his experience in the moment. It further argues on behalf of an attitude of fallibilism (Orange, 1995)—that is, that one hold one's "theory of reality" lightly enough to recognize that there is always more to be learned from an other.

"Truth as correspondence to facts" versus "truth as possible understanding": making the case for both/and

Eschewing the objectivist tradition of early psychoanalysis, contemporary psychoanalysts have taken differing positions regarding how they think about fantasy versus reality.[3] On this matter, intersubjective systems theorists such as Stolorow, Orange, and Atwood (2002) argue that the factual designation of truth is outside the province of psychoanalytic inquiry:

> We must attend to truth-as-possible-understanding and not truth-as-correspondence-to-fact. Whatever the facts may be, we must find ways to converse about the meanings, and arguments about reality and the associated insistence that the patient recognize the analyst's perspective are usually the quickest exit from the search for understanding.
>
> (p. 119)[4]

What I believe Stolorow et al. are at least in part arguing—a point with which most contemporary psychoanalysts would have little disagreement—is that psychoanalysis is not a science about the exactitude of facts (i.e., about objective reality). Indeed, citing Einstein, as human beings, we are always parsing the universe into our "optical delusions." In essence, our use of language is always operating in the realm of fictions,[5] some more useful in some contexts, some more useful in others. Still, Stolorow et al. seem to interpret that, absent adhering to their admonition, contemporary psychoanalysis risks adopting an objectivist stance, especially where their language use puts analysts at risk of lapsing into the objectivist tradition of Freud's ambiguous legacy.[6] In their subversive fervor, I believe they go too far in their provocative language, accusing other contemporary analysts of engaging in a "God's-eye-view" of reality (Stolorow, Orange, & Atwood, 2002).

There is nothing, for example, in the relational canon that supports any version of a "Gods-eye-view" or any comparable allusion to a pure objectivist epistemology.[7] More to the point, what is at stake for the relational psychoanalysts is the need to distinguish the experiential subjective reality of the other as a separate subject from one's sense of self as subject. That means recognizing the other as having his own center of initiative, his own agency, his own mind, and that requires coming to terms with ways in which *one represents the other in fantasy as opposed to how that other actually experiences her subjective sense of reality.* To underscore, the relational psychoanalysts, at least as I read them, are not arguing about the patient's or the therapist's exactitude of factual representation, but how each accounts for the "facts" underpinning their deeply held narratives, emblematic of their deeply personal, often times deeply private, and deeply necessary "optical delusions." In short, "truth as possible understanding" simply cannot be fully apprehended without also attending to the "truth-as-corresponding-to-one's-organization-and-use/defense-of-one's-facts." Both versions of truth represent the "bricks and mortar" of the architecture of one's narrative truth. Collisions of "facts" involve intersubjective experiences of negation, and therefore of reparative mutual recognition, collaboration, and negotiation. Of course, when there are collisions of facts, couples often pressure the therapist into having to engage both elements of truth.[8]

Harold and Pauline

Recently married, Harold and Pauline entered treatment with some profound disagreements about how to rear Harold's 11-year-old daughter, Nicky. Both were clearly in love, and in fact Pauline was automatically drawn to co-parenting her new stepdaughter. Unfortunately, past their honeymoon phase, their attitudes regarding parenting turned out to be wildly in opposition to one another's. While Pauline had admirably connected with Nicky, she also had reservations about Harold's "permissive" parenting, especially around his adamant insistence that they always take Nicky's feelings into consideration.

Given how at odds their parenting styles were, it seemed important to flesh out what was the "truth" about their respective styles, both in terms of "truth-as-possible-understanding" and in terms of the actual facts of what each was doing. A thumbnail of their respective backgrounds gave me an imprint of what their developmental histories had had on their respective parenting styles. Harold's parents divorced when he was very young, at which point his father vanished from his life. Thereafter, his mother had multiple partnerships with a number of men. Though he enjoyed most of the men in his mother's life, her capricious style of breaking up with them without regard to his feelings of loss was pronounced. Compounding this developmental travesty was his mother's unwillingness to discuss these abrupt relationship terminations, much less the impact that they had on Harold. Indeed, worse than simply not discussing his feelings, his mother engaged in a mode of obfuscation that led to twisted and contradictory versions of the truth. The outcome of this for Harold was twofold: First, he was highly skeptical about the endurance of any long-term relationship, notwithstanding his "taking the plunge" a second time in marrying Pauline; second, he formed an indefatigable stance that any child of his would always have her feelings considered as penultimate. This latter position led to an almost "Herculean" attitude of patience with Nicky that was far beyond the pale for Pauline.

Although Pauline's upbringing was comparably chaotic to Harold's (her parents, too, divorced during her childhood), she had found solace in her mother's strident set of values about how children should behave. This ethic came close to the old world values that "children should be seen and not heard." Though she clearly did not ascribe to such a severe perspective, it was also clear that Nicky's entitled behavior was close to 180 degrees out of phase with values that Pauline cherished. Compounding matters was her desire to become pregnant for the first time in her life. Thus, she envisioned multiple collisions in their future with their own biological child, which petrified her.

Notwithstanding this potentially explosive situation, it was important to note that Nicky and Pauline actually had developed a considerable female bond. They mutually enjoyed fashion and loved watching the various celebrity shows (*TMZ* being a favorite), while playfully fighting over which of them would get the first look at every new issue of *People* magazine. They also loved teasing Harold for his absentmindedness and his ADD-like behaviors.

A developmental grasp of their personal histories enabled me to connect with them around their respective parenting styles, each in its own way bent upon correcting aspects of their own childhoods. Harold's "permissive" indulgence of Nicky regarding how she felt about all things—including commonly agreed upon chores—made Pauline, like a bull, see red. Meanwhile, Pauline's manner of intervening (at times when she'd had enough) was rife with shaming Nicky—a position that made Harold's blood boil!

Two things became factually apparent. First, Harold's emotional attunement impaired his capacity to insist Nicky do as told, as she agreed to. Hence, simple machinations of how a family works turn into a crippled and often stagnant way of functioning. Simple agreed-upon chores would routinely degenerate into recycled debates about her responsibilities, as if there had been no previous collaboration and negotiation. As these instances piled up, Harold began to recognize that what he had tried to achieve in encouraging Nicky to express her feelings had become disastrous, not only for Nicky but for someone like Pauline. Facing these facts, Harold agreed to work more diligently in changing his manner of engaging Nicky, while also becoming more supportive of Pauline's wishes.

A problem ensued, however, insofar as it was factually true that Pauline's style of arguing with Nicky bore more than a whiff of contempt. When Pauline bristled, the only words that came out of her mouth were words of condescension and sarcasm—both of which not only upset Nicky but enraged Harold. Still, it was extremely hard for her to stop behaving this way, in large part because she was profoundly ensconced in her objectivist standards about how children must be raised. She was so certain of these that she strongly expected me to agree with her on each and every one. With deepening exploration, however, it became ever apparent that her fear was that the way in which Nicky was being raised would doom her stepdaughter's future.

Pauline's fear electrified my curiosity about how Nicky actually did perform in the world. It was most edifying to learn that, in fact, Nicky was very well liked at school by her teachers and classmates. She also was very much liked by the parents of her friends, and her participation in all extracurricular activities made it clear that the borders of her sometimes obnoxious entitlement were indeed confined to the family home.

In short, the "problem of Nicky" was one specific to living with Harold and Pauline. On this basis, I reflected back to Harold and Pauline that, by and large,

Nicky sounded terrific, but that clearly something had to change at home. The good news, however, was that Pauline's fears for Nicky's future seemed unwarranted, though her fears about the intolerable situation at home most certainly did seem factually based.

It became clear to me that, while Harold seemed amenable to change, he would not be able to unless Pauline would change as well. The issue was less about Nicky's performance around the house, though that certainly mattered too, than about her attitude. Unfortunately, when irritated, Pauline's only response repertoire seemed horribly truncated to shaming her. Having developed a rich sense of how well Nicky got along with Pauline when they were in their "let's-be-girls" play mode, I suggested that Pauline shift from her position of sarcasm (and its deadly counterpart, contempt) to one more ensconced in playful irony.

Harold immediately latched upon this idea, pointing out a myriad of examples of how Pauline engaged Nicky playfully when she was not angry at her. We suddenly all began improvising ways for Pauline to engage Nicky. For example, at dinnertime, to playfully say, "Nicky, would you remind me to remind you to do the dishes after we are done with dinner tonight?" Or "I didn't know that Pedro [Nicky's parakeet] could talk!" And, then to Nicky's dumbfounded expression, to add, "He told me that tonight's the night that you clean his cage, and he said that it is none too soon." Here, Pauline could use irony as a form of humor, without devolving into sarcasm and its inherent contempt.

These playful rejoinders instantly appealed to Pauline, because they still accorded her belief that children should respect their elders and be held accountable for what is expected of them. More importantly, she also saw that this could actually feel empowering, since she was becoming aware that her approach, especially when angry, not only alienated Nicky and enraged Harold, it also left her feeling powerless and ineffectual. Meanwhile, hearing Pauline's willingness to stop using humiliation as her primary disciplinary tactic made Harold more amenable to recognizing that what he was doing with Nicky not only did not work for Pauline, it started to seem bad for Nicky as well. Indeed, he realized that his self-subjugation in the pursuit of perfect affect attunement to Nicky's every feeling might leave her with impossible expectations in future intimate relationships. He acknowledged that it was time for him to step up and introduce more alterity in his relationship with her and less constant affirming mirroring. This meant for him to become more firm in his expectations of Nicky and to not cater to her feelings about them. It also meant that he needed to become more selective about when to attune to Nicky and when to simply hold her to their agreement, irrespective of her protests.

Discordant levels of discourse: the "doer" and the "done-to" versus what the partners mean

In avoiding Stolorow, Orange, and Atwood's (2002) binary claim that psychoanalysis is only about "truth as possible understanding" and never about "truth as correspondence to facts," I wish to take up a third and more of a both/and position. This said, there certainly is a vulnerability in couple's discourse to degenerating into argumentation about the exactitude of "facts," such that it runs roughshod over any attempt at getting at the partners' meaning. "Facts," in this latter case, get employed in a highly accusatory and defensive manner that replicate a reciprocating system of the positions of the "doer and the done-to" (Benjamin, 2004). On this level of discourse, conversation is mired with declarations, appearing to be a fight to the death over whose factual version of reality is the correct one. Of course, what is at stake, as is in evidence throughout this volume, is "who is crazy and who is sane?" There is seldom anything of worth that comes from this, with the exception of couples who might employ such skirmishes less as veridical exercises in "life and death" examinations of the truth than as frothy forms of ventilation. In some cases, this kind of linguistic foreplay is a precursor to sex, as well as other intimate forms of relating. In the latter case, Gottman (1999) notes that these couples employ fighting as more or less a means of ventilating the affective complexities of daily living. As such, they involve safe means of "blowing off steam."

Where the discursive rupture of the doer and the done-to is much more serious, however, is where the sanity of the partners is being adjudicated in a veritable marital "court of law," based upon both conscious and unconscious rules governing the presentation of evidence. This form of discourse is seriously threatening, as the evidentiary proceedings of the doer and the done-to undermine a level of necessary conversation that takes up the in-depth examination of the meaning of the rupture between the two parties. Preoccupations with evidentiary-like hearings seriously undermine each partner's presentation of the "truth as potential understanding" regarding any particular argument or vignette of conflict. When this happens, it becomes imperative that the therapist helps the couple shift the focal point of their argumentation away from facts and back to the plausible meaning from which their positions can be understood, without perseveration about the factual accuracy of their assertions.

Fostering curiosity

Part of how therapists can move the partners off their discussion of facts is to cultivate their curiosity about their problematic situations. According to Mitchell (1997), in any psychoanalytic therapy, an atmosphere of curiosity needs to be cultivated. Stern (1997) goes even further than Mitchell, stating that it is each patient's (as well as therapist's) responsibility to cultivate curiosity. For Stern, this ethic represents a kind of psychoanalytic morality. As Stern argues, "Since we co-establish the field, we're only partially responsible for the shape it takes. But in psychoanalytic terms, we *are* responsible for being curious about it … We're responsible for turning back on our own experience in reflecting on the fields we have co-created and in which we live" (p. 160). Unformulated experience (experience for which one has not reflected on its meaning) is a hotbed for dissociation, and the unformulated relationship (field) is a hotbed for mutual dissociation.

Motivating such curiosity requires the therapist to exhibit two strong characteristics: cultivating a climate of deep empathic engagement with each partner's
experience, as well as cultivating a climate of safety for personal exploration and
meaning-making to occur. This arises from making sure *that each partner is
recognized as the arbiter of what is true within her/his experience in the moment.*
This, however, is much more than merely mirroring back to the patient his or her
version of reality. It is more about establishing the depth of meaning of their
experience. This entails illuminating unformulated or prereflective experiences by
helping each partner symbolize what has heretofore remained primarily in the
realm of a concrete "given." It further acknowledges that what is true in this
moment may well change in another, given both shifts in the context of meaning
as well as shifts in self-states.

This does not mean that the therapist abdicates her role as an interpreter of each
one's experience; however, she also does not pull rank in her interpretations. She
offers them as plausible explanations. An essential task is for her to also correctly
interpret each one to the other. So, for example, she might routinely say things
like, "I'm not sure I am hearing your husband/wife saying what you are hearing.
I have a different read on his/her intentions which I think is as follows ..."

Meanwhile, crucial to helping develop each partner's more accurate interpretations of one another is to begin with their sense of "fitness" between that therapist's
interpretations about them as well as one another. Donnel Stern's ideas about the
"fitness" of interpretations is especially germane to my arguments. Stern (1997)
writes:

> No patient accepts or rejects interpretation because it is "objectively" true
> or false, but because it is or is not subjectively convincing. The successful
> interpretation touches the patient in a way that the patient can identify in
> her own experience ... Because they know that only those observations
> that arouse the patient's recognition will be useful, analysts try to observe
> from within what they imagine the patient's frame of reference to be ...
> The patient always has a sense of whether or not the analyst's interpreta-
> tion "fits." Without the feeling of fit, the patient can develop no sense of
> conviction. And without conviction, the interpretation may as well but
> have appeared in the patient's morning newspaper, for all the good it will
> do ... What, then, accounts for the patient's feeling of fit? In certain
> instances that tend to be rare and dramatic, the perception of fit follows
> the patient's sudden feeling of always having known, in some vague way,
> what the analyst was trying to say. Or commonly, the patient feels that
> what the analyst says has "pulled something together," and is anchored
> (or better, is useful) in that respect.
>
> (pp. 169–171)[9]

Stern's compelling argument resonates with comparable observations by
Bollas (1989) about the "unthought known" and Stolorow and Atwood's (1992)

"pre-reflective unconscious." And, of course, all observations about the fitness of an interpretation are critically important to making contact with dissociated multiple self-states, because it is only in the intersubjective connection to each of these isolated "narcissistic islands" within each partner that the connecting space both "within" and "between" them can be achieved (Bromberg, 1998).

Ultimately, the gift of couples therapy is that the therapist has the partner available to confirm her interpretation. That is, is she getting each partner's intentions more accurately than their spouse understands them? Of course, it's important to find a way of empathically underscoring how the "offended" spouse could plausibly misconstrue their partner's meaning. This also lays down a format of investigation, which then facilitates how the spouses' misinterpretations of each other pertain to both of their transference organizations, and ultimately to how transference powerfully shapes one another's ways of seeing and being that ironically can result in self-fulfilling prophecies.

Countertransference reactions: the collapse of the therapist's perspective

Opening the couple's horizons to greater possibility is most readily challenged by the therapist's own constraints. After all, therapists have their own selfobject needs (Bacal & Thomson, 1996) as well as repetitive transference vulnerabilities, no matter how well analyzed they are. Historically, traditional analysts assumed that, because of their own analyses, they were prepared to conduct analyses objectively. Contemporary analysts see this as a pernicious myth that not only fostered erroneous idealization, but also isolated most problems arising in an analysis to the patient's neurosis. A contemporary view emboldens analysts to now acknowledge that each analytic pairing potentially exposes "blind, hard and soft spots" (McLaughlin, 1987, 1991) that potentially prejudice the interpretive capacity of both patient and therapist.

Thus, since all therapists have limitations, it is incumbent for them to constantly look at themselves in a self-reflective manner. Therapists exuding such curiosity about their own foibles helps cultivate their patients' examination of their own. Meanwhile, just as broad transference themes organize the marital partners' lives, so too do they organize the therapist's life—in the form of countertransference.

An important way to think about the limiting impingement of therapists' countertransference horizons upon their patients is in terms of what Stolorow and Atwood (1992, in collaboration with Trop) described as *intersubjective conjunctions* and *intersubjective disjunctions*. Both arise, respectively, when the therapist's organizing principles profoundly correspond to or, conversely, differ from the patient's organizing principles. Conjunctions and disjunctions between the therapist's countertransference and patient's transference are inevitable in all treatments. They are primarily problematic only when they go unrecognized.

For example, conjunctions between the therapist's and patient's organizing principles (as well as life experiences) can be an enormous source of information.

Such conjunctions can facilitate the therapist conceiving of analogues to her patient's experience that deeply resonate to it and therefore "fit." On the other hand, where there is too great a fit between the therapist's and patient's organizing principles, the therapist may be blind to the fact that she and her patient both share a point of view that obscures their understanding of what is meaningful to the partner's subjective perspective. Meanwhile, disjunctions can interfere with the therapist's capacity to get inside the patient's world of assumptions, because her organizing principles are too far at odds with her patient's. Indeed, because of this, she even is liable to judge her patient. When such conjunctions and disjunctions go unrecognized by the therapist—or, even if recognized, become fixed—impasses in the couple's therapy are likely to ensue. This is particularly the case when the therapist finds herself in a state of conjunction with one of the marital partners and a state of disjunction with the other.

Unrecognized conjunctions and disjunctions lead to the therapy becoming imbalanced; that is, with the therapist siding with one partner's perspective while finding herself at odds with the other's. Unchecked, the typical outcome of this is for the partner with whom the therapist is in a state of transference/countertransference conjunction to begin to look like the co-therapist, assisting the therapist in treating his or her mate (i.e., the partner with whom the therapist is in a state of disjunction). Thereafter, the treatment typically devolves into one of two forms: a) the identified patient partner becomes narcissistically enraged or threatens to quit (either aggressively or passive-aggressively through missed appointments); or b) the identified patient partner adopts a pathologically accommodative role (Brandchaft, 1997, 2007), submitting him- or herself as the problem to be fixed, while nevertheless quietly resisting the treatment. In this case, the therapist will end up colluding with the spouse in the conjunctive position in his or her futile project for fixing their mate.

Two points are extremely important regarding the topic of conjunctions and disjunctions. First, therapists must accept and anticipate their inevitability. When she is able to do so, she can embrace her experience as nonjudgmentally as possible. This will become especially evident to the degree to which she demonstrates her interest in the impact her own conjunctions and disjunctions may serve. Second, the therapist must acknowledge to the couple the possibility of such conjunctions and disjunctions arising, and that if either of them thinks this may be happening it will be most helpful for them to speak up about this. A particularly important outgrowth of such an open invitation is that the couple is disabused of the fantasy that anyone in the room can know everything—including the therapist—and in so doing the therapist actually models for the couple that the principle of fallibility is not something to be eschewed, but actually to be embraced.

Sally and Dan

An example of this occurred close to two decades ago, when I fell into a terrible disjunction with a wife, Sally, and an inadvertent conjunction with her husband,

Dan. I had seen them for a few months, and was becoming concerned by how withered Dan had become over Sally's seemingly unrelenting criticisms about his lack of availability to her and their kids. This is not an unfamiliar complaint, especially among partners—where one or both of whom are employed in pressure cooker careers like the Hollywood entertainment industry. Their complaint is an outgrowth of the extraordinary demands that can take over their lives, especially if one or both are key players at the height of some creative project, such as shooting a film or running a TV series. As a "show-runner," Dan had to work 16-hour days, at least five days a week for close to two-thirds of the year. Still, Dan also had to acknowledge that work provided an excuse to stay away from Sally, especially when he had become weary of her criticism.

In an effort to speak to Dan about his passivity (a considerable source of Sally's complaints), I attempted to euphemistically engage *his* experience of her, saying, "It seems like you feel that Sally 'wears the pants in the family.'" Although my intent was to speak of *his* experience and not to judge her (frankly, I saw her as strong, but not really as dominating in the fashion as Dan experienced her), Sally nevertheless heard me as judging her in both a sexist and condescending manner.

At the next appointment, Sally came into my office seething and began accusing me of being sexist. To support her accusation, she reminded me of her background in feminist studies with an emphasis on linguistics. No matter what I said to both apologize and attempt to clarify that my point was about Dan's subjective experience and not about her, she dug in her heels and became ever more insistent. Soon, I found myself feeling unusually defensive. Intensifying my discomfort, I noticed in the periphery that Dan was enjoying watching Sally and me go at it. There was an implicit note in his face that read to me like, "See?! See, Doc? See what I have to put up with?"

In short order, the treatment devolved into an impasse from which I could not extricate us. Ever more deeply Sally and I spiraled into a profound disjunction, while just as disquieting was watching Dan become my "silent wingman." His nonverbal gestures seemed to convey, "You get her, Doc! I got your back!" In the throes of this debacle, Sally called and left a message that the treatment had become untenable for her and that she felt certain that they would need to terminate. To her credit, however, she did not think it appropriate to end in a phone message, so they would be returning for their next and likely last appointment.

Confused and both profoundly estranged and curious, I experienced Sally's phone call a kind of liberation. Instead of making me more defensive, I got ever more curious about what the hell she was stirring up in me. Furthermore, since the "worst" had already occurred, that I was being fired, I felt strangely fearless.

I found myself tracking my dreams and awoke one morning to realize that Sally looked identical to my maternal grandmother, at least what she looked like in photos as a young woman. Curious about this connection, I began to free-associate. I knew how controlling my grandmother had been of my mother when she was growing up. She was hell-bent on having her daughter marry someone of wealth, and my grandmother registered my mother in beauty contests, swimming and diving contests, theatrical plays, and so on. Though my mother enjoyed aspects of these activities, she always came in second place, which many years later she concluded was her passive-aggressive way at getting back at her mother. Suddenly, I began to feel like, in some peculiar way, Dan, Sally, and I were "channeling" an ancient argument from my multigenerational developmental background. More precisely, there was a way in which I was organized to become implicitly insinu-ated in the dynamic that had led up to our impasse.

As the next session approached, I became surprisingly relaxed. I had a narrative that felt right to me, and felt that, since I had in essence already been fired, I had nothing to lose in sharing it. Shortly after the session began, I informed them that I had given a great deal of consideration to what was going on and wondered if they would be interested in what I had come to. Fortunately, they very much were and so I told them the tale just described. I said that I felt like, in some very implicit and unconscious manner, I was responding to Sally, perhaps like my mother might have liked to to her mother, but did not dare to. I took my time and shared a few additional anecdotes I had been told by my mother about my grandmother. I finally summed up that it seemed that we had found ourselves in a huge enactment, and as my nar-rative ended Sally began weeping. She confessed that, as angry as she was at me, she had a more private sense that there was something deeply disturbed about her, and that this realization had flooded her with a completely immobilizing sense of shame that she tried to combat through "blaming" me. Meanwhile, she was then able to see how this pattern might be affecting Dan, and that he was, not unlike my mother, passive-aggressively diverting his attention and affection away from Sally rather than more directly taking up his feelings. With a big "whew," I got rehired.

Some therapists might worry that engaging in such self-disclosure could under-mine the therapist's idealizability in the minds of the couple, idealization being something that some couples may truly need for their engagement in the treat-ment. In my experience, however, the degree to which couples need to idealize the therapist is not deterred by this, as they will merely incorporate the therapist's openness into their view of what makes her idealizable. Meanwhile, rectifying an interlude of conjunctive and disjunctive imbalance also serves as an important lesson to the couple on the essential nature of rupture and repair. When the therapist repairs a rupture she has been a part of creating, it can take on a special meaning to the couple, especially when she mends the fence with the partner with whom there has been the disjunction.

Over many years of practice, I have found it relatively easy to maintain what Boszormenyi-Nagy (1987) refers to as a kind of fluidly shifting "multidirectional partiality"—that is, while we can feel more or less partial to one partner's position in one moment, in another we find ourselves more or less partial to the other, while still at other times both positions suit our sensibility well enough. For me, this often manifests in what I have come to refer to as "of course, of course" responses.[10]

"Of course, of course" responses involve statements (often made more implic-itly than actually saying "of course, of course") that summarize each partner's perspective. The therapist instantiates her "of course" response by indicating that each partner's reaction to the other makes sense in relation to some developmental context of experience. On the relationship level, the "of course, of course" response "slides" back and forth, as the therapist recognizes each partner's perspective while subtly but deftly recruiting the other partner to grasp what the therapist is saying about each partner. An example of this is the case of Tom and Jane in Step One. As I conveyed to Tom how his experience of Jane is shaped by his background, I also turned my attention to her, both implicitly and explicitly, conveying "his experience makes sense—though not so much on your terms—but in relation to his background." Of course, the same process is repeated with Jane and in fact this very process is repeated over and over during the course of the treatment. In this manner, the therapist helps each one's experience begin to make sense to the other in a manner heretofore inaccessible to either of them, building upon each episode, a model of mutual recognition.

In this manner, over time, partners come to feel the therapist striving to be on both of their sides, as well as on the side of the relationship. So long as the therapist can look at her partiality, so as to not get swept away in unwitting conjunctions and disjunctions, the therapeutic milieu acquires an increasing sense of safety—a requisite condition for developing a capacity for intimate subject-to-subject relating. The circumstance that most typically challenges this is when one partner insists on the absolute correctness of his or her position, that is, that it represents the only possible interpretation of reality, and that anyone who dares to disagree is regarded as heretical at their best or a scheming liar at worst.

Usually, such an individual requires an enormous amount of patience and empathy from the therapist, and it can be very trying to gain entry into what is at stake in this partner's tenacious "absolutizing" grip on reality.[11] Indeed, the therapist can find it quite taxing in her attempt to loosen the grip of such absolutisms. This even can lead to the therapist becoming demoralized about helping facilitate new possibilities for the couple. Ultimately, therapeutic resilience can be sorely tested when one of the partners pushes a point of countertransference vulnerability in the therapist. This is what happened in the case of Kevin and Stacy.

Kevin and Stacy

Kevin and Stacy were the kind of couple whose level of interpersonal sensitivity was truly daunting. Every effort to reach out to the other, or to defend themselves against a slight, was experienced with the same wildly out of control pain one might expect from conducting a "touchy-feely" group on a hospital burn unit. Such couples often require considerable containment and soothing from the therapist, who must swiftly yet gently create a cool buffer zone of potential therapeutic space between the inflamed partners.

In Kevin and Stacy's case, once they could be sufficiently calmed, I could usually speak about their thwarted developmental longings, which were chronically reenacted in their relationship. For example, Stacy's repetitive transference themes embodied an upbringing with a mother who was chronically depressed and frequently heavily medicated. Absent a well-functioning mother and being the eldest daughter, she came to feel responsible for looking after her younger siblings. In reward for her efforts, she hungered for and sought solace from her father, who represented to her the only "sane" parent. Tragically, she waited in states of hunger and deprivation, trying to soothe herself by fanaticizing that her father would someday be more responsive to her than he actually ever was. Ultimately, her revelation that she was deluding herself filled her with sadness. Not surprisingly, therefore, she was prone to flying into abandonment rage whenever she experienced Kevin distancing from her, either through his preoccupation with his work or his self-absorption in his recurrent bouts of depression.

Meanwhile, Kevin's vulnerability to depressive episodes was born out of being a highly sensitive member of an otherwise brutally insensitive family. The quality of daily interaction in his family waxed from belittlement of his artistic talent to real acts of verbal and physical abuse. Most tormenting of all, however, was the collective obfuscation of the brutality in which his family members routinely engaged one another.

Though I was usually able to calm each sufficiently to begin less defensive examinations of what each was experiencing, I nevertheless felt like I was walking a tightrope over two pits of alligators. I constantly felt that my slightest misstep would pitch me into the rageful jaws of Stacy on the one side or of Kevin on the other.

One especially disruptive session began with Kevin and Stacy announcing that they had not spoken in days. Several evenings before, Stacy came home from an especially draining day of work. By stark contrast, she was greeted by Kevin, who had received some especially good news that his artwork had been accepted for an important exhibition. They had in fact discussed this by phone earlier in the day, and Stacy had felt she had acknowledged Kevin's triumph with considerable enthusiasm, including her wish to discuss it more when she got home that evening.

Unfortunately, by the time Stacy arrived home, she was completely depleted. Her emotional and physical states required her to eat, relax, and restore herself before she could fulfill her earlier enthusiastic claim that she wanted to hear Kevin's good news. Just like the airlines advise passengers—"in the event of cabin depressurization, put on your oxygen mask before assisting others"—Stacy needed to take care of herself before she could authentically fulfill Kevin's mirroring needs. On top of this, Stacy also acknowledged that sometimes she could become a little wary in relation to Kevin's achievements, since they provoked in her the fear that they would draw Kevin's attention from her own needs and trigger a repetition of her unrequited longing for more attention from her father in the past, and her husband in the present.

The absence of Stacy's enthusiastic response, however, meant something entirely different to Kevin. For him, it was tantamount to her committing a covertly hostile act bent upon spoiling his achievement and excitement. Making matters worse, Kevin was especially in need of Stacy's unbridled enthusiasm to elevate him out of a recent bout of depression. In the context of her deprivation, Kevin flew into a rage. Knowing what his achievement meant to him, and not deferring everything in her own life to celebrate it, could only mean one thing: She wanted to spoil it. Feeling battered, depleted, and completely misunderstood, Stacy became reciprocally enraged, though sadly—as often happens in such imbroglios—her reaction only confirmed Kevin's hypothesis that she was out to spoil his success.

Such encounters of gross misunderstanding are readily recognized by conjoint therapists as the "meat and potatoes" of the conjoint therapy process. My own approach is typically one of attempting to contextualize the disruptive interaction by illustrating how there is a quite understandable misinterpretation of the intentions of one partner that leads to a defensive counterattack by another, and that this round robin of destruction ensues as each one's behaviors are read through a repetitive lens that distorts their true intentions.

Hoping to mend their misinterpretations, I offered that Stacy sounded like she had arrived home longing for some emotional as well as physical sustenance of her own. I suggested that we might even imagine that, given her history of failures of this longing, both during her upbringing and episodically in this relationship too, Stacy would likely enter the house somewhat defensively, perhaps protectively withdrawn.

Understandably, I continued, her actions immediately clashed with Kevin's need for mirroring. Given his history of failure of this selfobject function, he too likely anticipated (albeit perhaps unconsciously) that upon her arrival his needs too would be rebuffed. Frequently, when the therapist can link these reciprocal interactive processes to the deep intrapsychic longings of each party, each can then begin to recognize that not only their own selfobject longings were understandably failed, but so too were those of their partner's. When this occurs, the process of repair immediately begins. Both the partners can take a breath and stop the cycle of being triggered by one another. Acceptance of such mutual responsibilities is enormously liberating. This process is illustrative of a kind "of course, of course" subject-to-subject intervention attempting to generate mutual recognition. The case of Stacy and Kevin, however, illustrates how the best-planned interventions can run afoul.

Instead of the soothing, containing effect that an "of course, of course" intervention often can have, Kevin became ever more agitated. Certain of his conviction that Stacy was intent upon spoiling his evening, he now insisted she confess that her deliberate plan was to usurp his glory. Full of conviction, he insisted that she apologize, since no other possible response was conceivable to Kevin, given his absolute conviction of his interpretation of the incident. Indeed, the assertion of any alternative points of view could only be understood as a replication of his family's maddening process of obfuscation.

The conditions that Kevin demanded, which it appeared would be the only thing to mollify him, were of course impossible for Stacy to provide unless she was willing to lie. While she could acknowledge that her response fell far short of what he insisted he needed, she refused to accept his attribution about her motivations.

As I listened carefully to her, her experience made sense to me (as did Kevin's from his perspective). I could also see, however, how frustrating and enraging it was becoming for her to state her case without spiraling into deeper, more perilous discord. She was damned if she confessed to something she did not feel she was a party to, but damned if she did not.

My pointing out Stacy's double bind to Kevin, however, only aggravated his feelings. Threatened by my alternative perspective regarding Stacy, he dug in more deeply and became utterly incapable of accepting a different interpretation. Ever more agitated, he exploded at me, rose, and paced around the room. He threatened to terminate treatment and insisted that there was clearly something pathological about me that I did not see the indisputable evidence of Stacy's hostile intent. Since Kevin had effectively disrupted my own professional need (i.e., to create a climate of safety in which *both* parties could speak passionately about their experiences), I too started feeling angry. Uncontrollably, my own voice rose to match the pitch of Kevin's.

Retrospectively, I believe such encounters capture moments wherein I powerfully identify with the person being "bullied." In this case, Kevin's treatment of both Stacy and me solidified this identification. My lifelong reaction to bullies picking on others has been to rapidly move into my own profoundly aversive motivational system (Lichtenberg, 1989), and to come to the victim's aid. My aroused reaction led to the session ending in a highly discordant state. Upset that I had gotten so upset, I nevertheless privately hoped that Kevin would make good on his threat to terminate the treatment. This wish was immediately followed with some guilt that my wish would entail abandoning Stacy. And, though less present in my mind at that moment, I felt some guilt over the thought of abandoning Kevin too.

The next day, while pondering calling Kevin, I received a phone call from him. He restated that he was not sure he could work with me, since he felt that I was so clearly against him, as evidenced by my inability to see the unequivocal truth about his perspective on Stacy. I acknowledged that I too had some questions about my ability to treat them, which he found surprising and a bit alarming. I shared that I found his mode of confrontation bullying. To my regrets, I acknowledged, it elicited in me an urge to fight back for my own beliefs, as well as the sanctity of the conjoint therapy environment. I speculated, however, about the possibility that something might have gotten enacted between Kevin and myself: that we had in fact engaged intersubjectively in something like a negating third—that is, in a process that felt like something co-created between us was negating of both of our subjective experiences. I wondered if what was occurring might entail a dramatic reenactment of his family life drama. I spoke of my own aversion to bullying situations and wondered if in our fights he was enabling me to experience more directly how each family member escalated into a more ferocious form of bullying than the other, attempting to not feel dominated by any other just as we had clearly experienced engaging each other the previous evening. I added that in the context of our engagement it was virtually impossible to uphold a sense of perspectivalism and safety as articulated in Step Two of my model of treatment. I then referred him back to my article (Ringstrom, 1994), which, at their request, I had given to both Kevin and Stacy shortly after treatment commenced. I asked him to do us both a favor and to seriously reread it. In a considerably calmer state, he agreed to do this.

The next session, both arrived in an entirely different frame of mind. Kevin had taken my suggestion seriously and reread my article. What emerged next was emblematic of the restoration of mutual recognition. The space had opened up for all of us to find a new way of experiencing ourselves and one another intersubjectively. My own reaction to Kevin seemed to convince him that he was powerful enough to destroy the fabric of important relationships in his life, both his marriage and his therapeutic one with me. My encouragement that we try to recognize a more effective use of his power than bullying created a dramatic shift for Kevin. It restored his sense of agency as opposed to perpetually feeling like a victim and striking back in his bullying manner.

In summarizing his position, Kevin was able to share what had so crazed him during the previous session. During his upbringing he felt his point of view was constantly under assault. What he experienced as most toxic was when the abuses he or other members of the family had suffered were then collectively denied. This seemed to be repeated in his experience of a conjunction between Stacy and me, and both of our disjunctions with him in which Kevin felt that Stacy and I had colluded against him. Worst of all, were challenging his sanity. In retrospect, he could see my intent: It would be impossible for me to do what I needed to help them, were I to cave in to either of their convictions as absolute truth rather than as an outgrowth of each of their subjective experiences. He further understood my need to maximize a climate in which both could not only air their differences, but also sort out both their intrapsychic as well as interpersonal meanings.

Unfortunately, there are times in which the disjunction between the therapist and one of the partners is so severe that it cannot be remedied. While this could conceivably happen around any issue, in my own experience it most often happens when, no matter how open-minded I try to be to bridge my half of the divide, one partner remains in an intractable state. This makes the person incapable of entertaining any perspective other than their own, no matter how much understanding is brought to bear about it. In other words, I am ultimately unable to help them adopt an attitude fitting with the sensibility outlined earlier in the chapter, one embracing perspectivalist realism and pursuing a process of dialogical truth building. In such cases, the therapist often gets caught in a similar pattern of split complementarity, reflective of the same enactment going on in the couple's relationship, finding it trickier and trickier to come up with a creative way to get out of it.

Tony and Margaret

Tony and Margaret were an example of a couple that presented me with such an impasse. They came to me as their fourth couples therapist. Each time a previous therapist had disagreed with Margaret's position, she steadily became disenchanted and the relationship would rapidly devolve into her firing the therapist. Forewarned, I worked extremely hard at not confronting her, and in fact to empathize with her in an effort to create a third space of dialogue and meaning. Despite my efforts, the dialogical space would always collapse into complementarity, with Margaret insisting on the correctness of her position, while completely disqualifying Tony's and eventually mine. Margaret reflected a style of "psychic equivalence," a dysfunctional form of mentalization described in the next chapter.

Like many couples I see, both Tony and Margaret had neglectful and abusive backgrounds. Tony's father had been abusive to all the family members, though least of all to him. Eventually, his father abandoned the family, leaving Tony, his mother, and sister to make ends meet on their own. His mother and considerably older sister pretty much neglected him, leaving him to attend to his own upbringing. Meanwhile, they struck out on their own entrepreneur path of boutique clothing sales in which they repeatedly made and lost fortunes. At age 12, a lonely and bored Tony sought janitorial employment at a local retail car/stereo store and installation shop. Being something of a waif, he was willing to hang around and do whatever tasks his employers needed. His desire to please them, as evidenced through a tenacious work ethic, led to his being embraced by the owners as the son they never had. Working for them night and day surpassed any other interest and ambition in Tony's life. He eventually dropped out of high school after barely passing the California state proficiency exam, and he proceeded to learn the business from bottom to top.

Eight years later, the owners decided to retire early and sold Tony the business. During the next two decades of lucrative car stereo sales, Tony parlayed the business into a series of stores all over the Los Angeles region, which made Tony extremely successful, an achievement all the more impressive given his relative lack of education and formal business training. Halfway through this 20-year phase, he met Margaret, and not only fell in love, but also found in her a second kind of mentorship. From Tony's perspective, Margaret appeared far more socially advanced than he, having been married and having already had children. From the beginning of their relationship, he deferred to her judgments on a host of matters, including her recruiting him into joining her in a number of 12-step programs, such as Overeater's Anonymous and Co-Dependency Now Groups.

Meanwhile, Margaret also grew up in an abusive and neglectful family. As the child who would defy her father and boldly voice her mind when other family members could not, she was routinely beaten. As often happens to the child who becomes the mother's mouthpiece against the father, Margaret was never protected by her mother, though also never dissuaded from speaking up. Indeed, the mother would even come to hold her after the beatings, but never interceded during them. She also, however, allowed Margaret to believe that she (Margaret) was the cause of all of the problems in the family. In fact, whenever Margaret confronted her mother, she was told, "You are just like your father."

Surviving her family meant resorting to something of a reaction formation against her impression of being all wrong, arriving at the conviction that if she was "ever wrong, or bad, it was someone else's fault." Though she acknowledged that this couldn't always be true, and in fact she had troubles of her own of which she was painfully aware, she also would stridently cling to a belief in what she referred to as her "painfully accurate intuitions." This made her emotional convictions beyond the range of doubt, speculation, curiosity, or alternative explanation. At such moments of "intuition," she behaved as though her point of view was virtually a "god's-eye view of reality," not one amenable to intellectual debate, but one embodying a purity of vision.

This was less of a problem in the early years of their relationship, since Tony deferred to what he believed was Margaret's vastly wiser and more mature worldview. However, after starting a family of their own, Tony began to develop his own parental intuitions and judgments, which were remarkably sound from everything I heard. Correspondingly, he began questioning many things that Margaret did with both his stepchildren and their own offspring. To make matters much, much worse, the upswing of competition in his car stereo market, coupled with the downturn in the economy, had seriously challenged his business, which deeply threatened Margaret's sense of security.

As he began raising questions in the household, she began raising questions about his business practices. I was not in a position to determine the efficacy of his business decisions, but I was clear about two things: First, Tony had been a bootstrap millionaire who succeeded through hard work and the seeking out of advisors when he was stumped; second, that Margaret's ideas did not in any way sound like improvements that Tony could or would be willing to do, since they simply were not at all in keeping with the business principles he was articulating. Furthermore, and most importantly, not only were Margaret's demands for change of dubious worth to him, they would also guarantee he would have to be away from his family much more, which would become another source of aggravation in their relationship, since he was very much a hands-on father that she relied upon to take over the moment he came home from work.

My point was not to judge the merits of their decisions, so much as to try to flesh out what they meant to each of them. While Tony was willing to do this, Margaret found such investigation very threatening, since it appeared to call into question the indisputability of her view of reality. Again, this is exemplary of the concept of psychic equivalence, and as such curiosity was not really in the realm of possibility for her. Feeling her anxiety, I empathized with how she might understandably feel threatened by the specter of financial insecurity. In this vein, I supported their taking steps that would protect them personally in the case of more extreme financial circumstances, including measures that might allocate certain assets in her name only. Nevertheless, she still found heretical for me to in any way agree with what Tony was doing. She was certain that she was the only one who was right.

Even empathizing with her loss of her "mentorship position" in their relationship was not sufficient to bandage the huge narcissistic injury she was suffering from Tony no longer relying upon her judgment. In the end, her intractable state of concretization of reality became the death knell of the treatment. This became especially the case given another powerfully destructive element that undermines the creation of perspectival realism: external support for the patient's psychic equivalence by one of the partner's individual therapists.

Although this has rarely happened in my practice, on the few occasions when it has it has had a virtually irreversibly destructive role in undermining the treatment. This is because it completely offsets the essential perspectival realism necessary for creating the condition for mutual recognition and the instantiation of thirdness, a topic taken up in detail in later chapters. Instead, the treatment degenerates even further into fruitless and destructive arguments about objectivity, reifying the worst aspect of the relationship and locking it into binaries, another topic for more detailed discussion later.

In this case, Margaret's therapist, Jim, fell directly into this trap. Though it was he who had referred them to me, and even initially attempted to be helpful in facilitating their staying in treatment, he ultimately compromised the treatment's course by reifying Margaret's point of view and turning her observations into objectified concretizations of fact. Jim's penchant for doing this was born of his own history with Tony, one long predating his becoming a therapist and working with Margaret. As a teenager, Jim had worked for the same car stereo company that Tony had almost two decades earlier. As a subordinate employee of Tony's, even though a few years older than him, Jim developed certain convictions of his own about Tony that ultimately carried over into his work with Margaret. While Jim clearly attempted to encourage Margaret to examine the meaning of what was occurring in the couple's treatment, he was also prone to excessively reinforce her point of view as being the more realistic one. There was even the implied suggestion that Tony may well not know what he was doing in his business and that his success had been simply a matter of luck.

Although Jim and I tried to collaborate in a way that would help the couple, eventually this broke down into our parodying the very problems emblematic of their relationship. It was apparent that Jim's countertransference conjunction with Margaret was as deep as my emerging disjunction was with her. Jim's suspicions that Tony may not be able to pull the business off the rocks, fueled by Margaret's fears, turned her demands for change into absolute requirements. Meanwhile, despite her worries about their finances, Margaret had been making a succession of expenditures solely for herself that deepened their economic crisis by tens of thousands of dollars. This point unfortunately did not seem ever to be addressed in her individual treatment. In no small measure of irony, her expenditures deprived them of the means to continue their couple's work with me.

Cases such as this one founder when the patterns of split complementarity cannot be resolved, since both perspectives are not allowed to emerge in the space they share. Mutual recognition, something that Tony sorely sought, was rejected by Margaret, and since her perspective was not held by her own therapist as merely *a* perspective but regrettably supported as *the* correct perspective, this imbalance could not be righted.

Summary

In the high stakes gambits of marital interaction, partners can often feel that "To feel sane I must forgo love and to feel loved I must forgo my sanity" (Davies, 2003). This often culminates in fights over whose version of reality is the correct one. The contemporary psychoanalytic perspectives of both relational and inter-subjectivity theories have challenged analysis' objectivist past, wherein the analyst was the interpreter of the truth about the patient's unconscious, against which a patient's protestations might be regarded as resistance. Freud's own impressive *oeuvre* is rife with examples in which the father of psychoanalysis insisted on this point with some of his more contentious patients.

Contemporary analytic thinking has adopted positions such as perspectival realism, wherein analysis involves a deeply empathic engagement with the individual's perspective and experience. It recognizes that each person operates out of their own perspective of reality, and that none of us can lay claim to an objectivist or god's-eye view of reality. Perspectival realism, however, does not concur with absolute relativism. Indeed, it accedes to the argument that some "propositional truth" (Cavell, 1998) points of view are better than others, but it also grasps that the very best way for us to come to an optimal version of what is truest among our perspectives at any given point in time is through a dialogical process in which each of our perspectives can be authentically represented, leading to our arrival at dialogically constructed truths. In this manner, the limitations of our own personal horizons can potentially be expanded.

Such dialogical truth finding, however, requires cultivating a quality of relating that is often lost on couples, particularly those in dire straits. It requires the cultivation of a sense of safety in speaking one's mind and creating a sense of curiosity about one's own subjective experiences and perspectives as well as one's partner's. Such a sense of safety and curiosity becomes especially crucial to the revealing of each one's personal narrative, which arises from each one's intimate personal history. The investigation of that history is undertaken in the next chapter.

In almost all couples treatments, one of the chief obstacles to this investigation is when the therapist enters an unwitting or intractable transference/countertrans-ference conjunction with one partner, which becomes acutely exacerbated when accompanied by a disjunction with the other. The former case arises when the organizing principles of the therapist and one partner are too similar and in the latter when they are too disparate. Such instances often arise in the course of longer-term conjoint therapies, and are important sources of information based upon expectable enactments within the treatment. They are only a cause for alarm when they go unrecognized and or unchecked.

Encouraging both partners to point out anytime they sense this happening goes far to mitigate damage. Furthermore, when the therapist non-defensively engages curiosity about such enactments, it helps reckon with the therapist's overall admonition in Step Two that none of the three participants in the therapy has a more correct (i.e., objective) view of reality than any of the others, and that each is the arbiter of what is true within her/his experience in the moment. Thus the therapist's acknowledgment of her participation in the enactments helps model an optimal attitude towards the partner's perspectives, as well as modeling how to engage in a process of dialogical truth finding. In short, the therapist's willingness to be fallible, to remain curious and non-defensive, and, when necessary, to authentically own her defensiveness as her own, all become processes that underscore that the principle of thirdness between partners can be created, and that the personal horizons of each can be greatly expanded.

Adherence to the principles of curiosity and non-defensiveness, albeit seriously challenging in many treatments, pays off remarkably. As noted, however, sometimes it becomes impossible to overcome the concretization of one of the partner's point of view. In my experience this problem has only become insurmountable when the concreteness of that partner's point of view is externally supported, for example, in the case of an outside therapist.

Notes

1 I am grateful to Shane, Shane, and Gales (1997) for introducing me to this quote.
2 From Dan Siegel's website (www.drdansiegel.com).
3 Mitchell (2000) noted that "Fantasy cut adrift from reality becomes irrelevant and threatening. Reality cut adrift from fantasy becomes vapid and empty. Meaning in human experience is generated in the mutual dialectically enriching tension between fantasy and reality; each requires the other to come alive" (p. 29). And, as Strenger (1998) indicates: "The more the individual's image of a life worth living is formed by images created in fantasy, the more the distance between actual life and a life informed by authorship is increased. The fantasy image transcendentalizes the idea of a 'real' life to the point where nothing in actual life could correspond to it anymore. In therapeutic work this manifests itself by the patient's contemptuous rejection of real-life options which could provide a step toward authorship, because he or she cannot see any connection between these steps and the image of real life they have gotten used to in fantasy" (p. 180).
4 Their radical position reads as overly relativistic, a position that their epistemological stance of perspectival realism argues against.
5 Rorty (1989) makes a comparable point about how all language is inextricably embedded in metaphor; the question then becomes which are more suitable to the elucidation given circumstances.
6 Adam Phillips (1993) captures Freud's ambiguity with respect to how much psychoanalysis was art versus science. Phillips writes: "Psychoanalysis, in its inception, had no texts, no institutions, and no rhetoric; ... [it] was improvised; but improvised ... out of a peculiarly indefinable set of conventions. Freud had to improvise between available analogies and he took them, sometimes despite himself, from the sciences and the arts ... With the invention of psychoanalysis—or rather, with the discovery of what he called the unconscious—Freud glimpsed a daunting prospect: a profession of improvisers. And in the ethos of Freud and his followers, improvisation was closer to the inspiration of artists than to the discipline of scientists" (pp. 2–3).
7 In fact, Benjamin (2005) writes, "The most troubling feature of the analyst's aspiration to objectivity is not only the scotomization of the analyst's subjectivity, that is, unconscious contribution, but the certainty that it will create relations of power. If the analyst clings to a need to be objective, to be the one who knows, this will tilt the relationship toward fostering compliance or defiance and will eventually undermine collaboration"

(pp. 451–452). Echoing Benjamin's comment, Aron (1996) writes: "Relational-perspectivism eschews the role of the authoritative analyst, who knows the truth and represents reality and therefore health, in favor of a view of the analyst as a coparticipant involved in a mutual if asymmetrical endeavor" (p. 258).

8 Meanwhile, Mitchell (2000), resurrecting Loewald's body of work, captures the essential and inextricably intertwined ways in which both fantasy and reality necessarily inform each other. In fact, when either is taken alone, it is at best an impoverished perspective, and at worst, possibly an endangering one.

9 Daniel Stern (2004) describes "fitness" in the following manner: "Another way to describe the 'moment of meeting' is to speak of the 'fittedness' of intentions. The term 'fittedness' applies to 'recognition of fittedness' and 'specificity of fittedness.' When this occurs there is an experience of a *shared feeling voyage*. The participants recall such 'present moments' as rich and emotional love stories" (p. 171).

10 I am grateful to Lynne Jacobs for the "of course, of course" response, which is an extension of how her analyst, the late Dede Socarides Stolorow, would bracket her deeply empathically attuned, penetrating interpretations.

11 This point will be further elaborated upon in Step Three, regarding the concept of mentalization.

4

STEP THREE

The exploration of how each partner's complaint arises from a multivariant developmental history that contextualizes what each partner brings to their relationship.

Those who cannot remember the past are condemned to repeat it.
George Santayana

"Why do we have to dwell in the past? Why can't we just move on?" "Whatever happened to, 'No sense crying over spilled milk'?" "I *don't* want to go into the past!!! It will only be destructive!" "The past is a bunch of psychoanalytic mumbo-jumbo! We need *real tools* in the present to help us, not a recitation of the past!" "I *don't* believe in the past!!" These are, of course, just a few of the laments psychoanalytically oriented psychotherapists routinely hear. Cognitive/behavioral therapists likely hear them as well, when they must explore repetitions of both cognitive and behavioral patterns in their patients' lives. As it is to all modes of practice, getting over this hurdle becomes an essential one, especially to the relationally oriented conjoint therapist.

Notwithstanding our cognizance of our temporal past and future, experientially, we exist in the here and now, although every present moment is saturated with the phenomenological shadow of the past—a part of our individual and collective memories—as well as our imaginings about our future.

There are multiple theoretical considerations that unfold in this chapter that help the conjoint therapist to actively assess features of each patient's personality organization that impede self-actualization, that undermine the couple's capacity for mutual recognition, and that play a role in constituting mutual negation (i.e., creating negative thirdness) in terms of the relationship having a (destructive) mind of its own. The remainder of this chapter takes up both *in vivo* and deliberate history-taking styles that illuminate each partner's developmental past, which becomes essential for increasing their capacity to experience emotions heretofore intolerable. It also enables their learning to reflect upon their states in a manner that enhances both their individual understanding of themselves as well as each other. Toward these ends, this chapter delves more deeply into information regarding each partner's attachment patterns and how these influence their capacity for mentalization (Fonagy & Target, 1997; Wallin, 2007). Finally, as we all grow up in families deeply ensconced in powerfully cultural and gendered ways, this chapter examines how those prejudices press upon the manner in which couples collaborate and negotiate an intersubjective reality. This is also viewed through the lens of the multigenerational transmission processes, whereby culture, gender, affect styles, and biological predisposition (temperament) all influence the processes of self-actualization, mutual recognition, and the quality of the relationship having a mind of its own.

History-taking

The first moments of the treatment are ripe with information about developmental patterns within and between the partners. Discernible interactional patterns about the couple are instantly evident in their nonverbal communication. The way the partners of a couple enter the consulting room, sit in proximity to one another, engage in turn-taking modes of speech versus interrupting, as well as the crescendos and decrescendos of their affectivity, are all highly patterned and therefore profoundly informative. Likewise, information about the backgrounds of each frequently spills out, with each partner holding the capacity to fill in dissociated pieces of the other (e.g., "That's because she's *just* like her mother!" or "Ever since his father died, he regards the man as a 'saint,' forgetting the years of abuse he perpetrated on his family!"). All of this represents the *in vivo* unveiling of background, which becomes substantive to the relational therapist's cataloging for both here and now and future exploration. Such *in vivo* data gathering, of course, continues throughout the therapy, becoming deeper and more enriched.

In addition to *in vivo* exploration, I also employ a more formalized method, in which I suggest to the couple that we take a number of sessions (at least two) in which I interview each partner, with the other there as a silent observer. The purpose for this is to derive from each one their personal history of relations.[1] I usually suggest doing this at the end of the first session, when I am satisfied that I have completed a solid enough Step One engagement, wherein I have captured something subjectively salient about the entanglement of their bidimensional transferences and how they are caught in a vicious circle of each of their selfobject longings, triggering each other's repetitive dimension transferences. Assuming that the partners feel that I have sufficiently grasped their dilemma, they are usually amenable to my proposal of taking time for gathering some background information. This is because I have in fact demonstrated the value of linking something about their thwarted longings in their relationship with their current crisis, as well as linking this to their concerns about their future and their disappointments in the past. Of course, this doesn't always happen in the first session. On occasion, I remain unclear and am only able to give them a partial formulation, but this is often sufficient for them to come again, and by the second session I am virtually always able to come up with a compelling relational interpretation.[2]

While the history-taking sessions typically only last one session with each partner, some couples have profited enormously by simply staying with describing each of their backgrounds in as detailed a manner as each feels necessary. For instance, a couple I saw two decades ago began their session in an affective firestorm that made me aware of how quickly I needed to engage them in affect regulation, including addressing their vicious-circle style of relating. Because I was able to quickly make interpretations about their thwarted selfobject longings and repetitive transference reactions all bound in a vicious circle, remarkably, they quickly calmed down and were surprisingly open to my suggestion that we engage in some structured history-taking. Aside from being an essential structured format for information gathering, the history-taking acts as a transitional space that held the promise of heretofore unimagined intersubjective engagement with one another.

What was especially exciting was how much they enjoyed the process of history-taking. Each of them ended up taking six sessions, going over in great detail all of the best and worst relational circumstances of their upbringings. In the calm and safety of our history-taking session, they began to be able to elaborate on how their backgrounds shaped their personalities, and how they played a great role in their prejudicial views of one another. What was especially outstanding was each one's complete willingness and interest in hearing the other's story. Even though they knew much of it already, they developed a renewed depth of appreciation for what they were hearing from one another—almost as if it was for the first time.

This course of lengthy history-taking appeared to profoundly change each one's view of the other. Following 12 sessions of historical review, we had three more sessions. At the end of these three sessions, they weren't sure if they needed to continue (though they were certainly willing to do so), since their hearing one another at such depth had generated a heretofore unknown level of mutual recognition. I agreed with them that it appeared that no more therapy was required for now, since they had created a remarkable intersubjective space to continue this work on their own.

Key areas of developmental concern

During the history-taking interviews, I typically ask each spouse what it was like to grow up in their family of origin. In an open-ended, somewhat free-floating style, I ask them for a brief autobiography—a personal narrative—in which the form and substance of how it is presented is frequently as important as its content. For example, does the person seem hurried to get through the history-taking? What is her affect in relation to sharing her life narrative? Is her history coherent, or are there major gaps and lapses of memory? Does it require a great deal of intervention on my part to help shape it with questions and intermittent comments?

I typically ask each partner to tell me who the principal members of their family are, including their names, birth order, and what their relationships were like—both positively and negatively. I also ask them to expand their focus to others outside their family of origin to include other relatives and other significant historical figures who they identified as both positively and negatively influential to them. I tell my patients that I am interested in what the relationships were like among all of the key players, especially as they related to closeness and distance, the quality of their emotionality, and to whom the patient would turn in times of emotional and physical need. I tell them I am looking for models of relationships that play a crucial role in shaping how each partner conceives of their marriage.

From this data, I am listening for styles of intersubjective relating—that is, how recognized each partner felt growing up, and to what extent there was evidence of intersubjective relating (i.e., the capacity for mutual recognition). This material often begins to fill in the background of each partner's bidimensional transference, which I often highlight briefly during this session as a way of relating it to our initial session. Most importantly, it begins to suggest the kinds of attachment patterns available during their upbringings.

Knowledge about attachment patterns can be crucial, because individuals coming from securely attached developmental backgrounds reflect a host of capacities that those coming from insecurely attached ones do not. According to Beebe and Lachmann (1994, 2002), individuals with insecurely attached, emotionally reactive backgrounds are more prone to either being occupied with self-regulation (at the expense of sensitivity to their partner) or excessive monitoring of their partner (at the expense of their own self-regulation). It is not hard to see how either form of attachment preoccupation can become a serious buzzkill to the partners' romantic and sexual lives. Likewise, gone unchecked, these tendencies undermine the capacity for mutual recognition and negotiation of differences.

Attachment styles vary tremendously, depending on the assessment of the degree to which a partner experienced a secure attachment growing up or in the manner and style of insecure attachment he experienced. A secure attachment prepares partners for a much greater freedom to explore the world in a much more self-actualizing manner (Wallin, 2007), to connect with others, and to be much more reflective. Insecure attachment patterns involve three characteristic styles: an *avoidant-dismissing* type, an *ambivalent-preoccupied* type, and a *disorganized-unresolved* type.

The avoidant-dismissive attachment pattern involves a relational style born of either a pattern of rejection of the child's early bids for physical and emotional contact, or of his caregivers' over-intrusive, over-controlling, or over-arousing manner of engagement (Wallin, 2007). This individual's adaptive strategy becomes one of avoiding having his emotional experience responded to, as well as dismissing the other having her own emotional needs. Wallin notes of these patients that they "seem to 'relocate' their own vulnerability and need in others, whom they then experience as weak, burdensome, and undesirable. More generally, the inflated self-esteem of these patients appears to be secured at the considerable cost of finding fault with those they might otherwise depend upon and love" (p. 91).

The ambivalent-preoccupied attachment pattern contrasts mightily with the avoidant, insofar as instead of being avoidant and dismissive, the adaptive strategy of this type involves under-regulation of affect, not over-regulation. Parents of such patients were neither consistently over-intrusive nor rejecting. Instead, born of their own severe anxiety, their manner of engagement was erratic. This resulted in their children becoming over-focused and preoccupied with their caregivers. The result, as Wallin writes, is an "alternatively clinging and angrily resistant [child], on the one hand, or reduced to helpless passivity on the other, the ambivalent infant [being] extremely hard to soothe" (p. 91). For these patients, intimacy in later life is like going to Las Vegas, each episode of engagement with an intimate other feels like roll of the interactional dice—that is, they are perpetually shooting for an accurate response from the intimate other while also anticipating "crapping out." Their preoccupation first with the caregiver and later with their intimate attachment figure sorely undermines their ability to feel secure in the activities of self-actualization, which require an interest in exploring their world, in being agentic, and in developing a sense of personal competence. They can be over-dependent at one moment and angry in the next, when their needs and expectations go unmet. They are highly prone to replicate the mixed messages they internalized growing up.

The disorganized-unresolved attachment pattern evinces the "scars of trauma and loss" (Wallin, 2007, p. 93) that remained unresolved in the lives of the child's parents. Since his/her parents' lives are constituted by highly dissociated narratives, the child becomes the recipient of a kind of perpetual "double bind" communication (Bateson, Jackson, Haley, & Weakland, 1956; Ringstrom, 1998a, 1998b). Driven by the vicissitudes of the child's fearful states, she is prone to seek out her caregiver, but when she does, she is met with displays of either sequential or simultaneous contradictory responses that create perpetual states of feeling damned if she seeks succor and damned if she doesn't. As an adaptive strategy, she comes to embody her own version of disorganization, seeking and rejecting care in a manner that confuses her partner.

All of the adaptive strategies of those with insecure attachment patterns are further complicated with an "as if" way of relating—that is, their repetitive transference dimensions are marked with styles that may well undermine that which they ostensibly claim they both need and desire (Seligman, 2000). What complicates this all the more is the paucity of reflectivity that they are able to bring to their situation—that is, their ability to mentalize what is happening to themselves, as well as what this gives rise to in their intimate relationships.

As a consequence of all of this, what I especially listen for in assessment interviews is each partner's capacity to mentalize. The inability to mentalize—to reflect upon, symbolize, and express their experiences—may stem from the interpersonal dimension (such as a lack of safety and a dread of shame), or it may represent a background in which there was a paucity of interactions with their caregivers that would facilitate their capacity to mentalize. Thus, during the history-taking sessions (as well as during all sessions), I listen intently to how well or poorly the pivotal caregivers in each patient's life recognized their subjective experiences and, in so doing, helped them develop minds of their own— their own "theory of mind" (Main, 2000). Describing how the caregiver helps the infant/toddler with developing a capacity for mentalization, Fonagy et al. (2004) note:

> The caregiver who is able to give form and meaning to the young child's affective and intentional states through facial and vocal mirroring and playful interactions provides the child with representations that will form the very core of his developing sense of selfhood. For normal development the child needs to experience a mind that is concerned with his mind and is able to reflect his feelings and intentions accurately, yet in a way which does not overwhelm him …This is the experience the psychologically neglected child might never have, even if there can be no doubts about the provision of adequate physical care. The child who does not experience the caregiver's integrative mirroring of his affect states cannot create representations of them, and may later struggle to differentiate reality from fantasy, and physical from psychic reality. This leaves the individual vulnerable to primitive modes of represented subjectivity and the agentive self which are not fully representational or reflective.
>
> (p. 427)

Impairment in one's capacity to mentalize challenges not only his emotional health, but also the health of his relationship to others. It undermines his capacity for affect regulation and impulse control, since the second-order representations (i.e., the ability to reflect upon emotions rather than knee-jerk enact them) are disabled or absent. It becomes difficult for the individual to grasp that he has a mind of his own. It further compromises his ability to recognize that his perspective on reality is only one perspective, and therefore represents one theory of mind—his view of reality—among those of many others.

Fonagy (2004) and colleagues note that patients with impaired capacities to mentalize tend to devolve into two modes of thought, both of which, in extremes, present dire consequences. The first mode, "psychic equivalence," involves equating one's internal image with the external world. A paragon of this is captured in the novel and film *The Great Santini*. Fonagy notes that in psychic equivalence "What exists in the mind must exist in the external world, and what exists out there must invariably also exist in mind" (p. 427). This mode can make the patient's fantasies about others extremely frightening, as in the case of the paranoid personality projecting his suspicions onto the world, and being convinced that they are correct, or with the lovesick patient who assumes that a prospective man is madly in love with her simply because she thinks it is so.

Another way of thinking about this is the state of "embeddedness," wherein one simply concludes that we are what we experience (Wallin, 2007). There is no second-guessing, no doubting. Obviously, this presents a rather daunting mode of engagement for a couple's relationship, not to mention a considerable challenge to a conjoint mode of treatment ensconced in perspectival realism.[3]

A second mode of thinking that can correspond with poor capacity for mentalization is the "pretend mode." In this mode, one's inner world is de-coupled from the outside world, and one lives predominantly in fantasy, utilizing this mode as a departure from the vicissitudes of external reality. Analogies to this might be thought of as the Blanche Dubois effect in the play *A Streetcar Named Desire* or from the HBO movie *Gray Gardens*.

Ultimately, Fonagy notes that neither mentalization mode works well because psychic equivalence is too possessed of certitude of what reality is, while pretend mode is possessed of functioning in the world of fantasy devoid of engaging reality. As Mitchell (2000) notes, "Fantasy cut adrift from reality becomes irrelevant and threatening. Reality cut adrift from fantasy becomes vapid and empty. Meaning in human experience is generated in the mutual dialectically enriching tension between fantasy and reality; each requires the other to come alive" (p. 29).[4]

In developmental circumstances that are optimal to an evolving capacity for mentalization, the child integrates these two modes to arrive at a more reflective one, in which thoughts and feelings can be experienced as representations. Even more importantly, rather than the pretend mode or psychic equivalence obscuring (negating) the other's subjective experience of reality (as well as one's own), optimal states of mentalization recognize that others also have an independent capacity for mentalization. Although originally designed for research purposes, Wallin (2007) argues that Fonagy et al.'s studies of reflective functioning can be informally used to enhance clinical judgments. Reflectivity enables us to see both ourselves and others in psychological terms that go beyond mere behaviors, but that enable us to infer desires, intentions, feelings, and beliefs. This capacity is fundamental to our capacity for insight and empathy.

This psychological capacity is also instrumental to our ability to play, a function that is crucial not only in child development but throughout life. As such, it becomes an important part of this model of conjoint treatment. Becoming able to play with their versions of reality, rather than embracing them as psychic equivalents of reality or dissociated fantasies, is critical to reinvigorating a couple's relationship. It also assists in mitigating the extremes of shame states, which corrode one's sense of self and one's sense of the other. As Fonagy (2003) notes: "unbearable shame is generated through the incongruity of having one's humanity negated, exactly when one is legitimately expecting to be cherished" (p. 445). This is a sure-fire pathway to invoking dissociation to maintain splits between one's versions of self, or invoking projection as a means of disavowing split-off versions of self and other and attributing them to the other.

While our capacity for mentalization depends sizably on the degree to which our caregivers could reflect back our state of mind in a manner that is accurate to our experience, there is no reason to believe that any of us has escaped the vicissitudes of malattunement. Fonagy (2003) notes that

> [e]ven the most sensitive caregiver is insensitive to the child's state of mind over 50 percent of the time. Thus we all have alien parts to our self-structure. The coherence of the self as many have noted, is somewhat illusory. This illusion is normally maintained by the continuous narrative commentary on behavior that mentalization provides, which fills in the gaps and makes us feel that our experiences are meaningful. In the absence of robust mentalizing capacity, with disorganized patterns of attachment, the disorganization of the self-structure is clearly revealed.
>
> (p. 446)

Bringing alien parts of self (Donnel Stern's 2006 "not me") into consciousness, by enhancing the couple's capacity for self-reflection, unearths unformulated versions of self that have interfered with their self-actualization, while expanding their potential range of ways of being by connecting to heretofore dissociated aspects of self. Restoring the reparative function of mentalization as a mode of self-reflection is crucial in couples therapy because it enables each partner to come to terms with his or her own theory of mind, sense of agency, and capacity for recognition of one's self and partner.

Kurt and Kathy

Kurt and Kathy were a lovely heartfelt couple in their early forties, whose family backgrounds significantly impaired their capacity for mentalization of their problems. Their relationship was in a serious state of demise, and they all but retreated from any form of intimacy, including simple conversation. Their lives were mostly composed of Kurt working long hours and Kathy being consumed with the upbringing of their two daughters, another source of controversy, since by their own admission they both often felt clueless about how to parent.

When I first met them, I was completely thrown. Kathy was a tall, vivacious, highly extroverted, athletic-looking woman, who was both extremely affable and outspoken. She did not wear make-up, had shortly cropped hair, and dressed predominantly in gym clothes much like a pre-teen, while conveying a kind of cheery engagement that would make almost anyone feel safe in her presence. Her lively manner suggested that she was someone interested in having a good time. However, she was also clearly worn out from having retired from her career to be a mother, especially one who often felt more like a single parent.

Kurt's physical contrast to Kathy was palpable. When I went to the waiting room to get them for our first consultation, I was frankly a bit worried at who these people must be, since Kurt, dressing like a 7-year-old boy in gym shoes, shorts, and a T-shirt, stared in space when I entered. When I invited them to come into my office, he literally shuffled his untied gym shoes across the oak wood floors, stooping deeply in a round-shouldered gait, and appearing very much like a boy brought in with his mommy to an elementary school principal's office for having committed some malfeasance. Once seated, Kurt stared vacantly into space as Kathy chatted away about what brought them to me.

I am going into this elaboration because this was a time when an *in vivo* observation alone could really throw the therapist off and, therefore, where the collection of historical data becomes so crucial. In fact, contrary to my observations, I discovered that Kurt was a brilliant and accomplished artist, whose expressionist works had brought him considerable renown. Kurt belied my initial concerns by being able to present a coherent narrative that enabled me to better understand the otherwise rather daunting limitations of his personality. In contrast to Kathy, Kurt was extremely introverted and one of the most shame-prone patients I had ever seen.

Kurt was the son of two high school dropouts, who had barely any time for the multiple offspring they had quickly brought into their devotedly Catholic family. Both parents worked two blue-collar jobs each, meaning he was primarily raised by his older brother and sister. When his father was at home, he would immediately begin drinking to "calm his nerves," but in fact it mostly seemed to inflame them. On Saturday nights, Kurt would frequently go to bed with a horrible stomachache, fearing that his parents would get into one of their drinking brawls. From his description, the fights were emblematic of his parents' exceedingly concrete style of mentalization. Both existed in their own realm of psychic equivalence from which each presumed that what they thought and felt *was* reality, and that therefore the other was crazy.

Kurt began working for his father at age 10 and resentfully missed out on almost all aspects of his childhood from then on. When he was not working, he frequently had to babysit his vastly younger little brothers and sisters, who were at least 12 years his junior. In the context of these duties, there was little room for reflecting upon his feelings, but even more importantly, even if he had, it was clear that there wasn't anyone available to help mark them as his own. Mostly, Kurt felt like chattel, forced into labor in his father's various menial services business, such as seasonally driven lawn care, snowplowing by day, and other janitorial services by night. Compounding Kurt's anguish over his dutiful enslavement, his father paid him poorly. In addition, having lost control over his life, he also had to stomach living with an older brother who managed to escape this enslavement. By contrast, his brother was the family black sheep, who was constantly in trouble at school, with girls, and ultimately even the law. Thus, while his big brother was having a good time, Kurt felt imprisoned in the role of the good son—a moniker he came to hate.

This moniker was born of the necessity of his having to live up to his mother's view of him as the good son. As a result, he felt flooded with envy over his brother getting to be the footloose fuck-up, and loathed his brother, himself, and ultimately also his mother—who Kathy had come to personify in his transference. Accordingly, since elementary school, Kurt's worth was measured totally by the success of his performance, whatever that would entail. Anything short of meeting high standards flooded him with shame, for which the only sure tonic was alcohol. Although in contrast to his belligerent father, alcohol made Kurt mellower than meaner, it also disconnected him from being emotionally present with Kathy. Given the pressures of his own work, much like his father, at the end of a long day he frequently took refuge in a bottle of vodka, which meant that he and Kathy had very little connection.

Kathy's background was comparably deprived. Her parents were both alcoholics. Both had flagrant affairs that turned the whole household into a giant disruptive emotional storm. Her mother was extremely critical to the point of being abusive to her father, until one day he simply left. At his departure, he told Kathy that she'd have to be the parent, though she was only 11. This threw her into a topsy-turvy relationship of both caretaking and enabling her mother. With no one to look out for her and her brother, she learned to simply become numb to her feelings.

One of the means to become enlivened while remaining numb was for Kathy to engage in a vividly imagined pretend world, which frequently had her in some calamitous situation or another, such as drowning in quicksand, and her mother saying what a wonderful girl she was for not complaining. This pretend mode replicated her mother's rather infantile ways of thinking, feeling, and believing. Together, they were almost more like sisters than mother and daughter, and, accordingly, she experienced her mother as both her best friend and worst enemy.

Kathy and Kurt had met about 12 years before, when she got the job of representing his artwork. She really fell for his shyness, which she liked because it made him very unpretentious about his artistic achievement. She also seemed to like his little-boy manner, which was not threatening to her. Much like her father, Kurt had extreme difficulty showing his anger, and much like her mother, Kathy could be prone to being critical, which was sulfuric acid for a man as shame-prone as Kurt.

In more recent years, Kathy had undergone a lengthy analytically oriented psychotherapy that had enabled her for the first time to be able to mentalize vast areas of her childhood, including the whole symbiotic nature of her relationship with her mother. In the course of her work, she had largely broken the pattern of enmeshment with her mother, though she admitted any visits could throw her for a loop. She also finally reconnected with her father after many years of not communicating. As frequently happens when one partner gets involved in an intensive psychotherapy while the other doesn't, Kathy was now opening up to an array of new possibilities that emerged from recovering many sequestered longings. She also began wanting the same for Kurt. Her attempts to foster this, however, came in a form that typically backfires in intimate relationships—her attempts to try to "analyze" him. Kurt found her interpretations to be bewildering and intrusive. Worse yet, they flooded him with a sense of shame. Most of the time, all he could decipher from her comments was that he was bad.

A persistent clash in their relationship came from Kathy trying to expand their horizons, but often in so doing she triggered a shame reaction in Kurt. Frequently, she would try to give Kurt and herself a backhanded compliment by pointing out how comfortable she could feel just ignoring his needs and being mindful of her own. This made total sense in the context of emancipation from being the caretaker to her own mother. Unfortunately, in his concreteness, Kurt only heard this as his being undesirable and easily dismissible, instead of Kathy's real meaning that she was feeling freer. Comparably, on occasion, she wanted and needed to express some feelings of disappointment, such as the time they had a date but Kurt had to miss it due to a project deadline. Kathy's expressed feelings, which were a triumph over her numbed past, activated in Kurt feelings of having been bad, compounded with a reactivation of his childhood feelings of never being sufficiently appreciated for his work.

Discerning implicit versus explicit communication

Thus far, it would be easy to read this book as emphasizing verbal communication, especially considering the importance of language generally and in therapy in particular. As Fonagy notes, "Language is the representational medium *par excellance* for mentalizing explicitly" (Allen, Fonagy & Bateman, 2008, p. 29). The challenge, however, is that the bulk of human communication is often *implicit*—it derives from implicit memory systems which operate automatically and often intangibly, at least in terms of explication. This is because implicit memory and implicit communication are linked to procedural versus declarative memory systems. Furthermore, since implicit communication is prereflective, it is automatically "prejudicial," insofar as it registers the huge array of cultural and gendered biases transmitted to us both from within and from outside our families of origin. All of this lends to what Stern (2004) refers to as our "implicit relational knowing."

This latter construct embodies many unquestioned meanings, including countless prereflective expectations of what patterns of behavior should follow from what. For example, if someone holds out their hand in a vertical position stretching it towards another, the other knows implicitly that a handshake is being gestured and there is an expectation of it being reciprocated. If it is not, one will automatically be regarded as rude.

The obvious problem that implicit communication stirs up for couples is when their assumptions about *what* is implicitly relationally known—as in how each imagines what any given situation calls for—turns out not to be automatically the same for both of them. Indeed, frequently, their assumptions are simply not known to one another until they are mismatched. When respective versions of what is presumed to be implicitly relationally known are in conflict, couples are vulnerable to getting into trouble, and when their respective versions are argued as objectified truths the "fat really hits the fire." Complicating this further is that, absent the capacity to reflectively mentalize, the couple spirals into deadly traps of mutual criticism and condemnation.

Four particularly "deadly" styles involve what Gottman (1999) and his colleagues refer to as the "Four Horsemen of the Apocalypse." These involve four especially toxic modes of communicating, including:

1. Criticism, which links a complaint with a personal attack, such as, "It bothers me that we are always late because of you, which is just the tip of the iceberg of all the ways you are so inconsiderate!"
2. Defensiveness, which involves turning one's partner's complaint back on him as a means of blaming him—"You're the one that actually makes us late—I just get involved in other things while waiting for you!"
3. Stonewalling, which involves one partner tuning out the other when they are complaining about something that makes the former feel defensive. According to Gottman, this defensive strategy is typically used by males vastly more than females, in fact, when in evidence in a couple it is employed 85 percent of the time by men;
4. Contempt, which ratchets up criticism by infusing it with sarcasm, often of a nonverbal implicit variety such as "rolling one's eyes," or repeating what was said in a mocking tone. Gottman calls contempt the "sulphuric acid of love," and cites it as a 97.5 percent predictor of divorce if the couple cannot stop engaging one another in this manner.

Clearly, then, the therapist's ability to assess the couple's uses and misuses of implicit communication, as well as what it takes to facilitate their reflectivity about it, becomes very crucial to all forms of couples treatment. Implicit communication is especially important in how it takes shape in enactments, or what I refer to as mutual inductive identification. However, before leaving the topic of implicit and explicit communication, it is important to note their relationship to affect regulation and affect tolerance.

Affect regulation and tolerance

Affect regulation is a critically important process in couples treatment. Dysregulated affect states almost always create an atmosphere that is profoundly unsafe, and, when safety goes out the window, so too does any semblance of reflection. Goldner's (2007) depiction captures this aptly:

> By the time the partners enact their drama in the therapist's office, every statement each one makes, every action either one of them takes, cannot

be read simply, or even primarily, as an expression of self. Powerful negative affects incite automatic negative responses, which elicit recip-rocal aversiveness or distance, creating an infernal circuitry of anger and alienation. Each iteration of the reactive struggle now moves so quickly that it cannot be processed symbolically, while procedurally coordi-nated, contagious affects and counter-affects create wave after wave of iatrogenic relational trauma. Communication is by impact, right brain to right brain, not one mind to another.

In this heightened state of arousal and dysregulation, the symbolic register in which therapy is primarily conducted in the early stages—questions, answers, commentary, can feel like an empty add-on, language itself a desiccated, pseudo-mature form of compliance. The real action is occurring below the radar on the procedural/implicit frequency. People flush, the blood drains, eyes avert or glare, a woman gasps for breath after lashing out at her husband in a sudden, lacerating one-liner. And it's only 10 minutes into the session.

(p. 5)

Ultimately, we hope that each of the partners in couples treatment will be able to express their feelings in a manner that is experienced as impactful (expressing agency), while also being able to listen to one another. Partners reflecting more insecure attachment patterns, with their compromised capacity for mentalization, are vulnerable to engaging one another in patterns that are avoidant, ambivalent, or preoccupied in manners that produce tremendous emotionally wrought defen-sive strategies. Moreover, most of these manifest as much in the implicit register as they do explicitly. As we will see in subsequent chapters, the substantive verbal content of many disagreements pales in strength compared to the manner (e.g., affective tone and presentation) in which that content is conveyed. As the adage says, "It is not so much what you say as how you say it." Indeed, all couples have to learn to parse out which of their problems are reconcilable and which are not, and, on this latter matter, how they will come to terms with the irreconcilable in a very different affective manner that lends to humility, surrender, and genuine acceptance versus seething warfare and mutual destruction of self-actualization, mutual negation, and the relational unconscious mired in negative thirdness.

Todd and Angela

Meanwhile, affectivity is seldom located in one spouse or the other, but systemi-cally intertwined. This was what appeared to happen with Todd and Angela. She reported that his routine temper outbursts filled the house and made any kind of contemplative, reflective conversation impossible. Fairly soon into our work, this mode of relating also surfaced with Todd rising in fury, pacing the room, scream-ing at the top of his lungs, and making wild gestures. Eventually it got so bad that I had to tell him to stop. When he didn't, I was forced literally to rise to my feet and, in an equivalent booming voice, insist he sit down and "shut up." He finally complied.

What surfaced thereafter was his statement that he did not think that his temper was manageable. However, something then shifted from his articulating this and my empathizing with his frightened feelings. I also underscored that it would be the end of his relationship if he didn't control himself, which led to him finally deciding to take charge of his outbursts. Though still present, they reduced to about 10 percent of what commonly had been the case. That notwithstanding, Angela lived with an around-the-clock expectation that Todd would explode, a point that I had to drive home to help her see that Todd's behavior had radically changed, though her expectation about it had not.

More interestingly, however, was that the degree to which Todd got more in control of his temper and outbursts, the more Angela's temper and outbursts started to become more out of control. What is fascinating about this is the manner in which it documents how affectivity is not isolated to one person or the other. It is a property distributed across the system, much like what is discussed about complexity theory in Chapter 1. As a result of this shift, it then became crucial to help Angela see how the quieting of Todd's rage made it possible for hers to emerge. Nevertheless, the emergence of her rage potentially had the same dire implications to their relationship as did Todd's unbridled temper.

The importance of trauma, along with the risk of it turning into a "morality gambit"

Over the past two decades, psychoanalysis has made an important correction to Freud's fateful turn away from his original trauma theory (embedded in his seduction theory) to his Oedipal theory of childhood sexual disturbances that haunt the patient well into adulthood. In his earlier seduction (trauma) theory, Freud posited that parents actually had behaved in an inappropriate sexualized manner, including sexual abuse. Though Freud never rejected this possibility in some cases, his Oedipal theory posited that the focus of psychoanalysis should take up the patient's neurosis, constituted by repressed *fantasies*—a prospective source of psychosexual conflict even in seemingly normal developmental circumstances. As such, even children who have not been abused or traumatized can have fantasies that embody the desire to "murder" one's same-sex parent, so as to have the opposite-sex parent to oneself to then bear children. With his revised Oedipal theory, Freud moved from the trauma of the actuality of seduction to the bedeviling world of the imaginary, which subjected the unanalyzed patient to a potential lifetime of hysterical misery.

So as not to muddy his burgeoning theory of psychoanalysis, Freud pretty much dropped all attention to real traumatic circumstances, leaving trauma to be dealt with by other psychological interventions. The pure gold of psychoanalysis was not to be alloyed with distracting elements. Not all analysts agreed, however. Sándor Ferenczi (1988), in particular, stood out, attempting to point out the importance of remaining open to psychogenic aspects of trauma in patients' lives, including and especially how a patient's trauma could be and often was inadvertently repeated by analysts misunderstanding their patients. Though Ferenczi was a close friend and early collaborator of Freud, he (and his ideas) were later rejected by Freud and his closest adherents. Ferenczi's early death from pernicious anemia meant that throughout most of the twentieth century his arguments, and much of his archived writings, were set aside and largely left out of the psychoanalytic conversation until they resurfaced in the late 1980s. Their revelation also gave rise to relational psychoanalysis.

Indeed, today, trauma is a very prominent etiological explanation in contemporary psychoanalysis, seemingly almost replacing Freud's emphasis on the role of fantasy—that is, the role of the imaginary in hysteric (neurotic) misery. Trauma now gets used (and misused) in understanding a great deal of the symptoms and distresses our patients present to us. The traumas they present run the gamut of sometimes being acute, sometimes chronic, and sometimes catastrophic. Of particular importance in examining trauma is also taking into consideration one of its key impacts: dissociation (Bromberg, 1998, 2006; Davies, 2003). Uncovering trauma while gathering historical information, whether *in vivo* or during the more deliberate mode of history-taking, frequently exposes processes of dissociation, sometimes including a patient's denial of trauma in his background.

An example of this occurred 25 years ago, when during the course of taking background history, the husband of a couple mentioned parenthetically that, while he was up in a tree trimming branches, he accidentally cut off the lower extremity of his left arm with the chainsaw he was holding in his right hand. Needless to say, my facial expression implicitly (at the very least) expressed my horror, which he pretty much shrugged off, saying that it wasn't that big a deal. He added that he was raced to the hospital, and after 16 hours of microsurgery his arm was reattached. Nowadays, he could pretty much use his left hand for most things he needed to, and he'd gotten used to the numbness in some of his fingers.

Having recovered from *my* own momentary shock in listening to him, I suddenly recalled a conspicuous pattern of speech towards his wife that surfaced especially during their arguments. She was "always cutting him off," "her actions made him think she wanted to sever their relationship," "parts of their relationship felt to him like they had gone numb," and on and on in a thematic manner astonishingly isomorphic to his traumatic incident. Clearly, his trauma, though unrecognized (dissociated) by him, was speaking very, very loudly. He was shocked by my pointing this out, but also found it hard to disagree. Meanwhile, his wife burst into tears; her experience of being on the receiving end of his invectives finally made her feel recognized.

Unfortunately, with the historical correction restoring trauma as an etiological explanation, it has almost become an explanatory cliché, referencing the roots of seemingly any psychic distress. To try to avoid this pitfall, I have found it especially useful to discuss the phenomenology of trauma in a more specific way, that is, in terms of the "assault of the unimaginable"[5] (Grotstein, 1997, 2000).

There are countless examples of the assault of the unimaginable (e.g., the sudden and unexpected death of a family member or friend to a car accident; a heart attack or a stroke in an otherwise healthy individual). The key idea is that trauma occurs when the victim is unable to imagine the event(s) that occurred before their occurrence so as to, at least in some manner, defensively prepare or, in a more primitive sense, to imagine one's role in the cause of the trauma.

What is especially useful in approaching trauma in this manner is that it helps distinguish events in the life of the couple that may be experienced as traumatic for one, though not so for the other. For example, in the late 1980s, my wife Marcia and I decided we were ready start a family. After many months of trying, we discovered Marcia was pregnant—but only two weeks later we suffered the first of what became several years of a protracted period of infertility, punctuated by a total of three miscarriages. For many reasons, mostly pertaining to my own yet to be analyzed omnipotent fantasy, what happened was inconceivable to me (at least regarding the first miscarriage). It was the assault of the unimaginable from which I was extremely traumatized. While what occurred was also horrible for Marcia, it was imminently imaginable to her, as it corresponded thematically with a host of losses she had endured throughout her life. Furthermore, the direct relationship of her body to the miscarriage made it impossible not to feel directly implicated in it, notwithstanding that miscarriages such as the ones we suffered most likely were the result of unviable embryos, having little or nothing to do with the mother's body. Consequently, unlike myself, Marcia was not traumatized, though profoundly emotionally affected. This experience (and many others like it) solidified for me that an extremely important way of thinking about trauma (along with other formulations) is that it involves an assault on one's state of mind *a priori* to the traumatic event—and this may be composed of both shattered assumptions as well as an incapacity to imagine and therefore be prepared.

Indeed, the sequelae of what happens to those who have been traumatized include what sometimes occurs with respect to their processes of mentalization. For example, Fonagy, Gergeley, Jurist, and Target (2002) assert that the effects of trauma can present in

> one or more of the following ways: (a) the persistence of a psychic equivalence mode of experiencing reality; (b) the propensity to continue to shift into a pretend mode (e.g., through dissociation), and (c) (the) partial inability to reflect on one's own mental states and those of one's objects.
>
> (p. 382)

In addition, the authors argue that such patterns of mentalization can result in rigidity in relationships involving the "petrification of systems of (self and other) representation" (p. 384). The theoretical perspectives of Fonagy et al. (2002), Siegel (1999), and Wallin (2007) strongly suggest that trauma may actually culminate in processes that *cause* the formation of "absolutisms," rather than being a byproduct of shattered ones. Fonagy et al., however, also write that "Psychoanalysis and psychotherapy can break the vicious cycles by reinforcing reflective capacity" (p. 477).

There are also versions of trauma that surface in some couples' relationships that are especially menacing, and these involve times when one partner does something that profoundly devastates the other in a manner that he or she could never have believed possible. We hear this in statements like "It's like I never really knew him or her." A not uncommon version of this is in the form of one of the spouses having an affair. Obviously, with this breach of trust ensues the potential awakening of new possibilities for understanding one another, but getting to this is often extremely difficult, if not in some cases virtually impossible.

There is, however, another insidious problem that sometimes overburdens a couples treatment—when the traumatic reaction, which certainly is known to have physiological correlates, intertwines with certain characterological issues the "victim" of the trauma has. In these cases, a kind of impasse is at risk of occurring with what I call the "morality gambit," a strategy (not necessarily conscious) for upending any form of argument. The trauma in this case gets used as a kind of moral authority, a veritable "morality trump card" strategically employed the moment one feels like he or she is losing an argument. At such points, they swiftly haul out statements like "Well, at least I am not the one who got caught cheating!"

What is interesting in these cases—and they apply equally to both genders in my experience—is that often the "offending spouses" have gone to extraordinary lengths to acknowledge their transgressions, and to not wrap them up in counter-defenses such as "I had to do this because you became so cold." On the contrary, many had gone to great lengths to apologize, to acknowledge the horrible pain and sense of betrayal they had inflicted, as well as to humble themselves by vulnerably displaying their terrible humiliation and shame. Even when they asked for forgiveness, they did not insist upon its immediate appearance. Finally, they frequently exhibited unceasingly state-congruent remorse, remorse that came through in both their explicit and their implicit communication. Yet, with all of this, the "victims" in these cases held on tightly to their "send their spouse to jail" card.

Even more remarkably the morality gambit seems to have no timeline, holding sway over the lives of some couples for years, if not decades. One of the problems is that the current theories of trauma often hold, quite convincingly, that trauma can change the architecture of the brain and alter core emotional convictions. So, it can be argued that the victim simply cannot respond otherwise. The assault of the unimaginable is in effect chiseled in memory-stone. Still, the same thing can be said about hysteria. Meanwhile, where the trauma gets employed as the morality trump card, it can represent a deeply disturbing prognosis for the couple.

All of the above caveats considered, I do think that it can be very helpful, at least in an early phase of the treatment, to speak of trauma having an enduring impact, both psychologically and physiologically. Sometimes this is helpful in working with the spouse who caused the trauma (e.g., had the affair), who initially cannot tolerate the haranguing he or she receives for his or her transgression, especially when they have done every conceivable thing they can to atone and to recognize their spouse's pain. It is important for the therapist to find a means of "holding" the "offending spouse" and keeping both of them from committing the psychological equivalent of *harakiri*. Without such holding, they start to feel helpless and hopeless. Eventually, they become resentful over their remorse not having any impact. Worse, they start to feel in a perpetual double bind in which they are harangued when they acknowledge their transgression and harangued when they don't.

Yet it is also extremely important to get the couple unlocked from their morality gambit. Both parties, at least implicitly, know how powerful this strategy is, because the shaming effect of reintroducing the traumatic affair brings out an extraordinarily powerful shame reaction in the offending spouse that completely disables his or her capacity to mentalize—that is, to respond reflectively.

Though I cannot claim to always be successful, I have found it helpful to encourage the couple to leave "morality court," and allow us to enter a playground of possibility. I speak with them about all of the above, including the sequelae of trauma, its emotional stickiness, the deleterious effects it has on the remorseful spouse when it is brought up extemporaneously in a fight, and then used for shaming and blaming often tangential to the substance of their argument. This makes it impossible for any reflective responsiveness to ensue. Finally, trauma can easily become conflated in loyalty versus betrayal gambits arising from collectivist cultures, wherein self-actualization can be regarded as a traumatizing mode of disloyalty to more "tribal"-based cultures.

Meanwhile, it appears that what is getting lost in the overuse of trauma is the role of expectation (the psychoanalytic domain of which being largely unconscious) captured in the literature on *expectancy systems*. Crucial in this literature is the topic of "violations of expectancy" and what role they play in common disturbances in life. Still, equally important is how such violations are also a part of the punch line of every joke as well as crucial in cultivating highly mutative moments in life in general and in psychotherapy in particular.[6]

Beebe and Lachmann (2002) define expectancy systems as expectable "sequences of reciprocal exchanges." They relate them to Stern's (1985) idea about RIGs ("representations of interaction generalized"). Both of these ideas are constituted by cognitive, affective, and communicative processes that are both *implicit* (procedural, emotional, and non-conscious process) and *explicit* (conscious, verbalizable, symbolic narrative), as these processes generalize to expectancies about interaction. It is a tiny leap to seeing how all of this is formative of what reveals itself as the patient's transference organization.[7]

Some of our expectancy systems, of course, can be pleasant, while many are unpleasant, even bad. Through them, over time, we cobble out a myriad of transference expectations that will arise in various relational contexts the remainder of our lives, defining how in different circumstances we come to expect something about our self in relationship to something about the fantasized other. Some expectancy

106

systems may well be piss-poor and really crappy. Children raised in families that are abusive expect abuse to be a way that affect is regulated. They grow up expecting to be abused, if not themselves becoming abusive, in all matters experienced as entailing coercion. Children who were neglected or abandoned grow up expecting this and may shy away from others, expecting neglect or abandonment. What they miss is the self-fulfilling prophecy that they have created by being neglectful and/ or abandoning of others in their lives. These and many other expectancy systems are ones from which we suffer (sometimes tremendously), but we would be misled to always codify them as trauma. This raises the question: What is so important about distinguishing expectancy systems from trauma?

Quite a lot actually, but first I need to situate my argument in the topic of binaries, a gravitational state into which dyads of all sorts can be easily drawn. Jessica Benjamin (2004) and Lew Aron (2006) have studied this dyadic phenomenon better than anyone else I can think of. They see this natural gravitational pull in terms of the dyadic systems' vulnerability to collapsing into patterns of dominance and submission whenever there are *essential* beliefs in conflict. On the intrapsychic level, it is found between dissociated self-states. On the intersubjective level of the dyadic structure of two people relating, it is easy for them to slip into the binary wherein one experiences being the "done-to" by another who is then deemed "the doer." (More importantly, a common experience of the person who feels done-to is that he sees the doer in a domineering position relative to his state of submission.) Of course, as frequently happens, both parties are convinced that they are the done-to, the "victim" as it were, not recognizing that in complementary (character) form each needs the other to define their own position. There can be no doer without a done-to, no sadist without a masochist, and in either of these cases there is an imminent reversibility of roles. The point is these conditions of dominance and submission are the death knell of play in general and of improvisation in particular. They can only be reckoned with through the introduction of a third unbound (non-binary) point of view, that recognizes that a much broader sense of the selfhood of each participant often involves *both* the positions of the doer and the done-to and even, sometimes, the sadist and the masochist. Absent this recognition, one is doomed to split off one half of the binary, project it, and induce the other to act in accordance with the projected half. It is the mutuality of this process that makes for the concept of mutual inductive identification (Ringstrom, 2007a, 2008b, 2011a, 2011b, in press). So, in answer to what is important about distinguishing expectancy systems from trauma, it is the attempt to not readily fall prey to the victim/abuser binary that can so easily happen once the trauma construct has been invoked.

The organizing functions of culture and gender

While attachment styles, affectivity, and in particular mentalization speak to the intrapsychic landscapes of each of the partners, another arena of crucial information to be gathered pertains to the extraordinary influence both culture and gender play in defining certain organizing principles of both partners, while fleshing out the substance of many of their conflicts. For example, regarding the influence of culture in intercultural relationships, Rubalcava and Waldman (2004) write: "Awareness of the unconscious cultural organizing principles facilitates the therapist's ability to help the individuals to understand their differences and co-construct their own distinct marital subculture" (pp. 127–128). Developing such awareness is becoming more and more critical as the phenomenon of intercultural marriages is exploding in the United States. In California alone, "about one out of every six marriages are with partners of different race or ethnicity. It is estimated that more than 20 percent of all marriages will be mixed by 2050" (p. 128).

As a largely unconscious organizing principle, Rubalcava and Waldman note that culture maps out a sense of one's reality vis-à-vis a relatively stable system of shared meanings; it instills directives on thinking, feeling, and behaving within the purview of readily recognizable norms of a given culture; and it functions evocatively in terms of the kinds and qualities of affectivity (or the constraint thereof) it stimulates. Correspondingly, intercultural marriages bear the additional necessity of acquiring emotional competency, the rudiments of which Rubalcava and Waldman have teased out of a work by Saarni (1993), which entail:

> the ability to discern other's emotions based on situational and expressive cues that have some degree of cultural consensus as to their emotional meaning; the ability to use the vocabulary of emotions and expressive terms commonly available in one's culture; awareness of cultural display roles; and capacity for empathic involvement in other's emotional experience. In order to sustain an optimal marriage, intercultural couples must learn to enhance their emotional competence by becoming aware of their respective cultural organizing principles centered around emotion and emotional expressiveness.
>
> (p. 134)

Rubalcava and Waldman note two primary types of cultural and familial organizing principles which shape perceptions, beliefs, and behaviors among specific group membership. The two types include *individualism*, represented strongly among many Eurocentric groups who have immigrated to North America, of which they noted as examples Germans, Greeks, Irish, Italians, Jews, Poles, Anglo-Saxons, and Scandinavians, versus *collectivism*, found among many American ethnic minority groups such as Asians, Africans, Latinos, and American Indians. Individualism is characterized by the subordination of a group's goals to an individual's own goals, while collectivism is just the opposite, the subordination of an individual's personal goals to those of the group's. The authors cautiously note: "We may safely posit that persons coming from individualistic cultures who are married to individuals from collectivist cultures will find it especially difficult making sense of each other and co-creating a harmonious family culture" (p. 135).

The bifurcation of culture into individualism and collectivism is also seen as paralleling the hegemony of gender; cultures based on individualist models privilege the ideals of individuation, separateness, and goal-directed behavior, commonly being described as "masculine," while collectivist cultures privilege the communal goals of connectedness, relatedness, and nonverbal attunement, often seen as corresponding to "feminine" qualities. For heuristic purposes, such a delineation begins a dialogue about how these psycho-social-sexual factors can become powerfully encoded invariant organizing principles, and, insofar as they are outside of awareness, can spell trouble for each partner's self-actualization, for their capacity to recognize each other's subjective experience, and for the relationship developing a mind of its own. They also have a profound influence in encoding on unconscious levels what is and isn't and can and cannot be desired sexually. These invariant unconscious propositions can clash mightily with ostensibly conscious wishes and desires. These clashes inevitably play out in enactments, wherein unconscious conflict over the clash of personal, bodily desire and cultural and gendered injunctions becomes part of the thematic question "Can love last?"

Layton (1999) takes up the examination of individualism and collectivism in terms of agency and relatedness. She notes that, when gender is hegemonically tied to these concepts, the potential for pathological narcissism ensues. Narcissistic pathology reveals itself in disturbances in seeing both oneself and the other as separate centers of subjectivity, centers of awareness and agency. It interferes with "the processes of negotiating connection and differentiation, dependence and independence" (p. 32). She writes:

> Narcissistic wounds are caused when cultural and familial gender expectations restrict the many ways that one can be agentic and relational to two ways: those that define hegemonic masculinity and femininity. These wounds are powerfully conveyed and sustained when parents and other important figures make the giving and withholding of love contingent on a child's gender or on a child's meeting gender expectations. But they are also conveyed in more subtle ways, for example, in the different ways parents hold, play with, or talk to boys and girls. These differences, too, create subjects whose relational and agentic possibilities become constricted and organized in particular ways.
>
> (p. 33)

Hegemonic masculinity, Layton notes, appears to promote a version of agency that "defensively splits off dependency to appear defiantly separate and independent" (p. 33). Citing the works of Benjamin (1988, 1995), Chodorow (1989, 1994, 1995), Greenson (1968), and Stoller (1965, 1968, 1975, 1985), as just a few examples, she notes that both boys' and girls' first identification is with mother and is therefore "proto-feminine." To establish their male gender, however, boys are induced to "dis-identify" with mother, while girls are encouraged to remain identified with her; "Thus, masculinity is constructed in relation to femininity—but as a repudiation of it" (p. 38). Under such conditions, she notes, the masculine self *in extremis* forms rigid boundaries, defends against intimacy because of the terror of losing one's identity to the feminine, and frequently seeks positions of domination with respect to both other men and in particular women and children. Success for the male is defined far more by autonomous activities than ones emanating from connectedness.

Conversely, hegemonic femininity approves of submissiveness, often withholding approval for differentiation. Under extreme versions of such circumstances "Autonomy strivings that are not approved of get split off and disavowed, or at least hidden" (p. 34). Layton's words bear sober warning for all couples therapists:

> When a girl splits off autonomy strivings or a boy splits off dependency needs, another is needed to fulfill a function that the self cannot fulfill, and this other is experienced as a part of the self and not as a separate subject. Subjects marked by the narcissistic injuries that bring for these modes of connection in agency, then, do not have a differentiated experience of self and other and thus have great difficulty experiencing their own multiplicity and in recognizing that of others. Narcissistic injury and the splitting that follows from it internally perpetuate the reduction of multiple gender/agency/relational options to two polarized but co-implicated complements. Subjects whose gender experience is marked by severe narcissistic injury can oscillate between the two poles but cannot break free of them. The degree of narcissistic injury determines how capable one will be of achieving a mode of relating and differentiating that does not depend on disavowal or splitting.
>
> (pp. 34–35)

Just as Rubalcava and Waldman capture both the richness of culture as well as how it might insinuate itself in invariant organizing principles, Layton cautions against postmodernists' total deconstruction of the binary opposites of gender "erasing the specificity and creativity of those who have elaborated a group identity over many years" (p. 61). Granting that men and women will likely have to live with powerful identifications with the gender models in which they were raised, their broader sense of creativity and imagination can be spawned by therapists enabling them to adopt and maintain multiple gender identities dispersed through multiple versions of self, allowing that these may represent fluid shifts in expressing one's multiple senses of agency and relatedness.

Linking all of this to mentalization, the question the conjoint therapist must be asking herself (as well as each of the partners) is: "How do any of their embedded constructions of both culture and gender either facilitate or impair their capacity to reflect upon, symbolize, and make meaning of their cultural and gendered experiences, so that they become more savvy in detecting incidents of otherwise prereflective self-coercion and interpersonal coercion?" It is only through this pathway that self-actualization, mutual recognition, and the thirdness of a relational mind can occur. Of course, dovetailing with Step Two, all such inquiry imposes upon the therapist both the exciting and perhaps daunting task of examining his own invariant organizing principles as they structure his attitudes about both gender and diversity of cultures.

"Loyalty gambits" and their corrosive effects on self-actualization, mutual recognition, and the relationship having a mind of its own

One of the problems that also constrains long-term relationships is the degree to which partners feel bound by "loyalty gambits" that are predicated on a sense of allegiance that surpasses either partner having a mind of his or her own. Although not exclusive to collectivist cultures, and sometimes in evidence in individualist cultures, the call for loyalty *über alles* sets in motion implicit structures of enforced enmeshment through a host of systemic ways that loyal members are expected to think, feel, and behave. This paradigm is all the more exaggerated when it is constituted by versions of religion that hold up principles of orthodoxy and fundamentalist tenets as sacred. In such groupings, deviating from the cultural norms is not simply forbidden, it is desecration, the defilement of the hallowed or holy. This can be seen as tantamount to painting graffiti on funeral markers, or rising up in protest during some liturgical service, such as Mass or Shabbat services.

All of this potentially undermines the three themes of this book. It undermines the relationship being constituted by two free thinkers who arrive at states of thirdness and congress, not out of obligation or fear-based alliance, but out of mutual recognition. The latter is hard won through an achievement that arises from the couple dealing with the inevitabilities of their mutual negation, as well as the inevitable process of misunderstanding one another, especially when a new form of differentiated selfhood occurs.

In addition to clouding the articulation of the three themes, the imminent accusation of betrayal occludes the development and articulation of a sense of devotion to another, one based on love and not on the coercive world of the performative. In this world, love must be evidenced by what one has done for the other and/or rests in the person demanding loyalty. Examples of performative requirements insinuate themselves in the life of a couple, both from within their relationship and from without—that is, in their connection to whatever constitutes "tribal" others. Though this is usually most personified in terms of multigenerational family systems, it can also surface in friendships, in business, in professional institutional and associational life, and so forth.

The essence of the gambit is that one or both of the partners assert that "if you do not comply with my requirement, you have proven yourself disloyal, a betrayer, and one from whom I will threaten to, if not actually, cut off ties. Further, to the extent that I am able, I will see to it that you are cut off from fellow members of the tribe." Such emotional cutoffs happen in all forms, from not performing obligatory favors, to speaking one's mind in a manner that differentiates one from the groupthink, to befriending others outside of the tribe, and on and on.

It is easy to see how this operates both implicitly and explicitly as a coercive process for inducing others to operate in accord with the dictates of what is deemed sacred by the group. Such cases can be very trying in therapy, especially of a psychoanalytic mode such as this which extols the virtues of both the individual and relational mind as they come into recognition. In short, this is a model that proffers that the only real basis of authentic loyalty emerges first and foremost from loyalty to one's mind, not loyalty on a basis of interpersonal requirement. Accordingly, interpersonal loyalty must flow out of one's loyalty to one's own mind. When it flows from the other direction, collapsing into dictates not of the individual's choice, it is too often vulnerable to the world of the cult.

Now, of course, there are family systems and couples who do indeed choose to live a life guided by observance of both orthodox and fundamentalist traditions, which, when freely chosen, pertains more to what I am speaking of as devotion and observance, but not loyalty. Their choice allows them a sense of peaceful coexistence in a world all too random and all too vexing, with a proliferation of choices that can be distracting from the calmer, more serene life of practice.

My point is not to single out collectivism or orthodoxy or fundamentalism as inherently the root of the problem in loyalty gambits. Indeed, it is to differentiate the latter from where, in human relationships, loyalty gets used perversely in a coercive and inductive manner. Devotion is about choice, about acceptance, about surrender. Loyalty, by contrast, risks engendering submissiveness, which immediately tilts any relationship into the risky business of split complementarity (i.e., dominance and submission).

Multigenerational transmission processes

One of the major contributors to the aforementioned loyalty gambits has to do with how the management of affect in general, and anxiety in particular, were modeled multigenerationally in each partner's family system. One of the most useful models for determining the vicissitudes of these processes arose from the Georgetown University Family Therapy Institute in the form of Bowenian Family Therapy, based on the progenitor of the model, Murray Bowen.

The basic premise of Bowen's theory is that the capacity of any individual family member to develop a sense of self (as defined by the ability to choose goals regarding work and relationships, and strive towards accomplishing both) depends on his or her capacity to differentiate emotional reactions from those of other family members, as well as to differentiate emotional from intellectual functioning. Since anxiety undermines differentiation, Bowen's model focused on both the arousal and mitigation of anxiety within a family system. In particular, he investigated this by doing intensive developmental history-takings of each partner in the couple. Bowen was especially interested in how emotional and physical closeness and distance were managed in the family, how patterns of triangulation exhibited themselves over multiple generations, including talking to one family member about another versus talking with the excluded party directly.[8]

According to Bowen, highly differentiated adults are less prone to anxiety, or at least are better able to manage it without displacing it or projecting it on others. By contrast, those who are much less differentiated are prone to "fuse" with others, drawing others in closely tied relationships, as well as allowing themselves to be drawn into the emotionally wrought dramas of other family members. Families with poor patterns of differentiation were notably highly "emotionally reactive," tending to do what feels right instead of pausing to think things through. They operate more as "pseudo-selves," ones who cannot distinguish what is truly important to their sense of self. Those who possess more of a sense of "solid self" better grasp what they believe and what they are therefore willing to push for in life, despite the anxiety it may produce within themselves or others.

It is likely that families constituted by more enmeshed or undifferentiated systems exhibit greater patterns of both overt (explicit) and covert (implicit) modes of coercion, in terms of keeping family members in line. These will likely manifest—again, both explicitly and implicitly—in terms of each member's loyalty to the tribe and the extent that one's partner is loyal as well. A brilliant example of this tension was exhibited in the 2010 Academy Award nominated film *The Fighter*, in which Welterweight Champion Micky Ward (Mark Wahlberg) fights his way to the top of his game only after his partner Charlene Fleming (Amy Adams) helps him differentiate from the exploitation of his family, who keep him in constant check by challenging his loyalty to them.

The impact of immigration on long-term intimate relationships

A final issue increasingly affecting American marriages is that of immigration. Increasingly, I have had to address what both Gita Zarnegar (personal communication, 2004) and Ipp (2010) labeled the "amputation effect" of immigration. As an analyst who emigrated from Iran as a teenager in 1979, Zarnegar speaks intimately about her sense of amputation from her motherland. Likewise, having emigrated from South Africa to Canada, Ipp confronted a profound awakening of loss when she began working with a fellow Afrikaaner, "Nell," the experience of which led to the following:

> I was now for the first time starkly confronted with my amputated self—
> that part of myself left behind, severed and frozen in a place and space that
> could not travel with me as I struggled to achieve a new sense of comfort
> for myself in my adopted country. As we know the land of our birth continues to reside deep within us long after we have exited. Bridging the
> experiences of there and here, then and now, is daunting, often impossible.
> While an abiding sense of self may prevail and many aspects of self do go
> forward together to face the novel, punctuating and enriching these new
> possibilities, something vital is left behind, lost, encapsulated in the complex and multilayered world of the land of one's birth.
>
> (p. 376)

From this experience, Ipp notes the following:

> Apart from providing me with the opportunity to dismantle many of my
> own prejudices and stereotypes, [Nell] has enabled me to reconnect with
> that part of me that I refer to as my amputated self, to grieve my losses
> and open new spheres of reflective space connecting me with dimensions
> of myself that had previously been so sequestered. Locating oneself
> within the other, with all the struggles and angst that that stimulates, is
> perhaps the essence of what we need to grapple with as contemporary
> psychoanalysts as we confront our countertransferential responses and
> inevitable blind spots.
>
> (p. 385)

Clearly, this phenomenon can arise in couples treatment relative to one or both
spouses' experience of being cut off from their homeland, feeling at times alienated in their new homeland and profoundly misunderstood outside their culture.
This was certainly the case for Shoshana and her husband, Elon. With youthful
ambitions to work in Hollywood, they left their homeland of Israel and moved to
Los Angeles, where they raised three children. Yet, for all the promise Hollywood
held for them, there was a chronic sense of loss of their homeland, along with a
sense of alienation from American values so frequently at odds with the sense of
community, culture, and values that they took for granted. Worse yet, they
(Shoshana and Elon) felt like two perpetually migrating birds suspended between
two homelands captured in Lea Goldberg's (1970) poem "Pine."

Shoshana and Elon's experience very much fit with this, feeling, similar to what
Ipp describes, a kind of guilt for leaving their homeland and therefore never quite
at home there, as well as the immediate sense of estrangement as perpetual
foreigners to their new homeland, America. Helping them discuss this enabled
them to see that this represented a kind of "deep structure" to many of their seemingly more superficial fights. Framed in this manner, they found a greater kinship
in their mutual sense of loss, since now they were confronting that which they had
both been dissociating. This enabled them to grieve together, while becoming
"fishermen," who "now engaged in the process of deciding what to keep and what
can be thrown back" (Corbett, 2010, p. 392). This very brief vignette serves as a
reminder that it can become an especially important issue in marriages in which
one spouse is an immigrant and the other is not.

Summary

Couples frequently wonder what the merits are of examining their personal histories, hoping instead that the therapist will simply change the other spouse. With
those especially resistant to delving into history, I will sometimes playfully query,
"How did you know how to get to my office?" They will say something about
using a map, or they pretty much knew where I was by my address. I will point

out to them that it appears that some historical model gave them directions on how to reach their destination (my office), and that that holds true for the historical relational models in their minds that are directing the journey of their relationship.

Gathering data for mapping the relationship can involve a kind of *in vivo* process of history-taking, asking deepening background questions regarding material emerging in the present moment. Another method I employ can involve having sessions in which I interview each about their developmental backgrounds and do so with their spouse listening silently. Whether derived *in vivo* or more deliberately, there are several key areas of developmental concern that I listen for.

For instance, I am interested in what I infer to be their attachment backgrounds. How secure versus insecure were they? By insecure, I mean is there evidence of avoidant-dismissing, ambivalent-preoccupied, or a disorganized-unresolved type? In relation to this I am also listening for each partner's capacity to mentalize, to recognize themselves and others as centers of their own initiative with their own unique subjective take on things, versus the two broad dysfunctional modes of mentalization: psychic equivalence (what is in my mind is an exact capturing of what reality is, and not an organized construction of it), and the pretend mode (wherein reality is assiduously replaced by fantasy). I also listen for shame and shaming processes, because, as every debate coach knows, nothing disrupts our capacity to mentalize than feeling ashamed, hence debaters' employment of snide tones at key points of the debate. Also, shame is hugely disruptive to our affect states, frequently provoking either cowering or rage. Finally, all data gathering is on both the implicit and explicit registers of communication, meaning nonverbal and verbal. Much more is commonly communicated in the implicit register—for example, an insidious version of contempt is rolling one's eyes at what a spouse says without saying anything.

Yet another area of considerable importance is trauma and what role it plays in either spouse's past or in the couple's history. Trauma, which I codify as the assault of the unimaginable, is distinguished from expectancy systems, the latter of which can be both good and bad. In the latter case—for example, abuse and neglect—either can have powerful impact on how one engages others, especially one's spouse. As bad as expectancy systems may be, they are expected, and have to be taken up with patients to help them stop engaging in self-fulfilling prophecies. Distinguishing expectancy systems from trauma[9] can be important because of trauma's potential to become concretized in terms of bifurcating the abuser and the abused (Ringstrom, 2013). Once this happens, the trauma victim (occasionally) discovers the power inherent in seizing the moral high ground. This leads to a binary of doer and the done-to, with the victim holding a perpetual trump card they can pull and use in any argument the couple is having.

Cultural and gendered backgrounds can also be extremely important, with the former discussed as involving individualist versus collectivist cultural backgrounds. Individualist cultures tend to privilege (at least to some extent) the rights and needs of the individual over those of the group's, collectivist cultures doing just the opposite. A couple constituted by spouses coming from each of these cultural forms will almost certainly be facing some difficulties with cultural clashes, notwithstanding their initial infatuation with each other's backgrounds. This will be exacerbated when there are strains on each one's loyalty to the family culture from which they hail. This often presents itself in a multigenerational form that defines (mostly implicitly) how affect states, especially anxiety, are dealt with. Finally, in a country defined by immigration, the phenomenon of immigrants feeling like "amputated selves" is noted; like migrating birds, some immigrants are forever suspended in the heartache of no longer belonging in either of their homelands.

Notes

1 This approach was deeply influenced by my exposure in the mid-1970s to Murray Bowen's Georgetown Family Therapy method, which he referred to as an approach for "differentiating oneself from one's family of origin."

2 During the first decade or so of my practice, I made a point of conducting genograms with as many of my couples as I could. I found this an excellent tool for learning about patterns of emotional relating that were transmitting multigenerationally, and highly advocate it to beginning couples therapists. However, not infrequently, I would begin treatment with a couple with whom it was essential to temporarily postpone the history-taking, as they are either in a profound crisis or are so emotionally reactive that affect containment became a priority. Over time, I found myself using this method more selectively, often finding that I could obtain much of this information in a more organic *in vivo* style of relating. I believe that my capacity to perform the latter, however, was greatly augmented from years of experience with collecting genograms.

3 It also captures some of the phenomenology of what the Kleinians refer to as the "paranoid-schizoid" position.

4 As Strenger (1998) indicates, "The more the individual's image of a life worth living is formed by images created in fantasy, the more the distance between actual life and a life informed by authorship is increased. The fantasy image transcendentalizes the idea of a 'real' life to the point where nothing in actual life could correspond to it anymore. In therapeutic work this manifests itself by the patient's contemptuous rejection of real-life options which could provide a step toward authorship, because he or she cannot see any connection between these steps and the image of real life they have gotten used to in fantasy" (p. 180).

5 Grotstein (1997) refers to this most basic form of fantasy informing our sense of authorship as "autochthony." That is, that from infancy forward our earliest versions of intrapsychic reality are based in our omnipotent fantasy of having created the world/universe of which we are a part. To some extent, Grotstein avers, we never fully outgrow this, and it is this that must be taken up in analysis for us to "earn" our sense of alterity, our sense of intersubjectivity. By "earn," Grotstein means that, over time in optimal development, we undergo the disillusionment of our autochthony, while correspondingly begin to develop a sense that others are centers of their own agency, initiative, and autobiography, all "written" independently of us, of our earliest solip-sistic sense. When this disillusionment occurs without too much shock (or trauma), there is even the built-in benefit of our fascination with the different worldview that others can bring to us.

6 The discourse on expectancy systems reunites us with earlier and perhaps today arcane psychoanalytic discourse on self-"deficits," as distinguished from intrapsychic conflict. Beebe and Lachmann (2002) updated the language of structural defects to that of

"patterns of experience," always in process and therefore potentially transformative. These patterns represent "expectancies of sequences of reciprocal exchanges" and are associated with "self-regulatory styles." They write: "The concept of expectancies shifts the focus to the *process* in which patterns of interaction became organized in the patient's history and are becoming organized in the treatment relationship" (p. 13).

7 And, of course, also the analyst's countertransference during the course of psycho-analytic treatment.

8 See Appendix A for further elaboration of Bowen's model.

9 Of course, one can have traumatic expectancy systems; the key point is that not all expectancy systems are born expectancy systems of trauma.

5

STEP FOUR

An awakening of a "slumbering giant" occurs when the "dread to repeat" negative repetitive transference states shifts into the "dread not to."

We are appalled by our sins when we discover them in others.

J. W. Goethe

Love is giving something you do not have to someone you do not know.

Jacques Lacan

The introduction of Step Four involves what I refer to as the *relational turn* of the overall model as it shifts from the "dread to repeat" negative transference (espoused in Step One) into the "dread not to repeat" it. This turn is critically important because it accounts for what many times appears to be "self-defeating" behavior on the couple's part. Step Four introduces an ironic twist that occurs after a period in which the model of mutual attunement seems to be furthering each partner's sense of self-actualization along with deepening their sense of mutual recognition. In many treatments, often after an interim "honeymoon" phase of the therapy, the partners find themselves engaged in a phenomenon perhaps best described as "seizing defeat from the jaws of victory," or, as in the lyrics of Irving Berlin, "When you get what you want, you don't want what you get."

In this latter case, evidence emerges of a kind of undermining of self-actualization, which Gentile (2001) has described as a "perversion of agency." Frequently, this phenomenon manifests in terms of "enactments"—a central concept in this chapter—or, as will be taken up momentarily, in terms of a highly relationalized version of enactments which I refer to as "mutual inductive identification" (Ringstrom, 2001a, 2001b, 2004, 2005, 2007a, 2007b, 2008a, 2008b, 2010e, 2011, 2012a, 2012b, 2012c). The perversion of agency is rooted in the intrusion of dissociated self-states that finally emerge, ironically, because many of the partners' initial complaints are starting to be attended to. In short, there is evidence of the partners beginning to get some of what they had originally wished for, along with a deeper appreciation of one another's needs, especially as their needs no longer so readily trigger repetitive (negative) transference reactions. Thus, in the context of this progress, other dissociated states begin to emerge through "implicit communication" that becomes deeply confusing and disruptive. It may seem to come out of the blue, especially in contrast to the more "explicit communication" of what they consciously declared they wished would happen. This declarative, explicit communication is, of course, what is more readily available to the attuned responsiveness so important to the opening step of this model.

Attuned discourse is reflective of what we might call "ego discourse," of which we are conscious when speaking one to another. It is typically univocal and doesn't always reflect the equivocality of the human unconscious.[1] Think of it this way: Each partner tells their story, typically borne of some complaint, something with which they are emotionally struggling. The therapist listens carefully, and following an attuned, empathic introspective method, searches herself for something that will reflect her empathic understanding of what each partner is saying. If she succeeds in her quest to be empathically attuned, each partner obtains some relief, especially in having their feelings understood, perhaps a rarefied moment in their lives. The therapist's story about each elaborates each one's tale, and this lends not only to each feeling understood, but also to an enhanced sense of coherence, continuity, and worth relative to each partner's personal narrative. As noted in Step One, this is a crucially important place to begin with patients. Absent this entry engagement, patients will likely not stay in the treatment. All of the above notwithstanding, there remains a cautionary tale. What the therapist has done is to consciously tell a story about the partners' consciously spoken stories. Now, what we know about storytelling is that all stories leave a huge amount of detail on the editing room floor. That is true for the patient's rendition as well as the therapist's.[2]

Still, what remains on the editing room floor doesn't go away. In fact, it may find substance in other multiple self-states. This dissociated material may not find its way into the consulting room, at least not early in the treatment, but may appear in the forms of enacted behavior—the "awakening of slumbering giants"—and this vulnerability applies not only to the two partners, but also to the therapist.

Yet another reason for the inevitability of enactments is that therapists are notorious for using empathic attunement for their own countertransference defensiveness. Therapists who are frightened by a patient's aggression (and there are few therapeutic modalities wherein aggression is more in evidence than in couples treatment) often use empathic attunement to mollify their patients. As a consequence, what is more menacing lands on the editing room floor, but remains there for only so long before it must be played out.

Still another reason dissociated material emerges as "sleeping giants" pertains to the topic of sexuality introduced in Chapter 1, the theoretical overview of the book. This is because many of our deepest and most persistent longings are embedded in our sense of sexuality, and primary among these is the dialectical tension that can be experienced between our fear of engulfment and our fear of abandonment. This dilemma arises out of our dual needs for both autonomy and connection. As Mitchell (2002) notes: "It is not that romance necessarily fades over time, but it becomes riskier" (p. 207). Given the dialectical tension between the illusion of security in attachment versus the illusion of the danger of romantic excitation and arousal, Mitchell notes that the fantasy of permanence frequently trumps that of passion.

Still, what can readily become dissociated is that, while we need togetherness, we also need separateness, and we need the latter because it is a precondition of intimate sex. For desire to be charged, for spontaneity to be possible, sex can require a certain element of selfishness versus the presumptive selflessness of love. Perel (2007) notes that desire and egalitarianism are not equal, at least sometimes not in the bedroom, and she further admonishes that there is no love where there is no possibility of hate, since our selfish, sometimes ruthless motives are bound to stub our partner's toes. It's not hard to see how much about sex can become split off, sequestered, and dissociated.

Such sequesterization and dissociation also pertains to the psychological background of our desire, namely, how it was responded to growing up: Was it met with rejection, humiliation, and abandonment, or was it held as important, both recognized and vivified? When it is in the former case, one's background can serve as a huge psycho-social-sexual inhibitor. Partners who come from backgrounds in which desire is seen as an expression of selfishness, where virtue is measured by selflessness, have an especially hard time accepting not only their partner's desire, but also their own. Their articulation of desire, something impossible to completely transcend, is weighted with "doublespeak" and plausible deniability. They are uniquely adept at skewering their partner for his or her selfish needs, while dissociatively denying their own. In this way, they are mired in conflict with a very central human need: agency. In this context, the perversion of agency is especially germane. The remainder of this chapter elaborates on all of the preceding themes, while making it especially clear that the perversion of agency is central to our thinking about the relational turn in psychoanalysis. It is a complicated concept, because, while it initially appears dysfunctional, it can also be crucial in bringing out sequestered self-states, thereby availing them to finally be articulated.

Another tenet of Step Four is that, once a dissociated self-state becomes enacted, it quickly becomes systematized. This means that, while enactments typically begin *asymmetrically* (i.e., regarding some issue vexing one partner more than the other), an *issue-dependent context* of discord,[3] they quickly turn into *symmetrical* enactments by triggering other latent concerns of the initially less invested partner. Rapidly, the couple devolves into a tit-for-tat engagement, and the issues begin to pile on top of one another like football players. At this point, the couple's burgeoning enactment is best conceived of as a system in which they are engaging in processes of mutual inductive identification. In short, the asymmetrical becomes symmetrical when the initial issue provokes an unearthing of other "buried" issues that now take on a kind of mutuality of influence and regulation (or more often dysregulation). The mutual inductive identification entails processes in which each partner begins to attempt (albeit unconsciously) to induce the other to think, feel, and behave in terms of some preset system of "scripts."

These processes entail what Donnel Stern (2013) refers to as the "interpersonalization of dissociation," which manifests in especially obscure implicit communication, wherein the process of the therapy both "gums up and bogs down." However, it is in the playing out of these mini-dramas that the therapist is finally able to find a way to get the couple to play with other possibilities—that is, to improvise, in contrast to rigidly repeating their historical manner of dysfunctional engagement. Of course, this working through usually necessitates the therapist examining her own participation in the three-part system of mutual inductive identification.[4]

Adam and Eloise

"Seizing defeat from the jaws of victory" is well illustrated in the case of Adam and Eloise, a couple locked in over a decade of marital disquietude. Upon their arrival to their first conjoint therapy session, it quickly became apparent that their relationship was in an advanced state of "cancer"—that is, the state of their relationship having a mind of its own was one that appeared frighteningly "terminal." In this manner, they represented the kind of case that has led to my encouraging conjoint therapists to see themselves metaphorically as "oncologists." Embracing this metaphor, I argue, enables us to use whatever we have in our clinical armamentarium in hopes that something might reverse the course of the couple's relational "illness." My metaphor, however, is also meant to help therapists brace themselves for what might not be salvageable, much like oncologists have to, to survive the anguish of treating the frequently terminally ill.

Married over 10 years, Eloise and Adam had two children, an older daughter in her teens (from a previous marriage) and another, 9 years old. Almost as soon as our initial session began, they exhibited little capacity to contain their volatility or to reflect long enough to get very much perspective on their own states, much less that of each other's. As I typically do in Step One, in my first session with them I was able to clarify what appeared to be their massive failings of any attuned responsiveness to one another, along with their engaging in a vicious circle, wherein each one's selfobject needs triggered each other's powerful repetitive transference reactions.

On the surface, their vicious circle engagement was a relatively common one. Eloise felt powerfully insecure and unprotected by Adam, who, by the nature of his work in the entertainment industry, was perpetually caught in "feast or famine" cycles entirely dependent on the availability of his kind of work. He had woefully been caught in an out-of-work cycle for close to a year, though he had a number of potential projects or, as he called them, "irons in the fire."

By contrast, Eloise's high-powered job was much steadier, more of the stable 9-to-5 variety. As such, she had become the primary, stable breadwinner, a position that felt emasculating to Adam. Compounding this, Adam longed for Eloise's encouragement and support for all of the projects he was trying to cultivate. Unfortunately, as money got tighter, both became ever more anxious. In her anxiety, Eloise became prone to both question and criticize Adam's efforts, eventually leading to her stating that she had lost any faith in his "pie-in-the-sky" ventures. Her response to him was the utter antithesis of the quality of mirroring support he hungered for as he suffered the daily slings and arrows of misfortune in which his hoped-for potentials turned into dismal disappointments.

Equally common for couples in such stressful times is that their vicious circle of engagement replicates scripted aspects of their past. For Eloise, Adam had become a character in her lifelong drama that involved having suffered an unreliable father who recurrently would explode over his defeats and lash out at all around him. For Adam, Eloise had become a veritable clone of his intrusive, meddlesome, and perpetually worried mother, who seldom served as any source of comfort or support, instead flooding him with her own anxiety about the world.

My interpretation of the above formulation served to interest them enough to return, though Eloise also muttered about having one foot out the door of both the therapy and the marriage. Still, despite her doubts, she showed up regularly, a point I underscored when Adam would attack her for not being committed to treatment.

For quite a while, our sessions were very heated and very loud. Adam did indeed have a penchant for exploding the moment he sensed any misunderstanding from either Eloise or me. Although Eloise was much quieter and calmer in demeanor and delivery, her nonverbal behavior was saturated with a "rolling her eyes" gesture while also making deep interruptive sighs and, finally, furtively attempting to engage me in eye contact that implicitly conveyed, "See what I have to put up with?!" All of this exemplified the quality of contempt that Gottman (1999) referred to as the "sulfuric acid of love." Given both of their destructive modes of engagement, my work with them required a great deal of affect down-regulating (Wallin, 2007) in an attempt to restore some sense of reflectivity. Once I could get their attention, I often interpreted something to them in a manner that exhibited a kind of "alterego" version of discourse, wherein I would speak for each in the manner of what I heard each saying about themselves and about each other. Of course, I always followed these sequences by checking to see if what I said fit, then modifying it where they made helpful corrections and additions.

The sessions proceeded in the above manner, until Adam and Eloise gradually started to settle down a little bit more each time we met. Their affective tone had calmed somewhat, and they started to get a little more perspective on how each felt misunderstood, let down, and ultimately criticized by the other. It was in this phase that the following session occurred, involving what Adam referred to as the problem of "musical beds."

His tale was rooted in the fact that all four of the members of the household suffered some form of sleeping disorder. Eloise and the eldest daughter could not go to sleep without having a television on. Adam could not go to sleep with it on.

And the youngest simply didn't want to go to sleep at all, requiring a great deal of assistance to do so. Although, with the use of the television, Eloise and the eldest daughter fell asleep almost instantly, in Eloise's case she was easily awakened, especially if Adam came in their bedroom and turned off the TV. Notwithstanding everyone's issues with sleep, the center of the storm appeared to be their problem in dealing with their youngest child, who simply refused to go to sleep unless someone was there to tell her stories to soothe her asleep. (They actually had attempted to allow her to use the TV, like her mother and older sister did, though in her case it served as an endless stimulus that actually kept her awake.)

As we explored this systemic chaos, I asked them for more details about their youngest daughter's sleep issues. They informed me that she had seen sleep specialists for a few years, was placed on medication to help her sleep, though she fought taking it, and pitched a fit unless one of them laid in bed with her until she finally dozed off—this taking typically between 20 and 30 minutes. The huge source of Adam's complaint was that their daughter's falling asleep "drill" fell primarily upon him. This entailed his having to make sure that she took her medication and that he lay in bed with her in the dark, telling her a story. Although Adam did not mind doing this, he also complained that he would then become sleepy, making it difficult for him to complete the couple of hours of work he still needed to do in preparation for the next day.

Their calamity struck me as an opportunity to see to what degree we might be able to create a quality of "thirdness," wherein they could find a common ground that would benefit both of them as well as their daughter. I began asking them detailed questions about her difficulties with sleeping, which gradually turned into us all collaborating in an analysis of some of the dynamics that might be underpinning her sleep anxieties. Over the course of much of the session, we were able to generate a host of hypotheses for which there was considerable corroborative evidence based on things she had told them. For example, commensurate with her age, she had become somewhat preoccupied with questions about death. These seemed to fit with some fears about her own and others' mortality, especially living in a household where blood-curdling screaming was a not uncommon feature of her parents fighting or arguing with her older sister. In addition, she seemed to also suffer from separation anxiety. Although it did not inhibit her daily functioning, such as being school-phobic, separation panic seemed to "awaken" in her precisely as her bedtime approached. Finally, a third element in her aversion to sleeping was her powerful hunger not to "miss out on anything." Hence, for this little girl, sleep was an enemy waging war from all sides.

Our collective engagement in this assessment suddenly made the three of us truly look like a highly functioning therapeutic team for the first time. We were effectively accessing the situation, collaborating about what might be tried, what shouldn't be attempted, and ultimately strategizing the best implementation of our emerging plan of action. The atmosphere was unusually calm and highly cooperative. Both Eloise and Adam were very amenable to my saying that their daughter clearly needed their help with sleep, and that if they could settle into a calming routine her need for their assistance very likely would eventually lessen. Supportive of Adam's grievance that this "drill" fell entirely upon him, Eloise quickly agreed that she too needed to become more available to help. This included making sure their daughter took her medication at the prescribed time, and sticking to a negotiated time-limited routine in which she could only watch 30 minutes of TV before it would have to be turned off. Finally, there would be a routine for when the lights were to go out, along with the disclosure that each parent would be taking turns on specified nights for helping her fall asleep.

I also underscored the importance of the two of them sitting down with their daughter and laying out how the whole bedtime ritual would occur. This we agreed would include creating a checklist of all that had to occur before getting into bed (e.g., brushing her teeth, going to the bathroom, getting a glass of water, and saying her "good nights" to her sister and whichever parent would not be helping her on that particular night—all of these were ploys she would use to get out of bed "just one more time"). We even took up an initial concern of Adam's that their youngest might feel that it was unfair that Mommy and sister got to fall asleep with their TVs on and that she didn't. However, after it was cleared up that the TV kept her up all night instead of putting her to sleep, it was clear that her argument involved a very different circumstance, and therefore it was perfectly justifiable to administer different rules regarding her use of the TV. Both Eloise and Adam seemed very satisfied with our solution, and both also agreed that they needed to be involved together in conveying all of this to her so there would be no "splitting" of them by the daughter saying, "Well, Mommy/Daddy said I could …," countermanding whichever parent was "on duty" that night. I emphasized that a house divided is not a calm house, and that the better the degree to which they could coordinate themselves on this one thing, the more likely solutions to other problems would follow.

Eloise's immediate agreement to all of this seemed to deeply move Adam, who exhibited the most serene and appreciative nonverbal expression I had yet witnessed in our sessions. Wisely, he elaborated that if they could just settle this sleep issue, many of their other issues might also get resolved. For example, their sexual intimacy (or lack thereof), their being able to sleep in the same bed (which was frequently interloped by the youngest when Adam was working late in another room), and their finally being able to turn the corner from being a household full of sleep-deprived individuals to one in which people actually could get the sleep they needed. Indeed, Adam drew a direct line of connection between his lack of sleep and his negativity and vulnerability to temper flare-ups.

Underscoring her new spirit of cooperation, Eloise even acknowledged that she had been slipshod in helping out, and that indeed most of the chores had unfairly fallen on Adam's shoulders, though partly out of her frustration with his not working and her having to be the sole breadwinner for the past year. Now, however, she professed an eagerness to pitch in, and on that point introduced another area that she thought needed their attention regarding their daughter: difficulties getting her up and ready to go to school in a timely fashion.

She stated that to work on this problem also required some cooperation from Adam, because on some of the nights in which he had put their daughter to sleep he too had fallen asleep in her bed. In the morning, when it was time for Eloise (the early riser of the family) to get their daughter ready for school, their little one would pitch a fit, not wanting to leave the warmth of her bed. Furthermore, from what I gathered about her separation anxiety, she was in no hurry to part from whoever was still in bed with her (which could on other occasions be her mother). What happened next, however, exemplifies "seizing defeat from the jaws of victory."

Adam, who had throughout the session sat calmly and very engaged, rose into a perched position on the edge of the sofa and started screaming. He accused Eloise of laying in wait, searching for some way to slam him and to point out what a crappy, good-for-nothing husband and derelict father he was. Eloise was at first "wide-eyed" incredulous, though I could see almost instantly her retreat into her "this is always what happens, no good deed goes unpunished" expression.

As we were now five minutes from the close of the session, I quite assertively asked Adam to calm down. He initially got angry at me, but at my insistence began to report his experience that Eloise was attempting to turn all of this around and blame him for the problems of the family. He then launched into a vitriolic, somewhat paranoid-sounding soliloquy, saying that it was clear that Eloise saw him as a "lazy, good for nothing fuck-up" who she secretly hated.

Seeing little time left on the clock, I forcefully said to Adam that, although I had heard enough to know that at times Eloise may teeter on feeling this way about him, and that in a moment of anger might regrettably say something that seems to support his interpretation, from what I heard—at least in this session—they both were exhibiting an unusual spirit of cooperation. On that basis, Eloise was now extending their collaborative efforts regarding what to do at night, to also include seeking some collaborative effort in the morning. Furthermore, although I couldn't be certain about Eloise's state of mind in that moment (she was being close-lipped), it was clear what Adam's was, which included his belief that he knew better than any of us what Eloise was thinking (clearly a violation of the Step Two principle of perspectival realism, in which each person is authorized to speak his or her mind and discouraged about speaking for their partner unless asked to).

I also pointed out to Adam that he seemed caught in a powerful negative repetitive transference state (not the terms that I used, but the idea behind how I conveyed this in plain English), compelling him to interpret that Eloise was out to get him. I coupled this with an earlier complaint of his from previous sessions, where he claimed that she never asked him for help. Reminding him of this, I pondered—in the form of a question—might it be possible that Eloise is reluctant to ask him for help, if she anticipates a misinterpretation of this kind? Eloise chimed in, "Exactly!" Suddenly, Adam's entire demeanor shifted. He quickly calmed and turned to me and then to his wife and apologized for his misinterpretation and outburst. He also acknowledged that it now made sense why she was "gun shy" around him, which usually looked to him more like she was aloof and superior.

Adam's outburst exemplifies the point that there needn't always be a trigger for a repetitive transference reaction, such as a selfobject failure. Indeed, in this case, much to his incredulity, Eloise turned around rather quickly to see that their daughter needed help and that she had admitted egregiously letting this issue slip through the cracks, thereby being a part of the chaos rather than helping to remedy it. Lastly, she acknowledged that she had unfairly left this whole "sleep detail" for Adam to handle. All of this constituted a clear and unusual "victory" for both Adam and Eloise, making it all the more conspicuous, especially right before the session was over, that Adam had to spoil it.

In subsequent sessions, it came out that Eloise's relative ease of agreement and wish to collaborate frightened Adam. Indeed, getting what he wanted felt very disorganizing to his otherwise predictable though miserable universe of expectations about Eloise's disdain for him, a disdain that was indeed too often in evidence, though one that he also frequently had a part of triggering. Other sequestered material that surfaced in later sessions was that if Eloise got involved in sharing this burden he would lose some of the moral high ground upon which he stood, feeling like the better parent. In the context of Eloise being the breadwinner, Adam had been "bootlegging" a private sense of self-esteem around not only being the best father, but also the better "mother."

Although Adam's outburst seems like an asymmetrical enactment, launched from one side by one person, without my intervention it would have just as easily become a symmetrical one, in which a whole bookcase of grievances that Eloise had towards Adam would have readily come crashing down. Meanwhile, working on the sleeping issue eventually enabled us to uncover a part of Eloise's collusion in the sleeping problem. Clearly, at least in part, it was a means for keeping Adam out of their bed. This was not something she was conscious of; in fact, she was quite dissociated about it. It initially seemed preposterous to her until we could begin to examine, step by step, the implicit payoffs she got from all of their sleep issues. Her required use of the TV, which Adam couldn't abide, kept him out. Her leaving it up to him to attend to their youngest daughter increased the likelihood he would end up falling asleep there and not in their bed. Her "allowing" their daughter to "sneak" into their bed when Adam was still working foreclosed there being any space for him, since, after all, neither of them would dare think of stirring their daughter once she was finally asleep. With all of this evidence, Eloise sheepishly acknowledged how her own ambivalence in her marriage was getting enacted in maintaining versus helping to resolve their multiple household sleep issues.

The case of Adam and Eloise represents something very familiar in couples therapy. The partners' enactments serve many purposes, not the least of which is to manage the sexual tension in their relationship. As Adam noted, a resolution to their "musical bed" problem might perhaps also enable them to tackle other issues in their relationship, one obvious one being their lack of sexual intimacy. It was increasingly apparent that this was an issue that both feared resolving, as it appeared that each had unconsciously projected onto the other what they found gravely lacking in themselves. Though both were quite attractive and fit, they both fretted over feeling unattractive. Eloise, for example, constantly felt that she was too heavy to be sexually appealing, though Adam had no complaints about her weight and indeed professed that he found her alluring. Adam, on the other hand, felt that he was too unsuccessful professionally to be feel fully potent in his masculinity and to therefore allow it to fuel his desire. They privately housed these impressions in ruminations that sounded something like "Adam, you find me too fat to desire me" and "Eloise, you find me professionally impotent and so I am afraid that I will become so in bed as well."

Since these were sequestered as undeclared fantasies, their defensive strategies for avoiding intimacy remained intact and inaccessible to refutation, such as Adam saying something like "Eloise, that's ridiculous, I love your body, you know I hate skinny women!" or her saying, "Adam stop beating up on yourself, you have had some great breaks in your work and some tough ones, but that doesn't mean I am not attracted to you! I know I sometimes am anxious about your work, but in truth, far more than anything it's your temper that scares me away." Absent this kind of intersubjective dialogue and ensuing mutual recognition, the couple remains frozen in highly incorrect though protective fantasies. Meanwhile, it is through the proverbial "onion peeling" of the couple's key complaints that, eventually, sequestered anxieties about their sexuality finally emerge.

Meanwhile, couples mired in backgrounds like Adam and Eloise require considerable work in recognizing dissociated aspects of themselves that undermine their sense of agency or that represent deviations from self-actualization. Often these aspects of self-experiencing are unconscious, and in fact represent aspects of self-states that are in disharmony, ones that manifest from self-states remaining incommunicado from one another. This strategy of keeping these states out of consciousness while another self-state is in ascendancy effectively preserves each from annihilation by the others, thereby conserving certain versions of self, albeit typically at the price of considerable misery.

Thus, Step Four of this model introduces what Bromberg (1998) has noted in many treatments as the wish "to stay the same while changing" (p. 183). Gentile (2001) helps explain this when she writes,

> The birth of agency and desire, inevitably, threatens to betray and to annihilate what has become a lifelong identity and, along with it, the only basis for meaning or purpose in one's life resulting in a devastating loss of identity, overwhelming experience of emptiness, and bewildering crisis of personal meaning.
>
> (p. 644)

Both Gentile (2008) and Bromberg are indicating that the price of change can be too high for many. Generalizing Bromberg's (1998) point to couples therapy, it's as if the partners are saying to each other and to the therapist, "I fully expect you to try to cure me and I am prepared to defeat you. I don't have an illness; I *am* my illness and I won't let you cure me of being who I am" (p. 208).

Perversion of agency

After a number of desired changes in the couple's relationship have occurred, a new threat can arise involving a host of interesting, albeit menacing deviations from personal agency and the fulfillment of self-actualization (i.e., "perversions of agency"; Gentile, 2001) which undermine personal and relational agency. Understandably, some may find the term *perversion* in this case a complicated word choice. Its relevance, however, is that it is currently under reexamination in relational literature as a means of seeking the expression of something developmental that cannot otherwise be expressed. Perversion, as used in the context of couples treatment, can also be seen as an unconscious attempt at experimentation—that is, of trying to find—through means that seemingly deviate from so-called normative behavior—ways of facilitating real personal and relational actualization. Here is a perfect place where the fetishization of some form of lust can be about trying to discover something "other" about oneself through objectifying something about one's partner (Frommer, 2006; Mitchell, 2002; Stein, 2006; Wolff Bernstein, 2006). This principle frequently asserts itself in the potentially playful realm of polymorphous sexual perversity in search of more authentic personal and interpersonal expression, versus versions of perversion that truncate self-actualization and genuine mutual recognition.

Perversion is recognized relationally as pathological when it represents a pact between two people against both their personal growth and intimate connection. In this case, their relationship founders on treating one another as objects, even fetishes, rather than another for whom each seeks deeper awareness of self and other through mutual interpenetration.

Meanwhile, perversion of agency (in the sense that Gentile is using it) applies to deviations in agency that undermine self-actualization. This can surface in both individual treatment and in couples therapy in a menacing manner. Gentile notes an example of this occurs when partners are more devoted to seeking recognition for their victimization than finding their role in what is occurring in their relationship. In the former case, claiming victimization, one seeks exoneration from involvement in his predicament, as well as assigning blame to one's partner. By contrast, in investigating one's agentic role in what occurs, one seeks both recognition and understanding for his part in co-creating their predicament.

Gentile (2001) notes several outcomes of the perversion of agency that ensue when the patient allies himself with the role of the victim, such as: a sense of pseudo-integration derived from an identification with the original aggressor; an adoption of moral superiority through the assignment of uncontestable versions of good and evil, thereby "objectively" determining who is always right and who is always wrong; and "a stifling omnipotence that precludes dependence and vulnerability and the expression of desires that may closely resemble those who had betrayed the patient in some form or another" (p. 20). Notably, these patterns correspond with the discourse of the "doer and the done-to" (Benjamin, 2004) versus what the partners actually meant.

In the tradition resembling object relations thinking (Dicks, 1964; Scharff, 1992; Scharff & Scharff, 1991, 1992; Slipp, 1984), Gentile notes that perversions of agency are implemented through mechanisms quite similar to splitting, the unconscious division of one's self-experience into different parts while disavowing some parts of self and attributing them to another. In the case of couples treatment, this involves partners disavowing aspects of themselves and attributing them to each other. In this manner, marital partners may preserve their sense of moral superiority. There is, nevertheless, a terrible price paid in terms of the loss of personal freedom, a sense of expansiveness, and of an appreciation of the creative multiplicity in each one's life as well as the relationship.

Gentile notes that individuals seeking recognition for their role as a victim can actually have aversive reactions to others recognizing their subjectivity. This entails a tragic irony in that such individuals end up perpetuating their own psychic annihilation as well as that of their partner. Compounding this tragedy is that, by disavowing their own subjective frailties as well as those of the others, they undermine an essential precondition to surrender into mutual recognition, as well as to renegotiate how to address one another's needs. Only through such responsibility taking (the subject of Steps Five and Six) can coming alive in the context of one another be a possibility.

Caren and Joe

Caren and Joe were a couple that puzzled me the moment I first met them. They were, as I would eventually discover, exemplary of Goethe's admonition, "We are appalled by our sins when we discover them in others." As documented in Step One, typically I have some formulation that I can offer the couple that identifies how their rupture constitutes a vicious circle pattern in which each one's selfobject longings triggers each other's repetitive transference states. With Caren and Joe, I was stumped and was concerned that they might elect to not return. Our second session was a little bit clearer but not much, though apparently sufficient to make them want to continue treatment. Primary to their complaint was Caren's conviction that her husband Joe was having a long-distance affair with a former girlfriend, Sheila. Caren produced suggestive email transcripts between them, along with documentation of their 2:30 a.m. long-distance phone conversations found on his cell phone bill.

Joe adamantly protested, saying that Sheila was only a friend and someone with whom he felt comfortable confiding, given the complete breakdown in his and Caren's communication. Still, nothing he said would calm Caren. Instead, she became increasingly prone to scream her accusations at him and get infuriated with me for not recognizing the obvious—that Joe was having an affair! Over time, I was able to reframe Caren's accusation in a manner that at least partially met both of their needs. I suggested that Joe was indeed having something of an "affair of the soul" that understandably would give rise to Caren's ire, but not one of the carnal nature that made her apoplectic. Joe agreed to this, and reiterated that in part it was a symptom of his despair about their lack of emotional intimacy, to which Caren had to agree.

Though Caren's explosions mitigated, she shifted to bringing up a wide range of complaints about Joe: about how absent he was with the children, about how lazy he was regarding housework, and about how out of shape he had become. One disparaging item followed another until suddenly one day Caren announced that her ire probably didn't have anything really to do with Joe. She concluded that it had more to do with a host of dissatisfactions with herself, both in her work and in virtually every aspect of her life, with the exception of her relationship with her kids. On this note, she said, she believed that it was time for her to really take seriously getting into individual treatment. Although she had requested an individual therapy referral before, which I provided her, it unfortunately did not work out. Given our history of work, she was convinced that I was the therapist she could most trust and therefore asked, in Joe's presence, if I would start to work with her individually. Frankly, her proposal made great sense to me. Meanwhile, Joe was thrilled by the proposition, and also requested an individual referral for himself. We further agreed to suspend our conjoint sessions, although with the proviso that if an emergency arose we could temporarily reconvene.

During our first session of individual psychotherapy, Caren confessed that in fact it was she who had been carrying on an affair with a family friend and colleague for several years. She went to great lengths to describe her rendezvous with her lover, including how she would arrange for them to have a secret hotel room in another part of the hotel they were staying in when their families traveled together.

Caren became very animated in telling me about her trysts with both men and women, clearly identifying with a profound sense of sexual power, which she used to her benefit wherever she needed to. It became apparent that she had engaged in a kind of "turning the tables" strategy, claiming victimhood when in fact she was the perpetrator. This corresponds closely to Gentile's connection of the "perversion of agency" with an "identification with the aggressor." Suddenly, what had been perpetually befuddling became instantly clear. Caren's intrasubjective world was fraught with splits, marked from being raised in a fundamentalist Christian family, one which saw sex as sinful but also powerfully arousing, testimony to which was that her uncles and cousins started having sex with her once she hit early puberty at age 12 (though she claimed that she looked much older and sexually mature than her youthful age).

Step Four of this model can be seen as involving something of a conservation of self model, not unlike that discussed in object relations theory.[5] According to this theory, we are driven to reenact past relational styles, in pursuit of the security of the familiarity of a known mode of relating. This line of thinking is supported by a host of adages, such as "better the devil you know than the devil you don't." Of the many considerations under Step Four, an especially critical one is for each partner to learn to "own" their own dysfunctional style of reenacting the past, especially so that they can find alternative ways of staying true to themselves in the face of having to initially disappoint one another.

For example, it is clear that Caren's fundamentalist background, as well as her multiple episodes of trauma, led to some profound splits within her that could be aptly described as highly incompatible self-states. One state condemned sex as evil, this becoming a self-state that she attempted to vanquish from herself by projecting it onto her husband. Another self-state embodied a tremendous sense of sexual power—a mechanism through which she could exercise control of others. On one occasion, she stated that if she so chose to she could come over and give me a blow job that would be so good I would be helpless to resist it. Noting a visible impact on me, she swiftly changed the subject. Though I did not worry that I would yield to her provocation, I must admit that I must have looked like a deer caught in headlights, since Caren was not only not without considerable sexual allure, she had on several occasions graphically commented on her seven-minute blow job that no man could outlast, exhibiting at least one self-state that could feel hugely empowering in relationship to a host of other vulnerable, powerless ones. For example, during a routine gynecological exam, her doctor had intercourse with her, with neither of them commenting on it. When it turned out that she became pregnant, she had him give her an abortion, again without either of them commenting on the source of her pregnancy.

Meanwhile, on the assumption that Joe was also conflicted sexually, a not unreasonable assumption from what she knew of his history, Caren conveniently attributed her own sexual "straying" behavior to him, and made the accusation stick with her hard evidence of his turning his attention to Sheila. Thus, Joe became Caren's "vessel" into which she could project her guilt and self-recrimination, ridding herself of those prohibitions. Having done this, she could then, much like her relatives, ruthlessly have her way with whomever she chose to, for whatever gain she might achieve.

Under these circumstances, no movement could be made in the couples treatment, hence the fortuitous move to individual therapy. Here at least we could begin to take up Caren's dissociated self-states and develop an intersubjective relationship to each (Bromberg, 1998), from which we could finally come to terms with what sex meant to her. Eventually, this enabled her to feel both powerful and agentic without having to employ sex in the manner upon which she had historically relied. It also created room for her to finally grieve the loss of her childhood, a childhood scarred by the sexual transgressions of her fundamentalist kin. Lastly, it enabled her to be open to a greater intimate connection with her husband, the kind that he had had to find elsewhere in his connection to Sheila.

Dissociative processes

Therapists often have to grapple with their own potential dread of defeat in the face of a couple's tenacious resistance. However, it can help to reframe resistance as a kind of agency in its own right, as an attempt to avoid the pathological accommodation to being therapeutically "appropriate" in a manner that risks inauthenticity. Hence, each partner's resistance needs to be openly welcomed and honored by the therapist as a most natural reaction to a threat of impending change—change often interpreted as suiting the needs of the therapist, or their partner, or both. This happens routinely when the therapist is in a *conjunctive* countertransference position with one partner and a *disjunctive* position with the so-called "resistant" patient.

This phenomenon is especially common when patients report histories of trauma, for, as Bromberg (1998) notes, "The anticipation of misfortune is the principal way the traumatized protects himself from future trauma, the promise of 'cure' makes the process of attempting to 'free' a traumatized patient from the expectation of misfortune probably the most complex treatment issue a psychoanalyst faces" (pp. 231–232). This form of omnipotent fantasy—to prophylactically imagine trauma before its reoccurrence—is one of the fundamental designs of the human mind (Schore, 1994; Siegel, 1999; Van der Kolk, 1996, 2007). In such states, we gear ourselves to imagine the worst, to live in that expectation, and sadly to inadvertently recreate it through self-fulfilling prophecy; for example, if I insist over and over and over that you are angry at me, even when this is initially not remotely true, you will likely become angry in response to my insisting on my version of your reality over yours.

Modes of resistance often involve processes of dissociation. As Bromberg notes, "dissociation is not inherently pathological, but it can become so" (p. 244). We all utilize dissociation to great effect to get through our day by filtering out a perpetual bombardment of anxiety-provoking images. One only has to listen to an obsessive-compulsive patient's endless perseverations about nuclear war, or of the imminent threat of a natural disaster or deaths from simple household accidents, or the invisible yet highly threatening world of germs, to grasp how constantly imagining danger informs us far more than we ever realize.

But dissociation can be menacing to oneself and to one's relationship when one has little or no access to one's dissociated self-states. What is especially confusing in couples' relationships as well as in couples therapy is that seemingly little things can trigger big reactions. This corresponds to the "principle of criticality" or "tipping point," discussed in terms of the nonlinear dynamic systems of complexity theory. This is because self-state changes can be triggered by shifts in affect states, as well as by physiological changes. All such shifts create contextual shifts in what any issue may mean to the partners. And, any of these can lend to unpredictable "tipping points" of dysregulation in the relationship. Of particular irony is that self-state changes usually manifest in affective expressions that may be readily noticeable to others, though often not noticed by the one in whom they are occurring. This is especially true when internal self-state shifts involve dissociation, lending to the rise of something in oneself, the expression of which is noticed and reacted to by one's partner before it is noticed by oneself. Although others are frequently able to more appropriately read our affect than we ourselves are, equally problematic is their potential incorrect or inappropriate interpretation about the content of our mind.

Still, it is remarkable to me how often a partner will interrupt him- or herself mid-sentence, exclaiming "What?!"—meaning they have detected some shift in their partner's affective expression before they have even completed what it is they intended to say. In essence, they have already assumed their partner's imminent counterattack before they have completed their own point. This immediately generates a self-fulfilling prophesy, since their partner, not having the benefit of their completed thought, is already being presumed to be antagonistic.

Of course, based upon some historical exchanges, a partner may have good reason to imagine their spouse's forthcoming objection. And, even when such objection has been linked to some implicit nonverbal expression in the past, they become highly prone to imagining only one outcome can be expected, rather than being open to seeing what else may occur. This is a perfect example of where the partners are so locked in their mutually inductive scripts, they induce one another to behave in static and repetitive modes instead of being able to improvise with new possibilities. This also foreshortens any opportunity to explore each one's initial intentions versus petrified, presumed ones.

In this manner, emotionally reactive couples have to be down-regulated by the therapist, who can then facilitate a more thorough examination of what each intends to say and what they are preemptively cutting off. Such intervention is essential to creating a communication system ensconced in the reflectiveness of mentalization and not locked in reactivity.

In a similar manner to what I am positing, Shimmerlik (2008) argues that so much of what must be attended to in couples therapy is often not in *what* is spoken, but in *how* it is spoken. She underscores that how things are spoken is embodied in implicit processes, ones occurring simultaneously with the explicit but frequently very different from it. She notes that these processes pertain to how we are able to do things, to carry out the routine procedures of our daily lives, without ever making them explicit—that is, without ever moving them into the realm of the symbolic or the realm of words, wherein we can reflect upon them, analyze them, and think about their meaning.

Referencing the Boston Change Process Study Group (BCPSG, 2002; Stern, 2004; Stern et al., 1998), Shimmerlik notes that much of our daily relating with one another functions implicitly, not explicitly. The BCPSG refers to this as "implicit relational knowing." It encompasses all the ways we implicitly and procedurally "know" how to relate to one another. This involves ways that remain non-declarative, unwitting, non-conscious, but ironically are there for public display. Indeed, part of our vulnerability to shame in life is when we finally catch glimpses of how others see us implicitly relating to the world in ways totally hidden to ourselves!

Shimmerlik fruitfully weds implicit relational knowing with the "dance" of marriage, how each partner's mode of implicit relational knowing intertwines with the other's in ways that over time become patterned much like a two-person dance routine. These implicit procedures for relating involve non-conscious "systems of expectations," along with ways of reacting to what is inferred of the other's intentions (D. N. Stern, 2004, 2007), often in manners that are wildly disparate from what their intentions may be. But, notwithstanding the maddening impact of the mutual negation that arises from mutually misconstrued intentions, there is another level on which the couple interacts, and that is seen in "mutually dissociative" (D. N. Stern, 2007) enactments. Enactments, reflective of implicit recursive interaction sequences, are ones that to the outside observer suggest thematically organized convergences arising from each partner's "implicit memory system." Experientially to the couple, they can feel like the relationship is driving the partners instead of their driving it. This is the focal point of Shimmerlik's argument, which she illustrates in her work with Bob and Debbie.

Bob and Debbie

Shimmerlik describes Debbie and Bob as highly accomplished professionals that are both on their second marriage. Bob "presents as distant and disconnected" (2008, p. 372) with limited capacity for self-reflection. By contrast, Debbie is easily aroused and becomes "highly emotional and extremely reactive" (p. 372) to feeling misunderstood. Still, stepping back and viewing the couple as a system having a mind of its own, Shimmerlik notices that Debbie gives Bob virtually no time or space to become reflective—something he would need protected for any self-reflection to occur.

Shimmerlik writes:

> [W]hat I witnessed was a highly patterned, mutually constructed, inter-active affective sequence, carried out through the implicit or enactive domain, in which Debbie is highly attuned to Bob's pain and Bob in some ways counts on her to divert him, enabling him not to experience his pain and allowing her to experience her pain via him. He complains of her intense reactivity but feels safer having her express feelings to which he has limited access and which make him feel out of control. On the other hand, she becomes extremely anxious when he exposes his vulnerability in any way.
>
> (p. 374)

What is so compelling about the picture Shimmerlik paints is how much implicit processes can be at odds with explicit ones. In introducing the implicit and explicit, Shimmerlik is bringing refined language to what has for decades been discussed as "incongruent communication," "double binds," "mystification," "crunches," and "relational knots" (Pizer, 2003; Ringstrom, 1998a, 1998b, 1998c, 2003; Slavin & Kriegman, 1998a, 1998b, 1998c). In short, where there are multiple levels of communication going on all at once, contradictions can loom on every horizon, both within and between the participants.

As Shimmerlik notes, the contradictions in levels of the implicit and explicit is certainly further complicated by multiple self-state theory (Bromberg, 1998, 2006; Davies, 1998, 2004, 2005; D. N. Stern, 1997, 2007). Surely, marital part-ners are powerfully challenged by what Bromberg (1998) poses as our human problem of attempting "to feel like one, while being many." Dissociated multiple-self-states result in enactments through which the implicit relational process of the couple orchestrates a dance of collusions that undermine what it is that they ostensibly wish for from one another. For example, Debbie wishes for a more vulnerable, more emotionally reflective and disclosing husband, but the moment he starts to venture into becoming this, Debbie commandeers his emotions and takes them on as her own.

Meanwhile, I use mutual inductive identification in an attempt to illustrate how mutually dissociative processes can arise.[6] These processes involve each participant inducing the other to take up a part of their agenda that they cannot see, tolerate, or recognize. Clearly, these inductive processes are much more prominent in the implicit than in the explicit domains of communicating.[7] Mutual inductive identification becomes the mini-dramas involving inducing engagement with one's partner and sometimes the therapist as well. The therapist's task, as will be elaborated upon in Steps Five and Six, is to give "directorial stage notes," if you will, to interpret what is enfolding in the drama between the partners, a drama that occasionally involves the therapist as well.[8]

It is important to recognize that these episodes of mutual inductive identification emanate from and reflect issue-dependent contexts—that is, a particular issue that arises in a particular context. As noted in an earlier chapter, if the issue of money is conflictual for one partner while sex is not, and the opposite is the case for the other partner, issues involving sex and money will trigger each partner quite differently. In this manner, it is their particular thematic perspectives on a given issue that initially contextualize their subsequent responses, and notably, their contextualizing perspectives may be quite askew, though this (if anything) tends to over-stimulate reactivity. Still, as already noted, the asymmetrical beginning of any issue rapidly becomes symmetrical (otherwise there wouldn't be a fight, merely a misunderstanding that is quickly rectified). Once the enactment goes symmetrical, each partner begins to anxiously anticipate (à la their repetitive transference "scripts") what the other's presumed reaction is going to be. All the more vexing is that this process begins on the implicit nonverbal register, leading to plausible deniability of meanings ("I didn't say that!"), which then spills rapidly into processes of mutual inductive identification.

Since issue-dependent contexts trigger different self-states in each of the partners, the therapist must become facile in relating to the variety of self-states emanating from each. The work of the conjoint therapist adopting these principles is less about producing some form of overall self-integration within each partner than it is addressing the various parts of each partner's sense of self. Bromberg (1998) notes that this is as much about "a linking of opposing set narratives held by different states of consciousness that have been dissociatively inaccessible to an experience of internal conflict" (p. 256). He continues: "Psychological 'integration' does not lead to a single 'really you' or 'true self,' it is the ability to stand in the spaces between realities without losing any of them, the capacity to *feel like oneself while being many*" (p. 256, italics in original). By making an intersubjective connection with each of the isolated self-states of both partners, the conjoint therapist begins demonstrating bridges among the isolated states within each partner, as well as between such states as they manifest between the partners.

This becomes critical in demonstrating the multiplicity of states each partner may enter and exit, as well as mitigating arguments over either one's seeming hypocrisy. It normalizes the experience that we can present many different faces, which can be as useful and exciting as it can be confusing and aggravating. As Gentile (2001) notes:

> It is in the capacity for multiplicity and its transitional experience and intersubjectivity that the analyst offers and the patient discovers a space for negotiation and an end to war, space in which analyst and patient may find relative harmony together and a means by which a patient's self-experience may find relative harmony amongst its conflicting, split, or dissociated aspects.
>
> (p. 647)

Bringing to each partner's attention so much unformulated experience (Stern, 1997) compels them to examine how they define and employ their own sense of agency as well as deviations from it. Enabling the partners to recognize how they are doing this can be especially crucial, and the primary place for discovering this is in facilitating their recognition of their enactments. As Bromberg (1998) notes:

> The process of enactment ... often occurs in a dissociated self-state that is designed to communicate the existence of the "truth" that the patient is experiencing about ... [their partner] and that cannot be thought or said within the context of the self-other representation that the relationship is based on at the moment.
>
> (p. 182)

In this manner, the therapist must listen closely to what each partner has at stake in an issue, and be able to point out and interpret to each one how aspects of their historical backgrounds (both developmentally and from the history of the relationship) underpin the transferential meanings of each one's engagement in their argument. The task at hand, then, is to help elevate each partner's curiosity as to what characters they are each reenacting from their personal dramas, as well as what characters they are recruiting each other to be.

Improvisational responses to mutual inductive identification

Engaging enactments is about as easy as disentangling fishing line, which as every fisherman knows can be truly daunting if not sometimes impossible. Likewise, when in frustration therapists "tug" on the loose threads of an enactment, at times involving some off-the-mark question or ham-handed interpretation, they usually tighten the knot in which the couple finds themself bound. Thus, whether engaged in an enactment or in between such engagements, I prefer a more playful method of gently "pulling here and there," attempting to loosen the tangle we are all to some extent co-creating—that is, to look for loose ends (i.e., new possibilities) while looking for what also gets stirred up next. Still, this requires coming to terms with my own involvement in a couple's enactment.

These ideas emanate from an evolution in psychoanalytic thought in the twenty-first century, including the promotion of an improvisatory way of imagining psychoanalytic treatment. Whereas the more traditional psychoanalytic mode of practice involved "preparation for interpretation," the historical *sine qua non* of psychoanalysis, followed by a "second force" of emphasis, "preparation for empathic attunement," contemporary psychoanalytic theory introduces a "third force" involving the place of "collaboration and negotiation."

Collaboration and negotiation emerges from an improvisational mode of engagement wherein both analysand and analyst are "playing-off-of-and-with" unconscious material emergent from within each. This material embodies the dynamics of transference and countertransference, elaborating how each participant contributes in a manner that is hopefully opening up new possibilities, while inevitably reckoning with how psychoanalytic process also gets constrained. As stated throughout this chapter, this latter pattern emerges in enactments, which thereafter set the stage for even deeper investigation of implicit memory systems.

An improvisatory method also makes psychoanalysis much more approachable to patients of all kinds while still preserving the essential values of our psychoanalytic venture. These include the illumination of both unconscious affective and symbolic meaning. Emanuel (2011) proves the enormous flexibility of working improvisationally in her working psychoanalytically with autistic patients, a population not typically seen as amenable to psychoanalytic treatment, where behavior socialization treatment typically rules the day. Emanuel captures something of the improvisatory that speaks to work with patients in general and quite specifically couples:

> Like in theatre or music, improvisation is a method of playing off of and with another person's material and occurs in psychoanalysis when we are playful with our patients. Affect is charged, the back and forth feeling occurs dramatically and rapidly, the experience privileges feeling before thinking, often the content is funny, but equally often it is deadly serious. The result of this type of work is to bring implicit material into the room, with greater knowledge of the patient's unconscious mind and enhanced recognition of self and other that results. To the extent that improvisation is a mode of therapeutic action that quickly and potently fosters emotional engagement with another person, it is helpful in pulling autistics into the affective aspect of relating to another person, helping them expand their repertoire from their preferred thinking state to one charged with previously unexpressed feeling and other implicit material. The improvisational

sensibility works particularly well in the groups I run for young adults with autism, where multiple individuals play off of and with each other, creating an ambiance of deep connection, meaning, and intimacy among the players.

(p. 27)

My approach to working improvisationally in both individual and couples psychotherapies stems from an understanding of field theory (Stern, 2013), where the fundamental question hovering over every treatment regards the relative degree of playfulness available within each intrasubjectively and intersubjectively constituted field versus the truncation, annihilation, and constraint of possibility. My improvisatory model concerns modes of interpersonal engagement that involve four modes divided into two pairings. The *first pairing* involves how the quotidian discourse of everyday human relationships can devolve into a kind of devitalized "scripted-ness," in contrast to what I refer to as the more spontaneous co-creativity of "i"mprovisation. The *second pairing* involves the phenomenon of mutual inductive identification (including the imminent threat of impasse), in contrast to what I refer to as "I"mprovisation.[9]

The first pairing involves the so-called scripted-ness[10] of everyday discourse in contrast with the creativity of a kind of everyday "i"mprovisational engagement, though we rarely are aware of these shifts, for as Stern (2013) notes we can't know the field directly. Still, we eventually derive some sense of them in terms of what feels implicitly permissible and what doesn't, since interpersonal systems tend to fall into fixed relational patterns of behaving. These processes go pretty much unnoticed, are pretty much unremarkable and, in a word, "natural." Stern declares that "As one kind of relatedness becomes natural (say, friendliness), other kinds of relatedness (say, irritability) fall into the background and feel less comfortable, easy, or natural to create in this environment, or are even actively avoided, sometimes with unconscious purpose (i.e., defensive intentions)".

This so-called "natural world," however, tends to become repetitive and predictable, and as such can also readily become stultifying because it elides the potential discourse of co-creativity, "i"mprovisation. "i"mprovisation in couples therapy is emblematic of moments in which two participants are readily playing-off-of-and-with one another's ideas and feelings. It exemplifies what Stern refers to as a quality of "relational freedom" in the field. Periodically, however, maybe even quite frequently, we begin to detect a lack of this freedom. For Stern, this detection comes to him in terms of a sense of "chafing," a kind of almost subliminal level irritation. Things start to feel kind of static, kind of boring. The sensation of chafing is an especially important means for sensing something constricting the field because, as noted earlier, it is exceedingly hard to ever know the field directly. What is at stake is the degree of relational freedom in the field versus relational inhibition, or what Marcia Steinberg (personal communication) refers to as "relational constipation." Our sense of those irritating, chafing, constipatingly bloated episodes in both life and in treatment frequently accompanies a quality of anxiety-binding dialogue taking over the discourse. Whether this comes into evidence in our consulting rooms or couples' bedrooms, we begin to see the undermining of the co-creativity of being "i"mprovisational—that is, how partners and therapist undermine potentially creative new possibilities, including a kind of play that leads to the development of the "relational unconscious."

Let us not forget, however, that it is the humdrum of daily discourse that ironically makes us feel safe, insofar as it can be anxiety-binding for both participants, though Mitchell questions: Isn't this sense of safety often a kind of self-deceiving illusion? Might it not be an attempt to evade the riskier territory of the unknown, something especially anxiety-provoking in some sexual couplings? Creativity, after all, introduces the new, the unfamiliar, the unknown, and, for many, that is a formula for high anxiety! However, let us also not forget that ultimately this kind of humdrum discourse backfires because of its pervasive whiff of inauthenticity, which ultimately leads to a kind of deadening of affect and vitality that Gabbard and Ogden (2009) and Stern (2004) have all described so eloquently.

From a countertransference point of view, this humdrum discourse can correspond to analysts beginning to feel entrapped. They begin noticing that their analytic dialogue has become mired in repetitive stories that undermine potentially profoundly rich and creative moments in psychoanalytic process.

Returning to the truncation of relational freedom in the field—the degree to which the field becomes dominated by a subliminal sense of something needing to be avoided[11] —we are discerning that something is amiss, although it is usually something only discernible in the rearview mirror. What we are starting to sense, however, is what becomes structured in terms of the processes of mutual inductive identification. What is most important from a field theory standpoint is that episodes of mutual inductive identification, depending on how they are dealt with, become important precursors to the more dramatically mutative moments of "I"mprovisation.[12]

Bearing in mind all three therapeutic participants' vulnerability to the anxiety-producing vicissitudes of the unknown, the idea of mutual inductive identification becomes a powerful way of describing a rupture in the field, one that is undetectable consciously, at least initially— until it erupts. Nevertheless, it is also one that is there to be sensed by all parties. In relation to the overall topic of improvisation, we might say that it is actually the very play of the improvisatory that potentially triggers an episode of mutual inductive identification. This can make perfect sense seen in relation to the parties' fear of the unknown that looms large in the evolving dimension of the treatment, an evolution that their play is fomenting.

Here's how that might look. The therapeutic system is engaging on the level of co-creative play of "i"mprovisation. Eventually, one (or more) of the parties starts to feel vulnerable and becomes anxious, even though they may not yet be particularly conscious of feeling so. Nevertheless, something in their play leads to feelings of being "too close," "crossing boundaries," inciting "incest taboos," stirring up conflictual feelings between multiple self-states, inciting fears of abandonment, triggering yet disclosed associations to trauma, and/or yet formulated identifications … The list of possible triggers is endless.

139

However, when anxiety is triggered in someone, the unconscious adaptation for the other is to revert to familiar (albeit highly unconscious) modes of "scripting"— *inducing* the other(s) into "role identifications" with "characters" that are part and parcel of some self-other relational matrix. Once the treatment system enters a state of mutual inductive identification, each participant has entered their respective co-created prison cells and are now in "lockdown." Their "get out of jail card" entails the event of "I"mprovisation.

"I"mprovisation often captures more the spirit of what I have referred to as "improvisational moments" (Ringstrom, 2007a, 2007b). This mode of "I"mprovisation entails Stern's (1997) "breaking the grip of the field," Mitchell's "outbursts," Bromberg's (2006) "safe surprises," and the BCPSG's and Stern's ideas regarding "moments of meeting." It embodies more of a high risk, high gain quality (Gabbard, personal communication; Knoblauch, 2001), but is seasoned with the potential for restoration of *yes/and* recognition embodied in playing-off-of-and-with what is implicitly arising between the partners.[13]

It is in these moments that restoring an overall improvisatory stance entails a number of implicit steps. Often, the first step is for the analyst to engage in a kind of "private" improvisational state of reflectivity, a state of reverie (Ogden, 1994; Ringstrom, 2001a). This might require the analyst to ask herself, "What is it that is getting induced in me that speaks to some dissociated aspect of the patient's experience, and how is this giving rise to my dissociation?"—that is, "What character am I becoming in my patient's drama?" Such reverie must then include, "And, how am I unwittingly [dissociatively] inducing my patient to become a 'cooperative' agent, a character in my drama—often likely the kind of patient I feel more comfortable working with?" Playing with the mutually emerging inductions can become a source for releasing the dyad from the stranglehold of the field, as well as opening possibilities on which it is otherwise rapidly foreclosing.

Another step to restoring improvisation frequently entails a kind of "meta-communication" (Pizer, 2003; Ringstrom, 2003) about the therapeutic system's process. It can involve the therapist noting that the way that she is trying to be helpful is actually exacerbating the patients' experience of feeling harmed. In this moment, the analyst is acknowledging something explicitly, but more importantly she is also indicating implicitly that she too is in the proverbial hot tub. *Often such a meta-communication begins by noting that both parties seem to have lost their sense of play.* Commenting on their mutuality of loss helps mitigate shaming or blaming the patient for the analytic quagmire. What is potentially extraordinarily healing in this moment is the acknowledgment that whatever shame and blame there is that is dominating and therefore constraining the field of creativity is spread across the broad shoulders of all of the participants, and needn't be seen as a weight borne by any one of them alone. This shift in the field ultimately leads to inviting the patient to jointly imagine how the therapy might proceed differently, as well as illuminating in what manner both parties came to feel constrained.

Thus, when I use the term *mutual inductive identification*, I am attempting to illustrate how mutually dissociative processes arise, resulting in each participant inducing the other to take up a part of their agenda that they can neither tolerate nor recognize. Clearly, these inductive processes are much more prominent in the implicit than in the explicit domains of communicating. As a process, mutual inductive identification illuminates the kind of recursive implicit modes of relating that Shimmerlik is illustrating in her work with Bob and Debbie.

The paradox in working with a couple like Bob and Debbie is that each is inducing the other into keeping them safe from feeling something about themselves, although it's obvious that their explosive engagement means they are being affectively reactive. As so frequently happens, however, their implicit strategy backfires horribly, since it is at odds with other ostensible wishes for how each wants the other to be (i.e., more open to the emotional world they are co-creating). As such, their agendas, as stated in the explicit realm of communication, egregiously conflict with their implicit ones. As a result, their implicit enactments undermine their explicit agendas. Of course, what happens next is that both end up feeling negated in some form or another. In short, the treatment bogs down and gums up. However, as Shimmerlik notes, it is in the investigation of the enactment (mutual inductive identification) that the couple can come to see their joint participation in their calamity.

Moving into this "I"mprovisational mode involves the emerging realization that the capacity to play has been somehow lost in the treatment system.[14] I say *system*, because what is always happening in analytic treatments (both individual and couples) is something of an ineffable exchange of the implicit mixed with the explicit, the non-symbolic co-mingling with the symbolic. Furthermore, it's often very hard—maybe sometimes impossible—to disentangle these levels of discourse, not to mention the risks involved in pointing out these contradictions, since doing so may inadvertently shame participants. None of these difficulties, however, prevent our detection that play has become enjoined, raising the questions: When and where in our process did it begin to stop? Did the derailment occur in the patients' process? In the therapist's? In between both? These questions then give rise to others, such as: Who had something greater at stake in some manner than the others, and how did the others so quickly get recruited in a manner wherein they too are now engaging in their versions of mutual inductive identification? I hope that it is apparent that discerning with whom the derailment first occurred (which is frankly often indiscernible) isn't about who laid the eggs or who is to blame, but merely to attempt to track where "fault lines" of vulnerability exist in any and all of the participants, so that scripted patterns of derailed self-actualization can more readily be discerned, as well as patterns of mutual negation and negative thirdness, which undermine the relationship's potential for having a more co-creative mind of its own.

Of course, any preliminary answer to these questions must be held very lightly, because, no matter where constraints may seem to first appear, they tend to be distributed throughout the therapeutic system (Coburn, 2002, 2006). For example, in tackling Debbie's rigid style of taking over Bob's feelings, constraints from all parts of the system soon revealed themselves. What began as seeming more like

Debbie's "issue" slowly emerged as tying into those of Shimmerlik's and Bob's, as well. So, what to do?

Among the many possibilities for how to restore or recreate a sense of play for me to address, here are a few.[15] The analyst might point out that the play (the collaborative process between all of them) seemed to have become constrained, and then ask the patient(s) to help her investigate why. This is, in essence, what Shimmerlik invited Bob and Debbie to do with her. This could be an entry into a form of meta-communication (how each participants' versions of transference have become mutually negating); we all feel "damned if we do and damned if we don't" (Ringstrom, 1998a, 1998b). It may entail some self-disclosure of what is constraining the analyst, as in the illustration of my countertransference disclosure in Step Two in the case of Sally and Dan. It may entail finding a way to surrender versus submit—a topic elaborated upon in Steps Five and Six (see Benjamin, 2004; Ghent, 1990).

Mostly, however, I think it requires some faith in play in psychotherapy. This then entails beginning to experiment with ways in which the constricted scripted-ness between (and within) each can be "rewritten." In effect, in Shimmerlik's work with Bob and Debbie, all three were mutually inducing each other into familiar roles vis-à-vis one another that corresponded with a kind of reaction to a group mutual dissociative process that had to be enacted, to then be investigated.

Shimmerlik notes that for a while such defensive, non-conscious collusiveness is actually necessary. She notes that there is a great deal happening between the therapist and the couple that remains unknowable until the moment that it is happening. So, for example, it required a number of months of her working with Bob and Debbie to understand their primary organizing patterns.

What I suspect did evolve over time, especially given the imagination of a therapist like Shimmerlik, is that her own creativity may have begun to feel a tad dulled, a bit constrained and scripted, sort of patterned, like a mini-drama in which mutual character assignments were going on and that all her efforts at improvising began to feel like she couldn't! This is actually a fruitful awakening, one that really prospectively moves the couple along, because it brings into the crosshairs the inchoate ineffability of the mutually dissociated implicit communications which were not yet available for explication. I submit, along with Slavin and Kriegman (1998a, 1998b), that it is at this juncture that the analyst too must change. That change emerges in doing something counter to the scripts one is co-participating in enacting, but also doing something that stems from them.

Ultimately, Shimmerlik's message to both Debbie and Bob was wise and clear. Enactments are inevitable, necessary, and a vital source of study for the uncovering of the implicit in a relationship and making it available for explication. It is unlikely that the couples therapist, or individual therapist for that matter, can escape them. Indeed, trying too hard may only press the implicit into deeper "hiding"—sort of over-compensating for what is missing through efforts at exquisite empathic attunement to what appears more accessible to explication. As such, enactments should be welcomed as expanding the dimensions of the play space of therapy, not to mention creating room for many new potential "playmates."

Summary

As the saying goes, you can't always get what you want, but you have to keep trying if you ever want to succeed. Couples benefiting from the wisdom of this saying recognize that, indeed, you can't always get all the selfobject provisions you want from your partner, because quite often your own split-off, unconscious, self-centered needs preclude this. However, couples can learn that frequently (though not always) they can get what they really need, especially if they are willing to try to understand their dissociated self-states and begin to reconcile conflicts between them, to discover what they need.

Learning this, however, often requires better understanding of oneself and one's partner suddenly "seizing defeat from the jaws of victory"—that is, either of them undermining their own progress by engaging in enactments reflective of dissociated self-states that remain in isolation from one another. It is then imperative that each of these is engaged by the therapist, and where they cannot be engaged explicitly, they have to be enacted implicitly. Such dissociated self-states often also reflect perversions of agency (Gentile, 2001), deviations from each partner's personal agency. Until this is disclosed, this leads to their attributing aspects of their own existential responsibility to the other. Learning to take back one's projections, while recognizing that they are one's own, is not only potentially liberating, it can also cultivate a greater sense of safety in the relationship as it mitigates how projections can appear so frightening. The next chapter, Step Five, takes up exactly how this is done in a manner that increases each partner's sense of self-reflexivity—most importantly, in the presence of the other—a phenomenon that does not result very often from individual psychotherapy.

Notes

1 Many of these ideas have emerged from my Thursday-night dialogues with my "Lacanian"-influenced friend and colleague, John Wayne.
2 This is basic to the linguistic constraints of human language. All language is conveyed in terms of a "surface structure" sentence, which implies a "deep structure" of implicit "arguments" upon which the "surface" or consciously spoken discourse is based. In this manner, all spoken language is constrained by a myriad of unconscious *deletions*, *distortions* and *generalizations*. This involves what is implicitly deleted, distorted, or over-generalized in a manner that leaves much more left out than reported. There is nothing nefarious about this; it is, as the "transformational grammarians" (Chomsky, 1957) would say, simply a fact of all languages.
3 The enactment might begin with a variety of issues, such as one partner having stronger feelings about having sex, dealing with finances, going to dinner at their in-laws, or figuring out how to discipline the children.
4 An earlier example of this is the case of Sally and Dan in Chapter 3.
5 As Stern (2002) notes, "Most accounts of pathological repetition, beginning with Freud's (1955a[/1920]), have implicated the conservative tendencies of the human

psyche: tendencies toward death (Freud, [1955a[/1920]), toward consistency and stability of the self organization (Gedo, 1988; Mitchell, 1988; Summers, 1996), or toward
stability and security in actual or internalized object relations (Fairbairn, 1952;
Mitchell, 1988). Freud also felt that the progressive motivation to master traumatic
experience played a role in some forms of repetition, but ultimately concluded that
conservative instinctual forces were the primary factor ([Freud, 1955a/1920,
1964/1937]). Some contemporary theorists, especially Weiss, Sampson, and the Mount
Zion Psychotherapy Research Group (1986) and Tolpin (1999) have picked up on and
developed this progressive element in Freud's thinking. But they are in the minority"
(pp. 726).

6 Mutual inductive identification is especially useful in addressing the ever-vexing question posed by complexity theory with respect to all systems, especially ones such as
those in couples therapy. That question regards the "ambiguous ownership" (Coburn,
2008) of character, agency, or any way by which we attempt to assign responsibility to
one person over another. Coburn highlights this vexing problem writing, "To para-
phrase Merleau-Ponty (1968), we can no longer say, 'this is mine and this is yours'"
(p. 7). Nevertheless, as Benjamin (1998) notes, the question of ownership and authorship of one's desire is critical; it plays mightily in our very sense of agency. This, then,
forces me to respond to Merleau-Ponty's admonition with, that the day we stop trying
to figure out our respective roles and responsibilities, it will be a very problematic day
indeed.

7 In a similar manner, Wallin argues: "Bion (1967) actually argued that projective identification was the most significant form of interaction between patients and therapists.
What I emphasize … is the complexity of projective identification: first, the fact that it
is bidirectional; and second, that as therapists, we must be wary of assuming too readily
that what we feel the patient has evoked in us belongs to the patient alone. Usually
human beings need a hook to hang their hat on" (2007, p. 128).

8 Expanding the dramaturgical metaphor, Gerson (2001) writes: "in couples/family
therapy the therapeutic task can be viewed as lighting a stage, and illuminating the
shared life-drama. Within the frame of a dramatic rendering, what systems theorists
have called redundancy—overly familiar and deeply grooved loops of interaction—
can serve as dramatic elements. Just as the stage setting frames a play, so the overly
familiar premises of a relationship can be abstracted and serve as props and settings for
a new dramatic development" (p. 340). Gerson notes that Landy (1994) writes: "Drama
is based in paradox, the most essential being that persons acting dramatically live
simultaneously within two levels of identity: that recognized as me and recognized as
not-me. This dramatic paradox is most clear in theater, the art of performing dramatic
texts to an audience, where the actor plays the role of the character who is not himself."

9 I am indebted to Lynne Preston (2007) for her original introduction of "i"mprovisation
and "I"mprovisation.

10 A key arena in which scripted-ness is in evidence is in the routine of a couple's sexuality, where private fantasy embodies key ways of objectifying one's partner and, in fact,
implicitly inducing him or her to unwittingly participate. In this manner, the "erotic
imagination" is truncated, rather than subject to being played with. Perel notes that the
degree to which partners can begin to feel safe in expressing their fantasies is the
degree to which they can begin to play with them, setting a stage for creative, heretofore unimagined sexual expression. One couple that Perel (2007) notes began to play
with their "whore–customer" fantasy by the wife insisting her husband pay her for a
blow job. In this manner, the wife was able to play with her fantasies of being a "sexually provocative, slutty woman who demanded to be paid" and not simply the mother
of her husband's children, the thought of which had appreciably diminished his sexual
drive. This role play suddenly infused their relationship with "blatant sexuality" in
which his "lustfulness was finally unleashed" (p. 150).

11 The "unformulated," as Don Stern (1997) might say, or what Christopher Bollas (1989) refers to as "unthought knowns"—all of which are being collusively avoided.

12 Speaking of such moments in a comparable manner to "E"nactments, Tony Bass (2003) describes them as "highly condensed precipitates of unconscious psychic elements in patient and in analyst that mobilize our full attention and define, and take hold of, analytic activity for periods of time" (p. 657). Black (2003) also elaborates on enactments in a compelling way.

13 As Gerson (2001) writes: "Here the creativity of intervention becomes apparent. Partners are encouraged to 'play' with new possibilities in any realm—behavioral, affective and ideational. The couple has an experience similar to the actor, remaining someone familiar, becoming someone slightly unknown, but drawing on the familiar persona. The experimentation is analogous to the fantasy elaboration of individual therapy, but is interactional" (p. 341).

14 Obviously, the capacity to play at all may be sorely missing in the individual patient or the couple, so then the effort at teaching them how to play, much as Winnicott averred, must take place.

15 See discussion of untangling "relational knots" (Pizer, 2003; Ringstrom, 2003).

6

STEP FIVE

The enrichment of each partner's capacity for self-actualization through enhanced introspection in the presence of the other.

> It is not the strongest of the species that survive, nor the most intelligent, but the one most responsive to change.
>
> Charles Darwin

> Every extension of knowledge arises from making conscious the unconscious.
>
> Friedrich Nietzsche

Psychoanalytically oriented couples therapy can frequently look like two parallel individual psychotherapies conducted simultaneously. To the extent that this is so, the couple's therapist must negotiate working with the subjective realities of two distinct individuals who are nevertheless inextricably intertwined. In essence, the therapist must address herself simultaneously to each partner as a part of a triadic system. How this task manifests is in the therapist's facilitation of each partner's capacity to reflect upon their own subjectivity, with particular focus on self-actualization versus self-truncation. To optimize this, she must do her best to make sure this reflexivity occurs in a safe enough circumstance such that each partner comes to recognize not only their subjective complexity, but their partner's as well. It means that the therapist makes it clear that self-actualization cannot be truly, fully experienced by one absent recognition by another. As Pizer and Pizer (2006) write:

> The need for recognition entails this fundamental paradox: At the very moment of realizing our independent will, we are dependent upon the other to recognize it. At the very moment we come to understand the meaning of *I, myself,* we are forced to see the limitations of that self. At the moment when we understand that separate minds can share similar feelings, we begin to learn that these minds can share and also disagree.
>
> (p. 78)

146

Thus, it is primarily in the arena of taking up the differences of each one's self-actualization that couples can feel most profoundly threatened. And, absent the means to take up what it is that makes them different, they can readily devolve in all the aforementioned maladies, including emotional reactivity, defensive devolution into evidentiary argumentation, and a variety of Gottman's (1999) dysfunctional communication patterns (e.g., "the Four Horsemen of the Apocalypse": criticism, defensiveness, stonewalling, and contempt). All of these conditions make the articulation of self-actualization a profound threat that undermines mutual recognition through pervasive mutual negation and that makes having any kind of positive relationship with a mind of its own a true challenge.

Step Five presages the conditions that will be necessary for fulfilling the tasks of Step Six. This is because what each partner begins to learn about how to negotiate *within* themselves is the precursor for what they will be able to negotiate *between* themselves. In short, anything negotiated between the partners must ultimately rest upon what they have negotiated within themselves—that is, with their complexly dissociated self-states. Such negotiation includes conflicts between their multiple self-states as well as, in some cases, irreconcilable paradoxes. In this latter case, they must take up what may come to be experienced as something non-negotiable, which may result in finding a means of surrender.

Several ideas axiomatic to the subjective experience of each have parallelisms to what must occur on the couple's (intersubjective) level of experience. The principles that facilitate this include: enhancing the processes of mentalization, through increased reflexivity and mindfulness; emphasizing unformulated (unrecognized) multiple self-states (and the dissociative processes that de-link them); and coming to terms with what one accepts he or she can negotiate, while also becoming clear about what one cannot. All of these processes lend to the work of the interpersonalized, intersubjective world of experience of the couple, the topic of Step Six.

The building blocks in this chapter and the next include how each partner recognizes more and more their contribution to what is going on in their relationship. This recognition folds into a greater appreciation of a quality of co-created thirdness (the relationship having a mind of its own), versus a negating thirdness that perpetually binds them in scripted repetitions of past relational models each has brought to their marriage and that have become further concretized over their years of dysfunctional interaction.

Self-reflexivity

Self-reflexivity, and its role in enriching self-actualization, is inherently relational, whether occurring in development, in an intimate relationship, or in a therapeutic one (Aron, 2000). Self-reflexivity entails both intrapsychic and intersubjective dimensions of human experiencing.[1] Though he was writing about individual psychotherapy, Aron captured phenomenologically not only what occurs between therapist and patient, but also what is descriptive of processes in long-term committed relationships. He notes that for psychic change to occur (again, whether in a therapeutic relationship or, for my purposes, in a long-term committed relationship), the partners will need to pass back and forth a wide range of roles, representations, and images that they both externalize and internalize. It is upon this naturally occurring phenomenon that they must become much more reflective.

To understand this in depth, we need to understand what Aron means by "subjective and objective aspects of both self and object." What he is getting at, to some degree or another (and this degree makes all the difference in the determination of psychopathology), are what he refers to as complementary modes of experience. This culminates in four complementary domains of experiencing that are constituted by our experience of being *self-as-subject* and *self-as-object*, as well as experiencing the *other-as-subject* and *other-as-object*. This can get a little confusing but is worth elaboration.

Beginning with self-experiencing, Aron speaks of self-as-subject and self-as-object. When speaking of self-as-subject, we are taking up what it means for any individual to be "self-as-knower" (i.e., to know how one knows oneself subjectively). This position is constituted by how *I* feel, what *I* think, and, as Aron notes, that which embodies one's sense of "an integrated sense of agency, continuity, distinctiveness, and reflection constituting the self that initiates, and interprets experience" (p. 672). In short, when we speak from the position of "I," we are speaking as self-as-subject.[2]

It is in this mode that each partner declares something about themselves, saying, "This is what I know to be true for me because this is how *I* think and feel." This is critically important to each partner in laying down their perspective regarding how they have come to believe something about themselves and how it comes to embody an emotional conviction. An example might be a husband declaring, "Sometimes I feel sad and sometimes I feel depressed. They sort of feel the same, and yet I also feel like they are different. I am not sure why, but I know that there is something true about my experience about all of this." When the patient speaks of his subjective experience in this manner, he avails himself to the possibility of his therapist saying, "I am wondering if the difference you have noticed is that when you are sad, you can identify a specific loss of something (e.g., a friend, a family member, a pet, or even something about one self, like a lessening of your athleticism due to aging), versus when you are depressed, you are frequently upset with something about yourself, some failing, or your inability to express something emotionally meaningful to you." Here, the domain of inquiry relates to the patient as self-as-subject taking up his state of how he knows himself subjectively, creating an opportunity for further elaboration.

A second perspective on self-experience is self-as-object. This is how one might experience "actual qualities that define the self-as-known" (Aron, 2000, p. 671). This is what we are referring to when we take up the aspects of our sense of self which we are referring to that we identify as *me*.[3] *Me* is self-as-object; *me* is constituted by "the person's self-concept, all that one could know about oneself through one's own observations or through feedback from others" (p. 671).[4]

In this mode each partner is speaking about how they believe to be known by themselves and by others. So, for example, a husband could say, "Oh, I've been known to tell some real whoppers in my day, but no one who truly knows me would ever call me a liar!" Or a wife might aver, "I know that I can be a bit of a flirt, but I know in my bones that I could never cheat on my husband." Here each party is speaking of what it is that they believe they know, what they believe to be true about them. Here each is appealing to what they deem to be an "objective" truth. Aron notes that self-as-subject and self-as object are experienced in dialectical tension, a "process of experiencing oneself as a subject as well as reflecting on oneself as an object" (p. 668). This dialectical experience is not merely an intellectual exercise; it is profoundly, affectively experiential. Still, maintaining this dialectical tension is part and parcel to balancing an observational mode about ourselves along with an experiential mode. Other-as-subject and other-as-object recognizes that others also experience themselves in *I* and *me* states. In so doing, each begins to recognize their partner's intrapsychic world of experience. When this is reciprocated, it lends to what constitutes a state of mutual recognition (i.e., Benjamin's relational version of intersubjectivity).

All of this would risk sounding like philosophical gibberish were it not for what is at stake when partners are unable to maintain the aforementioned dialectical balance. Therein potentially lays profound discord. Citing Bach (1994), Aron notes that when patients (partners) are unable to maintain appropriate tension between self-as-subject and self-as-object, they are vulnerable to states of borderline and narcissistic pathology. This is reflective of the partners' incapacity to tolerate ambiguity and paradox. It especially involves the incapacity to acknowledge, much less accept, contradictory multiple self-states.

When an individual is stuck in an extreme and intractable position of self-as-subject without any recognition of self-as-object, he is almost totally immersed in "a state of consciousness of subjective awareness" without the dialectical position of "a state of consciousness of objective awareness." Absent recognition of himself as object among others as objects, such a patient presents with a great deal of grandiosity and entitlement. The world is his proverbial "oyster"! He is virtually incapable of recognizing others in his life as also being subjects of agency and initiative, constituted by their own needs, longings, and desires. For this patient, others are merely selfobject extensions of his solipsistic worldview; as extensions of himself, they either succeed (or more often fail) in servicing the selfobject functions he requires.

By contrast, when the patient is immersed in the self-as-object position, and thereby is stuck in a "state of consciousness of objective self-awareness," he can only see himself as an object among other objects, unable to experience his own sense of agency or vitality. In this extreme position, he is consumed with accommodating others as his only means of deriving any sense of continuity and worth— however fleeting this may be, as he is only as good as his last good deed.

Taken together, these two extremes are suggestive of two forms of narcissistic pathology, one of which sometimes corresponding to borderline pathology. Indeed both Soloman (1989) and Lachkar (1992) have characterized beautifully how narcissists and borderlines are an almost over-determined match in couples evidencing severe personality disorders. Such couples are powerfully attracted because it is only in their coupling that they begin to represent one "whole person," a system in which self-as-subject and self-as-object attempt (albeit unsuccessfully) to coexist. Unfortunately, until the partners can learn to own within themselves their own dialectical tension of self-as-subject and self-as-object, they are doomed to fight it out hopelessly with neither of their subjectivities being recognized, much less fulfilled. They are perpetually mired in the position of reversible complementarity, the "doer and done-to" positions (Benjamin, 2004). So it is quite apparent that enhancing self-reflexivity is critical to a relational approach to couples therapy, and how challenging it can be with some couples.

Ray and Gladys

When Ray and Gladys first came to see me, they announced that I was the 12th couples therapist they had seen, and they had just about given up on conjoint therapy. Both were fundamentalist Christians, married for close to 20 years, and had a teenage daughter. They were initially powerfully drawn to one another because they had each had a great deal of difficulty finding a suitable partner with the same degree of fundamentalist fervor that they initially each found in the other. Gladys was particularly drawn to Ray because he appeared to be certain about his evangelical role as a Christian male, husband, and eventually father. This role, however, obscured the fact that Ray lived almost entirely in his self-as-subject position. Thus, he existed totally immersed in a "state of consciousness of subjective awareness," only without any sense of himself as an object among others. Others for Ray were merely believers who would accede to his holy testimony—that is, to his own embodiment of the gospel of Jesus Christ. Should they fail in their servitude to him, he summarily dismissed them.

Gladys dutifully followed Ray's teachings, adopting an extremely accommodative role to him. She felt it was her responsibility to be a good Christian woman, wife, and eventually mother. Over time, however, things changed in their relationship. Whereas Ray seemed to have shown considerable promise in excelling in his corporate workplace, his very public profession of his religious fervor soon became a big turnoff. Thereafter, he was relegated to a perpetually low level accounting position in a relatively obscure financial division of the company, where he became a "financial report generator" with minimal contact with other employees.

Meanwhile, given her accommodative mode of relating and her sweet enough false-self disposition, Gladys' career in real estate exploded exponentially. Soon she became five times the breadwinner that Ray was. This power imbalance started to surface in many ways in their relationship. One huge one was which evangelical church they would attend, as Gladys had discovered a preacher in a different church that spoke the word of God to her in a manner she could not receive in the church that Ray insisted they attend. For a while, in a pseudo-accommodation of his own, Ray started to attend Gladys' church only to—in his inimical narcissistic manner—turn off his fellow parishioners. As a consequence, he was "cordially" invited to no longer attend services.

Ray and Gladys' doer and done to pattern reached extraordinary sadomaso-chistic proportions, taking form in unrelenting "holier-than-thou" screaming matches. Ironically, the only thing that appeared to calm them down was when I would firmly confront them about how "un-Christian-like" they were being with one another! It was quite remarkable to see how shocked (into reason) they were by my confrontation. It was as if in the Lord's name I was bearing testimony to a Christian imperative that bore some verisimilitude to, of all things, mutual recognition!

Curiously, one thing that this intervention started doing was to confront Ray about his oblivion to others as subjects in their own right. A second confrontation arose when I pointed out how subjugated and therefore resentful Gladys had become in her pathological accommodation, not only to Ray, but also to their daughter and to a myriad of others in her life as well. In her case, her Christian subjugation through a life of sacrifice led to repetitive states of her self-as-object position, one that mired her almost exclusively in "a state of consciousness of objective awareness" with little recourse to her self-as-subject.

Testimony to the crucial importance of the distinction of self-as-subject and self-as-object arises from Gottman's (1999) understanding of how contempt is the "sulfuric acid of love." Contempt is phenomenologically constituted by an attack on the other as self-as-object, that is, how he or she presumes to be "known" in the world, by him or herself and by others. The experience of self-as-subject (i.e., what one believes that he knows about himself) by no means obviates one's fundamental need for recognition from others. This need makes us vulnerable to profound narcissistic injury when one's partner conveys, "What you believe about yourself is bullshit!" Is it any wonder that most homicides are byproducts of fights emergent among intimate others and much more rarely among strangers?

This overall subject/object distinction can also be extremely useful in working with individual patients, particularly in helping them take up problems that they are having in their intimate relationships. What I have found quite useful is help-ing them see when and how they are thinking of, feeling about, and treating the other with whom they hoped to bond as an object rather than treating them as a subject. An example of this arose in my work with Josh.

Josh and the subject/object distinction

Josh came to psychotherapy overwhelmed with obsessions about his former girl-friend, Erin. Their on-and-off relationship had reached a denouement close to a year earlier when, on the brink of Erin moving in with Josh, he proposed that this was too soon. Instead, he suggested, they would be better off breaking up and working on becoming more independent before prematurely taking on the commitment of moving in together. Not long after their separation, however, Josh found out that Erin was pursuing new lovers. In a classic iteration of Berlin's "When you get what you want, you don't want what you get," Josh was clearly ill prepared for his ensuing maddeningly obsessional jealousy.

My sense of Josh's upbringing was that it was far above average. By all credible accounts, his parents were very devoted and conscientious, remaining steadfastly available to support and soothe him in troubled times. Contrary to the more common developmental malady of a deficit in mirroring and idealization, Josh's folks provided a nearly optimal amount of both, creating an expectancy system that this was how people treated one another, the disappointment of which Josh would have to suffer over and over in his adult experiences away from home.

In the midst of our initial sessions, Erin resurfaced and began exhibiting some evidence of wanting to reconnect with Josh. Initially, this began through their texting and eventually through experimenting with some trial dating once a week. This threw Josh into a state of confusion about how engaged he should be with Erin. According to him, he would love to be texting her all the time, and he desperately wished that they could see one another more often. He had even begun fantasizing what they might do together over the holidays. It was becoming more and more difficult, given the urgencies of his needs and desires, for Josh to control himself. Meanwhile, Erin had made it quite clear to him that she still very much liked being single and was truly enjoying herself more than she could remember in a very long time. So, although she was enjoying some reconnection with Josh, she still needed her freedom to see others if she felt so inclined.

I asked Josh what Erin's declaration of being single meant, and after he got over his initial jealous worries he acknowledged it seemed she was valuing her independence and her ability therein to make up her own mind. This, I pointed out, seemed to be Erin's way of conveying her experience of herself as self-as-subject. Through lengthy exploration, it became more and more clear that Josh's desire to "nail down" the terms of their relationship was not taking into consideration Erin's position of self-as-subject, but treating her as an object. In short, he was treating her as one who would fulfill his basic need for soothing without recognizing how she saw herself. I suggested that if he precipitously pushed Erin to get closer than she was ready, he would be treating her like an object, and not a subject. By subject, I meant how Erin would identify as one who is driven by her own initiative, her own sense of agency, and her own sense of desire. I proposed that all of this appeared quite important to her so as not to subjugate herself to Josh. I added that, in so doing, she was actually fulfilling what he had proposed regarding their earlier breakup—for each to become more independent of the other. I also pointed out that he seemed to have his own ambivalence about getting what he ostensibly wanted, something I suggested was worthy of our deeper investigation. After all, given his stance that they should actually *be* more independent of one another, he clearly had a mixture of feelings, some of which were in conflict with one another.

More on self-reflexivity

Wallin (2007) offers several ideas about how to further enhance self-reflexivity. He begins by listening to his patients' narratives with particular focus on how well (or poorly) they can manifest a coherent accounting of their experience—that is, how well (or poorly) they present a coherent sense of self. He writes: "By that I mean a self that (1) makes sense rather than being riddled with inconsistencies; (2) hangs together as an integrated whole rather than being fractured by dissociations and disavowals; and (3) is capable of collaboration with other selves" (p. 133). Following Siegel (1999), Wallin writes," I suggest that a coherent self is also one that is stable, adaptive, flexible and energized" (p. 133).

Wallin argues that patients evince three primary stances relative to how they present their relationship to what they describe as their experience. These three stances involve what he refers to as *embeddedness*, *mentalizing*, and *mindfulness*. When a patient's description of experience reflects embeddedness, it is as if he-is-his-experience for as long as any particular experience is happening. Wallin notes that there are plenty of times in which embeddedness is the optimal mode of experiencing: for example, when we're immersed in the pleasures of music, or skiing, or making love. Second-guessing or going into a state of reflection about our experience during such moments can be disconnecting, at the very least, and in some cases (e.g., skiing) endangering.

Still, if embeddedness is the only (or at least primary) way an individual has for relating to his experience and his experience of others, he will discover enumerable difficulties. Among the first of these, Wallin writes, is that:

> Within such an unreflective frame of mind, somatic sensation, feelings and mental representations that might provide *information* about reality are felt instead *to be reality*. Here—and this is a crucial point—there is only a single perspective on experience, a single view, as if there were no interpretations but only perceptions, no beliefs that are not also facts.
>
> (p. 135)

Clearly, what Wallin is describing parallels what Fonagy and his collaborators refer to in terms of mentalization as the quality of psychic equivalence. This stance is deadly to the possibility of perspectival realism, the epistemological precursor to states of relational intersubjectivity and therefore to any capacity for mutual recognition. This is because when one is in a state of embeddedness there is no sense of reflection regarding the subjectivity of one's experience or that of the other—once again, a requisite condition for the experience of intersubjectivity. Embeddedness is thus a state in which one's experience personifies a hyper-objectified sense of reality. Wallin notes that "All of our patients are embedded in experience some of the time and some of our patients are embedded in experience all of the time" (p. 139). It is these latter patients who struggle most. They are also typically ruled by unmodulated affects, which also make them exceedingly poor appraisers of reality and how to negotiate it with others. This was evident in the case of Helen and Jerry.

Helen and Jerry

Helen and Jerry were a relatively newly married couple, each for a second time, in their late forties. While Jerry had never had children, Helen had a young adult daughter, Linda, with whom she was very close, but who also had had a fairly severe eating disorder with which she had struggled since early adolescence after her parents divorced. Linda had learned to manage her disorder, and had gotten on admirably in life, recently having graduated from college and thereafter setting out for a career in fashion design. Still, it was apparent to everyone, especially Linda, that her disorder could cast an ominous shadow over many potentialities in her life. There was some sense for her that, without carefully monitoring herself and participating in ongoing therapy, her eating disorder could rear its ugly head once again. It was therefore in relation to some of their concerns about Linda that Helen and Jerry, as newlyweds, initially came to see me.

For a variety of reasons, Helen's daughter did not care for Jerry, primarily because she thought he was a phony. Worse than that was that Jerry was a member of AA, 15 years sober, and was as much of a 12-step program evangelist as I had ever met. As a consequence, Jerry was unrelenting in giving Linda (and, for that matter, Helen also) reams of unsolicited dogmatic advice from the *AA Big Book* as well as pabulum derived from his multiple weekly AA meetings.

Since their issue with Linda seemed so pivotal, I decided to set up a consultation with all three of them. On top of her list of complaints about Jerry, Linda claimed that he was completely duplicitous, especially in his unremitting denial of his being judgmental about her, her disorder, and even about her decision to pursue a career in fashion design. It didn't take long to observe what Linda was referring to. Aghast at Linda's accusation, Jerry defended himself, saying that it was impossible for him to be judgmental—after all, he was member of AA! Nevertheless, I have rarely seen such an enormous incongruence between an individual's verbal and nonverbal communication. Whatever he verbally professed to be true about himself he betrayed in his gestures and facial expressions. For example, feigning interest and openness in what Linda had to say, he would almost simultaneously roll his eyes in a kind of contemptuous gesture suggestive of his thinking, "Can you believe this BS?!" Or, at other moments, he would furtively look to Helen for support, though she mostly sat in a state of dissociation, unable to reconcile within herself how to preserve these two important relationships. Jerry, after all, had been the only suitor to take her seriously and to eventually betroth her after nearly a decade of being a charter member of the lonely hearts club.

Initially, I tried to appeal to a sense of perspectival realism, emphasizing that it was important that each of them be able to speak about their subjective take on things, and not to presume, at least too quickly, that they knew what the others meant. I also pointed out that attitudes can come out unwittingly both verbally or nonverbally.

Jerry acted as though he understood what I was saying, and, since it was non-threat-ening enough, acceded to it in principle. But quickly thereafter, he began challenging Linda anew and, in fact, claiming that her disgruntled feelings about him were merely a smokescreen for her general dissatisfaction with herself. This, of course, was quickly followed with a lecture on how her upsets could and would be remedied the moment she got into a 12-step program, such as Overeaters Anonymous. It was this kind of statement that infuriated Linda, though her angry riposte only seemed to for-tify Jerry's dismissive position, in which again and again he presented himself as only having caring intentions, while his nonverbal behavior was saturated in contempt.

Eventually, I tried, as gently as possible, to point out to Jerry that there seemed to be something contradictory in his communication: His nonverbal communica-tion seemed to be conveying something in contradiction to his verbally expressed intentions of wishing to be open-minded, nonjudgmental, and a source of support (if not even guidance) to Linda and her mother. It was in relation to my pointing this out that I finally got the ferocity of Jerry's proneness to psychic equivalence in his style of mentalization, as well as the embeddedness of his experience. All of which is to say, if Jerry thought something was real to him, it should be unques-tionably so for everyone else, or otherwise they were in denial of some version of their own addiction, whether they were aware of it or not. Obviously, my pep talk about intersubjectivity, mutual recognition, and perspectival realism (all of which I discussed in plain English and not jargon) had "gone in one ear and out the other" (if it, in fact, had gotten into one ear at all!).

In the following session, with just Helen and Jerry, I was informed that he could not work with me because I had made it completely unsafe for him through my lack of support of his convictions. I am sure from his embedded perspective that was quite true. Meanwhile, Linda decided she wanted to try a new therapist and began individual sessions with me, which her mother was very much supportive of. Last I had heard, Jerry and Helen were preparing to visit their fifth couples therapist, the first four of us having abysmally failed.

Still yet another highly useful stance—when it can be achieved—is mindfulness (though surely at best it comes and goes even among the most "enlightened"). Mindfulness is about "be here now." It is about someone being really experientially present, yet also able to comment on their experience when needed. It is generally an open and flexible state of mind, capable of freeing one from being judgmental and critical about oneself and others. Mindfulness can create an optimal circum-stance in the generation of thirdness, discussed further in Step Six.

As is often the case, the evaluation of a patient's intrasubjective (intrapsychic) worldview is most optimal when he is capable of fluidly moving through all three stances. Clearly, as noted, embeddedness has an important place in our lives wherein we are living our experience and not abstracting ourselves from it in some mental-izing, reflective mode. Indeed, this is the state of nature approximating our earliest evolutionary ancestors, who, with the advent of symbolization and language, grew farther and farther away from our phylogenetic instinctual "species-based instruc-tions" on how to detect something (e.g., what to eat versus what is poisonous) or what to do without thought or reflection (e.g., leap into a tree upon hearing scurrying leaves from behind).

Still, mentalization, as we have seen and will see more, is critical to understanding ourselves, understanding our intrapsychic conflicts between our multiple self-states, and collaborating and negotiating within ourselves preparatory to collaborating and negotiating intersubjectively between ourselves and others. Wallin (2007) notes that "A mentalizing stance creates the potential for affective, cognitive, and behavioral flexibility, in large part because it allows us to envision multiple perspectives on any given experience, enhancing the likelihood that preexisting models can be updated and habitual patterns 'deautomatized'" (p. 136). Finally, mindfulness is an attempt to combine the preceding two by being in states of "onement," wherein the mind and body are inseparable; we can come much closer to states of experiencing that are both embodied and embedded while allowing for here-and-now reflection on that experience.

Nicole and Russell (Part One)

Nicole and Russell had, for some time, been mired in a recurrent argument over their distinctly different styles of engaging their 2-year-old daughter, Penelope, especially at times when she was being oppositional to their needs and desires for how she should behave. This manifested to a large extent around her sleep patterns; she needed some soothing time before taking her afternoon nap or in the evening before going to bed. Nicole's attitude involved a stricter approach—to spend no more than 10 minutes with Penelope, reading, telling a story, rocking her, and then putting her into her crib and off the parent should go. If Penelope was still awake, she might have to cry or be upset until she "put herself to sleep."

Russell's attitude was more attentive to Penelope's emotional state. This meant that he was more involved in helping her settle down to the point that she would become naturally sleepy and then fall asleep. Usually, or so Russell pointed out, his method of engaging Penelope would take somewhere between 10 minutes (Nicole's outer limit), though seldom more than 20 minutes. He argued that Penelope rarely ever required the latter. Moreover, if she did, it was typically not because she was being oppositional so much as her sleep routine had been disrupted by their long-distance travel, covering several time zones, or there being the occasional disruption of their pattern for putting her down for either naptime or nighttime.

Nicole and Russell's controversy regarding sleep patterns frequently surfaces in families with infants and toddlers and can be among the most contentious, since what is at stake is how each parent conceives of the care and nurturance of their newborn, toddler, or young child. It is in this arena that strong emotional convictions, emblematic of the family culture from which each parent hails, come into bold relief unlike almost any issues in the couple's life; this can be especially vexing when the parents possess (or so they believe) diametrically opposed styles of soothing their children. This problem, as it surfaces regarding sleep, is further exacerbated by the plethora of "self-help" guides that instruct parents on proper sleeping techniques for babies. Unfortunately, since these guides are also often diametrically opposed, they only fortify each parent's opposition to the other.

Given the rather daunting level of upset about this that Nicole and Russell initially brought to treatment, we had made considerable gains toward finding something of a common ground. I had been able to point out to them that, although they felt far apart, they were actually quite close in their determination of how much parental involvement Penelope could receive in readying her for nap and bedtime (10 versus 20 minutes). I also underscored Russell's observation that disruptions in Penelope's sleep patterns were not emblematic of opposition so much as reflective of her being unsettled by the disruption of her bedtime routines. Though this controversy was not totally resolved in our work, it had been sufficiently laid to rest that they seldom talked about it—until, that is, when it was used in relation to a larger theme of concern.

An example of such a theme revolved around Nicole's concern that Russell was a softer, gentler father than she was as a mother. Her first fear about this was that Penelope would grow up loving Russell more than her. Her second involved her conviction that children needed to be shown that anger is not something to be frightened of, that it was a normal human emotion. This latter point typically manifested in Nicole's style of expressing her anger with Penelope, typically when Penelope was "being naughty." Nicole felt that this was not only a proper way of disciplining her daughter, but it also served the function of "normalizing" the role of anger for Penelope (e.g., everyone at some time or another gets angry). Anger is normal; mommies can express it, toddlers can express it, and daddies can, too. It was on this latter point, however, that Nicole was upset, because Russell never exhibited anger, at least never towards Penelope, though if sufficiently agitated by Nicole he could become full of rage. Nicole described this as Russell's "roar!" which she would demonstrate, mimicking him loudly, roaring like a very angry lion.

Russell acknowledged that it was true that, having grown up with a rageful, tyrannizing father, he attempted to regulate his own anger, especially with his daughter. He also stipulated, however, that he did not get angry with Penelope because she was, after all, only 2 years old, and his expectations of her were geared accordingly. In short, he simply expected that, at her age, she would at times be oppositional, that she would have her protests and occasional tantrums, and mostly these induced in him the desire to address her feelings or the circumstance underlying Penelope's emotional storms. He was fully cognizant that the day would likely come that, as she got older, she would "push his buttons," and that he would very likely become angry at her, especially when she was old enough to "know better" or to be able to better handle herself.

Nicole had two reactions to Russell's comments. The first was that she had trouble believing him, though she accepted she would simply have to take him at his word and have a leap of faith that his assertion about the future would be true. That resolution, however, caused a second problem. In this case, her entertaining the idea that Russell could in fact become angry with his daughter made Nicole fear that he would express it in an unregulated manner. She feared Russell would

157

go from exhibiting no anger at Penelope to becoming the roaring lion that she feared. Russell conceded that this might be an issue for him when Penelope grew older, and added that he anticipated that might be something he would have to work on. For now, however, he simply didn't feel angry with Penelope in the manner that Nicole did.

As I was listening to them, I started to get a sense of their being constitutionally different when it came to anger—a point that I shared with them. It struck me that, in fact, Nicole was completely comfortable with anger, while Russell was not. I playfully offered that navigating her anger was for Nicole like driving on a Formula One race course, whereas for Russell it was more being in a drag race. In the former case, Nicole could readily regulate the contours of her anger, "up-shifting" (up-regulating her affect state) for top speed on the straight-aways, while "down-shifting" in the bends (down-regulating her affect state), always discerning (regulating) her level of affective expression with a great deal of finesse, and with maximum impact on the other.

Russell, on the other hand, had much greater difficulty regulating his anger. Like a drag racer, he would ride his brakes hard as his engine (temper) was soaring to higher and higher rpms until he could hold it no longer, and it would, explode launching him from zero to over 200 mph in mere seconds. My point in this playful exchange was to try to help them begin to grasp their constitutionally different styles, rather than feel pathologized or pathologizing each other. They both embraced the race car metaphor with playful comments of their own about themselves and each other, views that captured their capacity to distinguish senses of self-as-subject and self-as-object, while seeing this in each other as well.

Playing off of this, they both spontaneously spoke of their developmental backgrounds vis-à-vis how anger was treated in their family systems. Both had fathers who were prone to rage, especially when they felt the universe of their family was teetering on chaos (almost always more in fantasy than in fact), and as a consequence felt threatened. Their mothers, however, were radically different. Russell's mother was soft and quiet and despised anger, hence, for Russell, any expression of anger felt somewhere between unacceptable to flagrantly dangerous. Nicole's mother, however, encouraged her children to vent their anger, their rage, their tantrums, and seemed in a sense to frequently even be entertained by their furies.

In Nicole's home, anger was treated as something of a "catharsis"—a form of emotional ventilation that was good for the child to release pent up "poisonous" affect states. By and large, Nicole felt that her mother's encouragement of their expressing their anger was a very good thing. She also felt, however, betrayed by her mother when she would not protect her children from their father's rage. This was especially the case, she felt, when her mother had encouraged the children to speak their minds, thereby provoking their father's wrath, while her mother sat by impassively and did nothing to protect them.

As we were playfully moved back and forth regarding the theme of catharsis, Nicole became ever more animated, describing how she could turn her anger into a playful, though merciless means of teasing her mom. For example, she spoke of her mother's lady friends as being boring, "bovine-like," "unfeminine" "church ladies." Nicole took great pleasure in going into particularly degrading details about them, which, to her delight, her mother found quite funny. Although I pointed out that this teasing was about her mom's friends and not her mom *per se*, her mom could have become upset, as in inferring that there was something wrong with her that she had such friends. But, by and large, she accepted her daughter's more sadistically twisted commentaries on her with a good sense of humor. All of this seemed to reassure Nicole of the depth of their attachment. Indeed, it was becoming ever more apparent that anger, as an intense affect state, was quite important to Nicole in expressing an authentic sense of selfhood in a more spontaneous, unbridled, alive, and vitalized way. In short, Nicole used anger not simply for disciplinary purposes, or to press home an argument. She also employed it as a mode of play. Correspondingly, she hungered for a playmate to join her in her playful form of aggression.

What suddenly became apparent was that, given his own discomfort with anger, Russell was tapping on Nicole's brakes, trying to slow her down. This became absolutely infuriating to her. She said that anticipating Russell doing this made her start braking (inhibiting) herself, as she felt the impending humiliation of his taking the moral high ground, a kind of "calmer than thou" position, made him Buddha-like rather than the robust "rough and tumble playmate" she hungered for.

Whereas anger frightened, even disoriented, Russell, it energized Nicole, making her feel more alive, vital, and sexy. For Russell, anger felt like a race car out of control; for Nicole, anger felt like the race is on and it became thrilling. Suddenly, Russell saw a whole new side to their situation, and recognized how his anxiety about anger was constraining his very dramatic and fun-loving wife. And, with this acknowledgment, Nicole stopped feeling quite so much like the "identified patient" in their relationship (i.e., the crazy and inappropriate one).

All of this seemed to lend itself to a new perspective on the place of anger and aggression. Russell even recalled that in the beginning of their relationship Nicole would at times be quite provocative and aggressive in her teasing. Clearly, she was seeking to get a rise out of him—though much of the time she got her real desired effect, which was that he actually found her both amusing and sexy. We then sorted out the progression of changes in their lives. Both had significant professional challenges as they excelled in their respective careers, but in each case their careers began to overwhelm them. Then, with the advent of having Penelope, their sense of playfulness had become rudely undermined.

In the improvisatory mode of play, couples are able to play-off-of-and-with one another's creative associations, which then lends to a more spirited, though risky, engagement. When couples lose this playful capacity, or when they never had it, they are reduced to a kind of scripted engagement born out of the host of unconscious family scripts that are constituted by injunctions about how to think, feel, and behave, not to mention how relationships are to take form.

No couple can escape the vicissitudes of such tightly organized pasts. All couples will at times revert to their scripted modes, especially in stressful, conflictual times.

But combining reflective knowledge of these repetitive transference states, along with how to become more playful about them, enables them to develop more of a sense of "Oops! There I/we go again." Their past scripts (i.e., past patterned ways of being) can become playful launching pads for taking on exaggerated versions of themselves, such that they are no longer held hostage to their over-determined enactments or mutually inductive identifications. Instead, they are using these identifications to play-off-of-and-with one another in a manner that potentially can take them into some new possibilities that their prereflective scripts would previously disallow.

Discerning multiple self-states and beginning collaboration and negotiation from within

The idea that the personality is partitioned into parts (frequently in dissonant, disconnected ones) is as fundamental to the psychoanalytic canon as any of its seminal ideas, including the unconscious and transference. Indeed, Freud proffered enumerable ways in which the human personality is divided, positing in multiple ways that any human being's experience is readily a house divided, whether in his tripartite model of the id, ego, and superego, or the unconscious, preconscious, and conscious, or the topographical, structural, or economic versions of mind, and so on. Indeed, Bromberg (1998) notes that Freud represented what may be thought of as "part-egos" (p. 59) for what relationalists refer to as multiple self-states. Thus, pretty much all psychoanalytic theories reflect aspects of how the human mind is at war from within, struggling for collaboration and negotiation of its "parts"— perhaps better stated as a multiplicity of self-state processes.

A progenitor to the relational psychoanalytic idea of multiple self-state theory is broadly recognized to have been Harry Stack Sullivan (1954), the father of Interpersonalism in psychoanalysis, who argued that we have as many different versions of self (e.g., of self-states) as we have different relationships. His work presaged the ideas of contextualism, wherein, depending on any given relational context, issues will generate what is at stake for each partner (the context-dependent issues in Step One) and, as such, differing relational contexts give rise to differing self-states—a point critical to working with couples. Thus, as noted throughout this volume, all of this underscores Bromberg's admonition that human experiencing is perpetually a condition in which human beings are attempting to "to feel like one, while being many."

That which separates (divides) self-states is dissociation, which keeps self-states incommunicado with one another. Although dissociation is commonly linked to trauma,[5] it is also completely normal. As Stern (2006) notes: "Normal dissociation is relative and often situational ... It makes life more comfortable, that's all" (p. 751). Thus a key task of Step Five is to facilitate each partner's recognition of their multiplicity of self-states, for as Bromberg (1998) notes:

> Pathological dissociation can be said to exist to the degree that the patient cannot simultaneously access self states that might modulate the "truth"

being held by the self-state that is the "real me" in the moment ... What we want is that his self experience becomes more complex by becoming safely enough linked to other self states. And what we discovered is that this linkage comes about through a process by which the patient uses the analyst's mind as a way of enlarging his own.

(pp. 72–73)

Fiona and Sam

An example of the illumination of multiple self-states arose in the case of Sam and Fiona. Our work began with her discovery that her husband of 20 years had been engaging in midlife crisis emails with younger women that dripped of sexual innuendo. His behavior seemed to come out of the blue, in what otherwise appeared to be a stable marriage that had grown over the years into one in which they were each other's best friend. They regaled in their success of raising two sons, one in college and the other in the application process. In this ostensible context, Sam's behavior did not make much sense to either his wife or himself, though he was massively humiliated, ashamed, and bereft with guilt. Clearly, Sam was grappling with some of the prohibitions about sex being exciting and desirous with Fiona, instead lusting for others much younger, in a sense in search for something youthful and vitalizing.

Thus, in the course of our initial explorations, it became apparent that Sam was enacting the clichéd "midlife crisis," or at least that was presumption that both Fiona and he were working from, desperately seeking some explanation for his aberrant behavior no matter how facile it might seem. Deeper inquiry revealed that Sam had lost both of his parents in the last few years. As a result, his sense of mortality was in one sense looming large, though just as mightily it was being sequestered into a largely dissociated self-state. In its place, an archaic self-state defensively appeared, resembling a resurrection of the "mad-bad-boy adolescent" of his youth. Thus, his mortality fears sequestered in one state were incommunicado with his resurrected youthful state. The latter worked beautifully, functioning like a combination of a "time machine"—transporting him back to his adolescence—along with his very own "fountain of youth" that could ward off the encroachment of his aging, loss, and mortality. He could, in this dissociated manner, now live out his boyish fantasy in a kind of fictional world of raunchy emails with attractive, ambitious women half his age (to whom he was exposed in his entertainment line of work) without acting this out in reality.

By maintaining the dalliances strictly on a texting and email exchange, Sam was able to rationalize that he was preserving the covenant of his marriage. Once we were able to link his disparate self-states and expose Sam to his self-deception, he became even more remorseful because he had a more genuine understanding of his behavior. Nevertheless, he remained very worried about the damage he may have done to his best friend above all other things—Fiona.

Fiona's feelings were as complicated as Sam's, since it quickly became clear that she had many conflictual reactions which were articulated in three discrete self-state versions of herself. Much like Sam, she was not aware of her disparate self-states; hence she felt like she was going crazy because her entire perspective on her marriage became torn in multiple directions, whereas historically it seemed to move along on a fairly even keel. First among the disparate states we uncovered was Fiona the "chump," who in reaction to Sam's betrayal should have summarily ended their relationship in one swift move and filed for divorce. Second was Fiona the "domestic protector," who felt compelled to stay the course, if not for herself, for the greater good of her children as well as their nuclear and extended family systems. Finally, there was the "hurt and bewildered" Fiona, who was having trouble finding her way back to loving Sam, though clearly she had been very in love with him in the years before.

At various moments in our sessions, either Sam's or Fiona's self-states could become dominant, obscuring access to any of their other states. As with many patients, I refer to this as the problem of the "committee of one's mind," in which, instead of an integrated sense of self, one has many competing versions embodied in disparate and incommunicado or poorly communicating self-states. The biggest problem occurs when one version of self-state becomes dominant over the others and appoints itself chair of the committee. For Sam, it seemed that his adolescent rebellious self had commandeered the committee of his mind, putting him in danger through his inability to reflect on the consequences of what he was doing. Meanwhile, the sequestering of his "mortality self-state" was tantamount to refusing it a place at the conference table of his mind.

In Fiona's case, there was an even trickier problem, since the discovery of Sam's behavior was an assault of the unimaginable—in short, a trauma. When there is trauma, the traumatized self-state takes over and other self-states recede into a dissociated background relative to the traumatic experience. This is because, as has been observed over and over, trauma emerges less in terms of what happened than in terms of preventing it from happening again. Hence, any moments in which the sense of imminent retraumatization is activated can run roughshod over all other self-states, undermining self-reflexivity in consequence. In this manner, the traumatized self-state dominates at least until the trauma is better understood and loosens its grip. For Fiona, the anxious question that kept resurfacing was: When would Sam once again stray, and this time, not simply in fantasy emails or in texts, but for real?

So much unintegrated affect from trauma allows it to bulldoze over other self-states that might lend perspective. In Fiona's case, her trauma over feeling that her trust was broken obscured the part of her that also recognized that something, for some time, actually had felt missing in their relationship. It further obscured the idea that what was amiss involved her as well. This wasn't a point that she was keen on investigating, but nevertheless knew that she must. After all, it was only going to be through examining the part of her that had been in denial that would better equip her to look at why the couple had been drifting apart.

There were enumerable things for her to contemplate. Why, for example, had their communication become so shallow? Why had they both neglected speaking up more openly and candidly about mortality? Especially, that is, as it related to their parents, not to mention themselves? And finally, what had prevented them from taking emotional stock in what remained of their prospective years together? In short, they both had to start examining how they had neglected themselves and each other regarding these crucial points of prospective emotional intersection. Only when they finally began to entertain these warded-off states of reflection was there any opening to begin to restore some sense of hope and worth for mending their relationship.

Fiona and Sam's experiences reflect that a very important source of conflict in marital relationships occurs not simply on the interpersonal plane, but on the intra-psychic one. This latter point exerts an even more powerful presence when each partner begins to recognize that they are a house divided from within as much as, if not more than, in their conflictual relationship. What must be taken up is how, within themselves, each is having self-state experiences which contradict other states. It is important to also note, however, that not only does this create mass con-fusion within the individual, but it also likely confuses the person's partner. So, for instance, Sam's self-states varied in degrees of being openly vulnerable and fighting for his relationship, as well as becoming humiliated, defensive, and then retreating. While, on the one hand, this latter state underscored Fiona's concerns about Sam's trustworthiness, on the other, his deeply vulnerable outpourings and entreaties for them to work on their relationship made her feel like he was trying to get by without penalty. This exacerbated her experience of herself as Fiona "the chump"!

Until partners can grasp that they may be over-representing one self-state without sufficient recognition of other ones, they are vulnerable to creating complementary self-states competing with another. The consequence of this is that one self-state, dominating within, comes to trigger a self-state in the other. As just demonstrated, Sam's shame-overloaded emergent defensive self-state could readily provoke Fiona's suspicious, withdrawing self-state. In both cases, their lack of the capacity to reflect upon their multiple self-states impaired their ability to see that they were becoming mutually reactive on the basis of each one's singular self-states, without opening up the possibility of taking up their true complexities as individuals, not to mention the complexity inherent in their relationship. This becomes the critical matter of concern.

Dialectics implicated in the formation of multiple self-states

As Slavin (2011) notes, because our sense of self is so dependent on our relation-ship to others, primarily our families of origin, we are prone to working out strate-gies in which our emerging self-interests (the substance of self-actualization) are often protected from the purview of others in our family of origin and culture at large. Slavin argues that we frequently come across to the world around us in a manner that involves our over-accommodation to what fits within the relational set-tings on which we are highly dependent, while simultaneously dividing our minds into self-states that are more hidden and sequestered, oftentimes even to ourselves. All of this manifests in invisible dialectic tensions between the fundamental duality of our needs for self-actualization and our dependency needs on the groups of which we are a part.

Taking up Winnicott's work on such dialectical positions, Pizer (1998) illuminates what he refers to as some fundamental contradictions and paradoxes that lend themselves to our difficulty in negotiating the contradictory parts of our intrasubjectively divided minds and our intersubjectively divided relationships. Here are the essential contradictions (and, in some cases, paradoxes) that Pizer reports:

1. We are confronted routinely with evidence of our "essential separateness" in relationship to our "essential relatedness."
2. We are perpetually vulnerable to being caught between our "irreducible need for personal privacy" and our "indispensible (need for) human relatedness," embodied in our need for recognition.
3. We are also confronted almost daily with "our ruthless self-interest" in relationship to our "caring and conscientiousness" regarding the needs and welfare of others.
4. To establish our sense of "subjectivity," we frequently must "deconstruct (destroy) the world of otherness" to evade its objectification of our experience, while we are almost instantly confronted thereby, by our profound need to "locate ourselves in relationship to the external reality" shared by others with us.

This fundamental human dilemma at the very least underscores the prevalence— one might dare say the necessity—of our divided minds. Our largely failed attempts at reconciling this dilemma divides us according to Slavin (2011) into being more conscious of more accessible states while sequestering our usually less conscious ones. He further intones, our "more conscious side comes to the foreground and fits within the relational settings on which we are highly dependent" while "we put whole aspects of ourselves out of reach, in places … that are less consciously accessible and also less visible to others—but not lost" (p. 403). Still, living in such a divided manner cannot only become problematic for ourselves; it is also very likely a source of emergent controversy and conflict between two long-term committed partners. And this remains the case, at least that is until, as Pizer notes, we as human beings begin to be able to negotiate these disparities within and between ourselves.

Tolerating the tension between one another's self-interests requires tolerating an essential paradox—that no matter how giving and generous each person imagines himself being in relation to the other, each of us is also motivated in their own paradoxically selfish manners. Achieving tolerance of such a paradox, according to Pizer (1998), can be regarded as nothing short of a "phylogenetic achievement." Such a developmental achievement represents "an evolved adaptive competence for each individual's negotiating with others the irreducible coexistence of utterly selfish and intrinsically overlapping survival interests" (pp. 139–140). Along the way toward developing this competency, however, most of us find ourselves confused about how to negotiate these dialectical, seemingly opposite tendencies in our nature.

In the course of couples treatment, the elucidation of this confusion, along with facilitating or negotiating aspects of self-experience, is critical.

What is important to remember among the tenets of Step Five is that, as conflictual and dissociative self-states become more recognizable, and therefore communicable to one another, each partner becomes increasingly able to make choices that would have heretofore felt untenable. For example, one spouse may be loath to visit her in-laws, but ultimately chooses to do so because she comes to recognize the value of her children getting to know their father's side of the family. In short, once competing self-states begin to collaborate, they are further able to negotiate new resolutions without devolving into split complementarity—dominance and submission gambits that can function both intrapsychically (one self-state dominating another depending on some context-dependent issue) as well as intersubjectively (domination and submission gambits that freeze the couple in impasse). As Pizer and Pizer (2006) note:

> None of these seemingly opposing needs are "either/or" juxtapositions. They are all "both/and." All are fundamental paradoxes of our existence and we are challenged to develop the competence to straddle them in a ceaseless back-and-forth dialectical process. However, the existence of such paradoxical conditions bedevils the mind and coerces ongoing negotiations that can only yield unstable and evanescent "solutions."
>
> (p. 77)

Paradox

Up to this point, the focus upon thwarted self-actualization and mutual recognition has pertained primarily to conflictual, dissociated, disconnected self-states. There is yet another conundrum, however, that can be far more befuddling—how self-states are not simply conflicted, but at times are mired in paradox. Paradox differs from conflict because paradox cannot be resolved by choice, only by surrendering to states of irreconcilability. Developing this capacity to tolerate paradox, Pizer (1998) notes, is not only a developmental achievement, it can be a rich source of personal creativity, since it compels the human mind to embrace and utilize irreconcilable opposites. An especially compelling example of one that Pizer notes is formulaic of "insecure attachment systems." This occurs when the caretaker the child turns to when he is hurt is the very person who hurt his feelings.

It is important to distinguish this paradox from an unavoidable aspect of child-rearing. We understand that mothers and fathers provide for their children in multiple ways, including physically, emotionally, and psychologically. However, they also take in the name of their own self-interests. In a sense, when a snarky teenager barks, "Well, it's not like I asked to be born!" he is tapping into a truth that parents have children for a host of narcissistic reasons, including phylogenetic and tribal imperatives, as well as fantasies of repairing their own childhood through how they parent, not to mention creating a legacy that supports their memorialization after they die. For these reasons, among others, parents may easily fall upon the petard with which our children can delightfully hoist them. Adolescents can be especially keen in arguing that they exist for our needs more than their own. And, though we have become an exceedingly youth-driven culture, we shouldn't forget that we are merely a century removed from when the primary social reason for having children was because they were the parents' only "social security" plan (prior to the 1930s). Thus, the purpose of raising children was that they would be the ones with the moral responsibility for parents' elder care.

Meanwhile, burdened by the normative tasks of parenting, mother (and father) hopefully nurture and soothe, but must also discipline and restrain their children. This occasion can involve disappointing and hurting their feelings. This seemingly contradictory tendency to nurture, soothe, and also withhold poses a similar contradiction in a long-term committed couple's relationship. Simply put, at times the same spouse to whom one ostensibly turns when one's feelings are hurt is the same one who is hurting them. Still, what distinguishes the potentially normal day-to-day conflicts from irreconcilable paradoxes (and sometimes impasses) is a host of both implicit and explicit capacities we have through meta-cognition and reflection, as well as meta-communication.

Meta-cognition entails "thinking about thoughts" such that they are taken to another level of abstraction, enabling a process reflection. Meta-communication involves moving to a level of speech wherein we can speak about that which we have spoken. This may seem like gibberish, until we realize that it is only by these processes that we are able to be cognizant of our multiple-self-states, much less to then be both meta-cognizant (reflective) and capable of communicating within ourselves, between our self-states. In short, meta-cognition and meta-communication actually create linkages between the multiplicity of one's self-states. They are what enable us to be aware of the negotiation that Pizer refers to as "healthy distributed multiple selves." From these states, we learn to negotiate experiences of periodically feeling decentered until linkages can be made between disparate aspects of our self-experiencing. This also enables the emerging process of negotiating differences within ourselves, such that we are better equipped to negotiate differences with our partner.

Pizer (1998) contrasts "distributed multiple selves" with "dissociated multiple self-states," the latter of which leads to experiences of fragmentation, the sequelae of severe paradoxical situations. Pizer poses an especially unsettling example, which he calls the "father's lap paradox," this being one instrumental to creating "disorganized insecure attachment patterns." Pizer writes: "Father's lap is protective and comfy. Father's lap has an erect penis" (p. 73). Pizer notes that such paradoxical situations are so severe as to be affectively and cognitively intolerable. They require a host of defensive strategies to be managed, beginning with dissociation followed by repudiation and disavowed splitting and ultimately projection. They culminate in what Stern (2006) refers to as "not me" experiences.

The collapse of such paradox means that one is no longer capable of maintaining a sense of one's multiplicity within oneself, and, absent this ability, one is ill equipped to recognize the differently and multiply constituted subjectivity of their partner as well. Partners in these circumstances are prone to kinds of mentalization reflective of psychic equivalence, with no tolerance for their partner's alternative vision of reality or to some version of "pretend mode," such as idealizations of self and other that are then vulnerable to collapsing into painful and frightening experiences of de-idealization. They also lose grasp of the necessary paradox of self-centeredness in relationship to mutuality, and as a result are vulnerable to collapsing into positions of dominance or submission versus mutual recognition. The world of such couples is occupied by either/or versions of reality, such as "my way or the highway," or the "doer or done to" (Benjamin, 2004) position. All of these disallow the possibility for both/and versions of reality, in which differences are appreciated as a rich asset and not as a depleting liability.

The heart of this breakdown of recognition is frequently a byproduct of the paradoxical nature of the vicissitudes of our self-centeredness in relation to our mutuality. By losing sight of this paradox, we lose sight that, over the course of a long-term committed relationship, we periodically must "destroy our partner" in fantasy to find him or her in reality. This is how we get beyond our over-determined and constrained transference versions of the other to discover what he or she is about, in terms of truly recognizing his/her intentions versus remaining stuck in our transference version of them. It is in this sense that *negation* of the other is paradoxically linked to an ultimate *recognition* of the other. In so doing, we also begin to recognize something different about ourselves. Furthermore, through this process we truly begin to see ourselves as constructers of reality. This recognition challenges not only how we view our partner, but ourselves as well; this can open us up to new vistas of creativity and play.

Thus, the conjoint therapist must find a way to engage the isolated islands of selfhood within each partner by entering an intersubjective engagement with each of them (Bromberg, 1998). This means that the therapist must hold in her mind the splits between these multiple self-states of the patient's personality, as well as speak for those that slip into the background behind those prominent in the foreground of each partner's experience. Doing so cultivates intrasubjective bridges between the former and latter states of being, and offers a way for them, much like a group of discordant committee members, to renegotiate their relationship to one another. It further helps patients cope with, accept, and embrace that which has heretofore been irreconcilable.

Donna and Herb

Donna opened our initial session stating that her life was over, and that she no longer knew who she was or what she wanted. She said that she had lost all will to live. Furthermore, she didn't have any secure sense about what the future would bring. Her collapse started two years earlier, with her discovery that Herb had been having an affair. They had by this point been married 30 years. Herb acknowledged that his affair was the worst mistake of his life, accounting for it as a combination of a midlife crisis and reckless abuse of amphetamines that had been prescribed to him as a middle-aged adult for the treatment for attention deficit disorder. Herb indicated that he had been unequivocally remorseful as well as thoroughly grateful that Donna had forgiven him and taken him back. Donna corroborated Herb's comments. Though this crisis was the first evidence of an affair, they had suffered a myriad of storms throughout their marriage regarding the complexities of raising two children, one of whom was diagnosed "special needs," as well as grappling with the severe ups and downs in Herb's entrepreneurial business ventures. Despite all of their struggles, they had remained quite devoted to one another, with Herb devoting virtually all of his attention to Donna. Having very comfortably retired after selling his last very successful enterprise, Herb had nothing but time on his hands to give to her. He was especially mindful of not wanting to make her feel insecure. Indeed, the affair that he had had was so utterly calamitous in its own right, and could not have served as a greater life lesson about what he would never want to do again nor what he would take for granted again. As a result, he thanked his lucky stars that Donna remained with him, and revised his life plan. Now into his "golden years," his new desire was to spend more time with their adult children and their grandkids.

While understanding how Donna was traumatized, he could not understand why she remained in the pall of such doom and gloom. Although he recognized that something about the affair still perturbed her, he also commented with some confusion that their life outside of our sessions appeared to him to be exceedingly enjoyable for both. On top of enjoying their semi-retirement, they were more sexually active than ever, traveled considerably, and relished a host of common interests from cooking to buying art to engaging in a multiplicity of cultural and charitable events. Nevertheless, at the commencement of every session, Donna broke into tears professing that her life was over.

In this context, we began to explore how Herb's affair had shattered certain fixed illusions of Donna's. During our history-taking, we had uncovered that she had been raised in a Orthodox Jewish family. From this perspective, the Ten Commandments were regarded as sacrosanct, including "Thou shall not commit adultery." I would venture that this commandment held greater sway in her mind than "Thou shall not kill." In relation to the commandment against adultery, her faith that Herb would never do such a thing was shattered. This made his actions traumatic, insofar as that which assaults one from the unimaginable tends to shatter one's illusion over being omnipotently in control of such events occurring in one's life (Ringstrom, 1999, 2010c). It destroys one's fantasy that, by feat of imagining the event before it happens, one can either avoid trauma or mitigate its damage.

As I probed more about the earlier periods of their marital life, I came upon some fascinating facts that led me to understand and interpret the untenable paradox in which Donna found herself. In the earliest years of their marriage, Donna was of the conviction that, despite there being a multitude of other attractive women at a party of some event, "she could have any man in the room." Notwithstanding this, she had chosen Herb. Thus, early in their relationship, she became furious whenever she sensed that he did not seem to appreciate the fact of her choice. Her fury was further compounded by his being flirtatious with other women at parties, rather than making clear to everyone his amorous feelings about his wife.

In response, Herb offered, as a means of explanation more than as an excuse, that in the early days of their marriage he was immature, naïve, and unappreciative. He further explained that, in those days, his focus was primarily on his anxiety over making a success of himself, which far overrode his capacity to attend to his wife and children as he should have. He also acknowledged that the pressures of supporting a family, running a business, and being consumed with his own immature "fucked-up-ness" did not bode well for his supplying Donna's needs for love and sexual attention. He added, however, "Aren't you getting all of that from me now? Aren't I giving you everything you ever wanted? Aren't I more attentive than ever?" To her affirmation to all his questions, he then posed, "So why are you dwelling in the past? Why can't you let it go?"

I felt that there was quite a bit of merit to his question. Indeed, I had to rein in some of my own countertransference conjunction with his logic, lest I enter a disjunction with Donna. Life, after all, is short, and it seems like an enormous waste to "cry over spilled milk," especially when refreshing new milk is pouring forth abundantly. They could be enjoying their "golden years," but instead they were at risk of becoming copper, coated in patina. Still, I also recognized that Donna was hurting deeply in a manner that was not of her choosing. Indeed, part of what I was hearing, over and over, was how she felt that she was now an "old hag." On top of this, she fixated on the question: "Why shouldn't I expect that Herb would end up seeking a far younger, healthier, and more beautiful woman than me?" I could understand her logic as well, though I took Herb at his word. Still, might her prophecy of doom and gloom eventually make that a self-fulfilling prophecy?

While I thought that her question underscored a true fear, more compelling to me was that she seemed to be totally fragmenting around a paradox that was taking her into the imponderable. In so doing, it was undermining every bit of faith she had in her own cognitive process. Accordingly, I made the following interpretations, saying, "Donna, I am wondering if what is happening is that you are faced with at least two propositions that are irreconcilable, and therefore untenable to you." This piqued both Herb's and her interest. I continued, "From what I hear, when you were young and beautiful, you felt that Herb didn't want you, but now that you are an old withered leper of a woman [of course she wasn't but she felt that way], it's impossible for you to imagine that Herb would now want you. It seems that something is seriously wrong with this picture. It violates your entire sensibility and, in fact, it so undermines your worldview that you have lost all faith in being able to make sense of anything. This accounts for what I was talking about a few weeks ago, that you have lost all sense of agency, all sense of personal authorship in your life. Perhaps this is why you feel so lost and vulnerable to collapse."

Donna lit up in reaction to these comments, and said that they were right on the target and that I had captured exactly what she was feeling, though she had been unable to put it in such words. I then asked her if she truly wanted to stay with Herb, and she unhesitatingly claimed that she did, while looking somewhat puzzled over my question. I commented then that although she felt like she didn't have any agency, in fact she had just demonstrated some in her will to remain with Herb. That being true, however, it appeared that, for now, we would need to help her simply contain and accept the irresolvable paradox that was befuddling her. Without being able to fully understand how it could be, the question would become: Could she entertain the possibility that she could enjoy her life with Herb anyway? This became an overarching question that she began to live with.

Negotiation

In his study of the negotiation of paradox in psychoanalytic treatment, Pizer (1998) draws from negotiation theory in examining destructive versus fruitful modes of negotiation, which he calls, respectively, "positional versus principled negotiation." I believe that when one's theory of mind hinges on the experiencing of a multiplicity of self-states, these same principles can be used as effectively when discussing intrasubjectivity as much as they apply to intersubjectivity. Positional negotiation is governed by individualistic needs, and is therefore of a self-centered nature. It lays claims to territoriality, power, categorical absolutes, and asymmetrical "win-lose" strategies. By contrast, principled negotiation bears in mind the interests of all the various parties involved, their needs, desires, and fears. It assures that all the personalities will get their due—that is, to at least speak their peace towards reconciliation that embraces both of their interests, even when their desires and needs cannot always be met.

To facilitate each partner's embracing their multiplicity, the conjoint therapist must be able, in a non-moralistic, nonjudgmental way, to help each negotiate the voices between their different states of self-experience. That is, to create an internal forum of mutual recognition between the disparate self-states within one's experiential self, while eschewing the complementarity of one self-state bullying others. This latter quality involves a positional negotiation within oneself. The therapist often has to be able to articulate a particular paradox that might be very hard for a patient to see—that an interpersonally submissive side within their personality is paradoxically dominating other aspects of the self that might otherwise stand up for one's autonomy. We see this enacted in patients who constantly engage in self-defeating behavior, chronically blaming others or circumstances, when the data indicates that time and again they have failed to embrace, if not even sabotage, every genuine opportunity that has come their way.

Each partner's capacity to take stock in what they do with their disparate versions of self creates fundamental building blocks for addressing what they do with one another. In essence, by engaging each patient's multiple self-parts, the conjoint therapist is modeling how to reflect upon a multiplicity of internal self-states without the exclusion of one self-state by another, nor the usurpation of any one state by others. In the course of doing this in couples treatment, the partners develop the capacity to recognize and negotiate elements of their intrasubjective world, including embracing their own sense of agency as well as taking responsibility for what were heretofore disavowed projections on their partner.

There is an important humbling quality to all of this that lends itself to a kind of personal liberation. It follows Walt Whitman's unabashed declaration of the essential and robust contradictory nature of a sense of self that is a complex composite of many personalities. He wrote in his poem, "Songs of Myself":

> Do I contradict myself?
> Very well then I contradict myself,
> (I am large, I contain multitudes.)[6]

This humble awakening, free of the absolute constraints of right and wrong or the implied shame of being hypocritical, is a precursor to surrender. And surrender is an essential intersubjective capacity, instrumental to holding, containing, accepting, and living with the basic human paradox that sometimes "I must ruthlessly be who I am," but in order for me to fully realize who I am, "I need you—as a separate subjectivity—to recognize me." In other words, I cannot be fully realized without you as a realizing other, nor can you be fully realized without my recognition of you.

Such surrender entails a potential relinquishment of pride and ego. In his seminal article on how submission and masochism are the perversion of surrender, Ghent (1990) notes that surrender distinguishes itself from submission in that it is reflective of growth. Surrender reflects an expansion of the limiting constraints of one's personality through their relaxation. By contrast, submission serves as a defensive adaptation in which one inauthentically accedes to the domineering demands (whether real or imagined) of the other (whether other be another person or a part of one's self). Submissiveness serves to defend "against anxiety, shame, guilt, anger… all deceptions, whether they take the form of denial, splitting, repression, rationalizations, evasions" (p. 110).

Ghent notes that, while one can surrender in the presence of another, one cannot surrender to another—that latter case involving submission. As Gottman (1999) notes of the "marital paradox—in order to change, it is necessary to feel that you do not have to change" (p. 97). Surrender is not an act of will. It is an experience of total absorption in the moment where past and present recedes from consciousness. In contrast to the puppetry of submission, surrender[7] exhibits the unreflective pre-consciousness of self-experiencing that is only available for commentary after the fact, but seldom during it. Ghent summarizes surrender, writing:

> The distinction I am making between surrender and submission helps clarify another pair that are often confused. Resignation accompanies

submission; it is heavy and lugubrious. Acceptance can only happen with surrender. It transcends the conditions that evoked it. It is joyous in spirit and, like surrender, it happens; it cannot be made to happen.

(p. 111)

John and Mary

An example of surrender came from a session with a couple named John and Mary. In reviewing their progress in couples treatment, they enthusiastically shared the following story. Three hours before trying to fly home from a lovely weekend vacation in Miami Beach, the two broke out into a terrible fight. Mary, an inveterate shopper, desperately wanted to return to a clothing boutique she had "poked her head into" the day before and that she was "dying to go back to before returning to Los Angeles." By her estimation, there was just enough time to go to the store by taxi and then return to the hotel, gather their luggage, and "sail" to the airport.

Since this was in the aftermath of 9/11, her fiancé John was skeptical as to whether her shopping junket would fit in the time remaining until they would have to board their plane. Feeling coerced into submitting to John, and feeling constrained by his concerns much in the way that she did with her first husband, Mary rebelliously asserted that John could go to the airport without her and that she would meet him there.

Her particular gambit smacked of a kind of positional negotiation, a kind of brinkmanship that compelled John to cave in submissively, or go angrily to the airport by himself, all the while imagining he would be flying home either with an empty seat next to him or one filled with a "victorious though resentful" Mary, who, just as she prophesied, had managed to make it to the store, back to the hotel, and then on time to the airport. In the throes of their fight, John suddenly realized that he did not have any real stake in getting to the airport besides assuaging his wounded ego—a product of his initially defensive and argumentative reaction to Mary's proposal. In truth, it was she that would be far more inconvenienced by their missed plane, since it was she who was more in need of getting home to her young children. Suddenly, it became clear to John that if they missed their flight, he could have yet another lovely evening in Miami with his beloved, along with a perfectly reasonable excuse for missing the next day at work.

Accordingly, John ran after and jumped into the cab that Mary hailed, telling her that he was fine with going with her. At first she was nonplussed and more than a bit suspicious. Though Mary was loath to being submissive herself, she did not have any interest in John's being submissive either. Although in the moment she needed to ruthlessly pursue her own plan, she was cognizant on some level that she was forcing her agenda on John. When he was able to explain his instantly revised position that their having another night in Miami would have been fine with him, he was able to convince Mary.

Interestingly, Mary literally swooned over his non-submissive change of mind. She thanked him profusely, and although they did in fact make their plane with some time to spare, she too shared John's wish that they hadn't. More than any-thing, she appreciated how his action (e.g., his surrender) recognized both of their needs and desires. It made her all the more convinced that they could work through whatever difficulties emerged between them. In her own language, she affirmed that she could count on John being different from her repetitive transference pro-jections (my terms, not hers, though they are conceptually apt) of his being a dominating force trying to coerce her into submission. She even acknowledged—not an easy thing for Mary to do—that it was more herself that was the pressuring force in this situation, and that in the context of John's response she was able to more readily consider her own pushiness.

Summary

The exploration of self-actualization in Step Five requires a capacity to successfully negotiate the multiplicity of one's self-states so as to "feel like one while being many" (Bromberg, 1998). Step Five focuses on how the therapist helps each partner recognize how to negotiate internal conflicts between multiple aspects of each one's self as they arise in relation to their partner. Equally important, however, is learning how to come to terms with (i.e., surrender to and accept) certain irreconcilable paradoxes that arise within oneself and therefore in relation to one's partner.

It can be helpful for the conjoint therapist to see the mind of each partner as analogous to a committee populated by numerous personalities, each unwittingly oscillating through positions of dominance and submission with the others (within oneself) as they contend for ascendancy to leading the "committee of one's mind." It is the unwitting aspect of this committee of the mind that bedevils oneself and, by extension, bedevils one's partner.

It is therefore the task of the couples therapist to facilitate each partner's self-reflection and to promote nascent curiosity within and between the partners. Multiplicity of self-states reflects an evolutionary strategy for negotiating within oneself the pervasive dialectical tensions that arise around separateness and relat-edness, ruthless self-interests and ruthful concerns for others, and the need to deconstruct (destroy) the relational world of which one is a part to discover one's subjectivity and not be swallowed up in objectivity. Multiplicity is critical to relat-ing to one's relational world. Once recognized and reckoned with, multiplicity helps negotiate the complex vicissitudes of reality that one inescapably occupy a couple's life together.

The capacity for such negotiating is also, in principle, grounded in each partner's capacity for self-reflexivity, and that capacity is influenced largely by each one's capacity for mentalization. Mentalization is crippled when one's mind collapses into a mode of psychic equivalence, wherein one is constrained by seeing the world in anything other than his rigidified (embedded) experience of it. One is equally con-strained when one collapses into the pretend mode, wherein one is mired purely in the world of fantasies about oneself and about the other. The pretend mode makes it impossible to recognize real aspects of one's own experience as well as their partner's.

By cultivating each partner's curiosity about the multiplicity of their experience, the therapist enables each to play with the "committee members of their respective minds," facilitating their recognition and negotiation. Besides conflicts between aspects of self, however, there arise certain irreconcilable paradoxes. Helping the partners distinguish between conflict and paradox is critical.

While conflict is often amenable to choice, paradox isn't, and is therefore manageable only by surrendering to its irreconcilability. Some paradox is simply endemic to development. Mother provides, but she also takes; mother nurtures and soothes, but she must also discipline and restrain her children. All of this closely mirrors paradoxes in a couple's relationship: the same spouse to whom one ostensibly turns to when one's feelings are hurt is the same one who is frequently hurting them.

Negotiating such paradoxes leads to a healthy distributed multiple self, which learns to negotiate experiences of periodically feeling decentered until linkages can be made between disparate aspects of one's self-experiencing. This contrasts with the dissociated multiple self, which experiences fragmentation from severe paradoxes. Paradoxes of this severity may not be tolerated within the mind, resulting in the necessary usage of such mechanisms of defense such as splitting, dissociation, repudiation, and projection, all of which collapse potential space.

When one is no longer capable of maintaining a sense of one's multiplicity, one is ill equipped to recognize the different and likewise multiply constituted subjective experiences of one's partner. The world of such couples is occupied by either/or versions of reality, such as "my way or the highway," or the "doer or done-to" position that disallows the possibility for both/and versions of reality in which differences are appreciated as a rich asset and not a depleting liability.

Based on the above, the conjoint therapist engages the isolated islands of selfhood within each partner by entering an intersubjective engagement with each of them (Bromberg, 1998). This means that the therapist must hold in her mind the differing aspects of the patient's personality, and speak for those that slip into the background behind those prominent in the foreground of each partner's experience. Doing so cultivates intrasubjective bridges between the former and latter states of being, and offers a way for them, much like discordant committee members, to renegotiate their relationship to one another. It also means that, when paradox makes such bridging impossible, patients have to be helped to cope with, accept, and embrace the irreconcilable.

From negotiation theory, we learned that there are destructive versus fruitful modes of negotiation respectively involving positional versus principled negotiation. I believe that when one's theory embraces multiplicity of self-states, these same negotiating principles can be used as effectively when accessing both the intrasubjective and the intersubjective. Positional negotiation, governed by individualistic self-centered needs laying claims to territoriality, power, categorical absolutes, and asymmetrical win/lose strategies, tends to be problematic. Principled negotiation bears in mind the interests of all the various parties involved, including their needs, desires, and fears, and assures that all personalities get their turn to speak even when their desires and needs cannot always be met.

To facilitate partners embracing their multiplicity, the conjoint therapist must negotiate the voices between different aspects of the partners' self-experience. Doing so creates an internal forum of mutual recognition between the disparate parts within one's experiential self, while eschewing the complementarity of one aspect of self-experience bullying others.

Each individual's capacity to take stock in what they do to their internal versions of self becomes a fundamental building block to their taking stock in what they do to one another. By engaging each patient's disparate self parts, the conjoint therapist is modeling how to reflect upon a multiplicity of internal self-states without the exclusion of one by another, nor the usurpation of one by others. In this manner, the partners develop the capacity to recognize and negotiate elements of their intrasubjective world, including embracing their own agency and taking responsibility for their use of projection.

The humble awakening to one's multiplicity helps free one from the absolute constraints of right and wrong or the implied shame of being hypocritical, all of which can be a precursor to surrender. Surrender involves an essential intersubjective capacity to hold, contain, accept, and live with the basic human paradox that "I must ruthlessly be who I am," but in order for me to fully realize who I am, I need you—as a separate subjectivity—to recognize me. As such, surrender entails a relinquishment of pride and ego, and distinguishes itself from submission in that it is reflective of growth. Surrender reflects an expansion of the limiting constraints of one's personality through their relaxation. It enables the fullest articulation of self-actualization, complemented by each of the partners' mutual recognition of one another's self-actualization.

Notes

1 Aron writes: "My technical use of the term *self-reflexivity*, or the self-reflexive function of the mind, needs to be carefully distinguished from the more usual understanding of self-reflection. Self-reflection ordinarily connotes a cognitive process in which one thinks about oneself with some distance, as if outside, that is, as if examining oneself as an object of thought. The way I use self-reflexivity here, by way of contrast, includes the dialectical process of experiencing oneself as subject as well as reflecting on oneself as an object. It is not, therefore, exclusively and intellectual observational function, but an experiential and affective function as well, and my focus of maintaining the tension between subjective and objective self-awareness includes as one aspect to this conceptualization the ability to integrate observing and experiencing functions, to connect thought and affect, mind and body, the observational and the experiential mode" (2000, pp. 668–669).
2 Here is where Fosshage's (1997) subject-centered listening position of empathic attunement can help the patient better develop his self-as-subject understanding.
3 Aron's declination of *I* versus *me* follows William James (1981/1890).
4 Here is where Fosshage's (1997) other-centered listening perspective might augment a patient's experience of his self-as-object understanding.
5 Dissociation related to trauma does have more severe implications resulting in "not-me" states. What the patient necessarily must ward off are states of recognition of me and not-me states because they cannot be held in conflict, they cancel one another out. When not-me states arise in the persons with highly vulnerable personality structures,

"the self is so seriously threatened and destabilized that experience can become psychotic" (p. 753).

6   Cited in Pizer (1998).

7   According to Safran (2007), "[For] Ghent, the experience of surrender involves a type of acceptance and 'letting go' of one's defensive need to control things, to impose one's preconceptions upon experience and to try to define oneself in opposition to the other. It involves an experience of 'being' rather than 'doing.' *Submission*, in contrast to *surrender*, involves a type of resignation. It involves a defensive, self protective subjugation of the needs of the self to the other. Submission occurs in response to dominance and control. This is not the case for surrender. One can choose to submit. One cannot, however, intentionally surrender, although one can prepare the psychological ground for it" (p. 18).

7

STEP SIX

The facilitation of each partner's capacity to attune to and support the other's introspection and personal growth.

It takes two to tango.
Anonymous

In the preceding chapter, we learned that the examination of each partner's intra-subjective multiplicity—their discovery of multiple versions of selfhood—helps facilitate each partner's ownership of and attempts at reconciliation of internal conflicts that can otherwise get projected by each one onto the other.[1] The therapist's engagement in that process attempts to facilitate each partner's recognition, acceptance, and capacity to better negotiate intrapsychic conflict between self-states. Also, on occasion, she helps the partners come to terms with surrendering to certain inevitable intrasubjective paradoxes when the negotiation of conflict is impossible. Step Six examines processes similar to those in Step Five, but focuses on how they take form interpersonally and therefore intersubjectively. As previously noted, that which is to be negotiated *between* the partners (Step Six) first needs to be negotiated *within* each partner (Step Five). Thus, the focus of this chapter shifts to the conflicts and paradoxes that emanate *between* the partners, though of course this also always includes the intrasubjective experiences of both of them. Special emphasis is placed on how poorly managed conflicts and paradoxes between the partners can manifest in negative thirdness, thereby truncating the couple's openness to their relationship developing a mind of its own.

Long before I had yet read about thirdness, the origins of my thinking about the relationship having a mind of its own grew out of a particular recurrent experience in extremely volatile couples treatment. What came out of this was a technique that I found useful in dealing with couples so mired in their fight that neither one could stop screaming at the other. Indeed, any attempt on my part to intervene with either one or the other would result in something akin to trying to break up a barroom brawl. In such a circumstance, any attempt to subdue one brawler leaves him vulnerable to the other sneaking in an extra punch. This calamitous scene makes the intervening party culpable of inadvertently making matters much worse, while also finding it impossible to not attempt some interruption, lest what is occurring devolves into something potentially deadlier.

Realizing that addressing either one of the partners was a doomed formula, I instead started to speak to (at) their relationship, focusing my attention literally on the space in between them. I believe some of the influence for this method came from what I had learned from my experience with Tavistock Groups, in which the group "consultant" (therapist) only addresses herself to the group's unconscious, speaking about how the group was failing to work as "working group."

In adopting a similar technique in my work with couples, especially when they were becoming out of control, I would find myself directing my full attention and interpretations to the space on the couch between the partners—ergo, to their relationship. In so doing, I would start making comments, such as "This relationship seems to be telling us that it is shear idiocy for anyone to dare to reveal anything vulnerable about themselves"; "This relationship is telling us that it is far too dangerous to do anything other than to hold to an aggressively defensive position"; "This relationship is telling us that instead of either partner daring to actually listen to the other, each can only consider their immediate strategy for defending themselves"; "This relationship appears to adhere tightly to Napoleon's admonition that 'the best defense, at times, is an offense.'"

Each time I engaged in this peculiar technique, I noticed something curious beginning to happen—both partners would begin to settle down a bit. Each would gradually stop attacking the other and begin to listen to what I had to say—not about either of them, but about their co-created relationship. Typically, as each partner quieted down, the energy in the room calmed. Color returned to their faces. They began to breathe more easily rather than in their quick-reactive, adrenaline-pumping "fight or flight" mode.

What dawned on me about why this worked, is that, instead of pinpointing either partner's specific contribution to what was promulgating their fight—a clear formula for instantiating shame and blame and therefore throwing ever more fat in the fire—I was speaking to them in a manner descriptive of how they operated as a "self-organizing (dyadic) system" (Coburn, 2002). As such, both were behaving in large part by how they were unwittingly being orchestrated to behave by the other.

It became apparent that if either partner felt singled out, they would likely devolve into more profoundly antagonistic states of humiliation, fueling their fight even more. Instead, I was suggesting that, in some ineffable way, their relationship was behaving as if it had a mind of its own. Therefore *it* was dictating their individual reactions. Posited this way, their individual experiences of shame and blame were suddenly distributed across both sets of their shoulders, not laid to rest on one or the other. Once this idea clicked—that the relationship could have a mind of its own, albeit in this case a very negative one—each partner could begin to gather a bit more curiosity about their own contributions. This point would nicely segue into what I had been extolling throughout the treatment: "You are each in a hopeless position attempting to control your partner. Your very best hope—and this is hard enough to achieve—is to attempt to gain control and perspective about what it is that you are doing!"

Subsequent to engaging in this intervention, I became much more interested in the relational psychoanalytic literature on thirdness. The more I read, the more I began to see that the theme of the relationship having a mind of its own could be especially useful in working with couples, not only in terms of their negative co-creation but potentially positive ones. It could be employed not only in pointing out how the couple's relationship can operate pathologically, but also how it can operate in a myriad of ways for the betterment of the couple. This especially includes how it sets a framework for enhancing self-actualization and mutual recognition. To develop these ideas even further, we must first take up the profound importance of the concept of thirdness and demonstrate how essential it is to the couple achieving a more alive, creative relationship with a mind of its own.

To think about thirdness in long-term committed relationships, we must first consider the plight of relationships when they are in trouble. As has been discussed enumerable times in this book, the dyadic relationship is in dire straits when it collapses into "complementarity," Benjamin's (2004) "doer and done-to" position. Similar versions of this idea are elaborated in the positions of the "victim and victimizer," the "sadist and the masochist," and so forth. These relational styles are mired in complementarity, since each style requires the other to exist. Complementarity preserves the binary of opposites that *remain the same while changing* by simply reversing each partner's respective position. Aron (2003) sums up the point accordingly:

> [D]yads, couples, and systems tend to get stuck in complementary relations. This complementarity is characterized by a variety of splitting in which one side takes a position complementary to—the polar opposite of—the other side. If one is experienced as the doer, then the other becomes the done to [Benjamin 2004]; if one is the sadist, then the other becomes the masochist; if one is the victim, then the other becomes the victimizer; if one is male, then the other becomes female; if one is active, then the other becomes passive. Polarities are split between two members, and the more each one locks into a singular position, the more rigidly the other is locked into the opposing, complementary position, thus heightening the splitting and tightening the polarization. At anytime, the split may be reversed without significantly changing the structure of the complementarity. The active member may suddenly become passive while the passive member becomes active, thus their surface roles are switched, but the dyadic structure remains split between activity and passivity.
>
> (p. 353)

Aron (2003) introduced an extremely useful image to capture the plight of the dyad fixed in the binary of complementarity: the seesaw. Typically, on a seesaw, one partner is higher (up) and the other lower (down). Seen as an image of a long-term committed relationship, the positions reverse as each gathers the storm of their argument, lending weight to their side, attempting to upend the other. All that happens, however, is as one rises, the other lowers. Up and down, balancing on the fulcrum of their argument, the couple get nowhere in elucidating an intersubjective understanding of what it is they are even fighting about. In this manner, mutual recognition is a veritable impossibility. This is because each is trying disparately to prove that he or she is not the "doer" but the "done-to," not the "victimizer" but the "victim," not the "abuser" but the "abused."

We have seen this vexing pattern over and over throughout this book in a myriad of examples. An especially telling one is how partners will argue who is the most traumatized in a gambit to secure moral authority over the other. In line with Aron's seesaw image, for several decades I have illustrated to couples that when they are locked in some dyadically fixed, complementary position, it is as if they are at either end of a large drainpipe looking through it, trying to look for why the relationship is in trouble and what caused it. Of course, all they see to explain their misery is their partner, the one who did it.

Thirdness

The only way to move the couple off their seesaw of dyadically fixed and opposi-tional positions is to introduce a third point of view—that is, to introduce third-ness. Although thirdness has been discussed throughout this book, its instantiation is especially critical in Step Six, because it is in the couple's acquisition of third-ness that they are at a position to potentially terminate treatment. It means that they have finally achieved (through the assistance of the therapist as a transitional third) the ability to find a means of reflecting on their stuck complementary position. And, building on the intrasubjective work of Step Five, they are better prepared to take up a deeper truth about themselves—that is, for a host reasons already discussed, why they each can end up feeling they are on one end of the complementarity pole or the other. It is worth momentarily recapping why this must be so.

Couples can go for long periods evading self-reflectivity regarding their own conflicts, until they hit an unpredictable "tipping point." When this happens, one partner feels like she has had to "put up with, and put up with, and put up with" what her partner does (or doesn't do), until suddenly she has experienced the "last straw!" At this point, filled with moral indignation, she brings the entire history of her felt subjugation down upon him. Unfortunately, what is typically split off from this is her recognition of her own complicit perversion of agency (Gentile, 2001). In her mind, in her experience, she is the "done-to," she is the "victim," and she is going to have her day in court and seek indemnification for all of her losses without recognizing her role in co-creating them. In classic reversibility, there is a high likelihood that her husband will be readily tipped into his own profusion of "injustices," and with that the seesawing begins.

There are a myriad of definitions of the third or thirdness in psychoanalysis.[2] For my purposes, I will be concentrating on Benjamin and Aron's formulations (Aron, 2003; Aron & Benjamin, 1999; Benjamin, 2004). Returning to Aron's image of the seesaw, he observes that pictorially it resembles a flat line with occupants sitting on either end in various states of balance and imbalance. The key to this image is that there is no independent space or place to move to off the line; the line has no extra-observational space. Meanwhile, each occupant's slightest movement affects the other's. Thus, to move out of their complementarity, the couple has to be helped to move off the seesaw into a space from which they can look at it (i.e., look at what they are doing and the impact that they are having upon one another).[3]

Benjamin discusses a variety of states of thirdness. Although some of her terms can be a bit complicated to follow, they speak richly to the complexities of any dyadic relationship, and in particular to the perils and impasses of relationships lacking thirdness. She writes about two types of thirdness that are of particular interest to my subject (though she employs other names for these two essential types as well). The two versions of thirds are what she refers to as the "one-in-the-third" and the "third-in-the-one." These terms seem a bit cumbersome, but when their meaning is unpacked they become quite relevant. As we will see momentarily, the one-in-the-third pertains to something closer to partners in a dyad working in conjunction with each other, while the third-in-the-one pertains more to how they work out differentiating from one another while remaining (intimately) connected.

The one-in-the-third

One-in-the-third[4] is also referred to as the "rhythmic third," hence the epigraph in this chapter's beginning, "It takes two to tango." Aron (2003) notes that rhythmicity in a dyad requires a kind of mutual accommodation, wherein both partners surrender to a third form that is not about either of them exclusively, but requires both of their participation, participation marked by working-off-of-and-with one another. Thirdness as represented in the one-in-the-third is especially in evidence in the performance of the tango. The tango relies upon the intersubjective experience of the two dancers in relationship to the form of dance itself as the third subject that informs how they surrender to one another. This is critical, because the tango relies upon an agreement (a covenant) between the "leader" (typically the male dancer) and the "follower" (typically the female).

It could be quite easy for one who is insecure in adopting these roles to confuse this with the male invoking a position of dominance and the female a position of submission. No doubt with some naïve beginning dancers this might be the case. But the tango, in its true spirit, involves each partner's surrender to the third subject of the form its dancing takes. This is a prescriptive form that defines how the partners move closely in relationship to one another, off of which they might begin to improvise their own co-created version of thirdness. All of this occurs in a "play space," a "potential space," and a "transitional space" in which the elegance of the dance unfolds precisely because it is about surrender and the automatic mutual accommodation that ensues. In this manner, it is not remotely about a dueling mode of dominance and submission. This is because, paradoxically, the leader can only lead to the extent that the follower follows *and* vice versa. The partners are instantly and always defined by their exquisite mutual dependency upon one another. There can be no actual dominance and submission, notwithstanding what might from a gender-neutral perspective appear to be the male dominating the female. Neither can perform without the other, as they cannot perform without both surrendering to the thirdness of the tango (Kavaler-Adler, 2012; Metzl, 2012; Ringstrom, 2012b). Like making love, it involves a kind of embeddedness of experience (Wallin, 2007). In the tango, reflexivity is at a minimum. Being in the moment together is what counts. Talking about it later is a whole other level of discourse. (One might imagine professional tango dancers and their dance coach reviewing a video of their performance and reflexively critiquing what was working and was not.)

Jazz musicians also perform in this manner, typically sharing in common a rehearsed and well-known tune that becomes a third to which each musician takes turns improvising new riffs. And it is also most certainly the case that each player's riff potentially begins to inspire the others' creative riffs as well. This kind of thirdness is also in evidence in moments of improvisational theater. There, the actors surrender to one another's spontaneously suggested versions of reality. Off of these, they then play in a process that builds upon one another's suggested realities. In so doing, they begin co-creating an intersubjective reality of their own. This then becomes a mini-form of a whole spontaneously generated theatrical production. In this back-and-forth manner, each partner keeps furthering the intersubjective world that they are co-creating by taking one another's suggestions to heart, and building off of them until their story reaches its own organic conclusion, which is obvious to both of them and to the audience.

When sex or lovemaking occurs in a one-in-the-third manner, the partners begin to melt into one another's arms and legs and bodies and lips, and the reciprocating interpenetration of genitals makes the pleasuring of each other as important as it is to one's self. There is a vulnerability that is so taken for granted that it is not even thought about during sex. Nevertheless, the maintenance of this vulnerability is not so easy, and it's not hard to see how, over time, a myriad of quotidian conflicts may jeopardize this.

What is crucial in understanding this version of thirdness is that it corrects historically earlier applications of psychoanalysis to couples treatment that likely would have interpreted the phenomenon of one-in-the-third as a kind of "symbiosis" or "merger," a defense against individuation. Unfortunately, such an interpretation would be emblematic of a kind of pathological regression in the couple. This was particularly the case given psychoanalysis' historical tilt towards the importance of personal liberation and its implicit valuing of psychoanalytic cure, resulting in one becoming a more differentiated self. While the idea of differentiation, as seen through the lens of self-actualization, remains very important in this model of psychoanalysis, it is now grounded in the importance of mutual recognition, and therefore underscores that differentiation of self is always in some manner linked to thirdness. Hence, the one-in-the-third can be seen as a particularly compelling way to think about how differentiated, self-actualized selves can tango without totally losing their sense of self.

Since most couples seeking treatment typically present with wildly discordant points of view, emerging from what seem to be wildly discordant subjective versions of reality, what is the point of the concept of one-in-the-thirdness? If a couple can tango, why would they even need therapy? The reason the construct is important is that it is important for the couple's therapist to also look for places in discordant couples' relationships that exhibit actual "pockets" of one-in-the-thirdness, where they really can be more genuinely accommodative to one another and not submissive. It is often not easy to see this in discordant couples, but can be an amazing handhold on some potential zones of automatic collaboration and negotiation that are readily dismissible in the midst of the couple's seemingly intractable complaints.

For example, I have worked with couples whose intimacy had gradually diminished over the years, but who have a very long-established track record of having parented very cooperatively, as well as having been able to build a lovely and generative life together. Finding elements of one-in-the-thirdness can be a way of helping such couples to see what is of value in their relationship, including a partial explanation for their initial attraction as well as what has sustained them for many years, despite what might be seen as irreconcilable differences.

An interesting and not so unique example of the pursuit of certain developmental longings for one-in-the-thirdness can be taken up in the controversial nature of what might be thought of more conventionally as perversions: highly cooperative and accommodative versions of collaboration and negotiation employed by some couples, even when unwittingly, for the purpose of working through together otherwise prospectively shameful versions of self. This occurs in some cases in the form of mutually co-created sexual activities. In this manner, the partners' playful and improvisatory mode of relating seems to enable an increased degree of connection to one another and to themselves.

The role of sexual perversion in relationships

The place of sexual perversions has been radically reexamined in contemporary relational literature[5] as a profoundly significant way to take up and question the so-called normative nature of long-term intimate committed relationships. It has been especially useful in interrogating the presumptive version of intimate relationships that has been routinely defined and proscribed by certain idealized conventions of the heterosexual institution of marriage.

The advent of the twenty-first century has brought with it a multitude of alternative views on the normalcy of relationships, providing evidence of a huge diversity of sexual couplings. These alternative views challenge that the potential rigidity and inflexibility of the conventional model can be a symptom in its own right. Instead, the forward thrust of our contemporary psychoanalytic literature asserts that it is in our open-minded investigation of the so-called perverse that we create an opportunity to call into question some basic assumptions that dominate the nature of so-called normal love. Dimen's (2003) insights are especially germane to this. She writes:

> Perversion and that inadequately specific term normality construct each other ... How do you know what's normal unless you know what's not, unless you have a boundary? How do you know what's not normal unless you know what is? In the discourse of psychosexuality, perversion and heteronormity constitute each other's limits. Perversion marks the boundary across which you become an outlaw. Normality marks off the boundary that, if stayed inside, keeps you safe from shame, disgust, and anxiety. The binary thus formed is, however, only illusorily clear. Even people who engage in normal sexuality, Freud says, tend to include the perverse moment or two in their ordinary sexual practice ... The label of perversion is as clinically superfluous as we now understand the label of homosexuality to be. It is not a diagnostic category; it does not tell us what to do. Now we take our clinical cue not from disorders of desire from struggles of self and relationship—splits and psyche, maladies of object love, infirmities of intimacy.
>
> (pp. 271, 287)

Picking up on Dimen's theme and wedding it to earlier discussion of thirdness—in particular, one-in-the-thirdness—we can begin to see in the following two examples how couples worked out versions of this rhythmic thirdness in manners that created instances of self-actualization, mutual recognition, and the relationship having a mind of its own.

Rob and Donna

I had worked with Rob and Donna for about six months when they sheepishly introduced their concern about what they thought might reflect a symptom in their relationship regarding their sexual behavior. Notably, they had come into treatment regarding some differences about rearing their children. What was at stake for each, in terms of selfobject longings and the vicious circle triggering their repetitive dimensions of transference, was fairly easily discerned. Donna leaned toward a more protective orientation to parenting, while Rob leaned toward a somewhat more permissive one. Donna wanted Rob to be more of the idealizing protective father variety that her father had been. Rob wanted more mirroring or reflection of his attuned capacity as a parent, especially in terms of acknowledging the value of his version of what entailed a proper level of parental restraint on their children's adventures in the world: to be involved without hovering. Expectedly, part of what they were initially battling over was the children's preference for Dad's style, and therefore Mom feeling put down and put out.

Though they began treatment at one another's throats, they also quickly embraced the perspectivality of the model, and got curious about their backgrounds. Thus, they were quickly able to contextualize their quarrels in terms of the expectancies they had about child-rearing from their own development. For example, Donna grew up in an inner city where crime was a daily aspect of life, and both of her parents were unified in their admonitions about how to conduct oneself to remain safe. Conversely, Rob grew up in the rural Midwest, where exploration and even mischief were a routine aspect of personal growth. In his mind, development always must face some risks from which a child typically learns how to form better judgments about life without too much risk of harm.

Once their respective fears regarding over-protection versus under-protection could be contextualized in their upbringings, both let down their guard and treated one another's parenting perspective with greater empathy. On this basis, they could more easily collaborate and negotiate more common rules with their children. This entailed Dad no longer being the "good cop" and Mom being the "bad cop." Instead, they became parents with a clear collaborative front that could specify with their children what was negotiable and, equally importantly, what was not. Furthermore, any particular permission for one situation was never necessarily a binding precedent for any future circumstance.

It was in the context of this good work that Rob and Donna finally decided to confess what they thought of as their secret perversion. They were especially vexed by this confession, as it seemed so afield from their otherwise rather everyday problem with parenting.

Somewhat sheepishly, they shared what they called their secret penchant for engaging in sexual bondage. This had originated early in their relationship, from their mutual pleasure in watching pornography. Attempting to mitigate their shame, they reminded me that they were a devoted couple who were adamant that they would never cheat on one another. However, they also bemoaned that the luster of their early sexual attraction had developed a lot of "lack." Eventually, they incorporated the rental of pornographic videos at their corner video store to enliven their "date nights." As this was a very collaborative effort, it was quite normal for one or the other to pick up a video on his or her way home from work, depending upon whose schedule could more easily accommodate the errand. Over time, however, they noticed that their selections "accidentally" revealed that they preferred porn that involved bondage.

Early on, their episodes of bondage had been pretty light, though progressively they became more and more elaborate and involved. Eventually, one night after having shared a bottle of Chardonnay, they decided that this year's Christmas present to one another would involve whatever intriguing contraption they thought either would find exciting to experiment with. Eventually, they developed quite a "pleasure chest" of toys, strap-ons, restraints, whips, and a large variety of objects for mutual anal penetration. They were especially careful to hide their "goodies" (or "baddies," as they also playfully called them) from their children. They were also careful only to engage in their experimental play when they were home alone, for example, when their son and daughter had happily obtained sleepovers at friend's homes.

Their question to me, however, was: Was there something "sick" in their little perversion? What became apparent in our examination was that it was an implicit way in which they were playing with their discord over whose "dominant style of parenting" was being played out. For example, Rob was most inclined to be "the submissive" to Donna's domination after he had gotten his way regarding some real life parenting issue. Once this was disclosed, it suddenly dawned on them that Donna was doing something in return—asking to be the "submissive" on the occasions her parenting style triumphed over Rob's. In effect, each was "atoning" for the guilty pleasure of having gotten their way. Their little perversion had co-creatively enabled each of them to indulge the other submissively, as a way of in part concealing their turns at being the dominant parent.

I shared that their hypotheses made a lot of sense to me. Rather than seeing them as ill, I marveled at the creativity of their implicit minds, through which they had unwittingly arrived at such an exciting and mutually gratifying way to balance out their anxieties. I also noted, however, that as their children were approaching adolescence their parenting decisions, especially regarding safety, could involve much higher stakes. On that basis, I could see why they finally decided to come into therapy, as it was likely that their perversion was not offsetting some of the feelings regarding the very palpable temporary power imbalances that would arise from their fights. Hence, their need to come into treatment and to finally take up the heretofore inexplicable as it applied to many areas of their lives.

At this point, the treatment had evolved from each partner becoming more curious about their intrasubjective world and their inner conflicts, to beginning to focus more on their intersubjective world. In this latter world, they were becoming more curious about bearing witness to one another's personal development and to their interpersonal negotiations.

As this evolution in therapy had mitigated some of their dominance and submission issues, they also somewhat sadly found themselves less inclined to engage in their perversion, which after all had had a highly pleasurable aspect it. On the other hand, they also mentioned that they'd begun to develop more interest in other means of sensual pleasuring. Over the summer, while their children were in camp, they took a weeklong course in Tantric yoga, exploring the nature of mutual sensual massage, ejaculatory control, and a variety of techniques for intensifying each other's sexual experiences. Just for the hell of it, they added, they kept their bondage toys, which they now consciously brought out to play with once in a while—especially when, once again, one of them had won the parenting problem, he or she would have to recognize their being "bad" and accept their "due punishment." There seemed to be something joyously freeing in this choosing whether tonight it would be Tantric sex or good old S&M.

Bill and Desirée

Bill and Desirée were a couple in their early thirties who were contemplating marriage for the first time in their lives; hence they came to me for pre-marital therapy.

Much like Rob and Donna, their course of treatment moved fairly quickly through the assessment of their selfobject and repetitive dimension transferences. They were open to the idea of perspectivalism, since it seemed in keeping with their liberal arts and sciences undergraduate experiences in college. They also were open about sharing their backgrounds, which was most helpful in helping determine where they seemed to rather naturally fit, and what would likely be sources of controversy that would require a deeper understanding of themselves and of one another.

Also, like Rob and Donna, this plateau of understanding and trust and faith in treatment finally allowed them to feel safe enough to introduce their "dirty little secret" regarding their sex life. In their case, they were quick to point out that the word *dirty* was something of both a pun and a fact. Like Donna and Rob, they had indulged in watching a little porn, and to their shock and surprise both admitted their fascination with anal penetration. Each had had their own previous experiences with other partners, though their reactions to these experiences were at best mixed. Ultimately, the intermittent, potentially soiling aspects of these activities with previous partners felt hugely embarrassing.

Though privately neither Bill and Desirée seemed in any way in conflict with their "little perversion," in introducing it they wondered if there was something unconscious going on that might at some point in the future lend to the derailment of their relationship. As we explored their respective backgrounds, we uncovered that both had come from homes with overbearingly fastidious mothers and submissive fathers. Dirt and getting dirty were highly prohibited in each of their upbringings, which propelled each into a fascination with the "unclean," which for each represented something of the forbidden. Implicitly, they had found in each other a soulmate in the fascination of filth—one with whom they could play without fear of humiliation.

Outside of their little perversion, there was nothing either wasteful or filthy about Bill and Desirée. On the contrary, Bill was a patent attorney and Desirée was a cookbook editor. They enjoyed a life of fine wine and food, travel, and lovely attire, and by all accounts kept what sounded like a lovely and tidy home. It was in this context, however, that the trajectory of their private paths converged, exposing their secrets. In the case of Desirée and Bill, this little perversion was a portal into each other's private world. Because it was one vulnerable to shame, humiliation, and denigration, they paradoxically reinforced their trust in one another, along with their experience of pleasure. In their case, their perversion symbolized a mode of sexual play that deepened their trust in exit's exposing themselves to one another. In all of these ways, Bill and Desirée left therapy satisfied that their marriage could be a solid one.

The third-in-the-one

Aron (2003) notes a second version of thirdness according to Benjamin, which she refers to as the third-in-the-one. She also refers to this version of thirdness as the "symbolic," "moral," or "intentional third." Aron states that Benjamin employs these synonymous terms "in order to highlight that this third creates a space for differentiation in what is ordinarily called oneness" (p. 629). Differentiation from oneness occurs when one responds to another mirroring their experience by "marking" (Fonagy et al., 2004); as close as they may come to capturing something of the other's experience (implying sameness), while noting their own experience remains inextricably different. Marking is a way of indicating that "this is *my* experience of *your* experience." "My" experience may indicate that "I" sees things closely to how you see/experience them, but it is nevertheless never identical. We are not identical twins, hence the pursuit of twinship in intimate relationships is inevitably fraught with difficulty.[6]

At this point, it should become clearer how and why the concept of thirdness is so important to the third major theme of this book, the relationship having a mind of its own. The term *relationship* is the embodiment of connection between two people. That connection comes to a standstill when it founders in complementarity. It comes alive in thirdness, whether it's the tango of the rhythmicity in the one-in-the-third or the process of connecting through acknowledging difference, the third-in-the-one, crucial to self-actualization and its being mutually recognized by the couple.

From dialectics of difference to thirdness

Step Five in the previous chapter folds readily into Step Six, insofar as what each couple is learning about themselves intrapsychically (i.e., intrasubjectively) becomes the foundation from which they can speak of their differences in a clearer and more cogent manner than before. The "dialectics of difference," a concept from Bollas (1989), works beautifully: intrasubjectively in terms of differences between multiple self-states, and intersubjectively in terms of differences between the partners.

Ultimately, and of huge importance, is that the dialectics of difference become the foundation from which "dialogical truth" begins to emerge. This happens when co-creating interpretive versions of thirdness account for who the two partners are to one another. This is of course a point crucial to self-actualization. But, even more importantly, the dialectics of difference serve to extend one's interpretive horizons (Stern, 1997) by introducing one another's alternative perspectives. This is perhaps one of the greatest assets of a long-term committed relationship, especially when it becomes a recognized and useable feature of that relationship. It marks what is most unique not only of the two individuals, but also of what they have created together, what would never be the same with any other partners.[7] It further conveys who they have become together.

This point of view evolves out of their recognition of their relationship having a mind of its own, though one they have ineffably created together. It is in this manner—though the partners begin from positions of extraordinary difference—that they learn something much more in general that they have in common. This is exquisitely illustrated in the case of Ken and Courtney, whose original conflicts over sexual desire ended up sharing many common third properties; these would inform them as much of what they shared in common as that which they shared in difference. (This was a case that I supervised and was therefore privy to its audio recording, from which this transcript was produced.)

Courtney and Ken

Courtney: Should we talk about the other night?

Ken: It's why we're here, isn't it?

C: I know, but it's so embarrassing ... but no, you're right, it's why we're here.

K: My wife is embarrassed to tell you that I wanted to have sex with her the other night!

C: I'm *not* embarrassed about that! It's more about what happened.

K: So. Tell the doctor.

C: It's about how you came home drunk and wanted to have sex, it felt, it felt so "slam-bam-not-even-thank-you-ma'am!" It felt so disconnected, so, sort of degrading. That's the way it's been feeling lately the last couple of times you have wanted to have sex.

Dr. X: Wait, Courtney, are you saying that Ken has been *wanting* to have sex with you? [*She nods.*] Is that right, Ken? [*He nods.*] Because, I thought that you said recently that this *is* what you wanted to be happening—to be having sex—and also that you guys hadn't been, for some time, for several years? [*Her nod affirmed the therapist's questions.*] And, that it had been Ken who hadn't seemingly wanted it—sex, that is—buuut, now he does? [*More nodding from both.*] ... Sooo, I am sort of confused?

C: No, that has all changed ... for the good, but ...

K: [*Interrupting*] And, by the way, for the record, doc, there wasn't any "slam bam ... " I always take care of her needs, always! Right?! [*Looking at Courtney.*]

C: No, that's true, it's just, it's just I didn't want it, because it felt so, I don't know, like I said, disconnected. Like it wasn't me, like I was someone else, like an object. So I just rolled over and tried to go to sleep.

K: Like I said, you can't say that I ever ignored you, your needs, that is. I *always* made sure that you were satisfied, more than satisfied, right?! Don't lie.

C: No that's true, in the beginning, it was amazing. Our sex life was incredible!

Dr. X: Really, what made it incredible?

C: Ken always wanted me in those days.

K: Just like I have been again.

Dr. X: So what did go on in the beginning? What has been going on subsequently? And what's going on now?

K: For a long time, for years, I have had troubles with my back, serious, crippling, immobilizing problems. I sometimes couldn't work for long stretches. But in the last half-year or so, I have been working out. I have a new routine, a great new trainer, and it's been changing my life. I finally feel good in my body. I feel strong again, like a man, and that's making me feel worthier and hornier. So I have been wanting my wife.

C: The problem is, it's clear that you want sex, but it doesn't feel like it's about me, like I could be anybody, "a piece of meat."

K: That's ridiculous … you're the only woman I ever wanted or want to be with. You know that; that I would never cheat on you!

Dr. X: Well, let's hear Courtney out, find out what she's experiencing.

C: It's true, I never worry about that with Ken, never. It's just like in the beginning … you only wanted me if I was wearing lingerie.

K: What's wrong with lingerie? You look fantastic in it! Of course I did and do!

C: No, no, you're not getting me. I loved dressing up in lingerie. In fact, it was my idea! I loved it. It made me feel really sexy. It's just that after a while, it seemed like that was the only time, you know, that you wanted to have sex. It dawned on me, we only had sex when I initiated, you know, like that. Wearing stuff. I started thinking, "It's not me that Ken wants, it's the lingerie." I started thinking of myself as an object. So I suddenly stopped. And, I was right. So did you. You stopped wanting me! And, that was pretty much that, you know, except for, you know, once in a while, and well, enough to have a couple of kids, I guess.

Dr. X: What about that Ken?

K: Fuck. I didn't know that. When you stopped wearing the lingerie, I thought it was because you didn't want me anymore. You know, that I was a fuckup. I was having problems physically, financially, professionally. There was no way that I was going to pursue you then and be rejected, rejected one more time by life, one more time, now by the most important person … my wife.

Dr. X: Wait a minute! Let me see if I get this right. So in the beginning, you Courtney are loving feeling sexy and powerful and turning Ken on, getting all dolled up in lingerie and making him crazy with desire about you?

C: Uh huh, until I started feeling like an object, you know, like a manikin.

Dr. X: And you, Ken, were in fact feeling crazy nuts with desire for Courtney, just as long as she desired you?

K: Absolutely!

Dr. X: And, I take it, not experiencing her as an object, but in fact as powerful, as the woman of your desire?

K: Until she abruptly stopped, then I felt worthless. It just confirmed my worst fears about myself.

Dr. X: So suddenly, you felt undesirable.

K: That's right.

Dr. X: So this is interesting. Each of you were actually experiencing the other as powerful objects of desire [*Note: meaning, of course, as subjects of desire*], and each of you were experiencing yourself as the other's object of desire [*Note: again meaning subjects of desire*]. Until, that is—and this is a big "until"—you started each experiencing yourself as devalued objects in the other's eyes, hearts, hell, even genitals. It's like you suddenly stopped imagining yourself in that delicious way that you did, that you were the hungered-for-other, to be devoured and no one else would do. Suddenly, you became "fast food," "takeout," and that was gross after dining on gourmet for so long. What's interesting, dare I say tragic, is what happened next. As soon as you felt "objectified" in the mind of the other, you began treating yourselves and one another very quickly *in* that manner. That spelled the rapid end to what was genuinely delicious for both of you. In fact, at this point, it sounds like any renewed sense of desiring and wishing to be desired converts into the experience of something about requiring and being required.

C: That sounds so right!

K: To me, too.

Dr. X: So your relationship has stagnated there for a very long time. It's gathered its own sinking weight, lending to its drowning. Pregnancies, job pressures, losses and gains, injuries, body image problems, ugh. You both so readily imagine your undesirability and end up making it so.

[*Both are nodding appreciatively.*]

Dr. X: It's not all that hard to imagine what happened the other evening that you are describing to me. In a sense, Ken, you have had to overcome a lot to feel "good enough" about yourself to risk "coming on" to Courtney. Alcohol has been known to smooth the way for many a shamed ego. Though, Courtney, it's also not so hard to understand that you imagine yourself *still* only a sex "object" to Ken.

C: Well, it's not like I am feeling all *that* great about my body!

K: You're crazy! You're beautiful! You hear that, doc, my wife is crazy! She's the most beautiful woman I know. You can see for yourself.

Dr. X: So perhaps some of your doubt of Ken's desire is some self-doubt of your own about your desirability, Courtney?

C: Probably ... yeah.

K: Thank you!!!

Dr. X: And, perhaps the drinking and your manner of approach, a manner that might have been unusually "aggressive," was about overcoming some of your own doubts, Ken?

K: Probably ... yeah ... sure.

Dr. X: In a way, so much of what I am hearing here is how you are each turning your experiences of desiring and being desired into icky requirements. Real turnoffs, especially in relation to how you once experienced each other. The power you experienced as a woman, Courtney, especially playfully, but so powerfully seductive, devolved into a repulsive sense of demand, of requirement, of "objectification" as you say, that robbed you of this being about you! That killed it. And, Ken, when it seemed that Courtney no longer wanted you, that you were not worthy of her irresistible seduction, you felt a requirement to perform, to try to present yourself as worthy in a manner that felt too disingenuous to pull off. Very quickly, you both went on strike. To hell with requirements, to hell with each other, and, ultimately, to hell with yourselves. There are no beggars in this relationship; better to do without than suffer the humiliation of the rebuff. And, in this manner, where desire(ment) becomes a requirement, better to desist with need altogether. In a sense, although maybe an awkward renewal, there is a beginning, and not surprisingly all that icky humiliation has to follow, at least until you can return to feeling your desire and capacity to be desired.

Like so many couples, Ken and Courtney found that their desire had devolved into the "politics of desire," which quickly degenerated into the "politics of worth." Finally, all of this got abysmally displaced onto a world of the "politics of contribution," as in "who the hell is doing the most around here?" This is a rather common displacement born of negative thirdness. But as we look more closely, what becomes apparent is what resides beneath their story: deeper structures of common identification. These include comparable patterns of transference that are composed of longings and fears, hopes and dreads. These primary forms of complex identity structure within each partner become enacted through unconsciously instructing each other who we are to be in one scene after another; these scenes go on and on without discernible beginnings, middles, or ends, and are in fact episodically repetitive.

So what is happening with Courtney and Ken? At the simplest level, we see that each harbors self-states imagining their lack of desirability, in contrast to other self-states in which they can imagine it. As the transcript portrays, their self-states of imagined desirability are highly vulnerable to shifting at any moment into ones mired in doubt. The triggers for these self-state changes are relational, as in how each is treating the other, but also very much a part of their deeply private body images, as well as how these relate to their capacity to imagine being subjects of desire. Most importantly, these confusions of self-states readily lend to experiences of misrecognition and to mutual negation.

In Courtney's case, she was quick to interpret Ken's lust for her wearing lingerie as an insidious mode of objectification. In this case, she hadn't lost her sense of her desirability as much as she experienced herself, not as a subject, but as an object, a "piece of meat." The shift in Courtney lends to Ken's swift reaction—assuming Courtney does not desire him. This, of course, instantly generates his feelings of inadequacy. Evidence supporting his conclusion was confirmed as soon as she no longer dressed in an alluring manner. This confirmed to him that she no longer wanted him.

This kind of *folie-à-deux* is very common in couples who once upon a time had a very gratifying sex life, only to see it inexplicably dry up. Thereafter, it seems cordoned off by a host of rationalizations about too much stress, too little sleep, too many kids, too much work, and so forth. Of course, the latter conditions can impose themselves on couples, but are more readily worked around where there is less vulnerability to self-states constituted in fears of being unwanted.

Two things emerge: The couple's communication devolves into the factuality of what each is doing (or not), which rapidly devolves into doer-and-done-to discourse, leading swiftly to the reversibility of split complementarity of who is the dominant party and who is submissive (i.e., the "victim"; Benjamin, 2004). The reversibility arises almost immediately, with each claiming this later role. Locked into entrenched patterns of defensiveness, neither seems to get that which is all too apparent to me: In their own ways, each one is working his or her ass off while feeling mutually exhausted. As Benjamin notes, when the life of the dyad becomes mired in the reciprocating accusations of the doer and done-to, they enter into what seems to be an interminable abysmal binary encampment. In the face of this, the therapist must become the voice of the third. Benjamin locates the third as "a vantage point outside the two" (p. 7). The thirdness of the therapist came in her interpreting to the partners what they shared in common.

Thus, the thirdness of the therapist's interpretation creates the possibility of a beginning dialogue, which (at least now) could enable the couple to recognize the mutuality of their state. This, of course, also includes the caveat that more icky humiliation might follow. They are especially vulnerable to this around a resumption of feeling desire, including a felt capacity to be desired. In these latter cases, there is an increased vulnerability to potential rejection. Still, with the emergence of a third interpretive structure, the couple can begin to create something of a bridge of thirdness that will lend to greater meta-cognition and meta-communication in their future dialogue.

Intersubjective collaboration and negotiation

The discussion of thirdness thus far has fleshed out what is a fundamentally critical issue in the life of a couple: how the partners work out lives together, constituted in terms of the aesthetics of their sameness and difference. This tension can lead to an enormous amount of creativity and vigor in a relationship, or it can lead to the possibility of devolving into the "teeth-grinding" stasis of complementarity when it cannot be authentically negotiated. As Pizer (2003) noted, when relationships cannot be negotiated from a position of mutual recognition, they must be on the basis of power.

Power is the key differential in complementarity, each partner fighting to have it their own way, whether that way involves the moral authority of "victim" or the domineering authority of how meaning is made. Finally, this power can manifest in the most grotesque of manners (e.g., through physical force), which nevertheless remains a systemic issue, and not one isolated to the perpetrator and the victim. As Pizer (1998) intones:

Negotiation is intrapsychic, interpersonal, and intersubjective, and it is vital to our biological existence. Negotiation is intrapsychic in the sense

193

that we must each mediate within ourselves the containment and expression of drive and affect, or in our contradiction and multiplicity, as well as in tension in living between engagement in the fresh potentials of the present moment and in management in the conservative grip of repetition of our past experience. Negotiation is interpersonal in the sense that we're always arranging with one another matters of desire, safety, anxiety, power, convenience, fairness, and so on. Negotiation is intersubjective in the sense that we constantly influence one another, consciously and unconsciously, from infancy onward in a myriad of ways, from minute adjustments to gross adaptations.

(p. 2)

An example of such collaboration and negotiation in the case of Nicole and Russell emerged from their reckoning with discordant details in their relationship. This case illustration is a continuation of treatment with Nicole and Russell presented earlier in Step Five.

Nicole and Russell (Part Two)

One Monday morning, I received a totally atypical and urgent email from Russell, asking if I could see them sooner than their routine end-of-the-week appointment. As I had a free appointment hour, I encouraged them to come in. Nicole began the session stating that they had a terrible fight over the weekend that culminated in Russell flinging a butter plate against the wall, a physical display of anger that she had never witnessed in their entire relationship. This act, she said, was emblematic of how Russell's anger could go from zero to 200 miles per hour, much like we had discussed previously, which was something she both loathed and found very intimidating. His violent act truly frightened her this time, as she immediately equated it as a mere stepping stone to his becoming violent with her, and this was completely unacceptable. She exclaimed, "I will not stay in a marriage where such a thing might happen."

Although my own clinical intuition was that Russell would not be capable of physical violence toward anyone, much less Nicole, it was clear that her fear had to be embraced as very real—at least for her. Thus, I first attended to it by stating that, notwithstanding that Russell's violence was demonstrated through the destruction of an object—a far cry from physical violence perpetrated by one upon another—Nicole was clearly, profoundly scared and that that had to be taken very seriously.

Though initially defensive regarding Nicole's accusation, to his credit Russell quickly apologized for having given her such a scare. He reiterated that, although he seemed out of control, his act of breaking an object was more histrionic, to make a point, than truly being "out of control." His comment provoked Nicole to add that, prior to this incident, she had actually asked that they discontinue their fight and talk about it another day, perhaps even saving it for their next therapy appointment. Russell acknowledged this and openly regretted that he hadn't heeded her request.

Following this comment, I asked why he hadn't accepted Nicole's idea, especially given the numerous occasions he had been the one to suggest they stop an argument and to save it for a calmer, more rational moment. In reply, he once again apologized for his actions, but then began to account for his degree of upset, which was reflective of the depth of his hurt feelings over something Nicole had said.

In a passing conversation over the weekend, Nicole quite innocently spoke of an odd speech pattern Russell's father had, the nature of which was a source of sensitivity to his father. Hearing Nicole say this made him feel quite defensive of his father, which totally came as a surprise to her, since usually Russell spoke quite disparagingly about his dad. She literally never imagined he would ever take umbrage with her comment. Consequently, she was both powerfully confused and terribly thrown. One could argue that this scenario approximated circumstances formulaic of a way of thinking about trauma: the assault of the unimaginable (Ringstrom, 1999, 2010d).

The position that Russell took also supported Nicole's strong conviction that there was something about his family that made her feel very alienated, as she felt pressured to contain her spontaneity around them for fear of hurting their feelings. Thus, when Russell stated, "That wouldn't be a good thing to say to any of my siblings about our father, or for that matter to him," Nicole translated his admonishment into a proclamation, a veritable rule of behavior, and this was the very thing against which she most chafed in life (i.e., being told how to behave). Russell quickly clarified, "I never was nor am in any way saying that you can't be yourself. I'm not telling you not to say what you wish for that matter. It's simply that *you*, Nicole, are so anxious about what my family thinks about you! *You* are so fearful that they will not love you. Therefore, I was trying to advise you of what might be upsetting to them. Can't you see, at least in part, that I was trying to protect your interests, not mine, nor even theirs, for that matter?"

Nicole nevertheless continued in her rant that there was a power differential between their families. She argued that in her family everyone was encouraged to speak what they felt, including their anger (as discussed in Part One of this case illustration, in Step Five), whereas in Russell's family there was a code of politeness that obscured difference, a point that Russell had readily acknowledged in many sessions.

The tipping point for Russell was that he felt once again that Nicole was unfairly and unabashedly being critical of his family, whereas there were plenty of things about hers that he could readily call into question. For example, there was a business enterprise with which they were modestly involved with one of her siblings that had gone sour, and to which they were not privy until such time as it was too late to do anything about it. Nicole jumped in and protested, "Yes, and I took this up with my brother and really let him have it!" Russell acknowledged this, but retorted, "I am only trying to say that we both have things regarding each other's families about which we can complain, but you seem to single my family out as if there aren't things about your family that I also object to."

Russell's degree of narcissistic rage over what he experienced as a perpetually imbalanced and unfair lambasting of his family fomented into his feeling compelled to "get in the last word" through his hurling the butter plate against the wall, shattering it into pieces. I took a moment to speak about the principle of self-righting, wherein in rage and especially at moments of humiliation (one of which Russell was clearly suffering) a common reaction is a rageful outburst (Malin, 1997), much like the one Russell had spontaneously gotten swept away in.

Notwithstanding this point, I underscored that explanations are not excuses. Certain behaviors, while understandable, can remain unacceptable to one's spouse, though they may be fine to another couple. So, clearly, Russell's violent act of smashing an inanimate butter plate was simply unacceptable to Nicole, and that was in large part because, for her, she was unable to differentiate violence with respect to inanimate objects from violence between human beings. Worsening the effect was that in her futuristic fantasies, someday even their daughter Penelope might be subjected to this demonstration of violence. This latter thought arose from her own developmental history, in which Nicole had witnessed her father on numerous occasions become physical with some of her siblings, though never herself.

Part of what had been heating up their controversy over their families was their plan in the coming year to relocate on the East Coast and to live closer to them. This situation reminded me of a quote from one of the grandfathers of family therapy, Carl Whitaker, in which he said, "The fundamental question in every marriage, is, whose family are we going to recreate?" At least subliminally, this question was playing a major role in their marriage, especially given their radically different family cultures.

Clearly, few issues in a relationship are as compelling as the necessity for collaborating and negotiating the partners' family cultures, since they are the bedrock of all of the potentially contentious issues posited in Step Three (e.g., attachment style, multigenerational transmissions of affect management, gendered and cultural issues, etc.). All of these elements culminate in each one's largely unknown theory of mind.

Negotiating the stylistic differences of their backgrounds was enormous. Russell's family could be seen as reflecting what Beaver and Voeller (1983) described as a family system constituted by a "centripetal" force field as opposed to a "centrifugal" one. The centrifugal force field was more descriptive of Nicole's family, as it is one in which family members "fly" away from one another. A centripetal force field was more descriptive of Russell's family, which involves family members' tendency to automatically pull together.

How these cultures played out in their respective family systems was that in Russell's family, on any occasion in which some members of the family gathered, it was presumed that all the family members were also to be invited. This was clearly not the presumption of Nicole's family. A recurrent futuristic fantasy scenario that made Nicole bristle (and that had happened on occasion) was that they would invite some members of Russell's family for an afternoon visit, only to discover upon their opening the door that all his family members—including his

196

parents, his sisters, their husbands, and even some of their young adult children—were standing there.

In contrast to this centripetal style, Nicole's family exhibited more of a centrifugal force—the members behaved more independently of one another. Occasions could readily take place among two members without worry that others would feel left out. Likewise, in her family, members could more readily speak their minds without grave concern over hurting one another's feelings, since when feelings were hurt, they either repaired their ruptures or avoided one another until the issue slipped into the oblivion of repression. In the diagnostic of differences in each of their families, Russell's mother "stuck it out" with his father's episodic fits of rage, while Nicole's mother divorced her father after decades of a contentious marriage, having endured only so long as the final launching of the youngest child into adulthood.

So, as Russell and Nicole thought more and more about moving back East, much closer to their family homes, the striking differences between their family cultures were making them both very anxious. They felt mightily adrift as to how they would collaborate and negotiate their differences; indeed, they seemed almost oblivious to the idea that collaboration and negotiation was even a possibility. What seemed acutely lost on them was that they could (and would absolutely need to) come to terms with creating their own family culture, one synergistically influenced by both of their families of origin, while also structured and presented to the world on their own terms. This version of thirdness—a complexly created family culture of their own—would therefore require considerable reflection, collaboration, and ultimately negotiation.

One enormous hurdle they had to overcome was Nicole's dual fears of being invaded *en masse* by Russell's family, and her dread of having to be "nice and polite" around them while degenerating depressively into a dreadfully self-conscious version of herself. Russell argued instead that their home was their castle, and that he was perfectly comfortable with making private, exclusive invitations to parts of his family, with the directive that others were not presumed to also be welcome at the specified visit.

Nicole immediately rebutted, "But what about when they just show up?!" Russell calmly asserted, "Then after that occasion I will take up with them how upset I was with them, and that this simply cannot keep happening." I added, "I suspect that this would start to be sufficiently humiliating to the family members that they would start to learn how to behave." Russell also added, however, that he simply couldn't be expected by Nicole to control his family's behavior in their own homes. So, if they were invited to his folks' house and suddenly his sisters or others showed up, he couldn't stop that. Nicole asked, "But can't you perhaps ask them not to have the others come over, that the visit be kept to just us and Penelope, especially since she prefers having time with her grandma and granddad and not have so many people?" Russell agreed to this as well, to which I added that their instituting new rules of decorum may have a system-wide effect.[8]

Something that kept striking me, however, was that while Russell was largely very congenial and forthcoming about some possible solutions about Nicole's urgent and anxious requests, he also seemed implicitly hurt. I commented on my observation, saying, "Russell, while you seem quite on board, even creatively coming up with solutions to at least some of Nicole's concerns, you nevertheless still seem upset. Am I accurately detecting something?" He acknowledged what I was stating, adding, "The thing that is so hurtful, Nicole, is how much you hate my family!"

Nicole countered that it was true. She acknowledged quite openly that she felt a considerable degree of hatred towards Russell's siblings, though not his parents, whom she loved, notwithstanding finding them terribly boring. Fascinatingly, rather than defending her hatred of Russell's siblings, she expressed astonishment about her own feelings! She continued to her own amazement that she'd become absolutely beside herself at the thought of their having done so little with their lives (especially in contrast to their highly successful brother Russell, who was the only one who moved away from home).

Indeed, part of what "burned her up" about Russell's family "cluster-fucks" was that they signified to Nicole that his siblings were "losers" with little to do in their lives, and therefore simply always deferring to the "cluster" mode rather than striking out on their own, exhibiting the kind of initiative that both she and Russell had. But, to her credit, she said that she was mostly confused with herself: "Why should I give a shit about what they are or aren't doing with their lives?!" Russell added gently, "Well, right, and after all it's not like your siblings did all that much with their lives. Right?"

Instead of becoming defensive, Nicole pondered Russell's comment, and she began describing her own childhood. The second of four children, she had by far done the most with her academic and artistic talents. She graduated with honors from her university, and had taken up her father's offer for economic support to all four children to study abroad. She was the only one that ever did. Instead, they all remained close to home, living their lackluster existences. She then reflected that an especially bitter pill to swallow from childhood was that her parents always tried to make a "secret" of her success. They insisted, for example, that she not speak of her accomplishments around her siblings. Growing up, her routinely stellar report cards had to be opened in private with her parents, who would then give her faint praise, lest she develop too big a head. Even more a matter of concern, she suddenly pondered, was their fear her siblings would develop even worse self-esteem, in relation to her accomplishments, than they already had. The irony, of course, was only so much of this could be kept private. Her siblings knew of her accomplishments, hated her for them, and ruthlessly mocked her *en masse*.

Years later, in adulthood, Nicole's siblings for the most part lived reasonably accomplished middle-class lives in their own right. Russell even noted that they seem to have come around to actually admiring their sister's achievements. What was becoming apparent, then (and so I proposed to Nicole), was that her own self-claimed "irrational" hatred of Russell's siblings was a displacement of feelings about her own from a much earlier age. What seemed to fuel her contempt was her fantasy about all her siblings-in-law presumed hateful envy of her. Though Russell conceded that of course his siblings might have some envy of both him and Nicole, in large part their concern was the degree to which he was happy with his marriage. To the degree he was, they would feel love towards Nicole.

This two-part illustration of Nicole and Russell seeks to examine how the therapeutic processes of developing a couple's capacity to be more reflective in the presence of one another (i.e., to take up conflictual self-states along with disavowed, unformulated dissociated ones) enables them to begin to collaborate and negotiate their relationship on an entirely different basis, one that also retains links to their developmental past, both in memory and in new manners of engaging their families of origin.

Paradox and surrender

Pizer (1998) notes that the:

> Negotiation of paradox and negotiation of conflict can be discriminated as subjective experiences. Conflict connotes dichotomous (or "trichotomous," and so on) interests or tugs between people and groups; or, in individuals, between divergent tendencies within a bounded nucleus of the self. On the other hand, paradox resides in the multiplicity of bounded nuclei within the self, where simultaneously coexisting nuclei (self-states, affect, self-other representations, and so on) reciprocally contradict or negate each other. Conflict can be resolved through interpersonal negotiation and meditation (you give and I give a little, or we are both helped or required to make concessions, and we arrive somewhere we can both live with or even codify by contract or treaty). Intrapsychic conflict may be resolved through choice (I'll accept *this* college) or renunciation (I'll let Dad keep Mom) or repression ("and never was heard a discouraging word"). On the other hand, paradox cannot be resolved; mutually negating elements continue to coexist, and the negotiation of paradox yields not resolution but a straddling or bridging, of contradictory perspectives.
>
> (p. 65)

The resolution—or perhaps better stated, the management—of paradox is noted by many (Benjamin, 2004; Ghent, 1990; Pizer, 1998; Safran, 2007) as frequently having to involve surrender. Surrender, as will be recalled from Step Five, may have a verisimilitude of appearance with submission, but is remarkably different in extremely important ways. Mitchell and Aron (1999) write:

> Whereas submission carries the connotation of defeat and is accompanied by resignation, surrender means, not subjugation, but transcendence and acceptance. The critical insight of [Ghent's] paper is that masochism is a perversion or distortion of this longing to surrender, to let go of

defensiveness, of the wish to be penetrated, for one's essence to be known and recognized. "Submission, losing oneself in the power of the other, becoming enslaved in one or other way to the master, is the ever available lookalike to surrender," Ghent writes.

(p. 212)

Bromberg (2006) notes that Ghent's concept of surrender is a highly creative and healthy one in the face of the inevitability of loss and pain in life, much of which cannot be controlled and therefore must be accepted. Herein the idea of transcendence is of such crucial importance, because it is only in this regard that the ego, notorious for its penchant to omnipotent control, can finally be surrendered. Until this happens, however, pride and therefore shame rule, especially in relationship to feelings of submission. Is it any wonder that the position of submissiveness in masochism so quickly reverts to its complementary position of sadism, a pattern that vexes couples—especially, that is, when they are looking for their partner (or themselves) to resolve paradoxes that can only really be taken up through acceptance of something that is negotiable neither within oneself nor between the partners?

Surrender, however, can be a tricky concept, insofar as it may pertain to some self-state that in a different relational context—and therefore in a different self-state—would no longer fit. Gentile (2007) writes:

> Submission, masochism, and sadism not only masquerade as surrender, they co-exist. One is always submitting or surrendering in relation to not only individual bodies but also the cultural bodies that provide meaning for experience. Thus, a critical analysis of power is imperative in order to explore the many different levels of submitting/surrendering. Resistance, goes hand in hand with power, often functioning to make it more visible.
>
> (p. 191)[9]

The case of Nicole and Russell demonstrates how, out of fiery confrontation with the non-negotiable, couples eventually must cobble together a means of surrender that enables them to accept insurmountable conditions in their relationship (which exist in all relationships) by ceasing to need to surmount them. Instead, they must find a means to accept these indelible aspects of their relationship and to understand that, indeed, they represented something unique about their congress.

The collaboration and negotiation of both the intrasubjective and the intersubjective sometimes can generate paradoxes that ultimately lead to states of surrender. Along the way, however, partners in a relationship can become extraordinarily confused, believing for example that they are doing something very positive for one another that abysmally backfires, much to their bewilderment and chagrin. Such was the case with Russell and Nicole.

Nicole and Russell (Part Three)

Although our work together had made some inroads in addressing their concerns about moving back East, there remained some aggravating issues over the differences in their family cultures. One in particular was that Nicole had recognized that she was powerfully jealous of Russell. Her jealousy reared its ugly head whenever she experienced him as placing something or someone ahead of her in his list of priorities. She had begrudgingly resigned herself to his career being his primary preoccupation, especially when he faced deadlines on multiple projects. And, though she had struggled with her jealousy a little, for the most part she had come to appreciate his devotion to their daughter, Penelope, with whom he was extraordinarily patient and attentive during the times he could break from his work and be with her.

In both of these ways, although Nicole still felt that she was in "third place," she had come more and more to accept what neither she nor Russell could change. However, when it came to considering their move back East, including the likelihood that Russell would be spending more time with his family, Nicole faced her proverbial "tipping point." This was something she feared surpassed anything that she could possibly accept. In the language of complexity theory, this became a point of "criticality," more commonly known as "the straw that broke the camel's back."

Fundamental to Nicole's complaint was her conviction that when she married Russell he would be exclusively devoted to her. Supportive of this illusion was the fact that when he courted, then proposed, then married Nicole, he had been clear that his family's proneness to merger could only be broken away from by his moving a continent away from them. Nicole concluded from this that Russell was all hers, unencumbered by any inclination, much less devotion to his family. The birth of their daughter had rudely awakened her to the fact that this was not the case. Now their discussions of their involvement with Russell's family felt tantamount to a betrayal.

Understandably, Russell felt profoundly misunderstood, and defensively described Nicole's "fantasies" as "irrational." The problem with this, I pointed out, was it located Nicole's irrationality as a problem of her "isolated mind," rather than taking up the complexity of dynamics they had co-constructed and in which they were now profoundly mired. Russell quickly embraced my point, perhaps as much as anything because he could see that what he said only made Nicole mad as hell; she fired back, "I feel like I am a nutcase! That this is all my fault! That you have nothing to do with this, nor any responsibility whatsoever for this issue."

Russell retorted, "Now hang on, Nicole! I'm not the one protesting seeing your family, but you are the one who is upset with seeing mine or, more to the point, my having any relationship with them at all." She blasted, "Well, don't you have issues with my family?" To which he rebutted, "Of course! They can be very irritating! Especially your mom! But I don't hate them. Nor do I feel obliged to see them all the time when you and Penelope do. Unlike you, I simply don't hate your family, so I can take them and leave them, which is what I say that you can do with my family!"

201

Clearly, Russell felt that what he was offering to Nicole was completely fair. He was indicating that as far as he was concerned, she was under no obligation to be with his family. Paradoxically, this claim appeared to backfire terribly. Although I could hear that Russell felt that he was liberating Nicole from a "toxic obligation" for being around his family, I sensed she heard this very differently.

Inadvertently, Russell was reinforcing Nicole's worst fear—that she was not important to him. Improvising, I said to Russell, "I think that you may have this all upside down, that in liberating Nicole from her obligation to you and your family, you make her feel unimportant; perhaps she'd rather hear something like, 'Now goddammit, Nicole! I expect you to suck it up and to come with me and Penelope this weekend to see my family! You're the *most* important person in my life and I'll be damned if I am not going to have my wife with me and by my side so that my family can see how proud of you I am and exactly where you stand in my life in relationship to them!'"

Playing off of what I said, Nicole injected, "Well, one thing for sure Russell is that *you* are the one with difficulties with obligation, not me! In fact, that's what really burns me up, that now it seems that you are obliged to see your family, when you never were before. In fact, you constantly talk about hating this 'obligation' to do something with friends for example, whereas I am fine with obligation." Nodding quietly, Russell agreed to Nicole's points.

This exchange reinforced my point that, while Russell felt he was doing the right thing by not obliging Nicole, he was in fact communicating or, so she interpreted it, that she was free to do as she wished because she wasn't important. As far as Nicole was concerned, she was either in third or fourth place of importance to him at best. Nicole vigorously nodded to my point.

Somewhat confused, perhaps somewhat testing and certainly being somewhat provocative, Russell said, "So, Nicole, is what you are saying that to feel number one, you should be able to call all of the shots regarding my family and their involvement in our lives?" Clearly, what he was venturing with this question was his worst fear, since he was convinced that he'd be giving away his family to Nicole's interests. And Nicole, at least initially, did not disabuse him of his worst fear. She volleyed back, "Pretty much," but then just as quickly, she said something that seemed to have caught herself, Russell, and me by surprise. She continued, "You know, if that were the case, that I got to 'call all the shots,' I would actually be insisting that you see your parents and family, and I would be insisting that Penelope see them too. Remember, I *am* the one in our relationship with a keen sense of obligation, including to one's family and, of course, I couldn't imagine either you or Penelope or even myself for that matter not being involved with them. That wouldn't be right."

What got clarified in this session, paradoxically, was that using his own frame of reference about how to convey Nicole's importance by liberating her from any obligation to be with his family only reinforced, in her mind, her lack in importance to Russell. Coupling this latter construct with what now appeared to be Russell's imminent obligation to his family reinforced her panic that as they came closer to moving back home, he was being pulled back into his family's centripetal force field and losing his mind. However, once their upside-down understanding could be turned right side up, Nicole began to surrender her vigilance and aversion to Russell's family. Likewise, he could begin to see that, in reacting to the wrong concern of Nicole's, he was sorely missing what she really hungered for: the reassurance of her central place of importance to him.

Correspondingly, Russell began to surrender his own sense of defensiveness, beginning to see that Nicole's aggravation was a byproduct of her jealousy, and that, although this was embedded in important historical roots which we had been uncovering, it also meant that less than wanting to control him she was hungering for him to value her as much as she did him. It was in her sense of imbalance in their respective valuing that her protests emerged. Once he could accept this, he could better look at his own proneness to judge her for her jealousy, instead of responding to it as emblematic of her desire.

By creating a mental play space for the partners to imagine the ramifications of trying on each other's positions, the therapist deftly maneuvers them out their respective collapse into psychic equivalence and into more of an imaginative, reflective mode of mentalization—that is, she moves them out of the former mode of "that which I think (and which all my 'objective' expert friends agree with) *is* the correct way to think about something" into the latter mode of "imagine what you might feel if you were to play with your partner's position."

The therapist's encouragement of the partners starting to play with one another's positions must include assuring them that they do not ultimately have to relinquish their own. It creates, however, a transitional open space for other ways of thinking and feeling. It facilitates a surrender of strident opposition without inducing pathological accommodation into submission. Of course, this does not happen in one session, but must happen over and over again before the partners begin to develop a more intuitive grasp of considering the other without the automatic fear of losing themselves.

The couple's increased capacity to use one another in a host of multiple functions instills an increasing vitalization of their relationship. With increased capacity to repair ruptures, the couple also can have the increased capacity to risk their occurrence by allowing their self-centeredness and usage of one another to emerge more readily. This comes along with the therapist's insistence that Step Six is never an end of the treatment, but just a part of the process of the relationship which leads back to Step One, much like the Escher print or Möbius Strip analogies introduced earlier in the book.

Step Six also marks the generation of and recognition of the couple having a mind of its own. Part of this results from the therapist speaking to the relational mind, especially at times when it appears that it is in a state of negating the subjectivities of both parties. Since the relational mind cannot speak for itself, it requires the therapist to imagine her way into it and to speak for it. This often involves picking up on something more in the realm of the procedural than the declarative (Stern et al., 1998).

Over time, the couple gradually begin to build new procedural patterns, ones where risk-taking is more possible. Often, however, such spontaneous "moments of meeting" (Stern et al., 1998) have to be demonstrated improvisationally by the therapist. For example, I find playing with each of the partners can be very helpful with many couples. It establishes potential levels of emotional excitation that are available to them that they either didn't know they had, or have long since forgotten they had, or never were there but can be co-created. Encouraging such playful, sometimes outrageous or absurd engagement with me then slips over into encouraging the same kind of playfulness to the couple, especially in hammering out their differences.[10] On the promising aspect of this point, Stern et al. (1998) write:

> Once an expansion of the range (of mutually created positive excitement) has occurred, and there is the mutual recognition that the two partners have successfully interacted together in a higher orbit of joy, their subsequent interactions will be conducted within this altered intersubjective environment. It is not the simple fact of each having done it before, but the sense that the two have been here before. The domain of *implicit relational knowing* has been altered.
>
> (p. 909)

Engaging in such a manner cannot be technically prescribed, as it is necessarily individualistic, bearing the personal signature of the therapist. It also cannot become "routine, habitual, or technical; [such moments of meeting] must be novel and fashioned to meet the singularity of the moment" (p. 913). This is the essence of good improvisation.

When spontaneity becomes compromised and the relational mind of the couple becomes scripted, it is generally a sign that a quality of anxiety has resumed, and it becomes incumbent upon the therapist to explore this. Doing so may well trigger controversy, but as this is a model built upon the expectation of rupture and repair, immediately reengaging in the processes of attunement identified from Steps One through Six begins to create a procedurally based relational structure upon which such controversy can be examined and worked through.

The partnership function of bearing witness

In Step Six, each partner is beginning to sufficiently internalize the conceptual tools of the entire model, such that he or she can become not only a self-reflective observer of their own process, but of that of their partner's. This entails taking on a host of therapeutic functions vis-à-vis each other, such as becoming a witness-bearer of one another's lives, a confidant to deeply private aspects of each other's personal narrative, a memorializer of each one's history, as well as a commentator introducing an alternative perspective on one another's lives. This largely evolves from the quality of engagement that the therapist has had with the couple, in which she is modeling all of these functions.

Witness-bearing is a chief function that partners in long-term committed relationships provide to one another on the occasion of visiting one of their families of origin. As each partner has begun to non-defensively take back their projections, they begin to become more open to looking at how their own and each other's family of origin has impacted them. There is a deep therapeutic function that spouses serve for one another in this regard. For example, being able to discuss one's experience with one's spouse of visiting one's family can be enormously helpful in not falling into the unconscious patterns of thinking, feeling and relating in scripted repetitions. One readily sees this in the illustrations of Larry and Sharrie and Samantha and Randall. Another example of the outcome of becoming witness-bearers is to become one another's closest confidant, as Allen and Shelby became.

Larry and Sharrie

Larry and Sharrie returned from a holiday visit with her parents in the Midwest. Sharrie commented that, being back there less than a day, she started feeling the emotional tug of her family's anxiety. Her anxiety was exacerbated by the fact that nothing emotionally charged could ever be discussed. As a consequence, everyone would lapse into dissociative states, as manifested by overeating and drinking to excess, followed by one member after another falling like a domino with whatever contagious seasonal illness beset them. In the context of her "collapse," Larry usually felt totally ignored, and therefore had come to resent their compulsory visits.

On this visit, however, Sharrie and Larry took my advice that they go for a walk at some point every day so that they could get away from her family's emotional gravity, as well as debrief one another regarding their respective experiences on the trip. Because they were now discussing daily what each was experiencing, Larry no longer felt left out and Sharrie was less drawn into her dissociation. Also, because they could remain relatively independent of the centripetal tug of her family, they became interesting purveyors of alternative activities and interests that drew the family out of its redundant "safe" grooves of playing such relationally trivializing games as Trivial Pursuit.

Most importantly, bearing witness to the *in vivo* reenactment of "model scenes" (Lichtenberg, Lachmann, & Fosshage, 1992, 1996) from Sharrie's development, Larry was experiencing something that enabled him to help formulate some of what Sharrie could not on her own. In essence, he could give voice to some of the most numbing aspects of her family: their need for constant mirroring and affirmation with little capacity to return this in any way that felt comparably nurturing to either of them. Sharrie could feel this, but had not yet been able to articulate it as clearly as Larry was able to. This allowed him to nudge her therapeutically out of her position of feeling doomed in the repetition of her role of making all her family members feel good about themselves with little in return.

Samantha and Randall

In my work with Samantha and Randall, I facilitated Samantha's capacity to become a memorializer of Randall's loss experiences, since although his family was terribly saturated with experiences of loss, it was fundamentally ill equipped to reckon with them. Like Larry's experience with Sharrie, Samantha found visiting Randall's family truly toxic, since she seemed to be the only one emotionally receptive to affect states of loss. In effect, she was bombarded with their transmission of loss and yet profoundly enjoined from commenting on them. On the rare occasion that she did comment, she was derided as being too thin-skinned in a manner that would leave her feeling accused of being overly fragile.

In our earlier work, Samantha was seething with anger over constantly being told by Randall that she was "too delicate." By helping Randall recognize that his shaming rebukes of Sam were reenactments from his family's response to loss, he began to see that he, along with his family, had lived in great disavowal about the early death of his mother, his father's failed subsequent marriages with a host of inadequate stepmothers, and the trauma of being perpetually uprooted from each familiar living experience to which he had ever become accustomed.

Finally recognizing Samantha's reactions as a compassionate memorializer of things lost but disavowed, he stopped feeling that she was hysterical, even though his family still maintained this claim. In fact, he now began experiencing her as his one true soulmate, a concept he realized that he had long ago sensed he wished for, but had given up after his closest confidante in childhood, his mother, died. Because they now could grieve his losses together, their own relationship was not only deepened and fortified, but their conflicts with his family completely attenuated, since against this dynamic duo, the impact of the dissociatively splitting and projecting features of his family was dramatically mitigated.

Allen and Shelby

Allen and Shelby hadn't developed the capacity to be one another's closest confidants, a position unfamiliar to each, until we discovered that they had come from families where dyadic pairings were regarded with a great deal of suspicion and jealousy. The proof of the pudding for Allen came when he went through the worst career setback of his life. As chief financial officer for a major corporation, he had drawn attention to the board of directors a problem with the corporation's organizational chart, which reflected too many linkages of power between certain departments that were in fact also connected by a host of familial relationships. While not casting any suspicions about their practices, he unveiled that the perception of their hiring and promoting practices was beginning to create a deeply threatening morale problem and that if it went unaddressed it could cause the corporation to spiral into serious financial upheaval.

Having enjoyed the good graces of all the corporate executives, the board of directors, and many members of the middle management team, Allen thought that he was in the optimal role to present this bold assessment of the corporation's organization. Unfortunately, as the messenger, he was "crucified," though not actually terminated. Still, the outcome was that he was terrified that all that he had built up in his career was now going to dissolve. Worst of all, however, was that for several weeks he hid all of this from Shelby.

Finally, a serious panic attack forced him into the emergency room, fearing he was having a heart attack. The emergency room doctors correctly diagnosed Allen's condition as non-life-threatening, and rather a reaction to anxiety that needed to be treated by psychotherapy. In our very first session, it came out that Allen was terrified that Shelby would challenge his actions and berate him instead of supporting him. To his shock and deep appreciation, Shelby sympathetically listened in detail without any of the judgment he feared. In subsequent weeks, with little effort on my part, Shelby encouraged Allen to keep expressing his concerns. Initially, I had to help her hold off on giving him unsolicited advice and to just stay in a listening role. However, over time, she learned to ask him if he would appreciate her alternative perspective, which when he did, he found enormously helpful as she found a host of ways of reassuring him that eventually the storm would pass.

Indeed, it did. In less than six months, everything he had predicted had come true, in fact much worse than he had estimated. A major corporate shakeup ensued that initially threatened to throw the company into bankruptcy. In fact, this calamity was only barely averted because the corporation took the very actions that Allen had outlined six months earlier. More importantly, his foresight and courage to speak the unspeakable not only exonerated him, but made him an even more trusted executive in the overall corporation. Despite the toll it had taken on him, Allen offered that he could have not gotten through this period without Shelby's confidence, her intimately sharing his private world, and her offering, where necessary, her alternative perspective.

The capacity to terminate

The capacity to terminate begins to emerge as the couple shows evidence of having internalized aspects of all Six Steps of the model:

1. To attune to one another's selfobject longings for attunement, to their disappointment, and to when such longings cannot be authentically met;
2. To grasp the perspectivality of one another's subjective experience and to learn thereby to not pull rank, or at least to repair such ruptures when they find themselves devolving into this old habit of dysfunctional fighting;
3. To take into account the organizing features of their respective developmental, cultural, and gendered backgrounds, as well as with the sometimes mind-boggling implications of these disparate backgrounds;
4. To begin to recognize their joint participation in their enactments;
5. To discern conflicts between their own multiple self-states; and
6. To begin to collaborate and negotiate on a basis of a much more sophisticated understanding of their individual make-up, as well as their unique thirdness.

In short, the couple should have developed what Pizer (1998), quoting Rubin and Rubin (1991), referred to as an "enlightened self-interest," and to which I would also add an "enlightened interest in one another" as well.

The capacity for termination is by no means measured by the couple no longer fighting or relinquishing disagreement in substantial ways. Indeed, the fundamental assumption of this model is that controversy will never cease, although the couple's capacity to negotiate it will have advanced considerably. Evidence of this will be the emergence of a kind of embedded structure in the relationship that now embodies their mutual understanding of where past unformulated and incomprehensible arguments are prone to take them once they arise. With this implicit as well as explicit understanding, there is a tendency for one or the other of the partners to say, "Let's not go there … " (meaning automatically repeating their dysfunctional mode of relating), instead looking at the transferential issues that they would otherwise be reenacting. This doesn't guarantee that they "won't go there," but it pretty much equips them to look back at what they are repeating and to realize that they have some choice about this repetition. This awareness becomes a new structure of understanding in their relationship and allows them to talk through what heretofore eluded them.

Phil and Syria

Toward the end of a very lengthy treatment, Phil and Syria exhibited all of the aforementioned characteristics, including surrendering to aspects of their relationship that had heretofore been simply non-negotiable. Deeply satisfied with what we accomplished, they terminated treatment, and with the exception of an occasional holiday greeting card and newsy letter or an intermittent referral, I did not hear from them for many years—until, right as I was beginning my winter holiday break out of the office, I received a panicked call from them. They were approaching their 25th wedding anniversary when, all of a sudden, all hell broke loose. This revisitation of the horrors of the past can lead to people thinking that all that they had accomplished in treatment was for nought.

Though I try to assiduously protect my vacation time, even when I remain in town, I quickly returned their call and told them I could see them on Monday (they had called on a Saturday evening). I indicated that I was on break, but that their circumstances made me want to see them as soon as possible. On Sunday, however, I received another call from them. They said that there was no need for us to meet. Instead, they had resolved their issue and were planning to take their exotic anniversary trip after all. What they said—and what had caught my ear then and have heard enumerable times since—was, "We decided to just sit down on our couch at home and imagine what it would be like to be in your office—what you would be asking each of us, and what you might be saying to us. In a short period of time, we had completely come to understand what was at stake in our fight, and suddenly realized—no offense, Phil—we don't need you!! So have a happy holiday and we're on our way on our trip and you'll hear from us anon." And so I have intermittently over the years.

The result of our treatment was that Phil and Syria had clearly co-created a quality of thirdness, as well as therapeutic alliance from which their conflicts and occasional paradoxical, non-negotiable situations could be contained, recognized, and ultimately accepted. From this vantage point, they were equipped to examine the binaries their argumentation could devolve into, and instead find a third point of reference from which to extricate themselves. Although that thirdness initially arose from me—from my therapeutic vantage point—it slowly but surely became internalized by both of them, and became an implicit structural aspect of their relationship having a mind of its own.

Ferenczi has been noted as averring that therapy terminates when the work has pretty much been exhausted (Salberg, 2011).[11] This makes quite a bit of sense to me. A crucial feature of that exhaustion, on top of the internalization of the overall model of treatment, is that the beginning idealizing transference toward the therapist evolves into more or less seeing her as just another human being, albeit one who has provided them with an indispensable means for considering their heretofore impossible problems.

In Step One, I noted that one of the results of the couple being "hooked" is that they tend to engage in an idealizing transference towards the therapist, while largely remaining in states of repetitive transference towards one another, though these repetitive states are now informed by a greater hope that this third party can understand and help both of them. Over the course of treatment, however, their need for the therapist diminishes as the third perspective she brings to their complementarity gradually becomes their own.

The first whiffs of possible termination often come with some playful de-idealizing comments about how costly the therapy is both in terms of money and time. These comments also begin to have a hint of playful sarcasm, wherein the therapist's formerly idealized position as the "magician" or "wizard" turns into a more realistically appreciative position of "I/we bet you and your wife really can get into it, too!!" This, of course, is not a position which I try to disabuse my patients of, even, on occasion, where appropriate, disclosing a "real doozy" of a quarrel my wife and I have had. Indeed, I think that it is extremely important that conjoint therapists be able to own their own borderline and narcissistic self-states, along with some understanding of what can trigger them thematically in their own relationships.[12] Whether these ever get disclosed to the couple or not, it is in this humbling awareness that the couples therapist can maneuver around the constantly shifting terrain of what couples will bring her way upon admission to treatment.

Traditional psychoanalysis had some rather procrustean notions about termination, not the least of which was that there would not be any contact after the treatment ended, because any suggested possibility of it would undermine the resolution of the patient's infantile wishes for merger, or of the Oedipal wish to bed with one's parents, or of undermining, by metaphoric example, confrontation with the inescapability of death. These were all fascinating ideas and deserve consideration. However, contemporary psychoanalytic views (Salberg, 2010) suggest, much like the Paul Simon song and lyric, there are "fifty ways to leave your lover," and that includes terminating therapy.

Of the multitude of ways to leave treatment, it seems almost certainly the case for analytic couples work (and, in many cases, individual psychotherapy too) that the door remains open for the couple to return as needed. Most specifically, the need to return arises when they falter in being able to restore a position of thirdness, and therefore devolve back into the binary: the complementarity of their doer and done-to position. My experience with couples returning is that the degree to which the structural vantage point of thirdness has been instantiated is the degree to which they quickly resume it and are often quickly done with this short course of treatment. With couples who have not sufficiently internalized it in the first round of work (often having had to leave prematurely for a host of real-world issues), our work quickly resumes and builds swiftly upon what had been begun to be established before.[13]

In the end, Harry Stack Sullivan's prophetic observation is especially comforting: "We are all more simply human than otherwise." The de-idealization of the therapist—and even of the therapy itself—helps cultivate this humble mutuality of understanding—that is, that life is a little easier to embrace when we are no longer so busy chasing illusions about ourselves and about our relationships. Instead, we can live in more playful spontaneity, until death do us part.

Summary

Step Six moves our discussion of dealing with conflict and paradox into the intersubjective realm. Special emphasis is placed on how these conflicts and paradoxes can manifest in negative thirdness, thereby truncating the couple's openness to their relationship developing a mind of its own. Helping cultivate open thirdness is critical to each partner's self-actualization. Repeated success in helping the couple develop a mutually recognizing mindset sets the ultimate stage for the transmission of the therapist's function to the couple, such that they gradually become one another's "quasi-therapeutic" partner in adult development. Indeed, in optimal outcomes, they develop something of a therapeutic alliance (Safran & Muran, 2000), obviating the need for the therapist.

In Step Six, each partner is beginning to sufficiently internalize the conceptual tools of the entire treatment model. This means that one is not only becoming a self-reflective observer of one's own process, but also potentially comparably observant of their partner's as well. This entails their taking on a host of therapeutic functions vis-à-vis each other. These include becoming a witness-bearer of one another's life, a confidant to deeply private aspects of each other's personal narrative, a memorializer of each one's history, as well as a commentator introducing an alternative perspective on one another's lives. This largely evolves from the quality of engagement that the therapist has had with the couple, in which she is modeling all of these functions and many more as well.

The development of the couple having a relational mind of their own is assisted by encouraging them to "play" with one another's opposite position—literally to imagine what it would be like to temporarily adopt the other's perspective. They must be assured, however, that they do not have to ultimately relinquish their own. The further development of the couple's relational mind also comes from the therapist speaking directly to it. He does so by discerning and speaking to its procedural level, the implicit affective relational style in which openness to one another can foreclose. This often takes the form of articulating the partners' composite of fears, such as saying, "This relationship is telling me that it is not safe to be open and vulnerable."

As Winnicott averred, if the patient cannot play, he must be taught, and that admonition holds for the conjoint therapist's work with the couple. Encouraging emotional excitation potentially creates new procedural patterns of enhanced emotional engagement. Doing so means that every therapist will engage each couple in his own signature style that cannot be prescribed technically or habitually lest, in the latter case, it will rob the couple of learning about developing spontaneity and leave them subject only to the routine and habitual.

Fortifying the strength of the relational mind includes reminding partners that breakdowns in their process are inevitable, and that this model is about the authenticity of their rupture and repair, not about fostering any illusions of the permanence of repair. Nevertheless, couples must develop a special sensitivity to the particularly powerful stranglehold that trauma can have on their interpersonal process.

The topic of termination is often introduced playfully, and comes in conjunction with the partners' internalization of the model, such that they have developed greater enlightened self-interest as well as enlightened interest in their relationship. There is a marked shift from the beginning idealization of the therapist to a more playful de-idealization that comes along with "We really don't need you anymore," but "Through what we learned with you, you will always be remembered." This is a shift from idealization to admiration, from fantasy to a realistic appraisal. And, in this latter vein, there typically is a sense of grief over the pending loss that termination brings, one that in my experience can be as strong for the therapist as for the couple. As this, too, gets processed, so do thoughts about what might be circumstances wherein a return visit might make sense, as well as reassurance that the door remains open. I have had many terminations over the years of both individual patients and couples, and not infrequently it is the couples termination that saddens me more (though I also am typically saddened at the end of an individual treatment), because with the couple I am not only saying goodbye to two individuals but also to their relationship (that now has a mind of its own) and to a plethora of connections that any triangle assumes with far greater levels of complexity that can ever happen in a single dyad.

Notes

1 Such projective processes might be better explained in terms of attribution and induction of certain unrecognized, disavowed self-states.

2 The *psychoanalytic third* is a term that is unfortunately riddled with all the vagaries and multiplicities of meanings. Some authors, for example, of the Lacanian persuasion, treat

the third like a system of rules that governs the dyad through an unconscious medium of laws linguistically, culturally, and in terms of gender. These operate through the deep structure of language that enables the dyad to relate. This version of the third structurally grounds the dyad (Muller, 1999; Wolff-Bernstein, 1999). For other authors, the third is an unconsciously co-created state of intersubjectivity. It is unpredictable, and therefore seems less tied to an emphasis on an *a priori* structure and more upon the *a posteriori* engagement of the dyad (Ogden, 1994). Still others see the third as a kind of theory of mind and/or professional association to which the analyst is married and therefore imposes some form of symbolic Oedipal partnership between the analyst and the analysand (Aron, 1999; Crastnopol, 1999; Hoffman, 1994, 1998).

3 Aron (2003) writes: "The two participants must find a way to go from being positioned along a line toward opening up space. I am referring, of course, to psychic space, transitional space, space to think, space to breathe, to live, to move spontaneously in relation to each other interpersonally. The conceptualization of the third attempts to model this state in that a line has no space, whereas a triangle does" (pp. 354–355).

4 The phenomenon of one-in-the-third begins very, very early in life, as Aron (2003) suggests when he writes: "Think of the rhythms established by the mother-infant dyad, in eye-gaze, reciprocal speech, gestures, movements, and mutual mirroring" (p. 356). This leads to a natural human sense of life evolving episodically, in perpetual successions of present moment experiences that are implicitly structured in beginnings, middles, and endings, awaiting further ensuing episodes (Stern, 2004).

5 See, for example, Wolff Bernstein (2006), Blechner (2006), Corbett (2001), Dimen (2003), Frommer (2006), Gentile (2001), Goldner (2006), Harris (2009), Perel (2007), and Stein (2006).

6 Aron (2003) writes: "Thirdness thus emerges here from within the dyad without needing a literal third object to intervene ... This is what Benjamin and I aver (Aron & Benjamin, 1999) describing the origins of self-reflexivity in intersubjective space, called an incipient third. It is in this way that mirroring creates a third symbolic intersubjective space of representation between infant and parent allowing for and facilitating mentalization and affect-regulation. The marked response is thus an excellent example of the third-in-the-one or intentional third in that it facilitates the differentiation of self and other within their very connectedness" (p. 358).

7 This last point, of course, is predicated on the degree to which they can become an open system for one another, as opposed to a closed system perpetually vexed in immutable processes of mutual inductive identification. If upon divorce neither partner has learned anything about themselves, it is then likely that they might continue to perpetuate similar dramas to the ones that foundered their marriage.

8 This point is derivative of the Bowenian Family Therapy model that is discussed in Appendix A. Families that are prone to merging over anxiety about differentiating simply have little exposure to what it's like not to always be together. That proposition is entirely too anxiety-producing. However, when one member of the family gradually institutes such change, the family members see that it's not as fatal as expected; indeed, it can be rather pleasant to be in smaller configurations and not always clustered.

9 Gentile (2001) further writes: "This makes surrender a very tricky concept. After all, power and aggression can only emerge gendered male in relation to victimization which is gendered female. One can surrender in the moment with a partner, but if that partner has more power within the culture (based on identified gender, race, class sexual orientation, etc.), then one is also necessarily submitting to them" (p. 190).

10 Stern et al. (1998) write: "Now moments [of shifting procedurally relational engagement] may occur when the traditional therapeutic frame risks being, or is, or should be broken" (p. 912).

11 "The proper ending of an analysis is when neither the physician nor the patient puts an end to it, but when it dies of exhaustion ... A truly cured patient frees himself from

analysis slowly but surely; so long as he wishes to come to analysis, he should continue to do so" (Ferenczi, 1927, p. 85).

12 Indeed, I lament the observation that the reason so many analysts are intolerant of doing couples therapy is that they are too frightened by what it stirs up in terms of the borderline and narcissistic aspects of their own personalities.

13 Cooper (2009) notes that in terminating treatment, "it is my sense that some of the most successful analyses … feature a revisiting of some of the same points of entanglement that accompanied analysis or that even fueled the initial decision to stop" (p. 590). This underscores the fundamental idea in my Six Step model that the couple perpetually recycles through all six steps over and over during the course of a long-term relationship that is inevitably fraught with ruptures requiring repair, from which intimacy gradually deepens.

8

MICHAEL AND CARMEN
An illustration of the Six Steps

Step One

In our initial session, I learned that Michael was 48 years old and Carmen had just turned 41. They had both been married before. Carmen had a son and daughter who were pre-teens, and Michael had an adolescent son recently enrolled in college in another state. They met via an internet dating service, and their "cyber-connection" quickly led to a coffee date from which they both left feeling "swept off of their feet." Their romance was fast and furious, leading to marriage six months later, two years before they came to me.

Carmen had grown up in an upper-middle-class section of Mexico City. Her family immigrated to the United States when she was 11 years old, when her father was offered a position in a prestigious architectural firm in Southern California. Her family were devout Catholics, a tradition which she passionately embraced, while also rejecting many aspects of it. These included the church's positions on divorce, birth control, women in the clergy, and even abortion, though she was adamant that she could never choose to have one.

Carmen described her family, which included aunts, uncles, and cousins, as passionately interdependent, a style of relating that was evidenced by their rapid oscillation between love and hate. This could manifest in heated exchanges, culminating in "wishing each other dead" or threatening to "never speak to one another again," juxtaposed with a fiery sense of loyalty. When not in one of their "never speaking to one another" modes, they were in daily contact, and few if any significant life decisions could be made without consulting one another. Individual strivings were often met with sarcasm and humiliation for having a "big head" (e.g., ego) or feeling that one was becoming too important to care about his or her family.

Despite these constraints on her autonomy, Carmen was able to follow in her father's highly educated footsteps, and was by far the most educated of her generation. Both she and Michael were attorneys. In Carmen's case, her expertise involved immigration law. She was especially involved in the Latino community in Los Angeles, with whom she felt a profound connection. Michael was a litigator.

Michael came from a Midwestern Protestant family from the suburbs of Chicago. His family had immigrated two generations earlier. His grandfather was a minister who devoutly studied the Bible every night. His grandfather's greatest wish was that his son (Michael's father) would also become a minister. This dream was thwarted by Michael's father, who rebelled by becoming a strident atheist who flirted with affiliations in the Communist Party. After Michael's grandfather died, he felt guilty about having been so oppositional towards his father. On top of this, his rebellion came to a screeching halt with the rise of Senator Joseph McCarthy's Committee on Anti-American Activities. Somewhat lost and scared, he enrolled in law school and settled into the quiet cover of becoming a corporate attorney.

Michael's identification with Protestantism was very weak. Indeed, his first wife was an atheist like his father. Despite so many contaminating factors to his own beliefs, Michael had begun to reconsider his ties to his spirituality in recent years, having lost a number of friends, colleagues, and older relatives. In this vein, Carmen's devotion to her Catholic faith intrigued him, especially given the passion he witnessed in her spirituality.

Carmen described her first marriage as extremely volatile and heated. Proud of her Hispanic heritage, it was important to her that she marry a Hispanic professional with a family background comparable to her own. Regrettably, it was a poor match. After years of faking it between their explosive fights, Carmen and her ex decided (in what was an unusually amicable manner) that they had married for all the wrong reasons. For the first time in years, they settled their differences, agreed to let one another go, and in so doing remained cooperative parents regarding the rearing of their children.

Carmen had a kind of radiant beauty, as well as being an attractive and stylish woman. It was her sparkling personality, however, that was instantly captivating. I could readily see why Michael became smitten so quickly with her. When she spoke, there was a glimmer in her brown eyes that reflected a brightness of mind, heart, and soul. She was very intense, oscillating in our initial session between moments of fiery anger, gut-wrenching laughter, and intense listening, evincing a desperate wish to understand what was going wrong between them.

Michael was comparably appealing. Though he was showing a bit of middle-age bulge, he was in reasonably good shape, which reflected a desire to take care of himself without devolving into the kind of obsession about fitness that many middle-aged Angelenos suffer. His hazel green eyes and sandy brown hair had a kind of softening effect compared to Carmen's dark and passionate looks, which made her look much like a gypsy and had the effect of dramatizing her affective swings. When it came to emotional regulation, each complemented the other. They seemed to rely on Carmen heating things up and Michael cooling them down. When either one's temperature became excessive, however, they could really throw one another out of whack. Although it appeared that Carmen could be the fierier of the two, Michael could be driven to his own intense reactions when he was narcissistically injured. In short, he could react as dramatically as Carmen.

What was most apparent in our first session was how in love Michael was with Carmen. It's not merely that he unhesitatingly said so; it was even more apparent in how he looked at her, how he reached for her hand, and how he beamed whenever he made her laugh. Similarly, I could see how much Carmen was in love with Michael, though she also made it clear that professing her love to someone other than her children was extremely difficult for her, since she felt such expressions made her look weak. Nevertheless, without saying so, her degree of vulnerability to Michael was palpable despite how reluctant she was to share it with him. For someone who had had as much therapy and who seemed as open and as passionate as Carmen was, her level of guardedness remained truly compelling.

Both agreed that, for the past six months, they had been on a perpetual emotional roller coaster. Their sex life was a testimony to the old adage "The best part of breaking up is making up." The regularity of their ruptures seemed to have more to do with the core ways in which each one's selfobject longings were repeatedly being ruptured. More to the point was how poorly they repaired their ruptures. When a couple continues to suffer ruptures without repairs, the extraordinarily complicated unconscious fibers of their connection gradually become more and more worn out, threatening permanent and divisive tears.

According to Michael, their relationship had been a wonderful romance resulting in their very quick marriage. Of late, he was worried that their impulsive connection may have placed their romantic bond in jeopardy, as he felt that no matter what he did, it often was either not good enough or, if it was recognized as good enough, it did not have any staying power. In short, he began to feel that he was only as good as his last good deed. Correspondingly, anytime he disappointed Carmen, it seemed to be having a more enduring effect on her negative regard of him. He also claimed that he felt caught in a perpetual Catch-22, that he was "damned if he did and damned if he didn't" do a whole host of particular things. The predictable outcome of his acts seemed to shift in a mercurial fashion in Carmen's eyes, lending to very little predictability of what it was that she expected from him. In sum, their relationship felt patently unfair to him, insofar as there was a pernicious double standard that required him to be nicer, more loving, more caring, and more giving than Carmen was expected to be. On top of this, he was expected to be capable of withstanding her frequent emotional outbursts. All of this, he confessed, was beginning to wear him out.

To her credit, Carmen acknowledged that there was considerable truth to Michael's position. This was something about which she was not proud, and she confessed that she did not fully understand it. Nevertheless, she did need him to conform to her requirements. In a moment of reflection, she acknowledged that being in love with a man like Michael truly overwhelmed and frightened her. She said, "Look, better that I quit than get fired by Michael. It is way too humiliating to be so in love with someone who might reject me." She then added that she "did not 'do' fear well."

Fear, Carmen continued, provoked in her a fight-or-flight response, which, she had discovered in her psychotherapy, was the principal adaptive pattern she had learned growing up. Indeed, she briefly described how, in her family, malfeasances could rapidly generate huge blood-curdling screaming matches from which family members wished one another dead. They would swear that they would never speak to one another again, only to reconnect at the next family event as if nothing had happened.

With this background, I asked them if they could be more specific about what brought them into treatment. Carmen took the lead and said that she could be rather critical of Michael, because there were some things about him that made her anxious. Principal among her concerns was her wondering if he would be able to take care of her, her children, and her extended family. She also said that, at times, she would obsess about Michael's health care, fretting over his occasional indulgence in a cigarette or a cigar, and his even more occasional enjoyment of smoking marijuana. These latter anxieties seemed to wax and wane relative to her state of mind. When she was not feeling threatened, she seemed to care very little about his small indulgences; however, when she began having doubts about Michael as protector, everything he did that called into question his judgment became unsettling, sometimes even unraveling.

It was a painfully mixed experience for Michael to listen to Carmen, but he added that Carmen's "compulsive honesty" was for him one of her best and worst traits. The positive side of it was how powerfully enlivening it could be, in contrast to the "lives of quiet desperation" he had witnessed in his parents' marriage, his two older sisters' marriages, and to some extent his first one. On the negative side, he frequently felt blindsided by Carmen's honesty. Worst of all, he did not feel that it was safe for him to be comparably honest with her. He professed that his periodic attempts to do so had frequently gone extremely badly, with Carmen provocatively goading him to leave her if, for example, he was critical about something about her.

Ultimately, Michael acknowledged that while his own therapy had convinced him that his desire for Carmen was meaningful and not neurotic, he remained uncertain as to what it was about her that drew him to want to meet her unabashed demands. The best he'd come up with was that he seemed to experience pleasing Carmen to be an amazing elixir, that it was something comparable to how he could capture a gleam in his mother's eye, as well as (on very rare occasions) even his father's. Up until recently, he had felt it worth doing, but lately, he was becoming weary of too frequently feeling "blown up." He had begun to wonder if there was some masochistic enactment in which he was engaging.

Contemplating the forward edge of Michael's and Carmen's developmental, reparative transference led me to hypothesize the following: It was evident that Carmen longed for the protective function of an idealizing transference. Correspondingly, whenever Michael fulfilled her image of a man who was capable in the world, and who could not only protect her and her kin, but also adore her from the bottom of his heart, she was momentarily insulated from the terror of having to manage all these relationships alone.

Carmen agreed with my interpretation while adding a critical puzzle piece of her own. Shortly after her father brought her family to America, he started evidencing symptoms of Parkinson's disease, which appeared with an unusually rapid and devastating onset of incapacitating symptoms. Eventually, his condition became very grave, leading to his having to be institutionalized. Mercifully for him and all that knew and loved him, he died shortly thereafter. Nevertheless, over the ensuing decades, because of her proficiency in English, Carmen assumed the role of the family's surrogate father. Notwithstanding the power and pride this position conveyed to her, she also powerfully longed for a man to unburden her of it. Still, she was also loath to let go of this role for a host of reasons that would gradually become apparent later in our work.

In comparison to what Carmen longed for, I suggested that Michael longed for affirmation (mirroring) regarding his legitimate areas of competency. These included his robustness of personality, his generosity, his sense of humor, and, more than anything else, his ability to make Carmen happy. Although I acknowledged his contention that these drives were not necessarily neurotic, I quickly encouraged his curiosity over what more might be understood about them. This included his emerging insight that perhaps there was something masochistic being played out in how he was behaving. I suggested that until he knew what he had at stake in this conundrum, it was likely that he would feel jerked around, as opposed to seizing control of his own initiative and sense of agency.

Given what Carmen and Michael were telling me, I also was able to understand the repetitive or trailing edges of the transference. Clearly, Michael hated being criticized by Carmen, and his defense against this led to his efforts to extract from her what his malfeasance was. Tragically, his defensive position sometimes fortified her anxieties that he could not readily handle her. If that was the case, she wondered, how could he protect her from a world full of malice?

Despite her protests, Carmen also acknowledged that she believed that Michael would never actually let her run away. In fact, it was in his adamancy that they connect and talk, as well as his insistence that Carmen tell him what was going on, that she was gradually developing a picture of him as far more resilient than she initially imagined. The crisis question for this couple, then, was: Would Carmen overcome her repetitive transference fantasy about Michael's insufficiencies in time for him not to have become fed up with her?

In this context, I hypothesized that any time Michael failed in his attempts at being Carmen's idealizing selfobject, one from whom she sought security and adulation, she could be thrown into a repetitive transference state. In it, not only would she begin to feel that she could not rely upon him, but also it was a reminder that she could not rely upon anyone. Once again, she'd have to become "the rock." In this repetitive state, she'd become embittered and highly critical.

For Michael, Carmen's criticisms began to undermine his sense of affirmation for how he was being regarded in their relationship. It also began to cause him momentary self-doubts. The problem was that emergent self-doubts further provoked Carmen's dreaded repetitive fantasy that he was only partially competent. They were caught up in a vicious circle, wherein each of their individual longings triggered their repetitive dreads. The more Michael sought Carmen's affirmation that he was in fact the man that she really ideally belonged with, the more she was prone to see this as a weakness. Conversely, the more she sought Michael to behave in manners that fulfilled her idealizing needs, the more he felt set up to fail. In short, not only was he deprived of the mirroring and affirmation of his goodness that he hungered for, in fact it triggered Carmen's criticism, which at its worse culminated in her sarcastic contempt. Clearly, their pattern of repetitive transference failings of selfobject longings had become an expectancy system of "vicious circle ruptures." Instead of seeking mutual recognition, in their lawyerly ways, they'd devolve into endless arguments over whose needs are more relevant. Ultimately, this relational structure degenerated into both partners battling against feelings of submissiveness.

In this context, their relationship appeared to have become constituted by many moments of reversible complementarity, wherein—at various points—each felt uncomfortably dominated by the needs of the other. This reciprocating quality lent itself to a kind of negative thirdness, wherein the relationship's mind of its own could be characterized as more negating than affirming and additive, that is, in evidence of a positive third. These latter ideas embody a relational mindset more amenable to dialogical truth building, wherein the subjectivities of both parties can be more fully actualized.

Finally, there was also some early evidence of each partner occupying multiple self-states that they were not aware of but were certainly playing out in the consulting room. Despite his desire to please Carmen and to feel very effective in doing so, there was also a very autonomous side to Michael that made him chafe at being pushed around. Likewise, Carmen seemed riveted in ambivalence, though she had not formulated this. On the other hand, she was deeply identified with her profession as an attorney, and much like Michael she valued having a mind of her own. Still, this position did not readily jibe with how she'd been raised in terms of her cultural background and gender, both of which bore a quality of enmeshment with her family system. In these ways, both Carmen and Michael could become confused within themselves as well as confusing to one another. Clearly, considerable work on Step Two was essential to this couple, since the whole realm of perspective about what is true and what isn't had—as it often does with most couples—become a bedrock to their either feeling sane or crazy.

Step Two

My treatment with Michael and Carmen had barely begun, when Michael laid out his greatest grievance with Carmen: at various points, her laying claim to knowing his mind better than he did. This was especially toxic for him, since he had felt that the most significant outcome of his many years in psychoanalytic psychotherapy had been to finally feel comfortable with having a mind of his own. This entailed grasping a depth of understanding of the heretofore unconscious contents of his mind. Indeed, he was a strong advocate that the cost of his analysis was truly the very best expenditure he had ever made, as it enabled him not only to trust the contents of his mind but also to be able to authentically speak it. On top of this, it made him increasingly comfortable with also knowing that there was much that remained unconscious to him. He certainly did not feel that he had a "god's-eye view" about anyone else's reality. In short, trusting his capacity for self-analysis in understanding issues as they arose in his life had become foundational to embracing wholeheartedly his own preferences and choices.

This accomplishment represented a hard-won victory for Michael, who had been inclined to defer to others' judgments most of his life. Often, he simply did not trust his own view of reality. This was quite ironic, because few people might have recognized him as having self-doubts. In fact, as a persuasive orator and an accomplished debater (hence his considerable success as an attorney), Michael was always more capable of convincing others about the correctness of his convictions than he was ever able to convince himself. Analytic psychotherapy had finally connected his mind and his voice, such that Carmen's claim to knowing his mind better than he did enraged him, and he experienced her assertions as annihilating. What he found especially toxic were her frequent abrupt interpretations about what Michael was *really* thinking and feeling, when in fact most of the time what she was claiming was very far from Michael's version of his truth. Often, Carmen's comments would come out of left field, though sometimes they were spurred by a thread of truth she then would weave into a larger, mostly erroneous argument.

For example, after responding to her complaint that he was too solicitous of her feelings, which she found humiliating and intrusive, Michael stopped asking her about them. Later on, however, Carmen misconstrued his actions to mean that Michael was distancing from her, when in fact he would have loved for her to share more with him. A more recent accusation corresponded with a period in which she was struggling, experiencing hormonal imbalances which resulted in weight gain. Gaining weight was always depressing to her and tended to provoke a certain degree of self-loathing, since Carmen counted on her physical fitness not only as a source of attraction, but even more as a form of self-righting and personal security. Because of Michael's lessened solicitations, she experienced an amplified self-loathing, and spinning off of this she began accusing him of being turned off to her because of her weight gain.

Michael was thunderstruck by this. He was especially incredulous over the example she came up with from the day before. To support her conviction that he was turned off, she claimed that he was looking at her in a manner in which she detected some dissatisfaction. The incident occurred when she rose to go to the bathroom shortly after they made love. She had noted what she believed to be a disdainful expression in the bedroom closet door mirror, and she was convinced that the expression coincided with his looking at her naked ass. While he acknowledged that maybe it had been true that his look bore less of the amorous afterglow to which she was typically accustomed—after all, her agitated mood of self-loathing had made her a bit prickly to be around—her interpretation nevertheless felt very far from Michael's truth.

Instead, Michael's accounting of the day before was that their lovemaking was as amorous as always, indeed, especially intense. He acknowledged that it was true that he'd noticed Carmen's slight weight gain but, if anything, marveled at how physically fit she looked in spite of it. In fact, he privately rejoiced over having such a strong appetite for her, such that any weight gain did not detract from his attraction to her. He was somewhat humiliated to say that this had not always been that way in earlier relationships in his life. His feelings for Carmen filled him with a sense of liberation from exactly the kind of body preoccupation that he might have shallowly felt at a much younger age. In this context, it was especially frustrating to have Carmen ensnaring him in this false accusation, which smacked of pure projection. But far more toxic than her false claim was her authoritative claim that she was right and that he wasn't; that Michael "simply didn't know his own mind."

Despite his protests, Carmen's proceeded with increasing volatility, stopping just short of calling Michael a liar. She interpreted his behavior in terms of his urgent need to get out of an emotionally uncomfortable situation. On this basis, he could "just go fuck himself," because she didn't have time for "wimps who were afraid of simply saying what was true." Above all, she couldn't stand men who were "nicey-nice" just to protect others' feelings and get along.

From Michael's point of view, Carmen's behavior was just one more dismissal of his reality, despite his having repeatedly implored her not to do this. In a state of rage, Michael exclaimed very loudly, "Well, that's just great! If that is what you think, if that is what you *really* think, then I suggest that you take a deep look at your assumptions, because either a) I am totally delusional, and have no idea at all of what I think or feel; or b) I am the world's greatest actor; or c) I am a fucking psychopath, who will do or say just about anything to get his way! If that is what you really believe, I don't see what the hell you are doing with me! Oh, and by the way, FUCK YOU!!!" Carmen, too, responded as she had on many occasions before: "Hey, if this is so hard for you, you can always leave me you know, nobody says you have to stay with me if I'm such a bitch."

In the beginning of our work, Carmen and Michael's outbursts stimulated a number of countertransference reactions in me. For instance, it was easier for me to experience a conjunctive identification with Michael's point of view, and a disjunctive one with Carmen. As mentioned earlier in the chapter, I have my own reactions to aggressive assertions by one partner that tend to obliterate the mind of the other. Such bullying engagement captures a certain quality of disrespect that is not only annihilating, but also constitutes a diminution of interpersonal safety, and ultimately impairs our capacity to mentalize. In truth, it was apparent to me that Carmen's style would likely provoke the opposite of what she seemed to want: the spontaneously open and authentic dialogue that I trusted she hungered for and had gotten more of from Michael than perhaps with any other individual in her life.

Thus, what became an immediate challenge for me was to circumvent both of their attempts to pull me in as a judge in favor of their respective versions of reality. Bolstering her case, Carmen averred that she was an astute student of psychology in college. She challenged my authenticity, suggesting that I was just trying to be nice to Michael. Meanwhile, she was convinced that I knew that she was right about him. Indeed, she couldn't fathom that I would disagree with her since, after all, I must have learned something from the hundreds of volumes shelved directly behind me. Surely all this education could help me understand Michael's self-deceptive bullshit—unless, of course, I was full of it as well. Meanwhile, although he was less dramatic in his manner of "courtroom" appeal, Michael was equally solicitous of my recognizing his "damned if he did, and damned if he didn't" life with Carmen. Since my own background was more like that of Michael's, wherein I was fighting more over abstractions of meaning than the concrete realm of abuse that Carmen had suffered, I could more readily identify with his existential outrage.

Feeling a countertransference imbalance, I decided to ask Carmen what her experience was that led her to attack Michael. To my surprise (and frankly relief), she informed me that she wasn't sure, but that when she was filled with rage, it meant that she was generally in a state of terror, one in which she afraid for herself, for Michael, and even fearful of her own volatility. I found her insight enormously helpful, as it helped me to reframe my understanding of her attacks as being about her state of terror and not really about her actual contempt of Michael.

In this state of greater reflectivity emerging in all of us, I was able to gently return to Michael's earlier story about the fury that came out over Carmen's weight gain. I was able to explore with her the meaning it had for her, which perhaps not surprisingly yielded multiple associations. Among the most compelling of them was the way in which her being in shape and physically fit represented both her power of attractiveness and her ability to defend herself against exploitation and attack from, in no small measure of irony, the kind of powerful men that might find her beauty especially alluring. Feeling strong versus overweight and out of shape (even by very small margins) helped Carmen combat self-doubt, as well as to fortify her sense of personal safety. Her disclosures readily led to a more empathic response, not only from me, but also from Michael, as evidenced by the softening of his nonverbal expression.

With this information, I was able to engage in an "of course, of course" mode of response, wherein I could move back and forth between both of them making empathic comments, while underscoring and fortifying for each that "of course" their reactions made so much sense in the context of how each of their backgrounds could so readily collide.

For example, with Carmen, I began commenting on how thrown she must have recently been feeling given the anomaly of her hormonal fluctuation, worst of all its impact on her temporary weight gain. I shared how understandably upset she must have felt given what I now understood about its meaning. As I was gaining corroboration on this from her and noticing her increased sense of calm, I looked at Michael with a kind of nonverbal nodding affirmation communicating that "It makes sense what Carmen is going through, right?" I added, to Carmen, that at such a time it must be especially hard to count on Michael, particularly since doing so could make her feel vulnerable exactly when she might most loathe feeling this way. Again, I nonverbally garnered Michael's recognition of Carmen's state of vulnerability.

Somewhere along in this, I gently shifted focus to Michael, commenting on how difficult it must be for him to feel mistrusted by Carmen, that when her mistrust manifested in her questioning the contents and integrity of his mind, he would doubtlessly find this toxic, especially after he had worked so long and hard in his analysis to achieve having a mind of his own. As I did in seeking some recognition for Carmen's position from Michael, I began to nonverbally do the same with Carmen regarding how Michael experienced feeling mistrusted. In conjunction with this, I also sought some recognition from Carmen regarding how her interpretations made Michael feel so badly.

Notably, as I was speaking to one of them, I was also intermittently punctuating my comments by looking at the other and conveying in my nonverbal facial expression, "It makes so much sense, doesn't it?" Later on, I underscored this verbally, suggesting that each one's position seemed especially true when seen from the viewpoint of their respective backgrounds. This mode of fluidly shifting empathic interpretations back and forth was meant not only to resonate with one, but also to carefully "sound-mix" recognition and resonance with the other. This begins to lay down tracks for intersubjective patterning, mutual recognition, and the relationship developing a mind of its own. Expanding the variability of the system in this manner, however, is as dramatically constrained when the therapist is unable to overcome her conjunctive and disjunctive countertransference biases. In short, the therapist is only equipped to expand the horizons of her patient's limited subjectivities when she can undertake a thorough examination of her own limitations.

Step Three

Most of the time, it is a humbling privilege to listen to the intimate details of a patient's personal narrative, and this was most certainly the case with Carmen and Michael. As already revealed, Carmen's upbringing was a powerful mixture of loss, tragedy, abuse, exuberance, creativity, and joy. She was the middle child of three, but had become the functional eldest after her father's demise from Parkinson's disease. In fact, her birth position would come to represent a powerful transferential point for Michael, as well as a powerful countertransferential one for me, as both of us were the youngest of three siblings.

Carmen's eldest brother, Manuel, was something of an enigma. Ten years her senior, he was out of the house while she was still in the equivalent of second grade in Mexico. Parting from the family tradition of enmeshment, he moved to Japan years ago and became involved in international exports. Carmen had learned as an adult that her mother had an emergency hysterectomy after giving birth to her youngest sister, Luisa. Compensating for her depression, her mother focused all of her attention on Luisa, which made Carmen feel second best. Thus, after moving to the United States and having become the surrogate father to her family, she experienced for the first time a sense of relevance and importance to her mother. Indeed, Carmen became essential to her mother, since her English was very poor, resulting in her becoming a veritable shut-in. It also meant that, though Carmen resented her father for "putting her in this surrogate paternal position," she also privately relished it. All of this left Carmen feeling guilty regarding her father, resentful of her mother's neediness, and jealous and envious of the attention lorded over Luisa, who after all did nothing for the attention she received, other than having been born when she was. By contrast, Carmen felt that she had to perform vital functions for her family to garner any comparable attention. The impact on her marriage to Michael was that Carmen could easily become enraged when she felt that Michael valued her more for what she did than for who she was, an accusation that Michael claimed was pure projection.

Carmen's promotion into the role of her family's functional father was a position over which she has been eternally conflicted. On the one hand, this status elevated her (at least partially) out of the constrictions of her hegemonically constrained role as a female by empowering her to have to think and behave like a man. On the other hand, it also burdened her with her collectivist-based value responsibility to take care of her "tribe." Finally, it flooded her with the impression that women are weak and must be taken care of, while confusing her about her own pressing urges and desires to express strongly felt qualities of femininity and the nascent desires of her female sexuality.

Ultimately, all of this responsibility imposed upon her a highly constricted orientation to her own adolescence and young adulthood. She was extremely studious, forsaking dating and the social life that surrounded her at college. While others experimented with alcohol, drugs, and sex, she hid in the library stacks, splitting off and denying the powerful sexual urges that would later command attention in her life. I found this story from such a vivacious and sexually passionate woman was one almost too hard to believe, but it also helped me understand some of what was at stake in her relationship with Michael.

As part of her burden to fulfill her role as a family provider, she got married right out of college to a veterinarian named Vicente, who was also of Mexican descent, though he was born and raised in the United States and barely spoke any Spanish. Immediately after she married him, she knew that she had made a huge, seemingly irrevocable mistake. Nevertheless, she and Vicente had two children, Esteban and Ramona. Since her entire adolescence had been marked by her responsibility to take care of her father, mother, and sister, as well as various aunts, uncles, and cousins, she swore to herself that she would do something more with her life than only being a mother. Accordingly, she enrolled in law school and was instantly highly praised for her intellectual acumen.

While in law school, Carmen also discovered that her male colleagues found her very attractive, and with that her sexuality finally blossomed. She began having casual coffee and lunch dates with several of them that would eventually evolve into sexual flirtations, and even in a few cases, brief, exciting but ultimately dissatisfying affairs. Although she never found sex with these men especially gratifying (except one man named "John"), her enjoyment of their attention made it ineluctably clear that her marriage was a sham. Against all elements of her religious background, she separated from Vicente, sought an annulment to their marriage, with which he happily cooperated, and soon thereafter they divorced. The shock of this horrified her mother as well as her extended family members. These complicating features added a burdensome layer to her new relationship with Michael that frequently insinuated itself into their arguments.

Michael's background, while basically free of the kinds of traumas that were routine in Carmen's life, bore its own complications. He was the youngest of three children and the only boy. Because he was the youngest, and because he was the only boy, Michael enjoyed something of a special status in his family, though he was also aware that this made him a frequent target of both envy and jealousy from his sisters. Like Carmen's relationship with her oldest brother, Michael barely knew his oldest sister, Diane, as she was away at college when he had just barely entered elementary school. Nevertheless, he recalled adoring and idolizing her. Although Diane was generally sweet to him, she was profoundly focused on her burgeoning young adulthood and barely gave him the time of day on the rare occasions that she was around.

By contrast, Michael's middle sister, Rae, was very much a part of his life. She was young enough to still be at home when Michael entered adolescence. She was also, however, old enough to lord her authority over him, and even to wield it abusively at times when their parents were away. Michael nevertheless also adored and idolized Rae. Because of their intense degree of involvement, he felt far more acutely pained by either her rebuff or her scolding. These came frequently throughout Michael's youth, as Rae was largely an unhappy child. Underpinning her disquietude was the fact that her eldest sister was the apple of her mother's eye, while Michael was the apple of his father's. This meant that his middle sister languished in a never-never-land where she was either jealous or envious, or both. Because of this, her moods were intemperate, shifting rapidly and sweeping over the entire family much like quickly changing weather fronts.

What Michael recalled most from his childhood was that when his middle sister was in a good mood, everything felt better. When she was in a bad mood, the entire focus and energy of the family was upon her. His parents never seemed to quite know what to do to console her. Michael consequently strove for two things growing up: pleasing his parents by not being yet another problem child, and trying to please Rae, a goal far more elusive than that of pleasing his folks.

In contrast to the volatility of Carmen's parents' relationship, Michael's parents seemed to live an outwardly pleasant enough existence. Still, although barely discernible, there nevertheless was an undercurrent of quiet desperation regarding issues ranging from the state of the family finances to the state of the world in the age of the nuclear bomb and population explosion. While he was somehow aware of his parents' private worries, he was incapable of articulating it. As such, this dim awareness represented what Bollas (1989) has described as an "unthought known."

Michael's father, an attorney who worked long hours, was away from home a lot, returning typically depleted and wanting his privacy. His mother, by contrast, was a housewife with a bit of a histrionic flair. She did very little with her college education other than pursuing and obtaining the proverbial "Mrs." degree. She married Michael's father shortly after graduation, and thereafter promptly had their first child.

All of this appeared to be driven by what a woman should do, and not by living out any personally chosen passionate design.

Michael's parents' lackluster relationship to religious faith left Michael wanting to investigate his own more. He was especially driven by seeing both of his sisters follow in their mother's footsteps—that is, they both started families immediately out of college and did little to pursue their own passions or interests either personally or spiritually. In fact, it was the discovery that he was on the verge of replicating aspects of this himself that drove Michael out of his marriage, an exit which finally became possible with his son Sam's near completion of high school.

The data gathered in our history-taking sessions became instrumental to my work with Michael and Carmen in the subsequent steps of this model. This preliminary data, of course, becomes richly filled in over the course of the treatment. Initially, however, our two history-taking sessions helped me begin to flesh out deeper elements of their longings, fears, as well as their capacity for mutual recognition. It also fueled my curiosity about a number of other areas for further exploration, ones that later on would also manifest in enactments.

The history-taking sessions also allowed me to assess under what conditions both Michael and Carmen evidenced fairly advanced capacities for mentalization—and under which ones they didn't. Certainly, both could symbolize and reflect upon their experience, as evidenced by their well-articulated personal narratives. The question became: Why were they sometimes more capable of thoughtful reflection and sometimes not?

In this vein, there were two circumstances in particular that could undermine their capacity to mentalize. One pertained to incidents of feeling ashamed, and the other pertained to overwhelming feelings that were triggered when their issues dovetailed with some traumatic experience. While both were prone to defend themselves when feeling shamed by the other's claim to holding the correct view of reality, Carmen's history of trauma made her more prone than Michael to lapse into temporary states of psychic equivalence. As Bromberg (1998, 2006) notes, trauma victims live in a perpetual state of vigilance that is always on the alert, anticipating trauma. Because of the prospective perils of being wrong, it is harder for such individuals to reserve a healthy sense of doubt when trauma states are triggered.

In contrast to Carmen's vulnerability to lapsing into a version of psychic equivalence, Michael's wishful pretend mode could be vexing, especially when he began imagining all the wonderful ways that he and Carmen would be able to be together, ways that did not necessarily jibe with Carmen's version of the future. In this manner, he was unwittingly setting himself up for disappointments regarding either her inability or lack of desire to fulfill his wishes.

Other historical data was helpful in clarifying the conflicts that arose from differences from their cultural backgrounds, as well as conflicts about gender. Carmen clarified that her Roman Catholic upbringing was very affiliative, and therefore adhered to principles of collectivism. She referred to her family and her extended culture as her tribe to whom she had become an ambivalent tribal chief. This created a multiplicity of dissociated self-states, which would move in and out of the experiential foreground and background of her consciousness. Each self-state would then operate as though no other ones existed except for the one in the foreground.

While it was clear that Carmen's autonomous strivings had found a place in her professional world, her family's collectivist demands exerted an enormous force upon her in a multitude of ways. As a mother, her children came above everyone else in the world, which seemed to reflect an admirable level of devotion. However, they also represented a kind of defensive stronghold to sometimes hide in, as they were the only relationships that she could trust that would never abandon her. Meanwhile, she often found that her responsibilities to the rest of her tribe could become smothering.

Much of Carmen's background flew in the face of the cultural emphasis on individualism with which Michael was raised. Michael's father had rejected his own father's urgings that he become a minister, while his mother virtually eschewed the religious world in which she had been raised. In short, his parents were quintessentially Americans, adopting what Michael referred to as a "WASP-lite" form of liberalism.

Although Michael found Carmen's passion for her faith profound and her connection with her tribe very appealing, he was concerned about what he felt was her unnecessary participation in all of the tribal functions of her family. In particular, he noted these seemed to "suffocate her and to make her miserable." Clearly, he wished for her emancipation from what appeared to be a stranglehold of obligations and how these interfered in their relationship.

Though less judgmental of Michael's background of individualism, Carmen was stalwart in protecting her collectivist culture. In fact, one of their biggest problems was that Carmen would not only assert the tribal dictums that governed her life, but, by extension, how these would dictate how Michael needed to be if he was going to be a part of her life. Her assertions often took on an absolutist, objectifying quality about reality, as in "what it is that a mother does," or "what it is that a father does," or "a husband," and so forth. These proclamations often seemed to assume an almost biblical text-like, quasi-fundamentalist quality. This, however, was not really how Carmen thought.

Instead, all of Carmen's years of therapy, and her interest in Michael, were testimony to her desire to have a mind of her own as well as to have it recognized. Nevertheless, given what Michael experienced as her stridency about many matters, he was not always able to so readily see this about her. This made him vulnerable to becoming defensive and responding in kind with his own cultural biases. It was clear, as Rubalcava and Waldman (2004) have indicated, that developing emotional competency regarding each other's cultural biases would be of the utmost importance to Michael and Carmen. Indeed, what was even more important was their learning what they each felt was missing from their own cultural backgrounds. It was these differences that led to each of them seeking out a partner from such different cultural persuasions.

Clearly, both Carmen and Michael were seeking emancipation from some of the more rigidified constraints of their gender orientations. Both longed for a partner who could be comfortable with the parts of themselves that stepped outside the hegemony of their gender identities; both needed to be able to do this without fearing the loss of their own complexly formulated gender identities. Concretely, Carmen hungered to be with a man who was strong enough to embrace her masculine side while also adoring her femininity. However, because of the dissociations between her personality self-states, these longings could often be at odds with one another. Meanwhile, Michael was seeking something from Carmen that would make him feel appreciated for his manhood, while also appreciating him for his genuine interest in the subjectivity and feelings of others. These latter characteristics had often made him vulnerable to being called a "feminist male."

All of this history set a foundation for examining how each defined their self-actualizing longings. It also underscored how each utilized (or didn't) processes of mentalization, which are instrumental to understanding how to negotiate the power struggles inherent in their cultural or gendered differences. In short, they gave me a foundation for understanding the repetitive constraints of their relationship. This laid the groundwork for helping them with freer expressions of non-destructive aggression, thoughtful reflection, non-submissive surrender, and negotiation.

Step Four

One of the important features of Michael and Carmen's intimacy was their sex life. Neither had had especially gratifying sexual histories, so both immediately felt a kind of magic insofar as they had both found in each other the best sexual partner they had ever known. In part, it worked beautifully, in terms of Carmen's longing to be "taken" by her man as symbolizing his capacity to take care of her in a more general way. It also worked for Michael in having his manhood so boldly affirmed. Throughout the course of our work, one thing they continuously maintained was that, no matter what was going on, their sex life remained quite active. In this context, however, Carmen had been becoming aware of something that was starting to concern her, though she didn't know exactly how to bring it up with Michael for fear of destroying something about their sex life. As it turns out, what she was detecting was the beginning of a huge enactment.

Over time, Carmen had noted a pattern: Precisely at the time of the month that Carmen was ovulating, Michael was scheduled to be out of town on business, or would become ill, or would profess to be too exhausted to have sex. This, of course, very much piqued my curiosity. What was most conspicuous to me was that Michael seemed quite oblivious to this pattern, even though Carmen felt that she had gently brought it to his attention on several occasions. Nevertheless, these were conversations that Michael professed not to remember. This seemed very unlike the Michael to whom I had become acquainted, since he was usually an adept tracker of their process, especially regarding anything that might cause Carmen some distress. This led me to wonder what state of dissociation he was in and from what other self-states he was dissociating. I asked both of them to recreate the circumstances surrounding Carmen's complaint.

Carmen began by explaining that one of the preconditions she had posed to Michael for their getting married was that she wanted to have yet another child and especially one with him. Indeed, this urgency was a part of their rather rapid decision to move from first date to marriage in six months!

The first complicating factor for getting pregnant, however, was Carmen's age. Though at 41 she was certainly a candidate for having another child, the odds were less in her favor than when she gave birth to her children years before. At her age, the likelihood of infertility complications requiring major intervention, possible miscarriages, and even birth defects loomed much more ominously than years before. And time was clearly not on her side, as her obstetrician had told her all of these complicating variables would be accelerating at a very fast pace with each passing birthday.

On top of all of this, an even more complicating factor than Carmen's age pertained to Michael. Toward the end of his first marriage, he had privately gotten a vasectomy to ensure that his wife would not become pregnant again. Though he felt a bit guilty over his secrecy, he also felt that his marriage was doomed, and was only invested in staying in it until his son was old enough for him to feel okay about separating. Thus, the idea of a complicating pregnancy was too overwhelming, and yet the announcement of his vasectomy might have led to a premature dissolution of his marriage. Ironically, during their separation and divorce, his wife did find out about his operation and told him that she was glad he had it, especially because (in the event she were to have gotten pregnant) an abortion would have been untenable for both of them.

Somewhat reluctant to have his vasectomy reversed, Michael also understood that Carmen held it up as a precondition for marriage. Thus, in accommodating her, Michael had unconsciously engaged in an act of submission. His dissociated behavior suggested he was far more in conflict about this than was apparent even to him. Hence, there was something of a sequestered "saboteur" self-state protecting Michael, "inadvertently" making sure that he was either not available or incapable to make love, especially with the urgent frequency upon which Carmen insisted when she was ovulating. Unconsciously, it appeared that Michael really did not want to have any more children, though in his dissociated state he wasn't able to convey this. Instead, he made up more excuses and acted as though he was still committed. Indeed, he did so in such a convincing manner that I too remained uncertain about what his real wish was.

Though enactments frequently begin asymmetrically, they quickly can become symmetrical, in this case involving an enactment of Carmen's as well. With her growing concern that Michael was being less amorous at exactly the time she needed him to be, Carmen started to worry that there was something about her that was making him less enthused. Doubting herself, she "friended" on Facebook her old lover, John, the one with whom she had had the best sex of her life prior to being with Michael. This was not about actually meeting with him, since he lived on the

East Coast; it was more about reclaiming a sense of her desirability that she hoped would somehow translate into something that might jump-start Michael's ardor. The fallout from this, however, was that on two occasions she unwittingly cried out John's name while having sex with Michael. He of course knew who John was, including that he was her first great lover. In this sense, John had served as a kind of competitor in Michael's mind. On occasion, Michael would even playfully query after he and Carmen had had sex, "That was a lot better than with John, right?" And although his prodding was always wrapped in the plausible deniability of "just kidding," these questions betrayed the gravity of his concern. Whether Carmen grasped this or not, she would just give him a demure smile, suggestive of "of course, you are the best ever," though she never actually said this.

Though Michael was dismayed the first time Carmen cried out John's name, it appeared she was oblivious to what she had done. The second time, however, Michael became quite suspicious. Although he would typically never violate any-one's privacy, including his wife's, his jealousy got the better of him. One day, while her email account was open, he quickly looked at her inbox folder, in which she had a couple of email correspondences with John that she had not deleted.

From what Michael could tell, the emails revealed that some flirtation was going on between Carmen and John, though there was no evidence of their actually having any direct physical contact. Still, Michael found the tone of their flirtatious intimacy very upsetting. The most painful exchange involved Carmen's confession to John that she had been fantasizing about him, especially around the time that she was ovulating. She mentioned that this was in part because she was always "horni-est" during this period of the month. But it was the next comment that Michael found most troubling: her disclosure that, at these times, Michael seemed to be the least interested in her.

Much like Carmen had been containing her thoughts about Michael's seeming "absenteeism" during her monthly ovulation cycles, Michael had kept his concerns about John to himself. While her decision to maintain her silence was about a fear of screwing something up sexually between them, his silence was more about his humil-iation over, first, snooping, and second, what he had discovered in Carmen's emails. In both cases, however, Michael and Carmen were simmering below the surface, unwittingly building up affectively charged tension that was just waiting to crack.

Interestingly, their implicit communication seemed to suggest that each had induced in the other a sense of "its best we not go there," that it was best that they not explore what was going on. While for many couples this evasive behavior might be common, for Michael and Carmen it was highly unusual.

None of what was brewing was apparent to me, though I was sensing that there was beginning to be some erosion in the positive work that had occurred over our many months together. In this context, I began to wonder what slumbering giants might be lurking. And it turned out my intuition was not only correct, it was soon realized.

On an especially stormy Monday afternoon, both arrived late, having driven in separate cars. In bad moods, ostensibly because of the traffic ("Nobody knows how to fucking drive in this town when it rains!"), and also expecting the other to chastise them for being late, the room was saturated with a powerful sense of agitated affect. It also came up later that Carmen had been ovulating since Thursday night, and Michael had not once initiated sex. When she finally insisted that they make love Sunday morning, he was unable to ejaculate.

On this latter point, Carmen began screaming, "What is up with this, Michael?! Are you intentionally trying to sabotage my getting pregnant? Because, if so, you know that would be a deal-breaker, Michael! I was crystal clear about this before we got married. It is an essential part of our covenant."

Michael was caught completely off guard by Carmen's barrage. After all, up to this point, he still was pretty much in denial about his pattern of absenteeism, with the exception of his recent discovery of Carmen's email complaint to John. Overwhelmed with humiliation, he blurted out defensively, "Oh, and is that something you're telling your friend John about?!" No sooner had he said this, than he knew his snooping had been revealed. Carmen screamed, "Have you been reading my emails?! You fucking asshole. That's my private correspondence and that's another covenant that we agreed to before taking our vows! We agreed that neither of us would *ever* pry into the other's privacy! You seem to be breaking our vows left and right, Michael! Dr. Ringstrom, I am not sure I can stay with a man like this!"

At this point, Michael's flagging defense was to turn to me and exclaim, "Well, what about it, Doc?! How would you feel if your wife cried out her old lover's name while you were having sex?! Not once, no sirree, but twice! And, this by the way, this John guy, was supposedly her best lover ever, and she has never even had the decency of disabusing me of my fantasies that she still prefers him over me! Not one fucking time!" Carmen cried out, "That's not true, I tell you that you were better all the time, you just never believed me!" (Later on, of course, it came out that she hadn't spoken this to him, in part, she said reflectively, because she enjoyed his jealousy, which seemed to be a turn on for both of them.)

Each was rapidly drawing me into a judgmental position vis-à-vis the other. On the one hand, I could certainly understand Carmen's sense of betrayal regarding their two covenants. On the other, I also could sense Michael's having unconsciously painted himself into a corner of pathological accommodation to Carmen's precondition that they try to have a baby if they were to be married. It struck me that the collaboration and negotiation that needed to have been dealt with before their marriage was finally coming out. In this context, Michael's behaviors, though unconscious, seemed to make sense. His behavior may not have been excusable, even to himself, but it certainly seemed explainable.

The problem now was that I was being sucked into the enactment, in this case having to become the moral arbiter of their mess. What was apparent was that, to pull out of this tailspin, there was much work to be done in Step Five. This would especially include assisting each of them to come to terms with their unwitting conflictual self-states. That would be a prerequisite to helping them then be able to negotiate between them what they had begun to negotiate within themselves.

Step Five

As often happens, the events that emerged (relative to Step Four) really threw Carmen and Michael and even me. They had made considerable progress with a deeper understanding of their states of bidimensional transference, the vicious cycles in which they would trigger one another. Additionally, they had developed a great regard for being attuned to one another, and were feeling increasingly positive about their marriage, which was an enormous relief given their dire concern when they first came to me. On top of this, they relaxed more into accepting one another's perspective about their own unique views of reality. The idea of this was suddenly more exciting than threatening. Also, with the illumination of the opposing dimensions of their backgrounds (e.g., coming from collectivist and individualist cultures), it helped them understand both what powerfully attracted them ("opposites attract") and what could readily repel them ("Whose culture are we going to follow?"). All of this work through the first three steps had made them feel more secure with one another. So the disruptions of their Step Four enactments sent them back to the proverbial drawing board. However, these enactments also presented us with the needed material functioning implicitly in each of their dissociated self-states. In order to progress with deeper authenticity in their negotiations, they had to become more aware of how they were each unwittingly in conflict within themselves, before they could negotiate certain issues between themselves.

Faced with the evidence that he had really dissociated his non-participation—indeed, his veritable absenteeism during Carmen's ovulation cycle—Michael had to confront what he was denying. This was not easy to do, since Carmen was not favorably disposed to hear anything from Michael other than his follow-up promise to do everything he could to give her the baby she felt so compelled to have. Given her reaction to sensing his betrayal of this promise and his fear that she might leave him (she threatened to, but I insisted she back off that point unless she really meant it), he was very cautious in how he proceeded. Interestingly, sensing her presence as a powerful inhibitor to Michael's exploration of his truth, Carmen suggested that we break with the routine of our conjoint treatment, and that I see Michael for a couple of sessions alone. This was a wise and generous act on her part, and with her strong support we did so. Of course, that was with the proviso that what was discussed would be shared with her in the manner that seemed most clinically advantageous.

In meeting with Michael—especially without his having to be on guard in front of Carmen—I began to see more readily that he was a man of many minds regarding her becoming pregnant. One self-state involved his promise to fulfill her wish to try to become pregnant. As smitten as he was with her, he would have practically guaranteed meeting any of her wishes, as he felt like he was so lucky at his age to meet such a compelling partner. It was in this self-state that he said, "I told myself, one baby, two babies, hell as many as she wants, so long as I can be with her."

There were other self-states that Michael was not so in touch with, which came into the foreground as we spoke in our private session. I had asked him to associate as freely as he could to all the different possible ways in which he could relate to the idea of having a baby. Something that popped up immediately, though he professed he'd not consciously thought of it before, was that both of his older sisters had had their last children around Carmen's age. In each case, their children were born with severely compromising conditions. His oldest sister's youngest child, a girl, had serious neurological birth defects. His middle sister's youngest son was eventually diagnosed as being on the Autistic spectrum. Michael suddenly also remembered that when he had his vasectomy a few years earlier he had been mindful of his sisters' traumas. In conjunction with not wanting to have any more children with his first wife, he especially did not want to have a special needs child which would shackle him to her forever.

It started to become clear, however, that in the context of Carmen's unequivocal demand that they at least try to have a baby together he could no longer allow such thoughts to permeate his consciousness. Consequently, he lost a connection to himself as a subject with his own thoughts, desires, and initiatives, which in this case were largely against having any more children. Having lost this connection, he submissively (without being clear about it) caved into feeling obliged to fulfill Carmen's more powerful desire to have a baby.

The more we talked, and the more he started to hear himself speak, the more he became aware that having another child was not something he wanted to do. He also gradually became aware that, as he was older than Carmen, he would eventually be reaching retirement sooner than her. This made him start to imagine what it would be like to be retired and to have a teenager. Suddenly, he was filled with dread by the prospect. Although his son was a late teen and most of the storms of their relationship had passed, he was quickly reminded of them. Thus, he began questioning if he'd have the wherewithal to go through that stage of development again, especially as he was becoming increasingly aware that he didn't want to go through it in his late sixties or early seventies.

Two things suddenly hit Michael very hard. The first was that he was astonished that, after all of the psychotherapy that he had had, he could still be so blind to his conflictual feelings. I assured him that there is no amount of analysis that will guarantee that all our blind spots will be illuminated. Furthermore, under the circumstances of Carmen having proposed a non-negotiable ultimatum to Michael about having a child, it may well have served a certain immediate need of his to be blind to all of his trepidations. Though my comments helped a little, nothing soothed his second dread: It was becoming obvious that he would now have to tell all of this to Carmen. He panicked, fearing that this would be the end of their relationship. I assured him that I would help him all I could, but I also had a sinking feeling, knowing how adamant Carmen was about doing everything within her power to have a baby.

In this context, Carmen called me and asked if she too might have a couple of individual sessions. With Michael's permission, I agreed, but also said that I would not share with her what Michael and I had discussed, as that was to be done with all of us together. I wasn't sure what Carmen would be bringing to me, but I felt like there might also be things she needed to examine which might be easier for her to contemplate absent worrying about how Michael might seize upon them to his advantage.

When we met, much as I had done with Michael, I asked Carmen to tell me as much as she could freely associate to what the meaning of having a baby was for her. Also, what meaning her long-distance enactment with John meant. Somewhat to my surprise, especially given her adamancy about having a baby, she said that she really wasn't sure—that is, although she felt certain that she "had to try to have another child," upon serious reflection, especially in the context of both hers and Michael's enactments, she said that she was no longer so sure she wanted another child. I privately breathed a little sigh of relief for both of them. There appeared to be some wiggle room in their respective conflicts about this topic that might enable us to open it up to the kind of collaboration and negotiation that had not yet been allowed.

One of the things Carmen told me (which she had yet to tell Michael) was that she had just recently been offered the possibility of becoming a judge, a dream she had imagined would never come true. She had been reluctant to tell Michael, especially in the context of their current acrimony, since she was afraid he'd use the information to discourage proceeding with trying to become pregnant. Nevertheless, it was apparent to Carmen that if she became pregnant and had a baby she would have to foreclose on the judgeship. This idea symbolically felt like a kind of miscarriage or, as I would submit, a submissive truncation of a powerful sense of self-actualization.

Bearing in mind her collectivist cultural tendency to accommodate the desires of members of her tribe, I asked Carmen if she could tell me who else had something at stake in whichever decision she made. This freed her to contemplate whose voice was pressing her regarding both the possibility of taking the judgeship and the possibility of having another child. Her answers came to her quickly and with considerable surprise. She said, "My deceased father would most certainly wish for me to take the judgeship, and my alive mother would insist on me having a baby. In fact, I can virtually hear my mother saying, 'Man creates careers, but God creates babies. It is a woman's duty to fulfill God's mission.'"

Surprised at hearing herself say this, she commented that she typically would allow her mother's biblical admonitions to go in one ear and out the other. Obviously, she realized she was deluding herself about the impact of her mother on her thinking and feeling. She quickly associated to her mother's inability to have any more children after Luisa was born, when she had to have a hysterectomy. Her mother had been depressed ever since then, and had spent countless hours going to Mass and praying for her children to have many, many babies. Manuel, who Carmen speculated was likely gay, had never married, and therefore had no children. Luisa had complications after the birth of her first child and, like her mother, had to have a hysterectomy. In short, the fulfillment of her mother's dream fell exclusively upon Carmen.

Suddenly, Carmen realized that she was a house divided. This was much like what had become apparent in the sessions with Michael; she also had several self-states competing for her attention. She had completely overlooked them in her compulsive drive to try to compensate for her mother's loss of her dream. Put in this light, however, she was filled suddenly with a pull to fulfill what she imagined might be her father's wish for her taking the judgeship as a kind of compensatory act for his own truncated career. Now, she realized, irrespective of their desires, she had to figure out what was true for her.

In answer to my query about John, she said that, as far as he was concerned, she saw their long-distance email dalliance as, at best, a somewhat pleasurable distraction from the tension she was now realizing she was feeling about all of these heretofore unknown conflictual thoughts. John, she said, was like a mini-time machine. She could enter it when writing to him and be spirited back to moments of comradeship that had helped her be distracted from what was so lacking in her relationship to her first husband, Vicente. However, in any contemporary sense, John meant very little to her. In her pretend mode of fantasy, he supplied temporary relief and also may have been a means for acting out her building anger over Michael's lackluster performance in bed, at least during her ovulation cycle.

The more she spoke, the more I heard in her voice that, although she wasn't quite ready to abandon the pursuit of becoming pregnant, she was undergoing a kind of internal negotiation between parts of herself. It started to become clear that what heretofore had been an unimaginable loss of trying to have another child opened up for her some possible gains she had not been allowing herself to see. It started to appear that surrendering her adamancy of becoming pregnant was a real possibility for Carmen. I allowed this to settle in without commenting, as I wanted Carmen to take in what she was saying without anyone adding any weight to her deliberations. I felt strongly that, however this was to come out for her, she needed very much to have her decision feel right to her.

It was apparent that, notwithstanding their considerable therapeutic experience, Carmen and Michael could readily find themselves becoming someone else's object while losing their own subjective sense of self. While this seemed especially the case for Carmen given her collectivist cultural background, it also could apply to Michael, who, in seeking something to compensate for the arid character of his individualist culture, could readily lose himself in his desire to accommodate Carmen. In the next step, we begin to see how all of their disparate self-states began to soft-assemble with each other, creating room for new internal negotiation between parts of themselves. This phenomenon made it possible for them to begin to become available intersubjectively to collaborate and negotiate with one another.

Step Six

Michael and Carmen's enactments in Step Four and their discoveries about the dissociated origins of them in Step Five set the stage for our work in Step Six. Returning to our conjoint work, both came into our session with a fair degree of trepidation.

Michael, of course, was imagining the worst, assuming that his disclosure of really not wanting another child might break up his marriage. Carmen, who was still trying to sort out her multiple decisions, feared that Michael might weigh in too heavily on any sign of her own second thoughts of maybe not trying to become pregnant before she had truly come to this decision herself.

As the session began, Carmen asked that Michael share first what he had figured out in his individual sessions with me. With my help, he explained to her his multiple reservations about having a child, as well as his initial desire to accommodate Carmen's wish. He discussed his recent revelations of fearing birth defects and other childhood abnormalities, much like those his sisters suffered. He then described what had become his emergent dread over imagining having to negotiate the stormy phase of the child's adolescence when he feared he'd neither have the patience nor energy to appropriately engage in it. With a lowered voice, he finally confessed that he'd concluded that he really did not want them to have another child. He proposed, instead, that their attention be focused more on rearing the children they had, as they still needed a lot of support. Finally, he also added his wish for them to put their energy into how they would plan for how they would live the remainder of their days together.

Carmen was visibly stunned and, much to Michael's chagrin, powerfully upset. She told him that she felt he had misled her, and that his decision felt like an enormous blow to her faith and respect in him. This repeated his worst fears that they had begun treatment with, clearly a profound assault on his need for her to be an affirming mirror to him.

As I asked Carmen to elaborate on her reaction, she said that what was so upsetting had less to do with what Michael was saying about the rationale for his change of mind, and more to do with its blow to a powerful conviction that she had about Michael. As far as his rationale went about birth defects, or being too old, she too had had some of these same thoughts and fears. Indeed, privately she was uncertain if she would even be able to get pregnant or, if she did, whether it would terminate in a miscarriage given her age.

Still, it was Carmen's sense of betrayal that was her undoing—that is, a betrayal of her undying belief in Michael's heretofore undying devotion to her. On this conviction, she assumed that if she felt there was something that mattered to her more than anything else in her life he would most certainly fulfill her wish. Up to this point in their relationship, she had not pressed him for anything except to accommodate her need to have another child. Whether they would ever be able to or not was, in a sense, secondary to the preservation of her conviction that Michael had proven himself as a devoted partner, notwithstanding her other earlier questions about his capacity to protect and to care for her and her tribe. Now, his new position dissolved her faith in this conviction. Michael was now visibly shaken. In this moment, the two of them entered a profound sense of grief over the apparent shattering of their version of the "perfect marriage" illusion that they had co-created.

What was also in evidence, however, was that Carmen, while bereft, was not becoming the stormy, demanding version of herself that she might well have become in the earlier phases of our work. I commented on this, and wondered how she might understand her shift. At this point, she acknowledged that what she had uncovered about her own multiply dissociated states about having a baby had made it clear to her that her over-determined drive may well have belonged to others and not so much her authentic sense of self. She recounted what she had said to me about compensating for her mother's losses, and additionally described being routinely pressured by her aunts and uncles and even a few cousins to continue to bring new life to the family as long as she possibly could.

Finally, she told Michael about the judgeship, about which he was initially elated, until she told him that his joy was premature and that it too easily felt like it was giving him an "out." He immediately became more subdued, appearing a little chastised, thinking that she was right, and that his upbeat reaction was ill timed in this moment. Carmen acknowledged that, at this point, she could see that they seriously needed to open up discussion whether having another child was the correct thing to attempt now. But she also said that she wasn't sure how to live with her shattered faith in Michael's devotion to her.

There arose in this moment a fundamental question at this intersection: How do two authentic selves coexist, in a devoted and committed relationship, in which each of their respective senses of self-actualization are respected? In hitting up against their most compelling test to date, Michael and Carmen each feared that the other would have a trump card that would override the other's autonomy, that they would come up against a paradox of such profound proportion that they would have to surrender to its implications or perhaps their relationship would indeed dissolve.

The paradox in their case was their collusion in the illusion that Michael could indemnify Carmen's losses through his assiduous accommodation to her most profound wish. Furthermore, as his reward, he would earn her indefatigable love and faith in his goodness, something that he remained uncertain about all his life despite seeming to have been a favored son. Each was forced to face their primary fantasies of what the other would do to ensure their redemption and salvation from their respective falls from grace that their backgrounds were heir to.

What was also becoming evident, however, is that the degree to which they could reckon with the loss of their respective fantasies was the degree to which they were freer to be themselves. Part of accomplishing this meant they had to openly grieve together what each had lost in relationship to the other. And yet, in this same moment, they were confronted with the realization that, as they both shared their profound losses, maybe they could begin to actually "be there" for one another in facing them.

In subsequent sessions, Carmen decided to forego attempting to have another baby, and ultimately accepted the appointment to become a judge. These decisions caused an enormous storm in her family. Now, however, she had Michael as her support, her comrade, and even her protector, especially in relation to her family's upset. Whereas she had been uncertain of his capacity to fulfill this role, he was becoming the man she knew that she ultimately needed. This was proven in his defending the actualization of both of their needs and desires.

In these manners, they had begun to create a therapeutic alliance of sorts. Having gotten through what seemed like an insurmountable impasse, they developed greater faith in their capacity to fight fairly. Out of this, they could finally come to some kind of collaboration and negotiation that worked for both of them. This pattern of resolution bespoke an emerging third position, relative to their vulnerability to devolving into binary arguments. Of course, this didn't mean they were no longer susceptible to degenerating into familiar binaries, but it did mean they were equipped to move away from them and into a position of thirdness to the ownership of their individual contributions to their meltdowns.

After several months of cultivating their own version of thirdness, they began speaking of no longer needing to see me. As is frequently the case, this came with playful comments about how I had become too expensive, both in fee and in the time required to dedicate to therapy. Our final few sessions were sad but also playful and full of deep feeling for the meaningful work that had occurred. Of course, when Michael and Carmen left, they did so knowing that they could return as needed, but for now they were well on their way.

9

FREQUENTLY ASKED QUESTIONS

Over the course of 30 years of developing, practicing, teaching, and supervising, I have been asked enumerable of questions regarding my model of couples therapy. Here are some questions that are frequently asked.

Your model, including your history-taking method, makes it appear as if you always see the partners together and never alone. Do you ever see one of the partners without the other?

Over the first decade and a half of my couples treatment practice, I adhered to a strict policy of never seeing one partner without the other. This, of course, could create some awkward moments, especially when one of the partners didn't show up or came egregiously late. This would result in my having to refuse to see the partner who had showed up, or leave them waiting until their partner finally arrived. This policy, however, also communicated something about the necessity of boundaries in relationships and the importance of their negotiation. During this period, my policy was still very much under the influence of early family systems theory; most of those models argued against seeing one partner without the other, or, as in the case of family therapy, ever seeing the family minus one of its members. This was seen as likely blinding the therapist to how the system as a totality worked. It also warded off colluding with the family in terms of leaving something disavowed and projected onto the non-attending member.

In addition to these theoretical considerations, I also discovered (through conducting many consultations and supervisions) that one of the fundamental factors related to a case going awry began with the therapist starting to see the partners individually. Rather quickly, it would become apparent that the therapist was engaging in a host of unwitting (and even sometimes witting) collusions with one partner in relation to the other. As described in Step Two, they would find themselves ensnared in a countertransference conjunction with one partner and a disjunction with the other. This predictably would lead to some version of impasse, with the partner in the disjunctive position engaging in "fight" (narcissistic outrage), "flight" (abrupt termination or the threat of it), or pathological accommodation to the conjunctive position held by the therapist and partner in which they begin to behave like "co-therapists." All of these considerations led to my strict adherence to only seeing the couple together.

Subsequent to my psychoanalytic training and many years of working with couples, I slowly began to bend my rule, at least in my own practice. (With more novice couples therapists, I would still caution against separating the partners.) Later still, as a relational psychoanalyst, I began to see the process of treatment as being far messier than I would have liked to have admitted before. Gradually, I found that because so much of my work appeared to look like treating two individuals in a conjoint treatment, at least some of the time, I could be comfortable with engaging them one at a time. Several principles of practice supported this rationale, and a few others emerged that have remained flags for when I would assiduously refuse to do it.

Central to what every patient experiences in my manner of treatment (at least hopefully) is that I am keenly interested in their unique subjective worldview of experience, as well as how this manifests (or not) in terms of their personal self-actualization. However, they also get a quick sense that for these criteria to be experienced fully, they must also involve their partners as the recognizing other. That, of course, can start with me as therapist, but if they are in couples therapy it becomes clear that their partner is powerfully implicated in this self-realization. Equally powerful is each partner seeing me tightly adhering to this stance with the other partner. The thematic principles of self-actualization, mutual recognition, and the relationship having a mind of its own are in operation from the moment a couple first walk through my door.

All of this leads to yet another question: How is the decision to see one partner without the other handled? First of all, it must be explicitly negotiated by all three of us; that is, that we are all in conscious agreement, bearing in mind that we must also be open to exploring what we might not be able to be conscious of in making this decision—most importantly, to be open to examining if something untoward arises from it. I make it clear, however, that if that turns out to be the case, there is nothing necessarily bad in our enactment. Rather, it would be emblematic of something needing to be awakened that was heretofore "out of sight," for example, a blindness to some kind of Oedipal issue regarding jealousy or competition that had somehow been obscured in "niceness" until this change of original venue could be fleshed out.

In addition to this, partners would also understand that the individual work we would be engaging in was about improving their relationship. If prolonged themes pertaining to either of them alone emerged, we would then begin talking about a referral for some individual psychotherapy. And, since the partners know that what is being discussed has to do with their self-actualization and their recognition of the same in each other, each counts on me to, in effect, also represent them, even in their absence from the room.

How such representation might occur is very important. It manifests in the following manner. If I hear someone describing their partner in a manner that seems different from how I imagine that partner feeling about themselves or at least wanting to be seen, I pay close attention to themes of transference. These include what might be being obscured (misrecognized) about the absent partner. This would typically be augmented by my movement in and out of the self-centered listening perspective and the other-centered listening perspective, which I discussed in Step One. By this, I mean that I would typically develop some sense of how the partner in the room was speaking about the absent partner—that is, the spouse was being turned into some transferentially projected version of self (subject) or projected version of other (object). This made it almost impossible for the projector to hold the other as a distinct subject with his or her own subjectivity.

When this occurs, I often ask the patient I am seeing alone if I might have their permission to share an alternative point of view. Typically, they are intrigued with what I might be thinking, especially as they have seen me with their partner and have experienced how I seem to "get something" about her that he frequently does not, especially when in a powerful state of transference. I say something like, "You know, that doesn't quite sound like Maggie, at least as I experience her in here with you and me. Whereas you seem to be imagining that she will, 'out of the gate,' reject your idea, indeed even willfully need to shut it down, I sense that she typically comes from a somewhat different place. By that, I mean that she seems more open to things, so long as she senses that you have considered her in your desire. It seems to me that the problem is that, since you are coming from a place of imagining being automatically shut down, you begin your expression of desire quite defensively. By that, I mean that you broadcast your disappointment in her, all the while treating her like an object, and not someone with a mind of her own—with her own sense of subjectivity and desire." Because this intervention is modeled on what we typically are already doing in the couples treatment when we are all together, it usually quickly takes hold and enables the one partner to develop a richer perspective regarding the other. The point is that, when meeting with one partner and not the other, the work of the couples treatment continues much like when they are in the room together.

Of course, this raises the question of when I won't see partners alone. This is usually the case when partners are embroiled in deeply vicious and affectively charged divisive battles that tend to split the room in some pernicious binary the moment they enter it. It happens when there is evidence of profoundly insecure attachment systems, primitive capacities to control affect, and pathological patterns of mentalization, especially psychic equivalence, though frequently the pretend mode can also be in evidence. With such couples, almost the only thing that they can discuss is the other as object. In so doing, they are vexed in binary positions, virtually always consumed with feeling the done-to in the doer and done-to binary.

In these latter cases, I find that there is so much regulation of affect, or turn-taking, or creative translating of what each means, that it has to occur with each in the presence of the other. As mentioned earlier, the typical "borderline/narcissistic" (Lachkar, 1992; Soloman, 1989) couples partnership presents much more like two half-people than two whole ones, vexed by repression, dissociation, and conflictual multiple self-states. The two half-partners are instead powerfully drawn together to create complementary vessels in which to project and ultimately recip-rocally induce, through the process of mutual inductive identification, what each has disavowed.

There are also other stipulations I state when I decide to see one partner alone. Typically, there is some understanding by all of us of what the topic will be. Meanwhile, sometimes meeting alone is a matter of convenience, as one partner is out of town and both agree that this presents a fortuitous opportunity for the one attending the session to take up something that has been disturbing him or her. Frequently, this is not so much about their relationship, though whatever the issue it likely has ramifications for their relationship. In this context, however, there is always the risk of some issue being raised that has not been brought up with the partner, specifically because of fear of their reaction.

This latter condition raises another frequently asked question: What do I do with secrets? This is one of the most vexing issues in couples therapy and has to be han-dled with great delicacy. Typically, I inform both parties that, in the main, every-thing discussed alone with me is open for our collective discussion. That said, when I meet with an individual partner and the topic of a secret or a yet-to-be-disclosed issue arises, I will, using the best clinical judgment I can muster, determine if, when, and how the topic should be brought up (or not). For example, if someone used their private time to disclose an affair that they had had in the past that had ended and is no longer in occurrence, but that now they wanted to unburden themselves of their guilt by disclosing it, I would want to seriously analyze their motivation in doing so. Is this about self-actualizing or unburdening a guilty conscience? I would also be judging what I imagined the impact might be on their partner: if the disclosure would generate something that might forward the other partner's self-actualization as well, or it might be shattering in a manner that undermines all that the therapy is attempting to mend and improve.

Thus, if I believed I knew (or at least could strongly imagine) that telling the secret would likely be harmful to them, I would advise against disclosing it. I would, however, investigate as much as possible what is keeping the guilt alive (e.g., a primitive superego function that serves little purpose in light of the fact that the affair is over, but could be harmful in expecting the partner to forgive one's past sin, a sin that they might very well prefer not to know about). I am also deeply interested in what their fantasies are about how their partner would react. This would be primary among many, many other questions. I would regard this as an opportunity to discover much about what was missing intrasubjectively and intersubjectively for the partner who had had the affair. Should it come to pass, I also would discuss my rationale for not disclosing the secret, and seek out the partner's reaction to my recommendation. Finally, I might very well encourage augmentation of our work by getting into individual therapy.

As a final note, at the beginning of couples therapy, I will almost never see one partner without simultaneously seeing the other. An example of a deviation from this was when one partner came in uncertain as to whether she should be in treatment herself or with her husband. Her questions on the phone seemed ambiguous enough to warrant granting a solitary consultation to sort out this serious question. Sometimes, I have ended up taking that partner in individual treatment and did not commence with couples therapy. On other occasions, it is apparent that couples treatment is what is called for, though if that is the case I then suggest having an initial session alone with the other partner to demonstrate immediately a sense of parity.

As stated earlier, relational psychoanalytic treatment, especially couples therapy, is a messy business. As long as we adhere to the convention of not being afraid of the messiness, but instead engage in curiosity about it, we can spread that curiosity like a helpful contagion. In this manner, both therapists and patients are better equipped to embrace these messy questions without being so afraid of them.

What do you do in cases of spousal (partner) abuse?

This is an especially serious and complicated question. We must first begin with severe cases and then work our way back from there. In severe cases, I agree very much with Dr. Paul Renn (2008, 2012), a relational psychoanalyst in London, who writes:

> Crime statistics show an egregious level of domestic violence by men against women. In many instances, the violence and psychological abuse is severe and frequent, with little or no sense of remorse for the harm inflicted. The abusive situation may be exacerbated because the male perpetrator misuses alcohol and/or illicit drugs, has mental health problems and is also violent outside of the family home. Couples therapy is strongly contraindicated in such cases.
>
> (p. 3)

I couldn't agree more. I also agree, however, with what Renn says about the broad and much more amorphous world of accusations of spousal/partner abuse. Many, many couples' relationships, at some time or another, evince some form of violence. Usually it is verbal. Sometimes it may be behavioral as in pertaining to objects (e.g., throwing a dish against a wall and shattering it). On more rare occasions, it occurs in terms of pushing, grabbing, and occasionally even hitting one another both offensively and defensively. In a sense, violence is not that surprising since, as I believe, our unconscious mind embodies all of the ages that we have ever been. Thus, when one thinks of the vicissitudes of violent reactions a toddler can muster in a fit of rage, a veritable temper tantrum, one gets a picture of what may occur for many intimately connected, long-term committed partners, especially when their relationship feels profoundly threatened.

As Renn (2012) notes, this is likely even more in evidence with partners exhibiting insecure attachment patterns. This is frequently also a context-dependent issue, as some more insecure self-states get activated in certain vulnerable contexts while others don't. Renn describes two notable versions of insecurity that are systematically prone to induce one another to violent engagement: "discomfort with closeness" and "anxiety over abandonment." Of course, these issues are ripe for occurrence in long-term committed relationships, especially around intimacy, since they create a powerful binary of pushes and pulls. She wants more (intimacy), which triggers his discomfort with closeness. He pulls back. She fears abandonment. She anxiously pushes for more connection and he distances further. She panics. He recoils. What is useful about this perspective is that it aids in assessing violence or abuse during the early stages of its development. From a relational psychoanalytic vantage point, what we are witnessing is the emergence of the couple as a self-organizing system that may have a propensity for turning to violence and abuse, especially if the partners come from backgrounds in which such behavior was in evidence.

I have treated many couples that look just like what I am describing above, including those in which the stereotypical gender roles are reversed; by this, I mean that the male partner wishes for more closeness and fears abandonment, while his female partner distances in the face of too much intimacy. The point in all of this is that, notwithstanding the fact that men are more prone to violence than are women, women are frequently systemically intertwined in the circumstances that create violence.

For example, Chaz and Lynda fit to a T the description above of systemically generated abuse. Adding fuel to the fire of their fights was their abuse of alcohol and, on occasion, cocaine. The degree of excess in their fights had led to police intervention, with Chaz being arrested. Their drama looked something like this. They would have been "partying" (abusing pot, cocaine, and alcohol), and, at a certain point, Lynda would start to become provocative. Frequently, this began with sexually teasing, while on other occasions with her becoming argumentative. The timing of her provocation coincided with her detecting Chaz slipping into a pleasantly inebriated state of solitude, his implicit conveyance of wanting to be left alone to enjoy his peaceful "buzz." This triggered a state of abandonment depression in Lynda, and because she was on a manic high from the cocaine she would become belligerent and start to antagonize Chaz.

When Lynda's provocations would not arouse her husband's attention, she would begin to scream, cry, and eventually throw fragile objects against the wall, shattering them. If Chaz in any way attempted to intervene and "talk her down," she would begin pushing, slapping, and punching him. As she was smaller and not nearly as strong or athletic as Chaz, her attempts to physically dominate him were typically ineffectual. This recognition made her feel even more humiliated and enraged, leading into more intense gambits. Chaz would finally flee, trying to escape by locking himself in a solitary room in their very large house. Somehow, Lynda was always able to unlock the door and barge in. At this point, the violence would really escalate, with her throwing herself mightily at Chaz, forcing him to have to defend himself by physically restraining her. Frequently, she would end up with bruises from Chaz's powerful grip in his attempt to restrain her attack. This was all the evidence she needed to then call the police. In this manner, she could exhibit her ultimate control over Chaz, and restore herself from her humiliation.

It was experiences like this that led to me stating three things very unambiguously when working with couples in which violence is in evidence: 1) it has to stop, *immediately*; 2) we have to understand why it's occurring, since it is most certainly occurring systemically. As such, no matter who appears more violent, this is a relational issue; 3) ever since the O. J. Simpson trial, men are especially at a disadvantage from a law enforcement standpoint. All it takes is one phone call and an accusation, and they will be immediately taken to jail, irrespective of their female partner's role in their violence. I emphasize this point to both partners as a means of making both have to reckon with this reality—that the husband will, very likely, be sent to jail, and that when things calm down this can have very bad implications for both of them, not only with respect to their relationship but also their standing (his in particular) in society. Such imprisonment can have very deleterious career ramifications.

The point I press home is that he must never become violent; however, she also must avoid provoking him. Furthermore, when either partner retreats and is trying to get away from provocation, their retreat must be respected and not pursued, as it is evidence of their knowing that they are close to their breaking point. I assure them that we will take up the rest in therapy regarding their particular vulnerabilities that are in evidence in terms of their approach/avoidance, distance/abandonment panic patterns. We will also come to understand their backgrounds from which these patterns emerged. Where augmentation to the treatment is necessary, I also will refer the couple for other kinds of support groups, including anger management and domestic violence groups, and, where drugs and alcohol are part of the problem, to substance management support, including (if especially egregious) Alcoholics Anonymous.

Most importantly, however, is that when couples are really interested in staying together, they are able to hear the gravity of what is at stake with episodes that can become violent. I include in this the destructiveness of verbal abuse, since it is often as disturbing as any physical act of violence. As Gottman (1999) reports, "our single best predictor of divorce is contempt," which led him to refer to contempt as "the sulfuric acid of love" (p. 47).

It is for this reason I also strongly advocate that neither partner ever use the word *divorce* or any verbal threat of leaving—at least, that is, until it is completely clear that one is done with a relationship, and visits to the attorneys are the next logical steps. But until that decision is made in a sober and deeply reflective manner, any pronouncement of divorce is one of the worst things couples can do. This is because nothing instantiates abandonment panic quicker than the invocation of this word. It is called up because it is the attention-grabber without comparison. But it is also very, very harmful. As a consequence, I encourage my patients to restrain their worst interactions to conventional weaponry of just being "shitty," but to absolutely restrain themselves from the violence of throwing down the divorce card. And if, as is likely still to happen despite my admonition, they impulsively assert divorce in an argument, they must, as soon as they are capable, apologize for having done so, and as rapidly as possible remove it from the discussion. We will then take up in therapy what it was that pushed the partner that far, and why this seemed to be the only way to get their partner's attention.

Do you ever self-disclose aspects of your private life to patients and, if so, under what circumstances?

Current trends in relational psychoanalytic thinking argue that it is impossible not to reveal something of ourselves; indeed, arguably, we are doing so all the time. As Aron (1996, 2003) points out, even a carefully considered and ostensibly objective interpretation, "purified" through the analyst's assiduous attention to remaining abstinent, neutral, and anonymous, is nevertheless rife with information about the analyst. To begin with, an interpretation clearly reflects, both implicitly and explicitly, the analyst's theory of mind. It very much reflects her predilections, prejudices, and attitude. It also reflects degrees of openness versus degrees of closed-mindness, ones especially emblematic of the analyst's faithful following of some theoretical persuasion. Her behavior also implicitly reflects her pensive contemplation versus her relative spontaneity in expressing an idea. The field of psychoanalysis has changed considerably from the former conceit to a greater openness to the latter. When I was in training at Menninger in the early 1970s, we were taught to think about an interpretation at least four times before sharing it. Notwithstanding the merits of reflexivity, by the time the "meat" has been chewed that many times, there isn't much flavor left! Sometimes it is better to speak of an idea while it's still fresh and not ground down.

As psychoanalysis has evolved, so too has the topic of self-disclosure. Over time, the dictum "never disclose" gradually became "only reveal something about yourself with a specific purpose in mind." Today, from an improvisational stand-point, disclosure can be an automatic aspect of playing along with the patient's iterations, as well as encouraging them to play with them as well. This leads to the co-creation of thirdness and very real and fresh states of intersubjectivity. It is on this latter note, then, that I want to discuss self-disclosure.

Much like improvisational theater, nothing works relationally when one actor overtakes the stage and begins to talk only about himself. The scene suffers a swift death, because the joy of improvisation is two (or more) persons working-off-of-and-with one another's subjective psychologies. So, from this vantage point, I share a fair amount, but typically mostly when it seems to playfully further something in the treatment, to generate some new possibility that might otherwise have been foreclosed upon in the couple's relationship. I might in fact discuss something from my own marriage. Here are a few examples.

Fighting has been commonplace in my marriage of 29 years. While it's not a daily occurrence, bickering can insinuate itself intermittently over a week's span. Indeed, I think that a third category positioned somewhere between submission and surrender might be called "bickering." Here I am talking about mini-instantiations of annoyances, typically over things one has come to know about one's partner, especially things that he or she will never comply with. Almost every long-term relationship has a myriad of annoyances on this scale. Many of them are simply a part of the inalterable fabric of the relationship. They constitute dimensions of its texture and design. The point is, however, that many of these things never change, nor do they stop being irritants. What they do stop doing is becoming deal-breakers or sources of major breakdown.

Then there are some tales that either my wife or I have disclosed of much greater magnitude. A favorite story of hers that she on occasion tells couples is the time we were in a rip-roaring argument, neither of us budging from our point of view, when one or the other of us (who can remember?) said, "You had enough?" to which the other said, "Sure, so where you wanna go for dinner tonight?" I like this story, too, because it speaks to the inevitable vulnerability to slip into borderline-like states which are inherently infused with binaries. Once the couple is trapped in a binary, everything becomes about whose version of reality will prevail. Knowing this and accepting this as aspects of both partner's multiple self-states can lead to a quicker "there we go again" resolution and an easier path to letting something go, rather than fighting to the death.

Playing-off-of-and-with what is spontaneously generated in couples sessions can be my best guide to disclosure, including a sense of reticence about disclosing something. This occurs when it does not seem that there is a playful enough relationship in which what one might disclose can be played with. In this latter case, I am typically more reserved, at least until there are moments in which this can change, and the idea of play can be reinstated.

How do you handle extra-marital affairs?

This is unquestionably one of the most commonly asked and utterly ambiguous questions that I encounter in presentations—ambiguous in the sense that the idea of affairs is a perfect example of the conceit of a binary and, in particular, one that on the surface seems beyond question and examination. Furthermore, when the term *affair* is invoked, the idea that it is a concept that holds still is ridiculous. Typically, it wiggles all over the place and ends up meaning so many different things to so many different people in so many different relational contexts. Affairs and what they represent is a topic that can easily fill an entire volume on its own.[1]

How affairs are handled in treatment has much to do with the partners' reactions to the discovery of an affair. The range of reactions can spread across a continuum that embodies a myriad of points roughly spread over mild, medium, and extreme. Affairs are milder when there is some conviction between the partners that the idea of a lifetime of monogamy and fidelity is a somewhat naïve and immature take on adult functioning. Some of these couples accede to the event of the affair as an inconvenient reality that then requires their taking up what it means, and what it may (or may not) mean about what is missing between them. Reactions are more extreme when there is a huge narcissistic injury triggered by the affair that then rapidly devolves into the binary of a villain and a victim. To the degree the victim clings to an image of himself as sacrificing and selfless, that he has always been bending and yielding (i.e., being submissive) to his partner, the perpetrator can be quickly positioned as the unforgivable villain.

Reactions to affairs in the middle range are characterized by the particulars of what the affair means to the couple, both characterologically and relationally. An affair or a suspicion of an affair, for example, can be highly titillating in some couples, though they likely will be extremely hard-pressed to recognize this about themselves, much less acknowledge it. For example, a fascinating phenomenon is when one partner insists on knowing all the lurid details of the affair (or suspected one) that moves beyond reasonable broad strokes of inquiry.

What starts to be in evidence with such an obsession is a kind of sadomasochistic enactment, wherein the revelation of the details can derive a kind of privately perverse level of intrigue and excitement for the victim. Meanwhile, they sadistically hold over the perpetrator's head that it is their right to perpetually interrogate him, anytime and anywhere. Nevertheless, what begins to emerge from the victim holding the accused perpetrator's feet to the fire is a kind of pornographic pleasure derived from hearing the gory details while then subsequently privately fantasizing about them.

In one such case, a husband discovered some flirtatious emails between his wife and a distant stranger. The evidence was solidly there that she was engaged in a kind of exciting fantasy flirtation, though because the man lived far away she was never at risk of acting upon their indelicate dialogue. Upon his discovery, however, her husband insisted on having access to all of her personal passwords for all of her social network accounts, email, cell phone, and the like. This requirement was still being held in the present, even though the emails in question occurred over five years before. Curiously, he would not allow her to have the same access to his private world of communications, though he routinely insisted on checking hers. This would most often occur without her knowing it until, she said, "He would suddenly start acting weird again." Each time he was in this state, it was after he had been checking up on her and had found something that appeared suspicious, even when there truly was never anything occurring that was of a nefarious nature.

Over time, it became apparent that there was greater evidence of his potentially straying than she ever had. Still, humiliated over being caught, she felt obliged to provide him complete access to her privacy and to not ask for the same conditions in turn. A telling sign of the pornographic fantasy her husband seemed to be deriving from this was that one of his favorite fantasies he would share during an episode in their very active sex life was about watching her get "gang-banged" by a group of men. In spite of this, whenever he pressed her with suspicion, she felt guilty and that she owed him explanations for whatever he was interrogating her about, notwithstanding that her explanations never seemed to soothe him at all. Of course, they never were going to soothe him, as it was apparent that his inquiries weren't about anything real. Rather, they served the function of creating the pornographic titillation he derived from all of them.

The conventional wisdom and therefore apparent knee-jerk reaction to affairs is typically that they are wrong. This convention suits a binary that is undergirded by the predisposition of church and state in its enforcement of the proper conditions for procreation and raising children. It follows from this logic—and it's not a bad logic—that children are typically (though not necessarily always) better off being raised in a two-parent household. Such a household shares certain advantages, including the enhanced possibility of better basic provisions (food, shelter, safety, education, etc.), as well as providing that potential for the greater psychological complexity of having two parents. In this case, the children have two parents to turn to in developing a mind of their own. This further obviates against the potential symbiosis of a one-parent household. And, clearly, the research holds this to be true, whether the two-parent household is represented by heterosexual or homosexual partners. The latter couples show every bit as much capacity for raising healthy children well as do the former. So, on this basis anything that threatens the couple, whether straight or gay, threatens the welfare of the offspring.

The ultimate threat to couples, however, seems less about affairs than about a host of other issues. For example, Gottman (1999) debunks the myth that affairs cause most divorces. Clearly, they don't, as affairs are reported in only about 25 percent of the cases in his research and only are cited as cause for divorce in somewhere between 20 and 27 percent of marriages. Severe or intense fighting, by contrast, represents 40 percent of the cause for the termination of unions, clearly a measurably larger phenomenon. As he further notes, while affairs typically involve sex, in fact sex is usually not their purpose. Rather, "affairs are usually about seeking friendship, support, understanding, and validation … they are about getting the acceptance that is missing in the marriage" (p. 24). And, on this latter point, we are forced to then take up the diversity of meanings that affairs represent relationally, in terms of self-actualization, recognition, and what the relationship (having a mind of its own) is doing creatively, or what is happening to create a world of stagnation. As a consequence, it is not the phenomenon of affairs that is so typically pressing (although on the emotional and societal level it can be made to feel so) as it is about the meaning of any affair in any particular relationship (Weeks, 1989).

The meaning of an affair is often interpreted in terms of the consequences of it to each partner. For instance, the consequences for the partner who wasn't having the affair may include lowered self-esteem, accompanied by a loss of sense of importance in the relationship. The consequences for the participating partner may include the problem of giving up a significant attachment to the other person with whom they are having an affair. Meanwhile, both married partners are forced to face a sense of loss of a version of their relationship that, in some cases, was regarded by themselves and others as the "perfect marriage." An affair can upend their earlier and more innocent states. It unveils how that state was naïvely composed of hope without the necessary recognition of dread: coming to terms with the dread to repeat something of one's past as well as the dread not to. All of these consequences are compounded to the degree other family members (and friends) are involved. Finally, the problems of an affair are far more amplified to the extent that the children are involved.

There is also considerable evidence that culture weighs in heavily in determining partners' reactions to affairs. Becoming ostracized from one's family culture for having an affair can be an example of extreme reactivity. This is perhaps even more likely in collectivist culture families than perhaps individualist ones.

On top of all of these points, however, is that most social science researchers question the accuracy of the self-reporting of affairs. As one researcher intoned, asking people to respond candidly about affairs is like asking 17-year-old boys about their sexual experience while they are standing in front of their peers (Westfall, 1989).

Still, it is probably in the arena of secrecy that affairs inflict their greatest damage. Until a suspected affair is finally disclosed, the non-participating partner can feel gaslighted. This can readily lend to their seemingly hyperbolic and over-the-top behavior, when in fact they feel tormented by a sense of being lied to—which ultimately turns out to have been in fact happening.

It is in this place that the couples therapist must be most careful in not getting entangled in a secret of an ongoing affair. Disclosure of a past one that has ended is another story, and is approached differently by different theorists. Some (Scharff, for instance) take an extreme position that any affair, past or present, needs to be disclosed "as basis to recommitment to the marriage by a knowing, mutual choice of both partners" (Westfall, 1989, p. 174). Others argue on behalf of that therapist's duty to preserve ethical neutrality regarding either partner's confidentiality (Humphrey, 1987). Therefore, disclosure is entirely determined by the partner. A more neutral position (Karpel, 1980) recommends "accountability with discretion" when it comes to handling secrecy. This seems more in trend with the contextuality and perspectivality of the relational psychoanalytic position. It is easy to imagine that the relational practitioner would be exercising her judgment in recommending whether past affairs should or shouldn't be disclosed.

Currently ongoing affairs are a stickier issue. For the most part, practitioners discourage couples therapy with couples when there is currently an ongoing affair. This is the position most take, according to Westfall, and is the position that Gottman and his marital clinic also take. While there might be exceptions to this rule, in the main, as long as an affair is currently in progress, it is likely to undermine all efforts at helping the couple. However, since 80 percent of the reason couples come to therapy is their "gradually growing apart and losing a sense of closeness, and not feeling loved and appreciated" (Gottman, 1999, p. 23), affairs which often are about seeking friendship, recognition, and the like are potential aggravators of the problems the couple is already suffering.

Still, despite how problematic they can be, the extraordinarily high statistics on infidelity regarding both sexes suggest that there is something often sought in an affair that may not necessarily be demonstrative of something so terribly wrong in the relationship. Indeed, individual therapists hear a great deal about how an affair may well have been a necessary part of an individual's personal growth and self-actualization, especially when he or she became involved in an affair not necessarily because of so much lacking in their relationship as in their personal development. Under-experienced partners may arrive in the second or third decade of their marriage wondering, as Peggy Lee sang, "Is that all there is?"

Finally, some affairs involve one partner trying to work out something developmentally that is too primitive for it to arise in the transference relationship they have with their actual partner (Steinberg, personal communication); that a primitive affect state can't get worked through with one's partner and has to be played out with someone else, typically, someone whose personality organization is more primitive than one's partner. This was the case of Herb and Donna in Step Five. Herb's midlife crisis necessitated his involvement with a drug-addicted former stripper, with whom he could initially play out some infantile attachment issues that were not present in his more mature relationship with Donna.

It is through the affair that they work through certain illusions about what turned out to be a not-perfect, but in the end a "good enough" state of marriage, much like Winnicott intoned about parenting and psychoanalysis. An affair may also become the signifier of something missing in the partners' recognition of one another. Getting an experience of what such recognition from another entails may jettison them back into seeking recognition from their marital partner, as well as starting to also recognize one's partner more.

In sum, affairs mean so many things. It is best not to assume anything about them until the therapist better understands their meaning to the partners. Deepening understanding is one of the essential values of this book and is critical to dismantling the binary that an affair, at least as typically codified in culture, tends to pull for. The relational analyst instead seeks a third position from which to understand the affair, and from which she then helps the couple understand it as well. Sometimes, this becomes implicit in the therapist's work when it has been determined that a past affair is better left undisclosed; other times, it involves taking up the meaning of the affair to the couple as a system when it has been discovered. Nevertheless, couples work with currently ongoing affairs usually isn't likely to have a very positive prognosis because of the gravitational pull of the party outside the marital therapy and the marriage. In these cases, individual treatments likely make more sense.

What do you do in cases where there is evidence that one of the partners is abusing drugs and/or alcohol, and that that is strongly implicated in the couple's problems?

As this relational model of couples therapy is founded on the principle of perspectival realism, the state of each partner's consciousness is extremely significant. Where mind-altering substances are used excessively, self-states induced by such chemical alteration can be wildly different from self-states constituted by more sober, reasonable states of consciousness. In short, the capacity for self-reflexivity, collaboration, negotiation, and confronting paradox and potential surrender can all be undermined by excessive abuse of substances. As a consequence, if one partner is abusing substances, the manner and degree of this occurrence must be investigated and addressed candidly. The same applies if both partners are engaged in substance abuse.

There are enumerable personal reasons why either partner may turn to alcohol or some other drug. It may have been a part of their culture or family history. It might

251

also signify a manner in which they are self-medicating. It most certainly can have interpersonal ramifications that are best examined relationally. After all, the classic family systems tale of yesteryear was "Her nagging drives me to drink!" and "His drinking turns me into a nag!" To some degree, they are likely both right.

Of course, very frequently, even when there isn't so much evidence of abusive (excessive) drug use, one still can discern patterns of self-medicating that are important to point out to couples. Sometimes this can result in a referral for a prescribed medication, but more often in my experience it can be a quick way of illuminating certain affect states one or both partners are attempting to control.

There is barely a month that goes by in my practice in which I don't have to give my little speech on alcohol, which begins with my comment, "Alcohol is unquestionably the fastest-acting neuroleptic agent there is for abating shame." I point out that many other drugs simply do not perform this function as quickly and as effectively as alcohol does—none. As a consequence, whenever I hear of alcohol having some relationship to an issue, either on the intrasubjective or the intersubjective level, I immediately begin looking for evidence of shame and/or humiliation for which drinking has become a quick remedy. This almost always encourages a great deal of curiosity on both partners' parts.

Of course, other drugs serve other functions. The examination of that topic exceeds the purposes of this chapter. The main idea is that relationality requires perspectivalism, and when that is disrupted by alcohol or substance use it becomes an immediate focus for the treatment. This is especially so insofar as drugs and alcohol abuse potentially undermine everything this model of treatment has to offer the partners. Usually, emphasizing this is enough to get one or both partners to reconsider their consumption of alcohol and or other recreational drugs. Where they find themselves incapable of such reconsideration, as in an intractable addiction, other drug related treatment resources have to be encouraged.

How do you typically talk with the partners about their sex lives?

For a field constituted by Freud's original dictum about the over-determination of the dual drives: sex and aggression, it might seem surprising how difficult it can be for the topic of sex to be raised by couples therapists. The importance of raising the topic has always been on my mind if not before, certainly ever since my clinical supervision with Stephen Mitchell between 1994 and 1996. Steve told me that, as a rule, he pretty much always asked his patients about their sex lives. When I asked why, he said something like, "I don't know, it just makes things more interesting. You know, people will tell you what they want you to hear, or what they think that you want to hear, but when you ask them about sex, it sort of throws them off their game. Plus it tells you a lot about how they regard their bodies and not just their minds."

As quoted in Chapter 1, Roland Barthes wrote, "What language conceals is said through my body. My body is a stubborn child; my language is a very civilized adult" (from Perel, 2007, pp. 111–112) Where the civilized adult may obfuscate points of discomfort, it is in the illumination of the partners' orientation to sex, in all its manifestations, with others, with oneself, in one's fantasies and so forth that more deeply penetrating material comes forth—both literally and figuratively. Despite this, therapists frequently can feel squeamish about this line of inquiry, not to mention be vexed with a variety of unwitting countertransferential prejudices about sex. Both of these propensities make it understandable that the topic of sex is one often avoided, albeit ironically when considered in relationship to couples therapy.

Perel (2007) provides an *in vivo* experience of what psychotherapists can face when addressing the topic of sex. She reports that several years ago she attended a national conference on couples therapy. The speaker on a particular panel described a case in which the couple reported a sharp decline in their sex lives. Prior to the birth of their second child, they had enjoyed years of mutually pleasurable sex, primarily entailing playing out their dominance and submission fantasies. The husband in particular missed these playful rituals; the therapist posed the couple would have to work through a lot of emotional dynamics in their relationship, especially in relationship to their new roles as parents. Perel continues, "But in the discussion that followed, the audience proved far less interested in the couple's overall relationship than in the disconcerting presence of domination and submission in their erotic life" (p. 53).

She noted that the ensuing audience discussion devolved into pathologizing the couple's sexual history. Why, they pondered, did the husband need to sexually objectify his wife and why did she desire being the object of bondage? From there the audience speculated that perhaps motherhood restored the wife's dignity, that the couple's history reflected problematic gender differences including an unwitting history of gender inequity. After a couple of hours of this form of interrogation, Perel finally raised the question that none, including the presenting therapist, had considered—that is, what was both pleasurable and erotic about the couple's past pattern of lovemaking? Her provocative question gave rise to a flurry of countertransference prejudices of her fellow couples therapists which ultimately underscored a central problem in the whole topic of sexuality—that is, the therapists' own pre- and unconscious preferences, predilections, and prohibitions when it came to talking about sexual union. Perel writes:

> The attitudes I saw in this meeting reflected deeper cultural assumptions. Did the clinicians in the room believe that this couple's sexual practices, even though consensual and completely nonviolent, were too "kinky," and therefore inappropriate and irresponsible for the ponderously serious business of maintaining a marriage and raising a family? It was as if sexual pleasure and eroticism that strayed onto slightly outer paths of fantasy and play, particularly games involving aggression and power, must be stricken from the repertoire of responsible adults in loving, committed relationships.
>
> (p. 55)

Clearly, the field of psychotherapy is fraught with politically correct assumptions about what constitutes appropriate sexual behavior. This may include tendencies to see romantic love as fleeting and immature in contrast to the hard work of the meaningful love of any long-term commitment. It may also include powerful prejudices about anything that bears a whiff of inequality along with a strong prejudice about what smacks of the objectification of one partner by another and vice versa. There can be an aversion to any aspect of sexual desire which can be selfish, even ruthless, but that paradoxically then elevates the object of such desire to such a potentially heightened state of being desired that it can be experienced as a kind of ambrosia so long as the P.C. police can be kept at bay. Discussion of sexuality can also become mired in gender politics, fears of aggression, aversions to a couple's use of porn and in general be discomforted with the "kinkier" side of the private sex lives of couples they see as somewhat mindboggling in relationship to their therapists less perversely—conversant mild-mannered selves.

To the question of how I talk about sex with my patients, I can only say, in whatever manner that facilitates their discussion of it. Expectantly, many couples I see struggle in their sex lives. For some there is a pattern of vicious circle. The withholding of sex by one partner generates a contemptuous response from the other which only degenerates into more withholding, a circular cause-and-effect pattern that has to be pointed out. For others, the degradation of their sex life mirrors their larger issue of a deeper fear of being vulnerable with one another that commonly manifests in many of the most plebeian aspects of their relationship. Still, for some, the topic of desire is complicated by a kind of morality play in which desire comes to constitute selfishness, while its minimization represents a kind of virtuous selflessness that ultimately grinds their sex life to a halt.

As hopefully has become apparent throughout this book, self-actualization of desire can often present as ruthless until one can see that being the object of desire can feel very empowering and a source of powerful reciprocation—especially, that is, when the couple can finally discuss this equitably. Desire can also easily be confused with expectation, which can degenerate into a sense of authority and dominance until once again desire can be unpacked from expectation and be seen as something powerfully attractive.

How sex gets discussed also pertains to what sexual relating may mean to a couple. Where it seems pre-Oedipal, the dynamics of merger versus separation need to be taken up. Where it is more Oedipal in nature, the topic of triangulation is huge. Sometimes sex grinds to a halt when the family bed goes on for years in a manner in which children are always literally between the partners. And, where there are not children, oftentimes there are pets! Oedipal couples are frequently fraught with issues of jealousy, which is dealt with in so many different ways, including purposive inclusion of third partners in "threesomes." Sometimes this actually works, though it also makes for some powerful moments of jealousy that have to then be mediated, sometimes with different negotiations than those originally practiced.

The topic of sex manifests in ways that far exceed what can be addressed in any of these instances. But fruitfully exploring them requires the therapist's tactful and curious and oftentimes playful inquiry into topics such as masturbation, whether separately or together. Sexual fantasy is also extremely fruitful—actually creating a safe place for its examination may prove to be one of the more illuminating arenas for the exploration of each partner's psyche as well as discovering something less obvious about their relationship. The sharing of their sexual fantasies can give rise to a host of things they had not realized about themselves; much more, about one another. By its very private nature, sexual fantasy is a mother lode of unexplored material that speaks volumes to how the partners may be inadvertently using—or wanting to use—one another in manners that facilitate the exploration of unknown aspects of themselves.

The most important thing for couples therapists to take to heart is to question their own inhibition to explore their patients' sexual worlds of experience, both in actuality and in fantasy. The couple is only as comfortable and as safe in venturing into this often anxiety-ridden territory as is the couples therapist. It is in this world of exploration that the treatment will almost certainly become more animated by stepping beyond their usual world of common everyday discourse.

Do you ever feel like a couple doesn't belong together, or that they would be better off divorcing?

My answer to this has multiple parts, often contingent upon the couple in question. Typically, if a couple comes to see me in earnest to help them with their relationship, I feel that it is bad faith on my part to judge their relationship as one that should end. Instead, I give them my all and, as mentioned earlier, I often liken myself to an oncologist who is treating a relationship afflicted by cancer, the severity or survivability of which is yet unknown.

I must admit, I have worked with couples in which I was deeply puzzled as to why the hell they were together. So, as this thought drifts through my consciousness, I find myself all the more curious about what drew the partners together and what makes their relationship work as well as what is plaguing it.

All of this said, I do have something of a tilt or prejudice in my work with couples who have children, especially young ones[2] —that is, if the marriage can be saved, the welfare of their children will typically be better off if the couple can stay together. Where there are no children, and in this sense each partner is a bit more of a "free agent" without the responsibilities of parenting, I might entertain more openly the idea of there being insurmountable obstacles that they would prefer to not attempt to change. Instead, they might prefer to end amicably and seek out new possibilities with others, predicated on what they have learned from their therapy.

One such case was a young couple I worked with over two decades ago. They were childless, and had a number of misfitted aspects between them that appeared to weigh in more with dread than with hope. We worked very hard in treatment, and indeed they each grew tremendously. Nevertheless, a year or so after they had seemingly successfully ended treatment, the wife decided she really didn't want to continue their marriage, and by then her husband pretty much agreed. They ended fairly well and maintained some common economic holdings for a number of years, as this worked out better than dissolving them in their divorce.

Each partner moved on and remarried; each had children with their new partners. Approximately a year ago, I spoke to the wife, who contacted me in seeking a referral for an out-of-town relative. During our conversation, she mentioned that her ex intermittently tells her, "You know the best thing we ever did was to get into therapy. I so thank you for dragging me kicking and screaming into it. I still use what I learned then in my marriage today." And she reiterated the same. The point is, it's always possible that some partners might do better in other relationships. As I have mentioned throughout this book, my job, if the couple elects to work with me, is to assure them that the outcome of the treatment will either be a better marriage or a better divorce. The only way I can approach this, however, is with as open mind an attitude as I can muster.

What do you do with couples who are affectively out of control in your office?

I allow a fair amount of rancor in my office, often, at least initially, to attempt to see how far it goes, what curtails it, and if there is anything that is useful about it or if it is simply destructive. Obviously, I am very curious about how couples manage their affect. This includes how they work with anger, disappointment, grief, joy, you name it. However, I am also clear that, while it is impossible, so far as I can tell, to be in a relationship in which feelings don't get hurt, behaving harmfully is another thing.

As a result, if I believe that something in the rancor and fighting has tipped over from hurtful to harmful, I am quick to intervene and to become as vocally and sometimes visibly forceful (by standing up) as I need to be in getting them to cease and desist. I tell the couple precisely what I am doing when I do so—that is, they will not, under my watch, destroy one another. I add that I have no control over what they do at home, but in my office the goal is to cultivate an atmosphere of safety, and harmful behavior is simply unacceptable.

There are also some occasions in which I have to insist on a contracted level of behavior at home, though this is no guarantee that it will happen. A case I worked with many years ago addresses this issue, along with the previous questions regarding violence and alcohol abuse. This involved a couple who appeared relatively reasonable in our sessions, but then would report carnage at home. This culminated in the wife finally reporting that a not infrequent cause of their fighting was that her husband would have drank pretty close to a whole fifth of Scotch, at which point he would become quite violent if his wife did not submit in any manner to whatever issue he needed to dominate. If there was any sign of her protest or a threat to leave, he would produce his loaded shotgun and force her to take the barrel in her mouth, saying that if she did not relent, he would blow her head off and then kill himself.

I was horrified, intimidated, and uncertain if I could work with this case. Ultimately, I decided that the only way I could do so was to write a letter and send it as certified mail to prove its reception. In it, I stipulated that all guns must be removed from the house and locked up in a separate location. Furthermore, they were not allowed to fight whenever there had been alcohol consumption. I required them to sign the contract in my presence at our next session, and to promise to abide by its dictates. If in any manner they were unable to do so, I would immediately terminate any further psychotherapeutic services.

Not surprisingly, at the next session, the husband was enraged with me, but actually I found little to be intimidated about since my contract was crystal clear and non-negotiable. Accordingly, they agreed to all its stipulations and signed the contract, and we continued to work for a few more months. Finally, overtime at the husband's work interrupted our sessions. Some months later, during our hiatus, I received a call from the wife from an undisclosed women's shelter, where her husband could not locate her. She said that fairly soon after they stopped seeing me, the guns were returned to the house and the violent intimidation resumed. When it reached the pitch as described above, she waited for her drunken husband to fall deeply asleep and slipped out of the house with the items she had packed to take to the shelter that she had discovered in a women's support group. She informed me that she was immediately filing for divorce, and thanked me for my forceful intervention, which gave her clarity about the violence and disabused her of her denial.

Notes

1 Esther Perel's examination of this in her book *Mating in Captivity* (2007) is especially useful.
2 In truth, there is seldom a good age for the children when their parents divorce, even if they are now adults.

Appendix A

A BRIEF SUMMARY OF FOUR MODELS OF FAMILY SYSTEMS THEORY AND THEIR IMPLICATIONS

Murray Bowen's theory

Of all the family systems theories, Bowen's was likely the most coherent and comprehensive. The basic premise of Bowen's theory is that the capacity of any individual family member to develop a sense of self (as defined by the ability to choose goals regarding work and relationships and strive towards accomplishing both) depends on his or her capacity to differentiate emotional reactions from those of other family members, as well as to differentiate emotional functioning from intellectual. Since anxiety undermines differentiation, Bowen's model focused on the arousal and mitigation of anxiety within a family system.

Highly differentiated adults, Bowen touted, are less prone to anxiety, or at least are better able to manage it without displacing it or projecting it on others. By contrast, those who are much less differentiated are prone to fuse with others, drawing others in closely tied relationships, as well as allowing themselves to be drawn into the emotionally wrought dramas of other family members. Families with poor patterns of differentiation were notably highly "emotionally reactive," tending to do what feels right instead of pausing to think things through. They operate more as "pseudo-selves"—that is, ones who cannot distinguish what is truly important to their sense of self-actualization. Those who possess more of a sense of solid self are better able to grasp what they believe and what they are therefore willing to push for in life, despite the anxiety it may produce within themselves or others. It is easier for them to know what is done is not readily negotiable, if negotiable at all, while others are anxiously trying to pressure them to do otherwise.

Undifferentiated family members engage in a host of symptoms to bind anxiety. A principal one is to engage in "triangulation," since "triangular relationships" are the "smallest stable relationship systems" in any family. Whenever anxiety arises between two partners, their tendency is to involve a third family member or an issue, thereby distracting themselves from the anxiety aroused by their conflicts over differentiating. A highly common example of triangulation is to "over-focus" on a child in the family, engaging in a "parent-child projection process," wherein one or more of the parents project their own anxieties on the child, making him or her the focal problem of the family while drawing attention away from their marital strife.

Being the focal point of anxiety in family systems also further impairs the child's capacity to differentiate. On the Bowenian differentiation scale of 0 to 100 (theoretically, from maximal fusion to maximal differentiation), the identified patient child will likely grow up scoring lower than his or her parents. Axiomatic to Bowenian theory is that because marital partners pick one another on a basis of "like levels of differentiation," over many generations families can produce members with lower and lower levels of functioning. This became Bowen's explanatory system for two of his more controversial ideas: that this multi-generational process eventually leads to onset of schizophrenia in a family member, as well as lending to what Bowen referred to as "societal regression."[1] Lack of differentiation results in family members either becoming emotionally fused to one another, in what was first referred to as the "family ego mass," or to becoming "emotionally cut off," going without contact with fellow family members for many years, if not for the remainder of one's life.

Bowen also argued that when marriages devolve into marital conflict they can rapidly escalate into patterns of competition or what he referred to as "pathological spousal adaptation," which results in a degeneration into fixed positions of one-upmanship or one-downmanship. These are characterized respectively as an "over-functioner" and an "under-functioner." An example of this is where one partner is a drug addict and the other becomes the enabler of their partner's addictive behavior by taking care of both of their needs.

Bowen's study of the influences of "sibling position" (i.e., birth order) also predicted the potential roles siblings might adopt in their undifferentiated family, especially with respect to their role in binding family anxiety. Eldest children, Bowen suggested, can become super responsibility caretakers. In so doing, they perpetuate a lack of differentiation in the family by taking care of others instead of insisting that these others learn how to better take care of themselves. Correspondingly, the youngest sibling might contribute to maintaining the lack of family differentiation, by offering him- or herself as the irresponsible member needing perpetual caretaking.

Particularly novel to Bowen's theory was that families could change simply through the therapist intervening with only one family member, since helping that member to differentiate has a ripple effect, forcing others to do the same while also providing them with a model for differentiating themselves. The therapeutic caveat was, however, that the individual patient's action should not be confrontational or in any way be anxiety-provoking. In fact, it was assumed that it is better that the rest of the family not know that one was in treatment. The therapist's task became one of coaching the patient to come up with strategies for how to engage his or her family differently, ones that would fortify his or her own differentiation, while doing so in the least anxiety-provoking way possible.

Salvador Minuchin's structural family therapy

Minuchin's structural family therapy model probably made the most use of systems concepts of all of the family theories. The basic premise of Minuchin's theory is that human beings cannot be understood outside the social context of which they are a part. Psychic life is as external as it is internal. Unconscious process perpetually makes itself evident in the verbal and nonverbal interactional patterns of the family members. Because the family is a system of interlocking members, change in any part of it will affect the whole.

Family systems are governed by rules, mostly unconsciously conveyed about what beliefs, feelings, and behaviors regarded as acceptable. These rules represent the "structures" or invisible sets of functional demands. The family system at large is constituted by subsystems, which are defined by boundaries. Normative boundaries in a family system should exhibit an "executive subsystem" (i.e., parental relationship), the normative children's relationship is called the "sibling subsystem" and in close extended families might be regarded as the "grandparental subsystem."

The key issue of assessment and intervention in this model is about the extent to which boundaries between, as well as within, the generations are respected. Boundary crossings and violations were evinced in extreme in either "enmeshed families," where boundaries were perpetually ignored, or conversely in "disengaged families," where the rigidity of boundaries keeps everyone at a distressingly detached distance from one another.

Symptoms, such as being construed as the identified child patient, would be confronted in family sessions by pointing out invisible collusions between members. For example, the functional purpose of the child's inconsolable tantrums would be unveiled in a family by showing how at least one of the supposedly hand-wringingly worried parents was secretly colluding in some manner with the child's tantrums. Structuralists have been known to say, "I am wondering whose shoulders this child is standing on, since no child is more powerful than two parents when they can effectively work together." The point of the confrontation would be to show that there is a breach in the boundaries between the executive and sibling subsystems in the form of "parent-child collusion." In contrast to Bowen's theory of change through the mitigation of anxiety, Minuchin's model was all about turning the heat up.

Interactional family therapy

Interactional family therapy is an amalgamation of a number of different authors, beginning with Bateson, Weakland, and Jackson's famous double bind project, later joined by Haley, Watzlawick, Sluzski, Satir, and many others who were most identified with the Mental Research Institute in Palo Alto. It incorporates the Strategic, Communications, and Interactional schools of family therapy. This group of collaborators focused closely on the actual communication style of the family, looking for functional versus dysfunctional styles of relating. Dysfunctional styles involve such characteristics as double binds and inconsistent or incongruent communication. The premise of the theory is much like the Structuralists: communication is constant and, like that so-called intrapsychic phenomenon, is seen as essentially being worn on the sleeves of every family member. Indeed, while the Interactionalists did not deny the unconscious, they eschewed delving into it, staying strictly conversant with visible communication patterns (both verbal and nonverbal).

Axiomatic to these thinkers is:

1. It is impossible not to communicate; even silence communicates something, sometimes something "deadly."
2. All messages convey both the *content* as well as a commentary on the *relationship* between the communicants.
3. How each communicator "punctuates" the message he or she receives will determine his or her cause-and-effect view of the relationship (e.g., "Her nagging drives me to drink!" versus "His drinking is turning me into a horrible nag!").
4. Communication is *always* both verbal and nonverbal.
5. Dysfunctional relationships tend toward escalating symmetry (competition over who is on top) versus "complementarity" (rigidly defined by who is one-up and who is one-down).

This theory is also assiduously embedded in systems theory, with its recognition that behavior is "circularly causal" (e.g., the husband and wife who are circularly driving each other to drink and to nag). Furthermore, change seen from its systems perspective entails *homeostasis* (i.e., "change that produces no change") as well as *morphogenesis* (i.e., "change that redefines the system"). Too much homeostasis creates stagnation in a family, while too little creates chaos. Real therapeutic change always involves morphogenesis.

The therapeutic approaches defined within this Interactional model focused on attempts to point out dysfunctional communication and correct it. Incongruities between verbal and nonverbal communication would be shown to the family as being at the root of their "crazy-making" behavior. So, for example, laughing while giving an order is doomed to undermine one's authority, just as saying "I love you" while hugging like a wooden plank makes the recipient of the verbal love message feel deeply confused by this process of obfuscation.

Eventually, educational principles for improving communication became regarded as neither very interesting nor very penetrating. The Interactional school was frankly far more interested in the use of paradoxical communication investigated by Bateson and his colleagues such as his double bind research, as well as the idea of a counter-paradox or a strategically configured therapeutic double bind (Palazzoli et al., 1978). This includes "paradoxical reframing," where some behavior was labeled contrary to the meaning it had in the family, such as stating that the runaway son is actually "pulling the family together" by getting the family to pay attention to its disturbances as opposed to being labeled by the family as "tearing it apart."

Even more controversial were the actual paradoxical injunctions, where behaviors were prescribed that would enjoin someone to change by making it impossible for them not to. An example might be the mother who was unable to say "no" to anyone in her life being ordered in a session to say "no" to everyone in her family. The paradoxical trap was that, if she refused to follow the therapist's order, she would in fact be saying "no" to him, presumably thereby undoing the impossibility of her symptom.

As exciting as that Interactional model could be, there remained controversy with its methods of treatment that were not only prescriptive, but were oftentimes authoritarian in their manner of prescription. In response to its authoritative style, symptoms may have initially disappeared due to pathological compliance. For example, one adolescent patient's trichotillomania (compulsive hair-pulling) was treated by a male therapist by having her count her extracted hairs and save them in an envelope, to be brought each week to their next session with the number of hairs written on the envelope's exterior. Though she never truly counted the hairs (as the clever therapist might have suspected), the symptom did eventually abate, which likely was counted as a therapeutic success—except for the fact that the patient never got to examine her profoundly disturbing eroticized transference towards her male therapist, which turned out to be a displacement of highly sexualized incestuous feelings toward her father. Though the patient had indeed stopped pulling out her hair to get out of continuing the therapy, the symptom had returned full force the following year when she reentered treatment with me.

Psychoanalytic object relations family therapy

With growing interest in the late 1960s and early 1970s in object relations theory, some psychoanalysts in the United States finally had a theory which spoke to the unconscious processes not only within an individual, but also about how these processes could become transferred between and among individual family members. Heretofore, Freudian analysts' tripartite model of id, ego, and superego, all linked in an internal psychic energy/reality testing model, provided no understanding for how one person's unconscious was directly influential to another's. The object relationist's introduction of the concept of "projective identification" finally made a theoretical link that enabled psychoanalysts to bring their ideas into the field of family and couples therapy.

Object relations theory put psychoanalysis one crucial step toward being recognized as a relational theory. It noted that the infant is first and foremost (instinctively) object seeking over and above simply seeking discharge of sexual and aggressive impulses. From the object relations perspective, the dual drives of aggression and sexuality were understood in terms of how the subject made use of the object vis-à-vis gratification versus frustration. When the basic psychological and physiological needs of the infant were met, the theory intoned that the infant could relax into pleasurable states of satisfaction. When they weren't, he or she would readily foment into a storm of agitated and frustrated affects.

Satisfying experiences were accordingly internalized as good object representations, while frustrating ones were internalized as bad ones. Bad object "memories" split into warring halves, hungering for merger and fusion with the "unrequited love object," on the one hand, while needing to spitefully reject it, on the other. Influenced by these ideas, family therapists started studying how immature adults tended to unconsciously project— that is, induce members of their marital relationship or their children to identify with split-off, disquieting parts of themselves. An example of this might be a father battling with his own disavowed antisocial behaviors by collusively promoting and rewarding such behavior in his delinquent son, while at the same time overtly punishing him for it.

The psychoanalytic term *transference* was now extended to the idea of "family transference" to capture the plethora of projections, introjections, displacements, and disavowals dominating the atmosphere of the dysfunctional family. Like the Bowenians and the Structuralists, these theoreticians saw great benefit in also studying the extended family background, as well as the current state of ties between generations, looking for over-involvement versus superficial ties or even complete disconnections. Like their other family therapy counterparts, the object relations family therapists sought to bring to the family members' consciousness how themes of exploitation, ostracism, and triangulation were founded in underdeveloped capacities to manage frustration, anxiety, and the host of emotions that we as human beings are heir to.

Clinical generalizations derived from the four family systems theories

While certain aspects of the four family therapy models conflict with one another, viewed at a distance, they each offer clinical observations which have considerable enduring value. Taken as a set, the following seven theoretical generalizations became themes that over two decades ago began to instruct all aspects of my clinical practice. As a result, they broke that theoretical ground from which the relational psychoanalytic theory in this book has sprouted. I will briefly outline these seven themes while acknowledging in parentheses the concepts of the respective family system theory models that underpin them.

First, in some way pertaining to all four models, the identified patient's symptoms (and by extension his or her subjective experience) cannot be completely understood independent of the family system from which they originated and to whom they are still connected. This principle also extends to the experiences of the other family members, even if asymptomatic, as each one's subjective experience exerts some form of reciprocal influence upon the others.

Second, in dysfunctional families, children are frequently called upon, albeit unconsciously (i.e., outside the "awareness" of the family), to become parents to their parents. (These processes of "parentification" are conceptualized in Bowen: parent-child projection process; object relations: projective identification, family transference and countertransference.)

A third but derivative generalization, similar to parentification, is that, when a family member finds certain affect states intolerable, he or she will sometimes employ another member (spouse or child) to take on—that is, to experience or reenact— said intolerable experience. (Bowen: parent-child projection process; object relations: projective identification; family transference and countertransference.)

Fourth, individuals' attempts to differentiate—that is, develop a sense of self independent from their family of origin—typically engender some degree of anxiety in everyone, and when found to be intolerable differentiation becomes muted or denied through fusion, triangulation, and other attempts to bind the fragmenting experience. (Bowen: differentiation of self and triangulation; structural and object relations: separation and individuation.)

Fifth, individual family members' experiences can and do become so fragmented as to manifest in confusing, incongruent communication. In more severe forms, their contradictory messages can present the individuals with the experience that they are damned if they do or don't respond. Coupling this with irrevocable dependency on their fellow family members, elements of psychopathogenic interaction become instantiated, including the inculcation of tormenting paradox. In such a climate, everyone is likely to begin to respond in similarly contradictory manners, ultimately double binding one another. (Interactional: incongruent communication and double bind.)

Sixth, linear causality is a fallacious way of examining complex human behavior (such as family interactions, couples relationships, and psychotherapy). When employed as an explanatory formulation of linear causality, it only promulgates labeling, blaming, shaming, and guilt-invoking by locating the cause of the problem in a particular individual in a given relationship system. (Interactional: circular causality.)

Seventh, dysfunctional patterns of relating are passed on generationally, thus blurring not only the articulation of self-boundaries between immediate family members, but also between those of each generation. (Bowen: multigenerational transmission process; structural: boundaries.)

Note

1 Bowen's family system's etiological assumptions about schizophrenia share a history with other family systems theories from the 1950s through the 1970s, in which the statistical and diagnostic criteria were rather unsophisticated. This resulted in a plethora of examples of patients being diagnosed with schizophrenia who were actually exhibiting severe personality disorders, major unipolar and bipolar disorders, as well as such symptoms of schizoaffective disorder. Furthermore, Bowen's concept of societal regression also commits the common error of over-extending a psychological theory to explain socio-political-economical and religious issues that are far too complex to be adequately captured in this highly reductionistic fashion.

Appendix B

PRACTICE QUESTIONS

Practice questions for Step One

1. What themes of self-actualization (or its truncation) are emergent in the first sessions and reemerge throughout the course of treatment?
2. What are the themes of hope and dread that manifest in the repetitive complaints the couple are bringing to therapy?
3. How do the couple's wishes and hopes conform to the developmental or selfobject dimension (forward edge) of the transference?
4. What disappointments, episodes of thwarted actualization, and trauma inform the repetitive (trailing edge) of the transference?
5. What evidence is there of each partner's selfobject transference longings triggering the repetitive dimension of transference in each other, creating a self-perpetuating vicious circle of engagement?
6. What are the early signs of conflicting multiple self-states?
7. To what degree is there evidence of the potential for mutual recognition (subject-to-subject relating versus subject-to-object relating)?
8. What evidence is there of the relationship having a mind of its own, including both negative and positive thirdness?

Practice questions for Step Two

1. What emerges in each of your patients' narratives that seems amenable to assuming a point of view embracing perspectival realism versus rejecting it?
2. If the couple reject perspectival realism, what appears too threatening for them to accept it?
3. What sources of anxiety within your patients and within yourself may be leading to any of you negating a perspectivalist position, and instead seizing upon an objectivist, god's-eye-view perspective?
4. What is getting in the way of you maintaining a stance of multidirectional partiality?
5. What episodes of countertransference conjunction and disjunction are in evidence in your treatment of the couple? What in your background might be contributing to this?

6. Is there evidence of morality gambits occurring, and what do you think you need to do to mitigate this and to instill an atmosphere of improvisational play?

Practice questions for Step Three

1. What capacity for mentalization does each partner exhibit?
2. Are they able to reflect upon their own subjectivity, as well as recognize that they are both discoverers and constructors of what they believe constitutes their sense of reality?
3. Do they also recognize this to be true of their partner?
4. Is there evidence of either partner lapsing into psychic equivalence or the pretend mode? If so, what are the circumstances that give rise to this?
5. How capable are they of restoring a sense of mentalization, and under what conditions?
6. What data can you glean about the attachment pattern (secure versus insecure) that each partner brings to the relationship?
7. How does the couple relate affectively? Are they prone to being reactors or responders, and under what circumstances are they prone to either style?
8. How readily can you restore a sense of affective safety by regulating the affect in the room?
9. What happens in terms of their communicating implicitly, and how congruent or not is this to their explicit communication?
10. Do they exhibit appreciable cultural differences that are affecting their relationship? Is one from a collectivist culture and another from an individualist one? Do some of these issues manifest in loyalty/betrayal issues?
11. Are they struggling with issues of gender?
12. Do they exhibit residual unresolved issues regarding immigration, such as what has been labeled amputated selfhood?
13. What evidence is there of multigenerational transmission processes that are constraining the relationship?

Practice questions for Step Four

1. What evidence is emergent of the process of seizing defeat from the jaws of victory?
2. Does this relate to some issue-dependent context?
3. Does it relate to thwarted self-actualization through a perversion of agency?
4. What evidence is there of an enactment?
5. How does the initially asymmetrical enactment devolve into a symmetrical enactment, or a case of mutual inductive identification?
6. What are the dissociative features of the enactment? What sequestered self-states are finally emerging?
7. How are they in evidence in implicit versus explicit styles of communication?

8. How are you as therapist also being inducted into the process of mutual inductive identification?
9. What do you notice happening when you too are losing your capacity to play with your own thoughts and feelings?

Practice questions for Step Five

1. What multiple self-states have come into perspective that are lending to each partner's internal conflicts? In other words, what is the state of each partner's committee of the mind?
2. What are the stumbling blocks to negotiating such internal conflict?
3. How do the partners incorporate one another in their conflicts through processes of projection and internalization?
4. How can each partner be reminded of and recruited to become reflective about the internal process versus being reactive?
5. How can each partner learn to get out of the way of the other's process, rather than become mired in it and thereby engaging in mutual enactment? In other words, how do partners recognize when they are treating the other as subjects versus as objects?
6. In what manner can each partner come to terms with what has heretofore felt irreconcilable vis-à-vis their internal conflict and that therefore has to be disavowed and dissociated?
7. How is the role of shame constraining each partner?
8. What evidence is there of the partners finally being able to engage in surrender (to the irreconcilable) versus feel doomed in submission?

Practice questions for Step Six

1. When is it useful to speak to the couple's devolution into binaries (complementarity) by speaking directly to the relationship instead of to either of the partners individually?
2. Is there evidence that the partners are engaging one another in binary positions?
3. What evidence of one-in-thirdness is there, as in ways in which the partners tango well together?
4. Is there evidence of some kinds of sexual perversions that serve creatively for the couple to work through issues otherwise embedded in developmental histories of shame and humiliation?
5. Where is there evidence of one-in-the-thirdness—the kind of thirdness that becomes the basis of dialectics of difference that pushes each of their otherwise limited horizons of subjectivity?
6. What are the key points of failure to collaborate and negotiate difference between the partners?
7. Where is there evidence of non-negotiable paradoxes in the couple's relationship that necessitate a capacity for intersubjective surrender?

8. What is the importance of establishing the couple's relationship as a form of therapeutic alliance instrumental to their functioning post-termination?
9. What are important points of bearing witness to one another's experiential realities?
10. In what manner is the couple evidencing a capacity to terminate treatment?

REFERENCES

Ackerman, N. (1958). *The psychodynamics of family life: Diagnosis and treatment of family relationships*. New York: Basic Books.

Ackerman, N. (1966). *Treating the troubled family*. New York: Basic Books.

Albee, E. (1962). *Who's afraid of Virginia Woolf?* New York: Dramatist's Play Service, Inc.

Allen, J., Fonagy, P., & Bateman, A. (2008). *Mentalizing in clinical practice*. Arlington VA: American Psychiatric Press.

Aron, L. (1996). *A meeting of minds: Mutuality in psychoanalysis*. Hillsdale, NJ: Analytic Press.

Aron, L. (1999). Clinical choices and the relational matrix. *Psychoanalytic Dialogues*, 9, 1–29.

Aron, L. (2000). Self-reflexivity and the therapeutic action of psychoanalysis. *Psychoanalytic Psychology*, 17, 667–689.

Aron, L. (2003). The paradoxical place of enactment in psychoanalysis: Introduction. *Psychoanalytic Dialogues*, 13, 623–632.

Aron, L. (2006). Analytic impasse and the third: Clinical implications of intersubjectivity theory. *International Journal of Psychoanalysis*, 87, 349–368.

Aron, L., & Benjamin, J. (1999, April). The development of intersubjectivity and the struggle to think. Paper presented at the annual meeting of the American Psychological Association, Division of Psychoanalysis (39), New York.

Atwood, G. E., & Stolorow, R. D. (1984). *Structures of subjectivity: Explorations in psychoanalytic phenomenology*. Hillsdale, NJ: Analytic Press.

Bacal, H. (1994). The selfobject relationship in psychoanalytic treatment. In A. Goldberg (ed.), *Progress in self psychology: A decade of progress* (Vol. 10, pp. 21–30). Hillsdale, NJ: Analytic Press.

Bacal, H. A., & Thomson, P. G. (1996). The psychoanalyst's selfobject needs and the effect of their frustration on the treatment: A new view of countertransference. *Progress in Self Psychology*, 12, 17–35.

Bach, S. (1994). *Narcissistic states and the therapeutic process*. New York: Jason Aronson.

Bader, M. (2002). *Arousal: The secret logic of sexual fantasies*. New York: St. Martin's.

Bass, A. (2003). "E" enactments in psychoanalysis: Another medium, another message. *Psychoanalytic Dialogues*, 13, 657–676.

Bateson, G., Jackson, D. D., Haley, J., & Weakland, J. (1956). Towards a theory of schizophrenia. *Behavioral Science*, 1, 251–264.

Beavers, W., & Voeller, M. (1983). Family models: Comparing and contrasting the Olson circumplex with the Beavers model. *Family Process*, 22, 85–98.

Beebe, B., & Lachmann, F. M. (1994). Representation and internalization in infancy: Three principles of salience. *Psychoanalytic Psychology*, 11, 127–166.

Beebe, B., & Lachmann, F. M. (2002). *Infant research and adult treatment: Co-constructing interactions*. Hillsdale, NJ: Analytic Press.

Benjamin, J. (1988). *The bonds of love: Psychoanalysis, feminism, and the problem of domination*. New York: Pantheon Books.

Benjamin, J. (1992). Recognition and destruction: An outline of intersubjectivity. In N. Skolnick & S. Warshaw (eds.), *Relational perspectives in psychoanalysis* (pp. 43–60). Hillsdale, NJ: Analytic Press.

Benjamin, J. (1995). *Like subjects, love objects: Essays on recognition and sexual difference*. New Haven, CT: Yale University Press.

Benjamin, J. (1998). Finding the way out: Commentary on papers by Malcolm Owen Slavin and Daniel Kriegman and by Philip A. Ringstrom. *Psychoanalytic Dialogues*, 8, 589–598.

Benjamin, J. (1999). Recognition and destruction: Afterword. In S. Mitchell & L. Aron (eds.), *Relational psychoanalysis: The emergence of a tradition* (pp. 181–210). Hillsdale, NJ: Analytic Press.

Benjamin, J. (2002). The rhythm of recognition: Comments on the work of Louis Sander. *Psychoanalytic Dialogues*, 12, 43–54.

Benjamin, J. (2004). Beyond doer and done to: Recognition and the intersubjective third. *Psychoanalytic Quarterly*, 73, 5–46.

Benjamin, J. (2005). Creating an intersubjective reality: Commentary on paper by Arnold Rothstein. *Psychoanalytic Dialogues*, 15, 447–457.

Bion, W. R. (1967). Notes on memory and desire. *Psychoanalytic Forum*, 2, 272–273.

Black, M. J. (2003). Enactment: Analytic musings on energy, language, and personal growth. *Psychoanalytic Dialogues*, 13, 633–655.

Blechner, M. (2006). Love, sex, romance, and psychoanalytic goals. *Psychoanalytic Dialogues*, 16, 779–791.

Bollas, C. (1989). *The forces of destiny*. Northvale, NJ: Jason Aronson.

Boston Change Process Study Group. (2002). Explicating the implicit: The local level and the microprocess of change in the analytic situation. *International Journal of Psychoanalysis*, 83, 1051–1062.

Boszormenyi-Nagy, I. (1987). *Foundations of contextual therapy: Collected papers of Ivan Boszormenyi-Nagy*. New York: Brunner/Mazel.

Bowen, M. (1978). *Family therapy in clinical practice*. New York: Jason Aronson.

Brandchaft, B. (1994). To free the spirit from its cell. In R. D. Stolorow, G. E. Atwood, & B. Brandchaft (eds.), *The intersubjective perspective* (pp. 57–76). Northvale, NJ: Jason Aronson.

Brandchaft, B. (2007). Systems of pathological accommodation and change in analysis. *Psychoanalytic Psychology*, 24, 667–687.

Breger, L. (1974). *From instinct to identity: The development of personality*. Englewood Cliffs, NJ: Prentice Hall.

Bromberg, P. M. (1998). *Standing in the spaces: Essays on dissociation, trauma, and clinical process*. Hillsdale, NJ: Analytic Press.

Bromberg, P. M. (2006). *Awakening the dreamer: Clinical journeys*. Mahwah, NJ: Analytic Press.

Bronowski, J. (1974). *The ascent of man*. New York: Little, Brown.

Bucci, W. (2002). The referential process, consciousness, and the sense of self. *Psychoanalytic Inquiry*, 22, 766–793.

Bucci, W. (2011). The interplay of subsymbolic and symbolic processes in psychoanalytic treatment: It takes two to tango. *Psychoanalytic Dialogues*, 21, 45–54.

Cavell, M. (1998). In response to Owen Renik's "The analyst's subjectivity and the analyst's objectivity." *International Journal of Psychoanalysis*, 79, 1195–1202.

Chodorow, N. (1989). *Feminism and psychoanalytic theory*. New Haven, CT: Yale University Press.

Chodorow, N. (1994). *Femininities, masculinities, sexualities: Freud and beyond*. Lexington, KY: University of Kentucky Press.

Chodorow, N. (1995). Gender as a personal and cultural construction. *Signs*, 20, 515–544.

Chomsky, N. (1957). *Syntactic structures*. Berlin: Mouton.

Coburn, W. (2002). A world of systems: The role of systemic patterns of experience in the therapeutic process. *Psychoanalytic Inquiry*, 22, 655–677.

Coburn, W. (2006). Terminations, self-states, and complexity in psychoanalysis: Commentary on paper by Jody Davies. *Psychoanalytic Dialogues*, 16, 603–610.

Coburn, W. (2008). Psychoanalytic complexity theory: Pouring new wine directly into one's mouth. In P. Buirski & A. Kottler (eds.), *New developments in self psychology practice* (pp. 3–22). Lanham, MD: Jason Aronson.

Cooper, S. (2009). Familiar and unfamiliar forms of interaction in the ending phases of analysis. *Psychoanalytic Dialogues*, 19, 588–603.

Corbett, K. (2001). More life: Centrality and marginality in human development. *Psychoanalytic Dialogues*, 11, 313–335.

Corbett, K. (2010). Mother country: Discussion of Hazel Ipp's "Nell: A bridge to the amputated self: The impact of immigration on continuities and discontinuities of self." *International Journal of Psychoanalytic Self Psychology*, 5, 387–393.

Crastnopol, M. (1999). The analyst's professional self as a "third" influence on the dyad: When the analyst writes about the treatment. *Psychoanalytic Dialogues*, 9, 445–470.

Crastnopol, M. (2006). The rub: Sexual interplay as a nexus of lust, romantic love, and emotional attachment. *Psychoanalytic Dialogues*, 16, 687–709.

Damasio, A. (1994). *Descartes' error: Emotion, reason, and the human brain*. New York: Putnam.

Damasio, A. (1999). *The feeling of what happens: Body and emotion in the making of consciousness*. New York: Harcourt.

Davies, J. M. (1998). Multiple perspectives on multiplicity. *Psychoanalytic Dialogues*, 8, 195–206.

Davies, J. M. (2003). Falling in love with love: Oedipal and postoedipal manifestations of idealization, mourning and erotic masochism. *Psychoanalytic Dialogues*, 13, 1–27.

Davies, J. M. (2004). Whose bad objects are we anyway? Repetition and our elusive love affair with evil. *Psychoanalytic Dialogues*, 14, 711–732.

Davies, J. M. (2005). Transformations of desire and despair: Reflections on the termination process from a relational perspective. *Psychoanalytic Dialogues*, 15, 779–805.

Davies, J. M. (2006). The times we sizzle, and the times we sigh: The multiple erotics of arousal, anticipation, and release. *Psychoanalytic Dialogues*, 16, 665–686.

Dicks, H. (1964). Concepts of marital diagnosis and therapy as developed at the Tavistock family psychiatric units, London, England. In E. Nash, L. Jessner, & D. Abse (eds.), *Marriage counseling in medical practice*. Chapel Hill: University of North Carolina Press.

Dimen, M. (2003). *Sexuality, intimacy, power*. Hillsdale, NJ: Analytic Press.

271

REFERENCES

Emanuel, C. (2011). An accidental Pokemon expert: My contemporary psychoanalytic work on the autism spectrum. Paper presented to the Institute of Contemporary Psychoanalysis, Los Angeles, CA, January 15, 2011.

Fairbairn, W. R. D. (1952). *An object-relations theory of the personality*. New York: Basic Books.

Ferenczi, S. (1927). The problem with termination of the analysis. In M. Balint (ed.) & E. Mosbacher (trans.), *Final contribution to the problems and methods of psychoanalysis* (pp. 77–86). London: Hogarth Press.

Ferenczi, S. (1988). *The clinical diary of Sándor Ferenczi* (ed. J. Dupont). Cambridge, MA: Harvard University Press.

Fonagy, P. (2003). Some complexities in the relationship of psychoanalytic theory to technique. *Psychoanalytic Quarterly*, 72, 13–48.

Fonagy, P., Gergeley, G., Jurist, E., & Target, M. (2004). *Affect regulation, mentalization, and the development of the self*. New York: Other Press.

Fonagy, P., & Target, M. (1997). Attachment and reflective function: Their role in self-organization. *Development and Psychopathology*, 9, 679–700.

Fosshage, J. L. (1997). Listening/experiencing perspectives and the quest for a facilitating responsiveness. In A. Goldberg (ed.), *Progress in self psychology: Conversations in self psychology* (Vol. 13, pp. 33–55). Hillsdale, NJ: Analytic Press.

Freud, S. (1955a). *Beyond the pleasure principle*. In J. Strachey (ed. & trans.), *The standard edition of the complete psychological works of Sigmund Freud* (Vol. 18, pp. 1–64). London: Hogarth Press. (Original work published 1920.)

Freud, S. (1955b). Group psychology and the analysis of the ego. In J. Strachey (ed. & trans.), *The standard edition of the complete psychological works of Sigmund Freud* (Vol. 18, pp. 67–144). London: Hogarth Press. (Original work published 1921.)

Freud, S. (1957a). On the universal tendency to debasement in the sphere of love. In J. Strachey (ed. & trans.), *The standard edition of the complete psychological works of Sigmund Freud* (Vol. 11, pp. 177–190). London: Hogarth Press. (Original work published 1912.)

Freud, S. (1957b). Mourning and melancholia. In J. Strachey (ed. & trans.), *The standard edition of the complete psychological works of Sigmund Freud* (Vol. 14, pp. 239–258). London: Hogarth Press. (Original work published 1917.)

Freud, S. (1961). *The ego and the id*. In J. Strachey (ed. & trans.), *The standard edition of the complete psychological works of Sigmund Freud* (Vol. 19, pp. 3–66). London: Hogarth Press. (Original work published 1923.)

Freud, S. (1964). Analysis terminable and interminable. In J. Strachey (ed. & trans.), *The standard edition of the complete psychological works of Sigmund Freud* (Vol. 23, pp. 209–253). London: Hogarth Press. (Original work published 1937.)

Frommer, M. (2006). On the subjectivity of lustful states of mind. *Psychoanalytic Dialogues*, 16, 639–664.

Gabbard, G. O. (1997). A reconsideration of objectivity in the analyst. *International Journal of Psychoanalysis*, 78, 15–26.

Gabbard, G. O. (2000). *Love and hate in the analytic setting*. New York: Jason Aronson.

Gabbard, G. O., & Ogden, T. H. (2009). On becoming a psychoanalyst. *International Journal of Psychoanalysis*, 90, 311–327.

Galatzer-Levy, R. (1995). Psychoanalysis and dynamic systems theory: Prediction. *Journal of the American Psychoanalytic Association*, 44, 981–986.

Gedo, J. E. (1988). *The mind in disorder: Psychoanalytic models of pathology*. Hillsdale, NJ: Analytic Press.

Gendlin, E. (no date). Improvisation provides. Unpublished article.

Gentile, J. (2001). Close but no cigar: The perversion of agency and the absence of thirdness. *Contemporary Psychoanalysis*, 37, 623–654.

Gentile, J. (2008). Agency and its clinical phenomenology. In R. Frie (ed.), *Psychological agency: Theory, practice, and culture* (pp. 117–135). Cambridge, MA: MIT Press.

Gentile, K. (2007). *Creating bodies: Eating disorders as self-destructive survival*. Mahwah, NJ: Analytic Press.

Gerson, M.-J. (2001). The drama of couples therapy. *Journal of Psychotherapy Integration*, 11, 333–347.

Gerson, M.-J. (2010). *The embedded self: An integrative psychodynamic and systemic perspective on couples and family therapy*, 2nd ed. New York: Routledge.

Ghent, E. (1990). Masochism, submission, and surrender. *Contemporary Psychoanalysis*, 26, 108–135.

Goldberg, L. (1970). Pine. In T. Rivner (ed.), *Collected poems* (p. 13). Tel Aviv: Iachov/Writers Association.

Goldner, V. (2006). Let's do it again: Further reflections on Eros and attachment. *Psychoanalytic Dialogues*, 16, 619–637.

Goldner, V. (2007). Untitled paper. Presented at Division 39 Spring Meeting of the American Psychological Association. April, 2007, New York City.

Goldstein, K. (1995). *The organism*. New York: Zone Books.

Gottman, J. (1999). *The marriage clinic: A scientifically based marital therapy*. New York: W. W. Norton.

Greenberg, J. (1991). *Oedipus and beyond: A clinical theory*. Cambridge, MA: Harvard University Press.

Greenberg, J., & Mitchell, S. A. (1983). *Object relations in psychoanalytic theory*. Cambridge, MA: Harvard University Press.

Greenson, R. (1968). Dis-identifying from mother: Its special importance for the boy. *International Journal of Psychoanalysis*, 45, 220–226.

Grotstein, J. (1997). Autochthony and alterity: Psychic reality in counterpoint. *Psychoanalytic Quarterly*, 66, 403–430.

Grotstein, J. (2000). *Who is the dreamer, who dreams the dream?* Hillsdale, NJ: Analytic Press.

Harris, A. (2009). *Gender as soft assembly*. New York: Routledge.

Hawking, S. (1988). *A brief history of time*. New York: Bantam-Dell.

Hegel, G. (1807). *Phenomenologie des Geistes*. Hamburg: Felix Meiner.

Heidegger, M. (1927). *Being and time*. New York: Harper & Row.

Hoffman, I. Z. (1991). Discussion: Toward a social-constructivist view of the psychoanalytic situation. *Psychoanalytic Dialogues*, 1, 74–105.

Hoffman, I. Z. (1994). Dialectical thinking and therapeutic action in the psychoanalytic process. *Psychoanalytic Quarterly*, 63, 187–218.

Hoffman, I. Z. (1998). *Ritual and spontaneity in the psychoanalytic process: A dialectical constructivist view*. Hillsdale, NJ: Analytic Press.

Humphrey, E. (1987). Treating extramarital relationships in sex and couples therapy. In G. R. Weeks & L. Hof (eds.), *Integrating sex and marital therapy: A clinical guide* (pp. 149–170). New York: Brunner-Routledge.

Ipp, H. (2010). Nell: A bridge to the amputated self: The impact of immigration on continuities and discontinuities of self. *International Journal of Psychoanalytic Self Psychology*, 5, 373–386.

Jacobs, L. (2010). Truth or what matters: Commentary on paper by Philip A. Ringstrom. *Psychoanalytic Dialogues*, 20, 224–230.

James, W. (1981). *The principles of psychology*. Cambridge, MA: Harvard University Press. (Original work published 1890.)

Jaynes, J. (1990). *The origin of consciousness in the breakdown of the bicameral mind*. New York: Houghton Mifflin.

Karpel, M. (1980). Family secrets: I. Conceptual and ethical issues in the relational context; II. Ethical and practical considerations in therapeutic management. *Family Process*, 19, 295–306.

Kavaler-Adler, S. (2012, April). In the arms of a stranger: In the moment, held in the embrace. Paper presented at the annual meeting of the American Psychological Association, Division of Psychoanalysis (39), Santa Fe, NM.

Kernberg, O. F. (1991a). Aggression and love in the relationship of the couple. *Journal of the American Psychoanalytic Association*, 39, 45–70.

Kernberg, O. F. (1991b). Sadomasochism, sexual excitement, and perversion. *Journal of the American Psychoanalytic Association*, 39, 333–362.

Kernberg, O. F. (1993). The couple's constructive and destructive superego functions. *Journal of the American Psychoanalytic Association*, 41, 653–677.

Klein, M. (1946). Notes on schizoid mechanisms. In M. Klein, P. Heimann, S. Isaacs, & J. Riviere (eds.), *Developments in psychoanalysis* (pp. 292–320). London: Hogarth Press.

Klein, M. (1952). On identification. In M. Klein, P. Heimann, & R. Money-Kyrle (eds.), *New directions in psychoanalysis: The significance of infant conflict in the pattern of adult behavior* (pp. 309–345). New York: Basic Books.

Knoblauch, S. (2001). High risk, high gain: Commentary on paper by Philip A. Ringstrom. *Psychoanalytic Dialogues*, 11, 785–795.

Kohut, H. (1959). Introspection, empathy, and psychoanalysis. In P. Ornstein (ed.), *Search for the self* (Vol. 1, pp. 205–232). Madison, CT: International Universities Press.

Kohut, H. (1977). *The restoration of self*. Madison, CT: International Universities Press.

Kohut, H. (1984). *How does analysis cure?* Chicago, IL: University of Chicago Press.

Korzybski, A. (1933). *Science and sanity*, 4th ed. Lakeville, CT: International Non-Aristotelian Library Publishing Company.

Lachkar, J. (1992). *The narcissistic/borderline couple: A psychoanalytic perspective on marital treatment*. New York: Brunner/Mazel.

Landy, R. (1994). *Drama therapy: Concepts, theories and practices*, 2nd ed. Springfield, IL: Charles C. Thomas.

Layton, L. (1999). *Who's that girl? Who's that boy? Clinical practice meets postmodern gender theory*. New York: Jason Aronson.

Leone, C. (2001). Toward a more optimal selfobject milieu: Family psychotherapy from the perspective of self psychology. *Clinical Social Work Journal*, 29, 269–289.

Lichtenberg, J. D., Lachmann, F. M., & Fosshage, J. L. (1992). *Self and motivational systems: Towards a theory of psychoanalytic technique*. Hillsdale, NJ: Analytic Press.

Lichtenberg, J. D., Lachmann, F. M., & Fosshage, J. L. (1996). *The clinical exchange: Techniques derived from self and motivational systems*. Hillsdale, NJ: Analytic Press.

Lillas, C., & Turnbull, J. (2009). *Infant/child mental health, early intervention, and relationship-based therapies: A neurorelational framework for interdisciplinary practice*. New York: W. W. Norton.

Livingston, M. (2007). Sustained empathic focus, intersubjectivity, and intimacy in the treatment of couples. *International Journal of Psychoanalytic Self Psychology*, 2, 315–338.

Locher, E. (1971). *The world of M. C. Escher*. New York: H. M. Abrams.

Loewald, H. (1980). *Papers in psychoanalysis*. New Haven, CT: Yale University Press.

Loewald, H. (1988). *Sublimation*. New Haven, CT: Yale University Press.

Magid, B. (2001). *Ordinary mind: Exploring the common ground of Zen and psychotherapy*. Boston, MA: Wisdom Publications.

Magid, B. (2008). *Ending the pursuit of happiness: A Zen guide*. Boston, MA: Wisdom Publications.

Main, M. (2000). The organized categories of infant, child, and adult attachment: Flexible vs. inflexible attention under attachment-related stress. *Journal of the American Psychoanalytic Association*, 48, 1055–1096.

Malin, B. (1997). Shameful and envious rage. In S. Alhanati & K. Kostoulas (eds.), *Primitive mental states: Across the lifespan* (pp. 205–220). Northvale, NJ: Jason Aronson.

Maslow, A. (1943). A theory of human motivation. *Psychological Review*, 50, 370–396.

McLaughlin, J. (1987). The play of transference: Some reflections on enactment in the psychoanalytic situation. *Journal of the American Psychoanalytic Association*, 35, 557–582.

McLaughlin, J. (1991). Clinical and theoretical aspects of enactment. *Journal of the American Psychoanalytic Association*, 39, 595–614.

Merleau-Ponty, M. (1968). *The visible and the invisible*. Evanston, IL: Northwestern University Press.

Metzl, M. (2012). Discussion of "In the arms of a stranger: In the moment, held in the embrace." Paper presented at the annual meeting of the American Psychological Association, Division of Psychoanalysis (39), Santa Fe, NM.

Minuchin, S. (1974). *Families and family therapy*. Cambridge, MA: Harvard University Press.

Mitchell, S. A. (1988). *Relational concepts in psychoanalysis*. Cambridge, MA: Harvard University Press.

Mitchell, S. A. (1993). *Hope and dread in psychoanalysis*. New York: Basic Books.

Mitchell, S. A. (1997). *Influence and autonomy in psychoanalysis*. Hillsdale, NJ: Analytic Press.

Mitchell, S. A. (2000). *Relationality: From attachment to intersubjectivity*. Hillsdale, NJ: Analytic Press.

Mitchell, S. A. (2002). *Can love last? The fate of romance over time*. New York: W. W. Norton.

Mitchell, S. A., & Aron, L. (eds.) (1999). *Relational psychoanalysis: The emergence of a tradition*. Hillsdale, NJ: Analytic Press.

Modell, A. (2008). Horse and rider revisited: The dynamic unconscious and the self as agent. *Contemporary Psychoanalysis*, 44, 351–366.

Muller, J. P. (1999). The third as holding the dyad: Commentary on paper by Margaret Crastnopol. *Psychoanalytic Dialogues*, 9, 471–480.

Ogden, T. H. (1994). *Subjects of analysis*. Northvale, NJ: Jason Aronson.

Ornstein, A. (1974). The dread to repeat and the new beginning. In J. Winer & J. Anderson (eds.), *The annual of psychoanalysis* (Vol. 2, pp. 231–248). Madison, CT: International Universities Press.

Palazzoli, M., Selvini, M., Cecchin, G., Prata, G. & Boscolo L. (1978). *Paradox and counterparadox: A new model in the therapy of the family in schizophrenic transaction.* New York: Jason Aronson.

Perel, E. (2007). *Mating in captivity: Unlocking erotic intelligence.* New York: Harper.

Phillips, A. (1993). *On kissing, tickling and being bored: Psychoanalytic essays on the unexamined life.* Cambridge, MA: Harvard University Press.

Piaget, J. (1973). *Memory and intelligence.* New York: Basic Books.

Pizer, B. (2003). When the crunch is a (k)not: A crimp in relational dialogue. *Psychoanalytic Dialogues*, 13, 193–204.

Pizer, B., & Pizer, S. (2006). The gift of an apple or the twist of an arm. *Psychoanalytic Dialogues*, 16, 71–92.

Pizer, S. (1998). *Building bridges: The negotiation of paradox in psychoanalysis.* Hillsdale, NJ: Analytic Press.

Preston, L. (2007, October). Improvisation provides a window into implicit processes: Thoughts on Philip Ringstrom's work in dialogue with Eugene Gendlin. Paper presented at the annual conference on the Psychology of the Self, Los Angeles, CA.

Racker, H. (1968). *Transference and countertransference.* New York: International Universities Press.

Renn, P. (2008). Understanding the links between adult attachment styles and violence in intimate relationships: When should couple therapy be the choice of intervention. Paper presented at a Violent Attachments CPD workshop, London, 2008.

Renn, P. (2012). *The silent past and the invisible present: Memory, trauma, and representation in psychotherapy.* New York: Routledge.

Ringstrom, P. (1994). An intersubjective approach to conjoint therapy. In A. Goldberg (ed.), *Progress in self psychology: A decade of progress* (Vol. 10, pp. 159–182). Hillsdale, NJ: Analytic Press.

Ringstrom, P. (1995). Exploring the model scene: Finding the focus in an intersubjective approach to brief psychotherapy. *Psychoanalytic Inquiry*, 15, 493–513.

Ringstrom, P. (1998a). Therapeutic impasses in contemporary psychoanalytic treatment: Revisiting the double bind hypothesis. *Psychoanalytic Dialogues*, 8, 297–315.

Ringstrom, P. (1998b). The pursuit of authenticity and the plight of self-deception: Commentary on paper by Slavin and Kriegman. *Psychoanalytic Dialogues*, 8, 285–292.

Ringstrom, P. (1998c). Competing selfobject functions: The bane of the conjoint therapist. *Bulletin of the Menninger Clinic*, 62, 314–325.

Ringstrom, P. (1999). Discussion of Robert Stolorow's paper "The phenomenology of trauma." Paper presented at the 22nd annual conference on the Psychology of the Self, Toronto, CA, October.

Ringstrom, P. (2001a). Cultivating the improvisational in psychoanalytic treatment. *Psychoanalytic Dialogues*, 11, 727–754.

Ringstrom, P. (2001b). "Yes, and …": How improvisation is the essence of good psycho-analytic dialogue: Reply to commentaries. *Psychoanalytic Dialogues*, 11, 797–806.

Ringstrom, P. (2003). "Crunches," "(k)nots," and double binds: When what isn't happen-ing is the most important thing: Commentary on paper by Barbara Pizer. *Psychoanalytic Dialogues*, 13, 193–204.

Ringstrom, P. (2004). Body rhythms and improvisation: Playing with the music behind the lyrics in psychoanalysis. Paper presented at the 27th Annual International Conference on the Psychology of the Self, San Diego, CA, October.

Ringstrom, P. (2007a). Scenes that write themselves: Improvisational moments in relational psychoanalysis. *Psychoanalytic Dialogues*, 17, 69–100.

Ringstrom, P. (2007b). Reply to commentary by Daniel N. Stern. *Psychoanalytic Dialogues*, 17, 105–113.

Ringstrom, P. (2008a). Improvisational moments in self-psychological relational psychoanalysis. In P. Buirski & A. Kottler (eds.), *New developments in self psychology practice* (pp. 223–235). Lanham, MD: Jason Aronson.

Ringstrom, P. (2008b). Improvisation and mutual inductive identification in couples therapy: A discussion of Susan Shimmerlik's article "Moments in relational psychoanalysis." *Psychoanalytic Dialogues*, 18, 390–402.

Ringstrom, P. (2009). Selfobject as dramatis persona: Cultivating the improvisational in self-psychological psychoanalysis. In W. Coburn & N. Van der Heide (eds.), *Self and systems: Explorations in contemporary self psychology* (pp. 174–188). New York: Annals of the New York Academy of Sciences.

Ringstrom, P. (2010a). Meeting Mitchell's challenge: A comparison of relational psychoanalysis and intersubjective systems theory. *Psychoanalytic Dialogues*, 20, 196–218.

Ringstrom, P. (2010b). Reply to commentaries. *Psychoanalytic Dialogues*, 20, 236–250.

Ringstrom, P. (2010c). Review of *Trauma and human existence: Autobiographical, psychological, and philosophical reflections* by Robert Stolorow. *Psychoanalytic Psychology*, 27, 241–249.

Ringstrom, P. (2010d). "Yes Alan!" and a few more thoughts about improvisation: A discussion of Alan Kindler's chapter "Spontaneity and improvisation in psychoanalysis." *Psychoanalytic Inquiry*, 30, 235–242.

Ringstrom, P. (2010e). Commentary on Donna Orange's, "Recognition as: Intersubjective Vulnerability" in the Psychoanalytic Dialogue." *International Journal of Psychoanalytic Self Psychology*, 5, 257–273.

Ringstrom, P. (2012a). Principles of improvisation: A model of therapeutic play in relational psychoanalysis. In L. Aron & A. Harris (eds.), *Relational psychoanalysis: Evolution of process* (Vol. 5, pp. 447–478). New York: Routledge.

Ringstrom, P. (2012c). A relational intersubjective approach to conjoint treatment. *International Journal of Psychoanalytic Self Psychology*, 7, 85–111.

Ringstrom, P. (in press). "Inductive identification" and improvisation in psychoanalytic practice: Some comments on Joye Weisel-Barth's article on complexity theory. *International Journal of Psychoanalytic Self Psychology*.

Rorty, R. (1989). *Contingency, irony, and solidarity*. Cambridge, UK: Cambridge University Press.

Rubalcava, L. A., & Waldman, K. M. (2004). Working with intercultural couples: An intersubjective-constructivist perspective. In W. Coburn (ed.), *Progress in self psychology: Transformations in self psychology* (Vol. 20, pp. 127–149). Hillsdale, NJ: Analytic Press.

Rubin, J., & Rubin, C. (1991). Conflict, negotiation, and change. In R. Curtis & G. Stricker (eds.), *How people change: Inside and outside therapy* (pp. 157–169). New York: Plenum Press.

Saarni, C. (1993). Socialization of emotion. In M. Lewis & J. M. Haviland (eds.), *Handbook of emotions* (pp. 435–446). New York: Guilford Press.

Safran, J. (2007). Will, surrender, and intersubjectivity. Paper presented at the annual meeting of the American Psychological Association, Division of Psychoanalysis (39), Toronto, CA.

Safran, J., & Muran, J. (2000). *Negotiating the therapeutic alliance: A relational treatment guide*. New York: Guilford Press.

Salberg, J. ed. (2010). *Good enough endings: Breaks, interruptions and terminations from contemporary relational perspectives*. New York: Taylor & Francis.

Satir, V. (1967). *Conjoint family therapy* (revised ed.). Palo Alto, CA: Science and Behavioral Sciences.

Scharff, D., & Scharff, J. (1991). *Object relations and couple therapy*. Northvale, NJ: Jason Aronson.

Scharff, J. (1992). *Projective identification and the use of the therapist's self*. Northvale, NJ: Jason Aronson.

Scharff, J., & Scharff, D. (1992). *Scharff notes: A primer of object relations therapy*. Northvale, NJ: Jason Aronson.

Schore, A. (1994). *Affect regulation and the origin of the self: The neurobiology of emotional development*. Hillsdale, NJ: Lawrence Erlbaum Associates.

Seligman, S. (2000). Clinical implications of attachment theory. *Journal of the American Psychoanalytic Association*, 48, 1189–1196.

Shaddock, D. (1998). *From impasse to intimacy: How understanding unconscious needs can transform relationships*. Northvale, NJ: Jason Aronson.

Shaddock, D. (2000). *Contexts and connections: An intersubjective systems approach to couples therapy*. New York: Basic Books.

Shane, M., Shane, E., & Gales, M. (1997). *Intimate attachments: Toward new self psychology*. New York: Guilford Press.

Shimmerlik, S. (2008). The implicit domain of couples and couple therapy. *Psychoanalytic Dialogues*, 18, 371–389.

Siegel, D. (1999). *The developing mind: How relationships and the brain interact to shape who we are*. New York: Guilford Press.

Slap, J. W., & Slap-Shelton, L. S. (1994). The schema model: A proposed replacement paradigm for psychoanalysis. *Psychoanalytic Review*, 81, 677–693.

Slavin, M. (2006). Tanya and the adaptive design of romantic passion and secure attachment. *Psychoanalytic Dialogues*, 16, 793–824.

Slavin, M. (2007). A natural history of existential anxiety and intersubjective conflict: Evolutionary origins and clinical implications. Paper presented at the annual meeting on the Psychology of the Self, Los Angeles, CA, October.

Slavin, M. (2011). Lullaby on the dark side: Existential anxiety, meaning making, and the dialectics of self and other. In L. Aron & A. Harris (eds.), *Relational psychoanalysis: Expansion of theory* (Vol. 4, pp. 391–413). New York: Routledge.

Slavin, M., & Kriegman, D. (1992). *The adaptive design of the human psyche: Psychoanalysis, evolutionary biology, and the therapeutic process*. New York: Guilford Press.

Slavin, M., & Kriegman, D. (1998a). Why the analyst needs to change: Toward a theory of conflict, negotiation, and mutual influence in the therapeutic process. *Psychoanalytic Dialogues*, 8, 247–284.

Slavin, M., & Kriegman, D. (1998b). Reply to commentary. *Psychoanalytic Dialogues*, 8, 293–296.

Slavin, M., & Kriegman, D. (1998c). Bigger than both of us: Double binds, conflicting interests, and the inherent paradoxes in human relating: Commentary on paper by Ringstrom. *Psychoanalytic Dialogues*, 8, 317–327.

Slipp, S. (1984). *Object relations: A dynamic bridge between individual and family treatment*. New York: Jason Aronson.

Soloman, M. (1989). *Narcissism and intimacy: Love and marriage in the age of confusion*. New York: W. W. Norton.

Stanislavski, C. (1932). *An actor prepares*. New York: Routledge.

Stein, R. (2006). Unforgetting and excess: The re-creation and re-finding of suppressed sexuality. *Psychoanalytic Dialogues*, 16, 763–778.

Stern, D. B. (1992). Commentary on constructivism in clinical psychoanalysis. *Psychoanalytic Dialogues*, 2, 331–363.

Stern, D. B. (1997). *Unformulated experience: From dissociation to imagination in psycho-analysis*. Hillsdale, NJ: Analytic Press.

Stern, D. B. (2006). Opening what has been closed, relaxing what has been clenched: Dissociation and enactment over time in committed relationships. *Psychoanalytic Dialogues*, 16, 747–761.

Stern, D. B. (2007). The eye sees itself: Dissociation, enactment, and the achievement of conflict. IARPP Online Colloquium.

Stern, D. B. (2012). Partners in thought: A clinical process theory of narrative. In L. Aron & A. Harris (eds.), *Relational psychoanalysis: Evolution of process* (Vol. 5, pp. 381–406). New York: Routledge.

Stern, D. B. (2013). Relational freedom and therapeutic action. *Journal of the American Psychoanalytic Association*, 61, 227–255.

Stern, D. N. (1985). *The interpersonal world of the infant: A view from psychoanalysis and developmental psychology*. New York: W. W. Norton.

Stern, D. N. (2004). *The present moment in psychotherapy and everyday life*. New York: W. W. Norton.

Stern, D. N. (2007). Commentary on paper by Philip A. Ringstrom. *Psychoanalytic Dialogues*, 17, 105–113.

Stern, D. N., Sander, L., Nahum, J., Harrison, A., Lyons-Ruth, K., Morgan, A., Bruschweiler-Stern, N., & Tronick, E. (1998). Non-interpretive mechanisms in psycho-analytic therapy: The "something more" than interpretation. *International Journal of Psychoanalysis*, 79, 903–921.

Stern, S. (2002). Identification, repetition, and psychological growth. *Psychoanalytic Psychology*, 19, 722–738.

Stoller, R. J. (1965). The sense of maleness. *Psychoanalytic Quarterly*, 34, 207–218.

Stoller, R. J. (1968). The sense of femaleness. *Psychoanalytic Quarterly*, 37, 42–55.

Stoller, R. J. (1975). *The language of psycho-analysis*: By J. Laplanche and J.-B. Pontalis (trans. Donald Nicholson-Smith). London: Hogarth Press; New York: Norton. 1973. p. 510. *International Journal of Psycho-Analysis*, 56, 103–104.

Stoller, R. (1985). *Observing the erotic imagination*. New Haven, CT: Yale University Press.

Stoller, R. (1991). *Porn: Myths for the twentieth century*. New Haven, CT: Yale University Press.

Stolorow, R. D., & Atwood, G. E. (1992). *Contexts of being: The intersubjective foundation of psychological life*. Hillsdale, NJ: Analytic Press.

Stolorow, R. D., Brandchaft, B., & Atwood, G. E. (1987). *Psychoanalytic treatment: An intersubjective approach*. Hillsdale, NJ: Analytic Press.

Stolorow, R. D., Orange, D., & Atwood, G. E. (2002). *Worlds of experience: Interweaving philosophical and clinical dimensions in psychoanalysis*. New York: Basic Books.

Storr, A. (1988). *Solitude: A return to the self*. New York: Free Press.

Strenger, C. (1998). *Individuality, the impossible project: Psychoanalysis and self-creation.* Madison, CT: International Universities Press.

Sullivan, H. S. (1954). *The psychiatric interview.* New York: Norton.

Summers, F. L. (1996). Existential guilt: An object relations concept. *Contemporary Psychoanalysis*, 32, 43–63.

Tolpin, M. (1999, September). Doing psychoanalysis of normal development: Forward edge transferences. Paper presented to the Cincinnati Psychoanalytic Society, Cincinnati, OH.

Tolpin, M. (2000). Discussion of plenary panel paper. Paper presented at the annual meeting on the Psychology of the Self, Chicago, October.

Tolpin, M. (2002). Doing psychoanalysis of normal development: Forward edge transferences. In A. Goldberg (ed.), *Progress in self psychology: Postmodern self psychology* (Vol. 18, pp. 167–190). Hillsdale, NJ: Analytic Press.

Vaihinger, H. (1924). *The philosophy of "as if."* London: Routledge and Kegan Paul.

Van der Kolk, B. (1996). The body keeps score: Approaches to the psychobiology of post-traumatic stress disorder. In B. Van der Kolk, A. McFarlane, & L. Weisaeth (eds.), *Traumatic stress: The effects of overwhelming experience on mind, body, and society* (pp. 214–241). New York: Guilford Press.

Van der Kolk, B. (2007). Paper presented at the annual meeting of the Los Angeles County Psychological Association, Los Angeles, CA, October.

Wallin, D. (2007). *Attachment in psychotherapy.* New York: Guilford Press.

Watzlawick, P., Weakland, J., & Fisch, R. (1974). *Change: Principles of problem formation and problem resolution.* New York: Norton.

Weeks, G. (ed.) (1989). *Treating couples: The intersystem model of the Marriage Council of Philadelphia.* New York: Brunner/Mazel.

Weisel-Barth, J. (2009). Stuck: Choice and agency in psychoanalysis. *International Journal of Psychoanalytic Self Psychology*, 4, 288–312.

Weiss, J., Sampson, H., & the Mount Zion Psychotherapy Research Group. (1986). *The psychoanalytic process: Theory, clinical observation and empirical research.* New York: Guilford Press.

Westfall, A. (1989). Extramarital sex: The treatment of the couple. In G. Weeks (ed.), *Treating couples: The intersystem model of the Marriage Council of Philadelphia* (pp. 163–190). New York: Brunner/Mazel.

Whitaker, C. (1977). Process techniques in family therapy. *Interaction*, 1, 4–19.

Winnicott, D.W. (1971). *Playing and reality.* London: Tavistock Publications.

Wolf, E. (1988). *Treating the self: Elements of clinical self psychology.* New York: Guilford Press.

Wolff Bernstein, J. (1999). Reply to commentaries. *Psychoanalytic Dialogues*, 9, 319–325.

Wolff Bernstein, J. (2006). Love, desire, jouissance: Two out of three ain't bad. *Psychoanalytic Dialogues*, 16, 711–724.

Wrye, H. (2006). Sitting with Eros and Psyche on a Buddhist psychoanalyst's cushion. *Psychoanalytic Dialogues*, 16, 725–746.

Wynne, L. (1970). Communication disorders and the quest for relatedness in families of schizophrenics. *American Journal of Psychoanalysis*, 30, 100–114.

INDEX

abandonment 19, 20, 26, 52, 63n2, 79, 81, 83, 107, 120, 245; anxiety over 244; fears of 139, 244
abortion 131, 214, 229
accommodation 14, 22, 40, 53, 236, 237; over- 22, 163; mutual 181–3; pathological 40, 131, 151, 203, 231, 239; pseudo- 151
Ackerman, Nathan W. 6n2
Adams, Amy 113
addictive/compulsive behavior 40, 259
affairs 98, 105–6, 129–30, 168, 224, 242, 247–51
affect regulation 46, 91, 93, 94, 100–1, 107, 112, 122, 212n6, 241, 256, 266
affective resonance 57
affectivity 51, 54, 90, 101, 102, 107, 108
agency 8, 9–11, 20, 50–1, 53, 56, 64n7, 68, 109, 110, 116n5, 120, 127, 128, 144n6, 148, 149, 171, 175; perversion of 51, 118, 120, 128–9, 130, 143, 180, 266; sense of 9, 10, 11, 34n3, 38, 52, 53, 55–6, 82, 96, 127, 152, 170, 218
aggression 13, 14, 20, 27, 41, 119, 130, 159, 212n9, 221, 228, 252, 253, 254, 262
aging 4, 148, 161
Albee, Edward 16
alcohol 9, 191, 243, 244, 245, 251–2, 256–7
Alcoholics Anonymous (AA) 154, 245
Allen, Jon 99
anger 38, 49, 54, 55, 71, 77, 79, 80, 81, 93, 98, 101, 102, 115, 125, 132, 157–9, 171, 194, 195, 196, 206, 215, 222, 235, 256
anger management groups 245
anxiety 34n4, 39, 58–60, 84, 93, 112–13, 122, 132, 138–40, 171, 184, 186, 194, 204, 205, 207, 217, 244, 255, 258, 263, 265; family 259, 264; separation 123, 125
anxiety disorders 33, 58
Aron, Lewis xii, 3, 11, 16, 34n5, 35n9, 66, 88n7, 107, 147–9, 175n1, n3, 179–80, 181, 187–8, 199–200, 212n2, n3, n4, n6, 246
assault of the unimaginable 103–4
attachment 1, 3, 18–23, 27, 28, 92, 107, 115, 120, 251
attachment patterns 52, 90; insecure 92–3, 101, 141, 166, 243, 266; secure 92, 266
attachment systems 21–2, 24; insecure 92, 165, 241
attention deficit disorder 54, 70, 168
attractor states 33; stable 31
attunement 3–5, 37, 39, 42–3, 49, 58, 63, 70, 71, 96, 118, 119, 142, 175n2, 184, 204, 207, 232; reciprocal 4
Atwood, George E. 2, 34n5, 39, 40, 41, 42, 49, 66, 67, 68, 71, 73, 74
authenticity 13, 29, 36n15, 48, 49, 128, 139, 159, 171, 211, 237
autism 137–8, 233
autochthony 50, 116n5

Bacal, Howard 43, 74
Bach, Sheldon 149
Bader, Michael 21
Barthes, Roland 27, 252
Bass, Tony 145n12
Bateman, Anthony 99
Bateson, Gregory 2, 93, 260, 261
Beavers, W. Robert 196
Beebe, Beatrice 12, 46, 51, 92, 106, 116–17n6

Benjamin, Jessica 3, 11–17, 19, 27, 32, 34n5, 36n15, 48, 51, 72, 87–8n7, 107, 109, 128, 142, 144n6, 149, 150, 167, 179, 181, 187, 193, 199, 212n6
Berlin, Irving 118
bickering 246
binaries 4, 41, 85, 107, 115, 209, 238, 241, 247, 248, 251, 267
Bion, Wilfred 63n2, 144n7
Black, Margaret J. 145n12
Blechner, Mark J. 18, 26, 212n5
Bollas, Christopher 19, 73, 145n11, 188, 225
bondage 185
borderline pathology 149–50, 209, 213n12, 241, 247
Boscolo, Luigi 17, 261
Boszormenyi-Nagy, Ivan 2, 77
Bowen, Murray 2, 35n7, 112, 116n1, 212n8, 258–9, 260, 263, 264n1
brain 10, 105; evolving 35n12
Brandchaft, Bernard 2, 34, 39, 40, 41, 42, 49, 75
Breger, Louis 39
Bromberg, Philip 3, 22, 34, 44, 52, 56, 74, 103, 127, 131, 132, 134, 135–6, 140, 160–1, 167, 173, 174, 200, 226
Bronowski, Jacob 35n12, 65, 66
Bruschweiler-Stern, Nadia 133, 203, 204, 212n10
Bucci, Wilma 9
Burt, Elisabeth V. 17

Catholicism 97, 214, 215, 226
Cavell, Marcia 40, 67, 86
Cecchin, Gianfranco 17, 261
chaos theories 28–9, 30
child development 12, 34n6, 42, 95
Chodorow, Nancy 109
Chomsky, Noam 143n2
civil rights 1
Coburn, William 29, 30, 34n5, 141, 144n6, 178
collectivism 106, 108–9, 111, 112, 114, 115, 224, 226–7, 232, 234, 235, 250, 266
communication 41, 67, 93, 99, 101, 129, 133, 154, 155, 162, 193, 248, 260–1; constricted 28; dysfunctional 147, 261; emotional 46; explicit 100, 105, 115, 119, 134–5, 141, 266; implicit 99–100, 105, 115, 119, 121, 134–5, 142, 230,

266; incongruent 134, 260, 264; levels of 134; meta- 140, 142, 166, 193; nonverbal 41, 46, 90, 133, 154, 155, 223, 261; paradoxical 261; paraverbal 41; proxemic 41; symbolic 35n12; verbal 99, 261
communism 36n13, 215
complementarity 41, 52, 83, 175, 180, 219, 261, 267; split 82, 85, 165, 179, 193, 209, 210
completeness 25
complexity theory 3, 4–5, 28–31, 102, 132, 144n6, 201
concretization 40, 85, 87
conflict 13–14, 22, 27, 28, 32, 37, 41, 63, 72, 107, 109, 120, 135–6, 139, 141, 143, 159, 161, 166, 174, 180, 182, 188, 199; inner 56, 177, 186; intrapsychic 116n6, 147, 152, 156, 163, 165, 173, 174, 177; negotiation of 177, 199; psychic 24; psychosexual 102; psychosocial 21–2; relational 4, 100, 163, 164, 173, 177; transference 54
consciousness 34n2, 66, 96, 127, 135, 149, 150, 151, 171, 227, 251; core- 9; extended 9; self- 63n1
containment 36n15, 63n2, 78, 116n2, 194
contempt 38, 59, 61, 64n4, 70, 71, 87n3, 100, 115, 116n4, 122, 147, 151, 154, 155, 198, 219, 222, 245, 254
context-dependent issues 48–9, 52, 58, 59, 62, 78, 80, 120, 126, 128, 129, 132, 135–6
contextualism 160
Cooper, Steven 213n13
Corbett, Ken 114, 212n5
countertransference xiii, 28, 48, 57, 74–5, 78, 85, 86, 114, 117n7, 137, 139, 142, 169, 221–2, 223, 239, 253, 263, 265; complementary 64n9
couples therapy 1, 2, 7, 14, 20, 28, 31, 34, 37–9, 44–5, 54, 57, 63n3, 67, 74–5, 82–3, 86, 96, 100–1, 105, 110, 114, 116n2, 119, 126–8, 131, 132, 138, 142, 144n8, 146, 150, 160, 165, 172, 173, 177–9, 182, 186, 213n12, 239–43, 247, 250, 252–3, 255, 262, 265–8; models of xiii, 29, 239, 251 see also psychotherapy; Six Steps model
Crastnopol, Margaret 18, 27, 35n9, 212n2
criticism (as toxic communication mode) 38, 100, 122, 147, 219

cultural studies 3
culture(s) 26, 55, 90, 108, 115–16, 207,
    212n9, 226–8, 251; collectivist 106,
    108–12, 114, 115, 224, 226–7, 232,
    234, 235, 250, 251, 266; family 108,
    116, 156, 196–8, 201, 214, 216–17,
    219, 226–7, 249–50, 251; individualist
    108–9, 111, 115, 227, 232, 235, 250,
    266
curiosity 28, 54, 62, 64n6, 72–4, 86, 87

Damasio, Antonio 9
Darwin, Charles 146
Davies, Jody 3, 26, 52, 65, 86, 103, 134
defensiveness 11, 19, 27, 30, 32, 33, 44,
    46, 47, 49, 51, 61, 72, 76, 79, 80, 87,
    100, 101, 127, 147, 166, 176n7, 178,
    193, 200, 203, 227, 241
dependency 20, 24, 27, 109, 110, 164, 264;
    mutual 182
depression 79, 80, 148, 223, 234;
    abandonment 244
designed interdependence 27
desire 7, 18, 20, 21, 24, 127, 144n6,
    152, 203, 241; sexual 23, 120, 184,
    190–2, 254
determinism, biological 10
dialogical truth 82, 86, 87, 188, 219
dialectics of difference 188, 267
Dicks, H. V. 2, 129
differentiation 17, 35n7, 109, 110, 112–13,
    116n1, 182, 188, 212n8, 258–9, 264
Dimen, Muriel 184, 212n5
disequilibration 39
dissociation 22–4, 48, 54, 56, 60, 72, 74,
    93, 96, 103, 120, 126, 127, 131, 132,
    135, 140, 153, 154, 160, 161, 166, 174,
    175n5, 205, 206, 227–9, 241, 266, 267;
    interpersonalization of 121; mutual 134;
    normal 22–3, 160; pathological 160–1
divorce 25, 64n4, 69, 100, 212n7, 224,
    229, 245, 249, 256, 257
domestic violence groups 245
dominance 16–17, 20, 23, 35n8, 37, 52,
    53, 55, 76, 107, 110, 112, 165, 167,
    170, 171, 173, 176n7, 181–2, 186, 193,
    253, 254
double binds 81, 93, 106, 134, 260,
    261, 264
drugs 43, 217, 244, 245, 251–2, 259
dual instinct theory 20
Duhl, Bunny 2

Duhl, Fred 2
dyadic systems 33, 107, 178
dynamic systems 28–9, 132

eating disorders 154
ecology 1
egalitarianism 20, 120
ego 12, 160, 171, 172, 175, 200, 214, 262;
    "part-" 160
ego defense 13
ego discourse 119
Einstein, Albert 66, 68
Emanuel, Christina 137–8
embeddedness 95, 153, 155, 182, 208
emotional convictions 67, 84, 105, 156
empathy 5, 48, 56–8, 61, 62, 64n8, 73,
    74, 78, 83, 84, 86, 88n10, 95, 102, 108,
    119, 137, 142, 175n2, 185, 222, 223
enactments 4, 23, 28, 34, 36n15, 48, 61,
    77, 81, 86–7, 100, 109, 118, 120, 126,
    134, 136–7, 141–3, 145n12, 160, 170,
    207, 217, 226, 228, 232, 235, 248, 266,
    267; asymmetrical 120, 229; sexual 63;
    symmetrical 120, 229
epigenetic life cycle theory 36n14
epistephilic instinct 64n6
Erikson, Erik 36n14
Eros 21, 22, 23, 63
erotic imagination 21, 22, 23, 144n10
erotic intelligence 21, 27
eroticism 21, 23
Escher, M. C. 5, 203
evolution 12, 13, 21, 27
expectancy systems 106–7, 115, 116n6,
    117n9, 126, 133, 152

Fairbairn, Ronald 144n5
fallibilism 68
family social systems 7, 17, 31, 112, 162,
    196–8, 202–3, 205–6, 212n8, 214,
    216–17, 219, 223–4, 237, 249–50, 252
family systems theory xiii, 1–2, 31, 34n4,
    112, 239, 258–64; and subsystems 260
family therapy 1, 2, 17, 42, 144n8, 196,
    239; Bowenian 2, 35n7, 112, 116n1,
    212n8, 258–9, 260, 263, 264n1; com-
    munications 260; interactional 2, 260–2;
    Minuchin's 2, 259–60; models of 260,
    263; object relations 262–3; strategic
    260; structural 2, 259–60, 263, 264
fantasy 14–15, 21, 44, 50–1, 61, 68, 75,
    87n3, 88n8, 94, 95, 102, 103, 106, 115,

116n4, 120, 127, 145n13, 167, 196,
235, 237, 242; omnipotent 14–15, 50–1,
104, 116n5, 168; sexual 20, 21, 23, 63,
144n10, 248, 253, 255
femininity 109–10, 224, 228
feminism 1, 76, 228
Ferenczi, Sandor 102–3, 209, 213n11
field theory 138, 139
Fighter, The 113
Fisch, Richard 55
Fonagy, Peter 9, 33, 39, 90, 94–6, 99,
104–5, 153, 188
Fosshage, James L. 56–7, 61, 175n2,
n4, 205
"Four Horsemen of the Apocalypse"
100, 147
Framo, James 2
"free will" 10, 14
Freud, Sigmund 12, 18, 27, 35n11, 36n14,
68, 86, 87n6, 102–3, 144n5, 160, 252
Frommer, Martin 18, 23–4, 25, 128,
212n5
fusion 12, 259, 262, 264

Gabbard, Glen O. 35n11, 40, 139, 140
Galatzer-Levy, Robert 33
Gales, Mary 44, 87n1
gay rights 1
gaze (Lacanian) 24–5
Gedo, John E. 144n5
gender 67, 90, 99, 107, 109–11, 207,
212n2, n9, 219, 228, 244, 253–4, 266
gender studies 3
genograms 116n2
Gentile, Jill 11, 51, 118, 127, 128, 130,
136, 143, 180, 200, 212n5, n9
Gergely, Gyorgy 94, 95, 104–5, 188
Gerson, Mary-Joan 144n8, 145n13
Ghent, Emmanuel 16, 142, 171, 176n7,
199–200
Goethe, J. W. 118, 129
Goldberg, Lea 114
Goldner, Virginia 18, 26, 27, 100, 212n5
Goldstein, Kurt 8
Gottman, John 61, 64n4, 72, 100, 122,
147, 151, 171–2, 245, 249, 250
grandiosity 149
Gray Gardens 95
Great Santini, The 95
Greenberg, Jay 11, 20
Greenson, Ralph 109
Grotstein, James 34, 50, 63, 103, 116n5

Haley, Jay 2, 93, 260
Harris, Adrienne 5
Harrison, Alexandra 133, 203, 204,
212n10
Hawking, Stephen 40, 66
Hegel, Georg 12, 14
Heidegger, Martin 22
hierarchy of needs (Maslow) 9
history-taking 90–2, 94, 112, 115, 116n2,
168, 226, 239
Hoffman, Irwin 3, 32, 35n9, 66, 212n2
homeostasis 261
homosexuality 184
humor 41, 71, 159, 218
Humphrey, E. 250
hyper-arousal 45, 53–4
hypo-arousal 45

id 12, 160, 262
idealization 14, 26, 42–3, 47, 48, 50,
53, 74, 77, 152, 167, 184, 209, 210,
217, 219
identification 17, 63, 81, 130; concordant
64n8; conjunctive 221; *see also* mutual
inductive identification
identity, sense of 9
illusions 10–11, 19, 24, 41, 168, 210,
211, 251
immigration 113, 116, 266; "amputation
effect" of 113–14, 116, 266
implicit relational knowing 99–100, 133,
135, 204
improvisation 29, 32, 33, 40, 41, 46, 54,
60–1, 87n6, 121, 137–9, 140, 182, 183,
204, 246, 266
"I'mprovisation" 138–40
improvisational moments 36n15, 140
incest 55, 139, 262
individualism 36n13, 108–9, 111, 115,
227, 232, 235, 250, 266
Industrial Revolution 7
infancy research 1, 3, 9
intentionality 11
interactional family therapy 2, 260–2
intersubjective conjunctions 74–5, 78
intersubjective dysjunctions 74–6, 78
intersubjectivity xiii, 11, 12, 29, 33, 34n5,
35n9, 39, 40, 42, 48, 51, 54–8, 68, 81,
86, 90–2, 116n5, 127, 131, 135–6, 138,
147, 149, 155, 167, 170, 174, 177, 180,
186, 200, 204, 212n2, n6, 235, 242,
246, 252, 267; relational 65, 153, 163

intimacy 28, 44, 96, 110, 124, 126, 128, 130, 131, 138, 183, 184, 213n13, 228, 244; psychic 12
intrasubjectivity xiii, 4, 11, 29, 51, 130, 138, 155, 163, 167, 170, 171, 174, 175, 177, 180, 186, 188, 200, 242, 252
introspection 3, 4, 57, 119, 146, 177
Ipp, Hazel 113–14

Jackson, Donald 93, 260
Jacobs, Lynne 88n10
James, William 175n3
Jaynes, Julian 34n2
jazz 182
jealousy 152, 201, 203, 206, 225, 231, 240, 254
Jesus Christ 150, 151
Jurist, Elliot 94, 95, 104–5, 188

Karpel, Mark 250
Kavaler-Adler, Susan 182
Kernberg, Otto F. 39
Klein, Melanie 12, 64n6, 116n3
Knoblauch, Steven 140
Kohut, Heinz 42–3
Korzybski, Alfred 65, 66
Kriegman, Daniel 12, 13, 134, 142

Lacan, Jacques 24–5, 35n9, 118, 143n1, 211n2
Lachkar, Joan 150, 241
Lachmann, Frank M. 12, 46, 51, 61, 92, 106, 116–17n6, 205
Landy, Robert J. 144n8
language 13, 21, 27, 35n9, 66, 87n5, 99, 101, 143n2, 155, 252
Layton, Lynne 109–10
Lichtenberg, Joseph D. 61, 81, 205
Lillas, Connie 46
listening stances 56–8, 61
Livingston, Martin 42
Locher, Johannes L. 5
Loewald, Hans 50, 88n8
love 7, 11, 18–20, 23, 25–6, 65, 109, 111, 120, 184, 199; attachment 5, 19, 62; falling in 25, 37; and hatred 24, 35n11, 61, 120; romantic 5, 19, 27, 62, 216, 253; sexual 20, 62; sustaining of 26, 109
loyalty gambits 111–13
lust 23–4, 27, 128, 145n10, 161
Lyons-Ruth, Karlen 133, 203, 204, 212n10

Magid, Barry 63n1
Mahler, Margaret 36n14
Main, Mary 94
marital therapy xii, 251
marriage xiii, 14, 19, 41, 92, 113–14, 121–2, 126, 133, 134, 147, 161, 171, 186, 196, 212n7, 214, 224, 229, 232, 236, 249–51, 253, 255–6, 259, 263; institution of 7, 18, 26, 183; intercultural 108
masculinity 109–10, 127, 228
Maslow, Abraham 9
masochism 16, 107, 171, 179, 199, 217, 218
masturbation 255
masturbatory fantasies 23
mate selection 7
McCarthy, Joseph 215
McLaughlin, James 74
meeting of minds xii
memory 90; autobiographical 10; declarative 10, 99; extended 10; implicit 10, 99, 137; procedural 10, 99; unconscious 34n2
mental health 26, 243
mentalization 3, 34, 52, 53, 83, 90, 93, 95–6, 97, 98, 101, 104, 106, 107, 110, 115, 147, 153, 155–6, 167, 173, 203, 212n6, 221, 226, 228, 241, 266
Merleau-Ponty, Maurice 144n6
meta-cognition 10, 166, 193
Metzl, Marilyn 182
midlife crisis 161, 168, 251
mindfulness 153, 155
Minuchin, Salvador 2, 259–60
"mirror that sees" 25, 26
mirroring 42–3, 45, 47, 53, 59, 71, 73, 79, 80, 94, 122, 152, 188, 205, 212n4, 218
Mitchell, Stephen A. 3, 5, 6n1, 7, 18–19, 20, 23, 25, 26, 27, 35n10, 72, 87n3, 88n8, 95, 120, 128, 139, 140, 144n5, 199–200, 252
Möbius loop model 10, 203
Modell, Arnold H. 8, 10, 34n3
moral authority 105, 180, 193
morality 12, 231, 254; psychoanalytic 72
morality gambits 105, 106, 266
Morgan, Alec 133, 203, 204, 212n10
morphogenesis 261
mother–infant relations 24–5, 212n4
Muller, John P. 35n9, 212n2
multidirectional partiality 77

Muran, J. Christopher 210
mutual inductive identification 33, 48, 63,
    100, 107, 118, 120–1, 135, 138–41,
    144n6, 160, 212n7, 242, 266, 267
mutual negation 15, 20, 53, 90, 101, 111,
    134, 141, 192
mutual recognition 3, 4, 5, 7, 11–18, 20,
    23, 25, 27, 28, 31, 34n5, 48, 50, 52–4,
    56, 58, 62, 66, 67, 69, 78, 80, 82, 85,
    90–2, 110–11, 118, 127, 128, 129, 147,
    149, 151, 153, 155, 165, 167, 170, 175,
    179, 180, 182, 184, 188, 193, 204, 210,
    219, 223, 226, 240, 265

Nahum, Jeremy 133, 203, 204, 212n10
narcissism 14–15, 24, 25, 26, 32, 54, 75,
    54, 166, 196, 209, 213n12, 239, 241;
    pathological 109, 149–50
narcissistic injury 38, 84, 109, 110, 151,
    215, 247
narcissistic islands 74
negative third 17, 53, 55, 81, 101, 147,
    192, 219, 265
negotiation theory 170, 174, 193–4, 199
neuropsychology 1
neuroscience 10–11
Nietzsche, Friedrich 146

obfuscation 17, 69, 79, 85, 95, 96,
    261, 277
object relations 2, 12, 23, 28, 36n15, 57,
    63n2, 129, 130, 144n5, 262, 263, 264
objectification 20, 23, 24, 25, 128, 164,
    191–2, 253, 254, 267
Oedipal partnership 35n9
Oedipal theory 102, 209, 212n2, 240, 254
"of course, of course" responses 77–8, 80,
    88n10, 228
Ogden, Thomas xii, 17, 32, 35n9, 139,
    140, 212n2
one-in-the-third 181–4, 188, 212n4, 267
Orange, Donna 34n5, 66, 67, 68, 71
organizing principles 39–41, 67, 74–5, 86,
    108–11; invariant 40–1; variant 40, 41
Ornstein, Anna 44
other-as-object 148–9
other-as-subject 148–9
otherness 13, 15, 23–4; of oneself 23–4
Overeaters Anonymous 154

Palazzoli, Mara S. 17, 261
panic patterns 245

paradox 5, 9, 14, 20, 29, 56, 141, 144n8,
    147, 149, 164–7, 171–5, 177, 251, 261,
    264, 267; counter- 261; management of
    199; negotiation of 199; of recognition
    13; resolution of 199
paranoia 95, 125
paranoid-schizoid position 116n3
parentification 263
parenting styles 69–71, 166, 184–6
patient–therapist dyad 29
Perel, Esther 7, 19–21, 27, 28, 120,
    144n10, 212n5, 253, 257n1
personal narrative xiii, 9, 70, 86, 90, 91,
    114, 119, 204, 210, 223, 226
personality disorders 38, 150, 264n1
personality organization 10, 39, 46, 48,
    57, 251
personhood, sense of 9
perspectival approaches 38, 66, 81, 88n7,
    187, 252
perspectival constructivism 66
perspectival realism 4, 11, 66–7, 82, 85,
    86, 87n4, 95, 125, 153, 154, 155, 251,
    265
perversion 128, 171, 183–7, 199, 267; of
    agency 51, 118, 120, 128–9, 130, 143,
    180, 266
Phillips, Adam 87n6
physical abuse 52, 79, 83
Piaget, Jean 39
"Pine" 114
Pizer, Barbara 146, 165
Pizer, Stuart A. 12, 51, 134, 140, 145n15,
    146, 164, 165, 166, 170, 176n6, 193–4,
    199, 208
play 11, 14, 21, 31–2, 41, 95, 139–40,
    142–3, 145n13, n14, 158, 159, 160,
    167, 185–7, 204, 210, 247, 253,
    266, 267
play space 143, 181, 203
playfulness 17, 46, 71, 94, 128, 137–8,
    159, 183, 204, 209, 210, 211, 238, 246,
    247, 253
pornography 185, 187, 248, 254
positive third 17, 53, 219, 265
postmodernism 110
potential space 53, 174, 181
Prata, Giuliana 17, 261
preconscious, the 160
Preston, Lynne 144n8
"pretend mode" 95, 98, 104, 115, 167,
    173, 226, 235, 241, 266

projection 4, 17, 25, 36n15, 96, 113, 126, 131, 143, 167, 173, 174, 175, 177, 204, 211n1, 221, 239, 241, 258, 263, 267; parent-child 263
projective identification 16, 35n9, 144n7, 262, 263
propositional truth 67, 86
psychic equivalence 39, 83, 85, 94–5, 97, 115, 153, 155, 167, 203, 226, 241, 266
psychoanalysis 1–2, 12, 18, 30, 35n11, 59, 63n3, 68, 71, 72, 87n6, 102, 105, 106, 112, 117n7, 137, 139, 160, 182, 209, 219, 220, 246, 251; contemporary xiii, 2, 16, 27, 42, 57, 65, 68, 86, 137, 184, 209; and improvisation 29, 32, 33, 137–9; interpersonal 57, 160; intersubjective 1, 86; object relations 57, 262; and paradox 170; relational 1, 3, 18, 20, 22, 26, 34n5, 57, 58, 68, 86, 103, 120, 160, 179, 240, 243–4, 246, 250, 263
psychoanalytic theory 2, 29, 54, 57, 137, 263
psychoanalytic third 16–17, 32–3, 35n9, 36n15, 54, 181, 211n2
psychology: ego 1, 12; evolutionary 35n12; one-person 1; self 12, 42–3, 56, 58
psychopathology 29, 33, 148, 264
psychosexual stage theory 36n14
psychosexuality 102, 184, 120
psychosocial conflict 13, 21, 120
psychotherapy xiii, 1, 30, 31, 39, 51, 63, 89, 98–9, 105, 106, 142, 151, 207, 216, 219, 220, 233, 253, 257, 264; asymmetric 63; conjoint 2–3, 4, 7, 16, 18, 37, 41, 42, 47, 48, 65, 80, 86, 89, 95, 110, 115, 121, 130, 136, 150, 167, 170, 173, 174, 211, 232, 240; couples 31, 138, 210; individual xiii, 57, 58, 64n3, 128, 130–1, 138, 141, 142, 143, 145n13, 155, 210, 233, 239, 240–2, 250; and intersubjectivity 12; relational 89–90; resistance to 86, 131–2; symmetric 63; termination of 207–11, 212n11, 213n13, 239, 268 see also couples therapy; Six Steps model

Racker, Heinrich 64n8, n9
reader–author relationship xii
reading xii–xiii

"real selves" 7
reflection 10
reflectivity 57, 93, 100, 105, 122, 140, 222; self- 38, 74, 180, 204, 210
reflexivity 146, 147, 246; self- 143, 147–8, 150, 153, 173, 175n1, 182, 212n6, 251
relational conflicts 4, 163
relationship(s) 16–17, 20, 29, 42–4, 51, 54, 57, 78, 82, 91, 92, 96, 105, 112, 115, 128, 129, 136, 138, 142–3, 147, 163, 174, 178, 184, 203, 210, 219, 242, 245, 255–6, 258, 261, 264, 268; author–reader xii; intimate 11–12, 34n2, 44, 51, 53, 71, 72, 93, 99, 151, 183, 188; long-term committed xii–xiii, 3, 7, 23, 24, 26, 27, 32, 33, 111, 113, 147–8, 166, 167, 179–80, 183, 188, 204, 213n13, 237, 243–4, 246–7, 253–4; and power 82, 115, 130–1, 150, 170, 174, 186, 191, 193–5, 253–4; ruptures in 4, 5, 7, 20, 24, 27, 51–2, 56, 62, 77, 197, 203, 204, 207, 211, 213n13, 216, 219; termination of 249; thirdness of 16–17, 27, 32–3, 50, 54, 179
relationship's "mind of its own" 3, 4, 5, 7, 16–17, 27, 28, 29, 31, 32, 53–4, 56, 90, 109, 111, 121, 134, 141, 147, 177, 178–9, 184, 188, 203, 209, 210, 211, 219, 223, 240, 249, 265; dysfunctional 16
relativist perspectives 66, 87n4
religion 36n13, 97, 214, 215, 226, 227; fundamentalist 66, 111, 112, 130–1, 150–1, 227
religious right 26
Renn, Paul 243
reversible complementarity 16
Ringstrom, Philip A. 29, 34n5, 42, 82, 93, 107, 115, 118, 134, 140, 142, 145n15, 168, 182, 195
romance 5, 18–19, 20, 22, 23, 26, 62, 92, 120, 216
Rorty, Richard 87n5
"rub, the" 27
Rubalcava, Luis A. 108, 110, 227
Rubin, Carol 208
Rubin, Jeffrey 208

Saarni, Carolyn 108
sadism 21, 107, 159, 179, 200, 248
sadomasochism 16, 151, 186, 248

safety xiii, 18, 56, 81, 91, 94, 100, 221; affective 266; climate of 73, 81, 256; sense of 11, 20, 78, 86, 139, 143, 144n10, 222
Safran, Jeremy 176n7, 199, 210
Salberg, Jill 209
Sampson, Harold 144n5
Sander, Louis 133, 181, 203, 204, 212n10
Santayana, George 89
Satir, Virginia 2, 260
Scharff, David E. 129, 250
Scharff, Jill Savege 129
schemas 39, 62
schizophrenia 259, 264n1
Schore, Allan 30, 46, 132
secular ideology 26
self 23, 101, 110, 129, 137, 140, 146, 176n5, 184, 237; assertion of 13; coherent 153; conservation of 127, 130; disappearance of 12; false 150; pseudo- 113; sense of xiii, 3, 8, 9, 10, 12, 13, 14, 22, 24, 29, 56, 94, 96, 112, 135, 153, 159, 163, 183, 235, 258, 264; "true" 15, 22, 135; unconscious 10
self-actualization 5, 7, 8–12, 15, 16, 20, 28, 29, 31, 34n2, 37, 38, 40, 43, 48, 50, 51, 64n5, 66, 90, 93, 96, 101, 106, 109, 110, 118, 127, 128, 141, 146–7, 163–5, 173, 175, 179, 183, 184, 188, 228, 234, 237, 240, 242, 249, 250, 254, 258, 265, 266
self-as-object 148–151
self-as-subject 148–152
self-deception 13, 161
self-experience 3, 24, 42, 62, 127, 129, 148, 165, 166, 170, 171, 174, 175
self-image states 23
self-organizing systems 29–31, 178, 244
self-states 33–4, 48, 63, 120, 130–1, 135–6, 160–1, 192–3, 199, 207, 211n1, 229, 232–3, 235, 243, 251, 266; archaic 161; borderline 209; competing 165, 235; conflictual 165, 199, 241, 265; dissociated 3, 4, 22, 107, 118, 120, 127, 132, 135–6, 143, 147, 161, 165, 166, 227–9, 237; multiple 4, 22, 27, 29, 33, 56, 64n5, 74, 110, 119, 134–6, 147, 149, 156, 160–3, 166, 167, 170–1, 173, 174, 175, 177, 219, 237, 241, 247, 265; narcissistic 209
selfishness 34n1, 120, 254

selfobject dimension 42–5, 47, 49–51, 56, 59, 62–3, 74, 80, 90, 125, 129, 143, 184, 187, 207, 216, 219, 265
Seligman, Stephen 93
separation–individuation stage theory 35n14
sequestered states 22–3, 120, 126, 127, 161, 164, 266
sex 19, 20, 22, 23, 26, 27–8, 37, 63, 72, 120, 124, 130–1, 135, 182, 185, 189–90, 216, 220, 224, 228, 229–31, 249, 252–5; anal 185, 187; discussion of 28, 252–5; Tantric 186
sexism 76
sexual abuse 52, 102
sexual perversity/perversion 128, 183–7, 253–4, 267
sexual power 130–1
sexuality 22, 27, 28, 63, 92, 119, 126–7, 131, 144n10, 184, 253, 254, 262; female 224
Shaddock, David 42
Shane, Estelle 44, 87n1
Shane, Morton 44, 87n1
Shimmerlik, Susan 133–4, 141–2
sibling position 259
Siegel, Daniel 30, 87n2, 104, 132, 153
Simon, Paul 210
Simpson, O. J. 245
Six Steps model (of conjoint psychotherapy) 3–5, 11, 18, 29, 33, 39, 48, 51, 52, 56, 59, 62–3, 67, 82, 86, 90, 111, 118, 120, 121, 125, 127, 129, 130, 135, 142, 143, 147, 155, 160, 165, 173, 177, 180, 188, 195, 199, 203, 204, 207, 209, 210, 213n13, 214–38, 239, 241; practice questions for 265–8; relational turn of 118
Slap, Joseph W. 39
Slap-Shelton, Laura 39
Slavin, Malcolm 12, 13–14, 18, 21–2, 134, 142, 163, 164
sleeping disorders 122–4
Slipp, Samuel 2, 129
"slumbering giants" 3, 118, 119, 230
Sluzski, Carlos 260
Socarides Stolorow, Daphne 88n10
socialization 21; over- 22
societal regression 259, 264n1
Soloman, Marion 150, 241
species survival 12
spirituality 215

split complementarity 16, 17, 112
splitting 96, 129, 130, 136, 143, 167, 171, 174, 179, 184, 206, 263
spontaneity 10, 18, 29, 40, 120, 138, 159, 182, 195, 203, 204, 210, 211, 212n3, 221, 246, 247
Stein, Ruth 18, 128, 212n5
Steinberg, Marcia 138
Stern, Daniel N. 11, 12, 29, 39, 44, 46, 64n6, 88n9, 99, 106, 133, 134, 139, 203, 204, 212n4, 212n10
Stern, Donnel 3, 11, 17, 18, 19, 22–3, 32, 36n15, 51, 54, 66, 67, 72, 73, 96, 121, 138, 140, 145n11, 160, 167, 188
Stern, Steven 143–4n5
Stoller, Robert 23, 109
Stolorow, Robert D. 2, 34n5, 39, 40, 41, 42, 43, 49, 66, 67, 68, 71, 73, 74
stonewalling 100, 147
Storr, Anthony 9
Streetcar Named Desire, A 95
Strenger, Carlo 87n3, 116n4
structuralism 260, 263, 264
subjectivity 3, 34n5, 35n8, 37, 129, 146, 148, 150, 153, 154, 175, 203, 219, 223, 228, 235, 241, 246, 263, 266; mutual recognition of 12–16, 171; sense of 164
subjugating third 17
submission 16–17, 20, 23, 35n8, 37, 52, 53, 107, 110, 112, 165, 167, 170–3, 175, 176n7, 181–2, 186, 187, 193, 199–200, 219, 229, 233, 246, 248, 253, 267
substance abuse see drugs
Sullivan, Harry Stack 160, 210
Summers, Frank 144n5
superego 160, 242, 262
surrender 4, 16–17, 101, 129, 142, 147, 171–3, 175, 176n7, 177, 181, 199–200, 212n9, 228, 246, 251, 267
symbolization 10, 21, 94, 101, 155, 226
symbols 13, 21, 41

Tantric yoga 186
Target, Mary 33, 90, 94, 95, 104–5, 188
Tavistock Groups 178
temper outbursts 101–2, 124, 127, 158, 221, 243, 260
theater 182, 246
theory of mind 35n9, 67, 94, 96, 170, 196, 212n2, 246
therapeutic alliance xiii, 209, 210, 238, 268

third-in-the-one 181, 187, 188
thirdness 16–17, 27, 32–3, 35n9, 36n15, 50, 53, 54, 64n5, 85, 110, 111, 123, 155, 179, 180–2, 184, 187–8, 197, 207, 210, 211n2, 212n6, 238, 246, 267; intentional 187; intersubjective 55; moral 36n15, 187; negative 17, 53, 55, 81, 101, 147, 192, 219, 265; positive 17, 53, 219, 265; rhythmic 181, 184; symbolic 187; of therapist 193
Thomson, Peter G. 74
Tolpin, Marian 42, 144n5
transcendence 18, 22, 199, 200
transference 3, 15, 22, 35n9, 42, 43–8, 50, 51, 57, 63n3, 64n5, n9, 74–5, 86, 98, 106, 137, 142, 160, 167, 208, 217, 223, 241, 251, 262, 265; bidimensional 41–2, 45, 48, 52, 53, 54, 62, 64n5, 67, 90, 92, 232; family 263; idealizing 48, 209, 217; negative 118, 119, 125; repetitive 3, 15, 42–5, 47, 48, 62, 74, 79, 90, 91, 93, 119, 125–6, 160, 173, 187, 209, 218, 219
transference neurosis 64n3
transitional space 91, 181, 212n3
trauma 15, 22, 34n3, 41, 43, 49, 52, 54, 93, 101, 102–7, 115, 117n9, 131, 132, 139, 162, 168, 175n5, 180, 195, 226, 260, 265; denial of 103; psychic 24
trauma theory 102, 226
triangulation 17, 67, 112, 254, 258, 263, 264
trichotillomania 262
Tronick, Edward 133, 203, 204, 212n10
Turnbull, Janiece 46
twinship 42–3

unconscious, the 7, 10, 30, 31–2, 87n6, 106, 119, 137, 146, 160, 178, 219–20, 243, 260, 262; pre-reflective 74; relational 139
unthought known, the 73, 145n11, 225

Vaihinger, Hans 65, 66
Van der Kolk, Bessel 132
verbal abuse 79, 98, 243, 245
vicarious introspection 57
vicious circles 45–6, 90, 91, 121–2, 129, 184, 218–19, 232, 254, 265
victimhood 38, 41, 82, 105, 107, 115, 128–9, 130, 179–80, 193, 212n9

Vietnam War 1
violence 194, 196, 243–5, 256–7;
    systemically generated 244–5
Voeller, Mark N. 196

Wahlberg, Mark 113
Waldman, Kenneth M. 108, 110, 227
Wallin, David 90, 92–3, 95, 104, 122,
    144n7, 153, 156, 182
Watzlawick, Paul 2, 55, 260
Wayne, John 143n1
Weakland, John 55, 93, 260
Weeks, Gerald 249
Weisel-Barth, Joye 11

Weiss, Joseph 144n5
Westfall, April 250
Whitaker, Carl 6n2, 196
Whitman, Walt 171
Winnicott, D. W. 12, 14, 15, 31, 63n2,
    145n14, 164, 211, 251
Wolf, Ernest 43
Wolff Bernstein, Jeanne 24, 26, 35n9, 128,
    212n2, n5
Wrye, Harriet 18
Wynne, Lyman C. 6n2

Zarnegar, Zohreh 113
Zen Buddhism 63n1